The Outlaw League and the Battle That Forged Modern Baseball

T0040490

The Outlaw League and the Battle That Forged Modern Baseball

DANIEL R. LEVITT

TAYLOR TRADE PUBLISHING
Lanham • Boulder • New York • Toronto • Plymouth, UK

Published by Taylor Trade Publishing
An imprint of Rowman & Littlefield
4501 Forbes Boulevard, Suite 200, Lanham, Maryland 20706
www.rowman.com

10 Thornbury Road, Plymouth PL6 7PP, United Kingdom

Distributed by NATIONAL BOOK NETWORK

British Library Cataloguing in Publication Information Available

The Library of Congress has cataloged the Ivan R. Dee hardcover edition as follows:

Levitt, Daniel R.
  The battle that forged modern baseball : the Federal League challenge and its legacy / Daniel R. Levitt.
    p. cm.
  Includes bibliographical references.
  1. Federal League of Base Ball Clubs—History. 2. Baseball—United States—History.
  3. Baseball players—United States—Statistics. I. Title.
  GV875.F43L48 2012
  796.3570973—dc23   2011047803

ISBN 978-1-58979-954-7 (pbk. : alk. paper)

∞™ The paper used in this publication meets the minimum requirements of American National Standard for Information Sciences—Permanence of Paper for Printed Library Materials, ANSI/NISO Z39.48-1992.

Printed in the United States of America

To my parents, for all their love and support

Contents

Preface

Today the idea of a new Major League in baseball or a serious rival to the National Football League is almost inconceivable. Where would the teams play? Could they possibly compete for players, considering the huge salaries paid to top athletes? This situation has not always been so. In three major professional team sports—football, basketball, and hockey—rival leagues have experienced some success in the past fifty years, forcing their way into the established leagues as recently as the 1960s and 1970s. These new ventures made headway when established leagues failed to expand quickly enough to satisfy the demand for Major League–quality sports. Entrepreneurs willing to gamble on forming a new league could occasionally gain traction, albeit while suffering huge financial losses.

Baseball experienced uncertainty over its eventual structure much earlier. By several decades the first established professional team sport in the United States, baseball's growing pains were particularly acute. In the nineteenth century there existed no blueprint as to what a sports league should look like. The National League, launched in 1876, became America's first modern sports league by granting territorial rights to teams and recognizing player contracts across the league. These two concepts revolutionized the way sports leagues and teams were perceived, and created valuable and exclusive franchise rights. Over the next twenty-five years the National League consolidated its position as the preeminent baseball league and brought the more recently established Minor Leagues under its umbrella. But the National League mismanaged its monopoly and failed to appreciate the growing demand for Major League baseball. In 1901 the American League successfully challenged the older league and the existing baseball hierarchy to qualify as a second Major League.

As America grew in the first decade of the twentieth century, the two Major Leagues reached a tentative peace accord. Revenues soared. By the early 1910s baseball owners were making large profits, partially at the expense of their players, who labored under harsh work rules and below-market salaries. At the same time, baseball had not yet moved beyond the small-business model of the Civil War era. Its ownership syndicates were generally made up of upper-middle-class professionals and businessmen. Most included local politicians or men well connected to urban machine politics, but not the nation's wealthiest upper crust. Thus the financial pockets of existing Major League owners did not appear prohibitively deep to affluent businessmen who looked to challenge Major League baseball. As the early rowdyism was cleansed from the sport and it gained popularity with middle-class crowds, a few of America's richest citizens began seriously considering baseball investment and ownership.

In late 1913 the newly formed Federal League declared itself a Major League. To compete, the eight-team circuit and its backers needed to place several franchises in large Minor League cities with Major League dreams. As the few truly wealthy citizens in these cities were often unwilling to invest in a franchise, the league's backers looked to recruit a large group of prosperous, upper-middle-class civic boosters to buy stock in a franchise (an ownership structure surviving today only in the NFL's Green Bay Packers). Eventually half the Federal League's franchises were backed by such syndicates of committed, well-heeled citizens. For the remainder, mostly in cities competing directly with existing Major League teams, the Federal League's organizers successfully lined up some of America's wealthiest merchants and industrialists. Once organized, the new league posed a real and substantial challenge to baseball's prevailing structure.

The existing American and National leagues, along with the Minor Leagues—together dubbed "Organized Baseball"—fought back furiously in the press, in the courts, and on the field. At the time and ever since, the nastiness of the struggle led the press to describe it in the metaphors of war. It continued for two years and represented the last, best chance that baseball's organizational structure, and that of U.S. sports leagues in general, would develop along a different path. After the final settlement with the Federal League, baseball's monopoly and hierarchical structure never again faced more than a token challenge. The story of this fascinating, complex, and historic battle centers on the machinations of both the owners and the players as the Federals struggled for profits and Major League status, the established leagues fought to stop them, and the players organized baseball's first real union.

When I refer to the various Federal League clubs throughout the text, I generally use the common construction of the time. The first syllable of the city was combined with "feds" to create a two-syllable name for each team—for example, Buffeds for Buffalo, Pittfeds for Pittsburgh, and Brookfeds for Brooklyn. The Kansas City club was the Kawfeds, Indianapolis the Hoofeds, and St. Louis the Sloufeds. Several teams had actual names, which are occasionally used to avoid repetitiveness, such as the St. Louis Terriers, Baltimore Terrapins, Kansas City Packers, and Pittsburgh Rebels. In all cases where these names appear, the club they refer to will be easily understood from the context.

There is no formal definition of what qualifies as a Major League. First and foremost, does the league itself consider itself Major? If so, do the fans and press treat it as such? Are their franchises based in major population centers? Do they have Major League–quality baseball players? If there is a competing Major League, does the league take the competition seriously? The Federal League, though it never achieved the talent level of the National and American leagues, qualified under these unofficial criteria. More officially, in 1968 the Special Baseball Records Committee, created to define standards in preparation for publishing baseball's first complete encyclopedia, ruled that the Federal League, along with several nineteenth-century leagues, was Major.

Many people have helped me tell this story. Mark Armour and Steve Steinberg reviewed the manuscript and provided detailed criticism. Trey Strecker, Marc Gullickson, Leif Jensen, Philip Veenhuis, Arnold Witt, and Mark Witt offered valuable suggestions. Ron Selter shared his extensive knowledge of deadball-era ballparks; the legal scholar Ed Edmonds offered his expertise on matters of law, and Rick Huhn shared his knowledge of player pursuits. Jeff Cruikshank, William Cook, and Robert Wiggins graciously responded to my inquiries. (For a more complete reference to events on the field in the Federal League, I recommend Wiggins's book, *The Federal League of Baseball Clubs*.) Dennis Goldstein, Mike Mumby, Pat Kelly, and Fred Buckland eased the process of finding interesting photographs. Gabriel Schechter helped me navigate the many resources at the National Baseball Hall of Fame Library, particularly the Garry Herrmann papers. Jon Sisk expertly guided the book through the editing process and Darcy Evans cheerfully helped me with the many details. Peter Morris introduced me to Ivan Dee, who believed in the project and provided valuable suggestions to help frame and edit it.

Dramatis Personae

William Baker	President and principal owner of the Philadelphia Phillies
Phil Ball	Ice plant builder and principal owner of the Sloufeds
Ed Barrow	President of the International League
Helene Britton	Owner of the St. Louis Cardinals
Schuyler Britton	Husband of Helene Britton and president of the St. Louis Cardinals
Mordecai "Three Finger" Brown	Aging Hall of Fame pitcher who jumped to the Sloufeds as player-manager
Dick Carrol	Buffeds executive; later business manager of the Brookfeds
Thomas Chivington	President of the American Association
Charles Comiskey	Owner of the Chicago White Sox
Corry Comstock	Architect for many of Robert Ward's bakery facilities and vice president of the Pittfeds
William Devery	Onetime disreputable New York City police chief; co-owner of the New York Yankees in 1914
Barney Dreyfuss	Owner of the Pittsburgh Pirates
Charles Ebbets	President and principal owner of the Brooklyn Dodgers
Frank Farrell	New York gambler; co-owner of the New York Yankees in 1914
Dave Fultz	Leader of the Players Fraternity; an attorney and former Major League outfielder

James Gaffney	Boston Braves owner and Tammany Hall–connected building contractor
Edward Gates	Lead Federal League attorney
James Gilmore	President of the Federal League
Clark Griffith	Manager and minority owner of the Washington Senators
Edward Gwinner	President and principal owner of the Pittfeds
Ned Hanlon	Key investor in the Baltfeds; nineteenth-century player and Hall of Fame manager for Baltimore in the 1890s
Robert Hedges	President and principal owner of the St. Louis Browns
Harry Hempstead	President and principal owner of the New York Giants
Garry Herrmann	President of the Cincinnati Reds and chairman of the National Commission, Organized Baseball's governing body
John Heydler	National League secretary
Tillinghast L'Hommedieu Huston	Wealthy engineer in the market for a baseball team
Ban Johnson	President of the American League
Kenesaw Mountain Landis	U.S. federal court judge presiding over the Federal League's anti-trust court challenge; became baseball's first commissioner in 1920
Joseph Lannin	Owner of the Boston Red Sox
Connie Mack	Manager and minority owner of the Philadelphia Athletics
Charles Madison	An attorney and president of the Kawfeds
Robert McRoy	Confidant of Ban Johnson; former minority owner of the Boston Red Sox
Ben Minor	President and principal owner of the Washington Senators
Charles Murphy	Owner of the Chicago Cubs; forced out by his fellow owners
Rebel Oakes	Player-manager of the Pittfeds
George Wharton Pepper	Lead attorney for Organized Baseball on the most important court cases; later a U.S. senator
Pat Powers	Longtime baseball executive and front man for Harry Sinclair
Carrol Rasin	President and principal owner of the Baltfeds

William Robertson	President and principal owner of the Buffeds
Jacob Ruppert	Wealthy New York brewer in the market for a baseball team
Larry Schlafly	Manager of the Buffeds
Harry Sinclair	Oil tycoon and owner of the Newark Peppers
Charles Somers	Owner of the Cleveland Indians; original financial backer of the American League
Otto Stifel	Brewer and wealthy early backer of the Sloufeds and Federal League
George Stovall	Aging player-manager; first generally recognizable name to jump to the Federal League
Charles Taft	Original financial backer of Cubs owner Charles Murphy; purchased Murphy's interest in the Cubs when Murphy was forced to sell; half-brother of former U.S. President William Howard Taft
John Tener	National League president and Pennsylvania governor
Joe Tinker	Star shortstop and manager; first star to jump to the Federal League
William Walker	Chicago businessman and part owner of the Chifeds
George Ward	Brother of Robert Ward and a minority owner of the Brookfeds
John Montgomery Ward	Nineteenth-century Hall of Fame player and union organizer; later became an attorney and business manager of the Brookfeds; no relation to Robert Ward
Robert Ward	Wealthy bread manufacturer and principal owner of the Brookfeds
Walter Ward	Son of George Ward and secretary of the Brookfeds
William Ward	Son of Robert Ward
Charles Weeghman	Chicago restaurateur and principal owner of the Chifeds

The Outlaw League and the Battle That Forged Modern Baseball

Prologue: The Opening Salvo— December 1913

Cincinnati Reds president Garry Herrmann should have been careful what he wished for. Before the 1913 season, in a trade with the Chicago Cubs, Herrmann finally landed the man he had long coveted as his manager: the quick-thinking shortstop Joe Tinker. One of the National League's greatest stars, Tinker had been immortalized several years earlier in Franklin P. Adams's poem "Baseball's Sad Lexicon," about the Cubs' double-play combination of "Tinker to Evers to Chance." Tinker, who had nurtured a friendship with Herrmann for some time, happily moved into his new player-manager role in Cincinnati. Although he loved Chicago, Tinker had little interest in playing under the constant scolding of his longtime teammate, second baseman Johnny Evers, recently named the Cubs manager. That Herrmann offered Tinker a $10,000 salary, one of the highest in baseball, didn't hurt either.

Herrmann had high hopes for his 1913 squad under Tinker, regarded as one of the National League's brainiest players. In 1912 the Reds had finished fourth in the eight-team National League and had played around .500 ball in the previous few years. Unfortunately, it quickly became apparent that the Tinker acquisition, made with such fanfare at the beginning of the year, was not working as expected. By the end of May Cincinnati was struggling in last place with a record of 15–26. The season quickly deteriorated for Tinker personally as well. In July he left the team for several weeks to return to Chicago to provide a blood transfusion for his seriously ill wife.

In August, back in Cincinnati, Tinker's frustrations boiled over. He chastised Herrmann in the press for dumping players for cash without receiving players in return:

> We are now in need of several good players who could be obtained if we had not been so anxious to dispose of some of our surplus for cash in a hurry. We sold [Hank] Severeid to Louisville, [Harry] Chapman to Atlanta, and [Rafael] Almeida to Montreal. . . .When I went to Louisville the other day I made a proposition about third baseman [Bert] Niehoff, who would help us out a lot and they laughed at me. A short time before we had sold them Severeid outright. If we had a string on him [optioned him to the minors and maintained his rights] we would have been in a position to deal with them for Niehoff. . . . A ball club cannot possibly be built up in this manner.[1]

Later in the month Tinker again complained to the sportswriters. He demanded a two-year contract and "complete control over my ballplayers and a guarantee that I will not be interfered with in my policies. I will insist that no waivers be asked without my knowledge and that no players be released or farmed out unless I know just what the transaction is."[2] Tinker knew better than to air his grievances in public, but they testified to his level of frustration with the Reds.

Herrmann was already disgruntled over the team's record and in no mood to tolerate his manager's venting. The club's directors, including the wealthy Fleischmann brothers and the machine politician George Cox, were likewise taken aback at the public complaints. When the Reds finished the season in seventh place, eleven games worse than in 1912, it was clear that Tinker had to go.

Once he realized he was on his way out of Cincinnati, Tinker hoped to return to Chicago. In late November while in Chicago, Tinker stopped by the Cubs offices to try to persuade them to reacquire him. Cubs owner Charles Murphy was in Europe at the time, but his office cabled him of Tinker's desire; Murphy then cabled Herrmann in Cincinnati to confirm his interest. Herrmann had planned to peddle his shortstop-manager at the National League meetings, beginning December 9 in New York, and may or may not have communicated this time frame to Murphy. Because of his travel schedule, Murphy would not return until well after the meetings had begun. In Murphy's stead, minority owner Harry Ackerland represented the Cubs for league business and negotiations with Herrmann. Several other owners, including Brooklyn's Charles Ebbets and Philadelphia's William Baker, also showed strong interest in Tinker when they found he was available.

Future Hall of Fame shortstop Joe Tinker, here shown as the manager of the Cincinnati Reds, would become the first Major League star to jump to the Federal League and one of the new league's key recruiters. (Courtesy of the Library of Congress)

The Tinker matter added to an already full plate for that year's National League meeting. The owners had long been factionalized and rarely agreed on important issues. League president Thomas Lynch, a onetime Major League umpire, had been elected president in 1910 as a compromise candidate. By late 1913 he had lost his support, and most owners wanted a new, higher-profile president, an outsider with prestige who could help guide them, mainly because they might actually pay attention to him. New Philadelphia owner William Baker was friendly with Pennsylvania governor John Tener and approached Tener regarding the job. Under Pennsylvania law a governor could not succeed himself, so Tener, whose term expired at the close of 1914, was willing to consider his future options. Once Baker received a positive reaction, he led a delegation of National League owners to sound out Tener officially. The governor proved a wily politician, and by feigning the reluctant office seeker he landed significantly better terms than his predecessor. The National League had paid Lynch $8,000 per year; for Tener, they happily coughed up a four-year contract at $25,000 per year.

Tener's stature gave the National League owners the prestige they craved, though no president could ever corral the fractious magnates into a harmonious relationship. At six feet four inches tall and 240 pounds, Tener was also physically imposing. Like many big men, he was quiet but forceful and tried to stay above the league's petty squabbles.

Tener had overcome a difficult childhood. He had come to Pittsburgh from Ireland with his mother and nine siblings in 1872. When she died one month later, Tener was left an orphan. He found a job in the steel mills and, aided by his size, began playing baseball. He developed into a capable pitcher and played several years in the Majors, his last in 1890 with Pittsburgh in the outlaw Players League. After his playing days he moved into a banking career and then into politics. The players hoped he would recall his comrades on the field fondly and offer a sympathetic ear to the concerns of the current generation.[3]

Tener later reminisced about how the pressure of his baseball-playing days helped steel him against the opposition in his campaign for governor:

> Our opponents, the Democrats, referred to us as "The Evil Ring," and I remember distinctly getting up to make a campaign speech in a big armory. The booing was terrific. I waited coolly to make myself heard, and then I said nonchalantly: "I have been booed to the echo on the ball field, so I am used to it and it does not bother me. I am going to say what I have to say here tonight, no matter how much hooting there is." That discouraged the hooters, and I finally achieved a degree of quiet. If I had not performed under tough conditions in baseball I might have flinched at that hostile reception, and my whole career would possibly have been changed.[4]

Nothing was ever simple in the National League boardroom, however. Tener still had one year remaining in his term as governor, so how could he run the National League? The owners agreed that for the year 1914 Tener would participate when available, and league secretary John Heydler would handle day-to-day operations. Thus, on the eve of what would prove to be one of the most critical baseball confrontations of the twentieth century, the National League might be left rudderless. In the event, Heydler proved an inspired choice: he had briefly served as league secretary and interim league president a couple of years earlier, understood how to maneuver within the dysfunctional National League boardroom, and later became league president himself.

But the National League owners needed adult supervision now. When Murphy returned from abroad and met with Garry Herrmann on December 11, he thought he had stolen a march on his competitors for Tinker. He believed he had obtained a verbal commitment from Herrmann for a forty-eight-hour exclusive

National League president John Tener, shown here throwing out the first pitch at Ebbets Field on Opening Day 1914. He would split 1914 between his baseball responsibilities and being governor of Pennsylvania. (Courtesy of the Library of Congress)

option to work out a deal, including a new contract with Tinker.[5] Although Murphy's claim seems highly unlikely—Herrmann would hardly limit his negotiating options in the middle of the National League meeting, and he disliked Murphy—Tinker also believed that Murphy would be allowed to negotiate a deal to bring Tinker back to Chicago.

Of the various offers Herrmann received for Tinker, the one from Brooklyn's Charles Ebbets seemed the most outlandish. Ebbets offered $25,000, a huge amount for the time. But even if this offer was legitimate, Herrmann and the Fleischmanns remained sensitive to the potential bad press following from an outright sale of Tinker. They demanded players, not just cash.

On December 12 in the early evening, while Herrmann was sitting around the hotel and buying drinks for owners and sportswriters, one scribe brought up the Tinker situation. He asked about the rumor that Ebbets wanted Tinker and was reportedly offering $25,000.

"Who do you want me to trade?" asked Herrmann.

"Ebbets says he wants Tinker; why don't you let him have Joe?" asked New York writer William McBeth.

"Oh, that's bunk," countered Herrmann. "Ebbets hasn't got the kind of money that has appeared in the papers. Say, how highly does Ebbets value Zack Wheat [Brooklyn's star outfielder]? I'd say about $25,000. Well, if you boys want to make a deal, tell Charley I'll trade him Tinker for Wheat."

The writers tracked down Ebbets at the hotel: "Herrmann says he'll trade you Tinker for Zack Wheat."

"Yes, and I'll trade him a nickel for a dollar bill any time," Ebbets responded.

"About that $25,000 you're supposed to have offered for Tinker; Herrmann says you haven't that kind of money," one writer piped up.

Ebbets reddened and walked over to Herrmann's table. With the writers looking on, Ebbets publicly confirmed he would pay $25,000 for Tinker. Cornered by his own bombast, Herrmann accepted.[6]

With the writers egging them on and the other executives watching in amusement, Herrmann and Ebbets signed a quickly drawn-up agreement: Ebbets would pay $25,000 for Tinker, of which Herrmann would pay Tinker $10,000 as an inducement for him to sign with Brooklyn. If Tinker refused to sign with Brooklyn, the $25,000 would be refunded to Ebbets.[7]

Not surprisingly, given the circus atmosphere in which the deal was cut, the Herrmann-Ebbets document did not end the Tinker saga. Julius Fleischmann and the Cincinnati board of directors repudiated it. They did not wish simply to sell Tinker, they wanted players, and they sent Ebbets a telegram to that effect. What's more, Tinker balked at the trade; he still wanted to go to Chicago. And Murphy encouraged him by publicly asserting that he was still in the hunt for Tinker.

Ebbets refused to back down, demanding that Cincinnati sell him Tinker and that Murphy quit interfering with the transaction. As pressure mounted on the Cincinnati board to honor the deal made by their authorized representative—none of the directors wanted to be in the baseball limelight—they relented.[8]

Although Tinker wanted Chicago, he would go to Brooklyn for the right price. He wired Ebbets, "If you wish an answer from me send me your highest terms for three years."[9] Once freed to sign him, Ebbets contacted Tinker. He naturally emphasized the $10,000 bonus Tinker was getting and suggested that they meet in Indianapolis a week or so later to discuss salary. Because of a scheduling misunderstanding, this meeting never came off, which Tinker took as a personal snub.

Brooklyn manager Wilbert Robinson followed up by long-distance telephone.

"Your telegram made Ebbets sore," Robinson told Tinker.

"Why should he be sore when I only asked what I would be paid for my services?" Tinker replied.

"Well, Ebbets has made up his mind what he will pay you," Robinson told him.

"Are my ideas in regard to salary not to be considered?"

"What are your ideas?"

"I won't consider anything less than $7,500 per year."

"I would like you to get all you can," Robinson told him, but then added, "Ebbets has stated that he will not pay more than he had made up his mind to pay. If you will not accept his offer, then Ebbets will take the chance of losing the $15,000 he paid Cincinnati."

Tinker refused to back down. "Well, you have lost the $15,000."[10]

At the time, players were not free agents when their contracts expired. All baseball contracts contained the infamous "reserve clause," granting the team an option to renew the contract for one year at terms and conditions—except for the salary—similar to those in the existing contract. Thus Tinker's 1913 contract contained fairly typical language: "In consideration of the compensation paid to the party of the second part by the party of the first part as recited in clause 1 hereof, the party of the second part agrees and obligates himself to contract with and continue in the service of said party of the first part for the succeeding season at a salary to be determined by the parties under such contract."

Because the new contract would also contain the reserve clause, the team essentially controlled a player forever. Most observers, both within and outside the baseball establishment, believed that the reserve clause was not legally binding because it was so one-sided and lacked specifics about something as central to the contract as salary. But as long as Organized Baseball operated as a virtual monopoly, the issue of legality was moot. No team within Organized Baseball would attempt to sign a player reserved by another team, and there was no active players union with an interest in challenging the clause. No individual player was likely to challenge the issue in court because he risked being blackballed from Organized Baseball. Even if he won a long court battle, he would have no assurance that other teams within Organized Baseball would actually bid for him.

Tinker had some leverage, despite the reserve clause, simply because of the controversy surrounding his sale to the Dodgers. The National League preferred to put this embarrassing situation behind it as quickly as possible yet had no leadership in place to push the owners to a collectively beneficial solution. Ebbets and Robinson, however, were unwilling to recognize Tinker's leverage and continued to bungle the negotiation. On December 23 Ebbets sent Tinker a letter in which he confirmed Robinson's statement that "your request for a three year contract at $7,500 is unreasonable." Later in the letter he at last made a concrete proposal: "The $10,000 bonus we will pay you will, with a yearly salary of $5,000, compensate you in great fashion for the part you play in the transaction."

Ebbets and Robinson also failed to understand that the environment they worked in was changing. A new Major League was now on the scene and looking to make a splash. In the fall of 1913 the Federal League's owners had decided to challenge the American and National leagues as a third Major League, and they needed big-name players. Chicago Federal League owner Lucky Charlie Weeghman and league president Jim Gilmore saw the Tinker debacle as a huge opportunity; they were not sitting idly by while Ebbets sent his star player a condescending letter. Once Weeghman and Gilmore realized that Tinker was in play, they quietly approached him, offering him an opportunity to return to Chicago.

On December 27, 1913, Weeghman officially fired the baseball war's first big salvo. In an announcement that shocked the baseball establishment, Weeghman revealed that he had signed Tinker to one of the largest contacts in baseball history, $36,000 over three years with $12,000 up front. Ironically, that same day Robinson had sent another letter to Tinker asking him to reconsider and accept Ebbets's terms.[11]

The Federals had their attorneys ready as well. To preempt a court challenge from Ebbets, attorney Edward Gates threatened that "any baseball club that attempts to secure an injunction to restrain a player from playing in the Federal League must come into court with clean hands. . . . The National Commission [baseball's governing body] if it goes into the court will immediately be confronted by two very serious propositions. First is the Commission a trust within the meaning of the Sherman antitrust act? And is not, in fact, a blacklist maintained?"[12]

When he heard the news, Ebbets was furious. He had lost his star, and Herrmann was now refusing to refund his $25,000. The two had long been among the more reasonable voices within the National League. Now the league's already quarrelsome ownership was being further stressed as the Federals pursued their players. Ebbets, not surprisingly, disregarded Gates's warning and threatened to sue Tinker for violating the reserve clause of his contract. The National Commission, based on legal advice, dissuaded Ebbets from suing. They didn't wish to test the reserve clause in court, where it would most likely be ruled invalid.

Until Tinker's signing, the Major League baseball owners had publicly ridiculed the new league, and privately most had remained dismissive as well. Tinker changed this casual attitude; it began to dawn on the Major League owners that they had a real battle on their hands. The Federals had landed their first star. They could no longer be ignored.

1

America Meets Sports Leagues

From the time the first openly professional baseball teams began appearing in the late 1860s, their backers struggled with the problem of organizing themselves. In 1857 sixteen clubs in metropolitan New York created the National Association of Base Ball Players. At the time the players were generally upper-middle- and middle-class amateurs playing baseball as a recreational activity. As the sport's popularity grew and the competition became more intense, teams began raiding one another's players, often by offering money. By 1870 several of the teams had become fully professional and had little in common with their brother amateur teams in the Association. (See the timeline at the end of this chapter for a chronological outline of important events.)

In 1871 the professional teams broke away and formed the National Association of Professional Base Ball Players. The new organization was not a league as we understand it today; any group of professional players could join the organization by paying a ten-dollar entry fee, and there was no limit on the number of teams from the same geographic location. Nor was there a common schedule or player contract. A player could jump between clubs; he simply had to be a team member for thirty days before he could play, and even this nominal restriction was not uniformly enforced. Not surprisingly, the association did not prosper. Ten fellows in Keokuk, Iowa, who might have kicked in a dollar each to join, had nothing in common with teams in Philadelphia or Boston that spent large amounts of money to assemble the best players in the country.

After the 1875 season William Hulbert, owner of the Chicago White Stockings and a member of the Chicago Board of Trade, signed several stars who were already under contract with other teams, a violation of the Association's rules. Rather than attempt to defend his actions, Hulbert decided to start a new organization. Hulbert's new arrangement, named the National League of Professional Baseball Clubs, would form the model for all professional sports leagues to come. The National League incorporated four tenets we now take for granted in defining a sports league: (1) most important, the league took control over its membership—two negative votes among the owners were sufficient to bar a new team from joining; (2) teams were granted exclusive territorial rights to their city; (3) a common schedule was created by the league so that each team played the same number of games against the other league teams; and (4) player contracts were registered at the league office so that all teams were on notice of other teams' rosters.

Despite Hulbert's innovations, the National League was surprisingly unstable its first few years. From 1876 to 1878, every team lost money, and in 1879 only league champion Providence turned a profit. With players generally on one-year contracts, teams continued to lure players from competing teams by offering higher pay. In this environment player salaries consumed nearly two-thirds of a team's operating budget. "Revolving" players also hurt fan interest. As the financial losses piled up, the league lost teams almost every year, their places usually taken by new hopefuls.[1]

Boston owner Arthur Soden thought he had a solution. To stabilize player rosters he proposed that each team be allowed to "reserve" five players for the next season. That is, the reserving team would have exclusive rights to negotiate with these players. On September 29, 1879, Soden's scheme was secretly adopted by the National League. Once implemented, the system had its desired effect. Salaries fell—in Boston they dropped between 16 and 32 percent—profits rose, and the franchises became more sturdy. The reserve system proved so successful for the owners that they eventually made it public and expanded it to nearly all players on every team.

As profits grew, rival leagues and investors wanted in. In 1882 the American Association organized the first successful challenge to the National League. After a year of conflict and swelling player salaries as the new league competed for players, the two leaguers reached a peace settlement, each recognizing the reserve lists and territorial rights of the other. The National League recognized the upstarts relatively quickly for several reasons. Most important, none of the cities in the six-team American Association overlapped with the Nationals; even after the American Association expanded to eight teams in 1883, the two leagues doubled-up only in New York and Philadelphia.* Also, because the American Association charged only 25 cents (the National charged 50 cents), served beer (the National did not), and played on Sundays (at this time the National League still prohibited Sunday baseball), the league had been fairly successful at the gate.

Even with sixteen Major League teams, other entrepreneurs saw an opportunity to create another Major League. In 1884 the wealthy St. Louis investor Henry Lucas started the Union Association, in which he owned the St. Louis franchise. Fighting back, the Majors blacklisted players who jumped their reserve, significantly curtailing the number of Major Leaguers willing to jump. The Minor Leagues suffered most, as Minor League players were much less likely to be deterred by the blacklist for a shot at the Majors. After the season the National League co-opted Lucas by offering him a St. Louis franchise in their league, and the Union Association quietly folded.

Of course, the players detested the reserve system. They had recently been able to jump from team to team for better salaries, but now they were tethered to one team, effectively forever, without any negotiating leverage. To counteract the owners' encroachment on their rights, the players, under the leadership of John Montgomery Ward, a star infielder with New York, formed the first real players union, the Brotherhood of Professional Baseball Players. In 1890 the players, with backing from wealthy investors, launched their own league, the Players League, taking most of their players from the National League. Once again salaries soared, but this time the National League fought back in the courts.

To hold on to its players, the National League claimed that the reserve clause in its contracts was legally binding and that its players could not sign with another team. The league won none of these cases. The courts unanimously held that the reserve clause was unenforceable, principally because it lacked definiteness (it failed to specify any of the terms of the next contract) and mutuality (it was too one-sided toward the club). "The right of reservation is nothing more or less than a prior exclusive right as against the other clubs to enter into a contract securing the players' services for another season," read one opinion. "Until the contract is made which fixes the compensation of the player, and the other conditions of his services, there is no definite or complete obligation upon his part to engage with that club. . . . [I]t is operative and valuable to the club. But

---

*In 1882 the eight-team National League consisted of Boston, Buffalo, Chicago, Cleveland, Detroit, Providence, Troy (New York), and Worcester (Massachusetts). The six-team American Association had teams in Baltimore, Cincinnati, Louisville, Philadelphia, Pittsburgh, and St. Louis. In 1883 the National League replaced the smaller Troy and Worcester with New York and Philadelphia. The American Association added Columbus (Ohio) and New York to become an eight-team league.

as a basis for an action to enforce specific performance it is wholly nugatory. In a legal sense, it is merely a contract to make a contract if the parties can agree."[2]

It is worth noting that while the reserve clause, in the form used at the time, was certainly unfair to the players, some form of player control was necessary for league success. Even today, with the reserve clause having been struck down by collective bargaining arbitration in 1975, and with one of the most powerful and influential unions in America, players remain under the control of their team for their first six years of Major League service. Only then are they free to sign with another club.

The Players League war of 1890 proved financially disastrous for all club owners. By one estimate the Players League and the National League together lost $500,000, and the American Association was weaker than either. Once again, to end the struggle, the National League co-opted the owners of the upstarts. Some owners were allowed to buy into the National League club in their city, a few were bought out, and two joined the American Association.[3]

The American Association, unhappy with their allotment of players from the settlement, abrogated their agreement with the National League, initiating a new baseball war. For another season the players would enjoy higher salaries as the two leagues competed for their services. The American Association, however, was too fragile financially to contest the Nationals for long; the Nationals also had little stomach for further strife. After the 1891 season the two leagues merged: the National League absorbed four of the American Association's franchises and paid $135,000 to buy out the other four. The expanded National League also negotiated an agreement with the Minor Leagues providing for recognition of each other's player and territorial rights and officially delineating a hierarchy of leagues, with the National League at the top as the sole Major League.[4]

After taking in four teams from the American Association, the National League operated as a twelve-team, single-division league through the rest of the decade. This unwieldy organization produced seasons in which many of the teams were well out of the pennant race by July 4, and the lack of a significant postseason series further depressed interest. By the end of the decade, despite holding its monopoly over Major League baseball, the National League was in disarray.

The game on the field had become the province of hoodlums. The Baltimore Orioles, one of the leading teams of the decade, often won by intimidation and outright cheating as much as by their skill. Managed by Ned Hanlon, the Orioles were known for their rule breaking and their violent side. They would resort to almost any tactic to win, including hiding balls in the outfield, intimidating umpires and opposing players with vicious verbal and physical abuse, cutting across the diamond from first to third when the umpire was not looking, and tripping or grabbing opposing base runners to slow them down. Other teams naturally imitated the Orioles' successful tactics, and the games became particularly riotous. Weak league leadership gave little support to the lone umpire who tried to arbitrate these games. Umpire Tom Lynch (later to serve as league president) was fired, though later reinstated, for complaining about the treatment of his fellow arbiters.

Off the field, the situation was even more unsettled. The National League's owners had little experience in working toward a common cause—except as it related to taking advantage of the players—and each maneuvered to his own advantage. For example, though all teams were supposed to charge 50 cents for admission to the grandstand, some cut secret deals with visiting teams so that they could charge only 25 cents. The Washington owner added forty hits to Gene DeMontreville's statistics to make him more attractive to other teams.[5] The league's warring factions, without a central leadership capable of controlling them, exacerbated all the conflicts.

League ownership issues festered throughout the decade. As unscrupulous as it seems today, at the time it was not uncommon for an owner of one franchise to own a piece of another. By the end of the decade the National League situation had become untenable. Several owners actually controlled two clubs. The ownership of the St. Louis and Cleveland franchises transferred all their best players to St. Louis; Pittsburgh and Louisville consolidated their stars in Pittsburgh, and the owners of Brooklyn and Baltimore created a juggernaut in Brooklyn. The owners of Boston and Cincinnati were minority investors in the Giants and occasionally funneled players to New York.

With declining attendance and negative press, even the National League leadership, such as it was, recognized that changes were imperative. Not surprisingly, they implemented precisely the wrong solution. During the 1880s and the heyday of the American Association, fans had generally supported sixteen Major League teams. And although many struggled at the gate, as recently as 1890 twenty-four teams had competed as Major League. The National League could easily have split into two or three divisions; they could have expanded to sixteen teams in two divisions; or they could have simply cleaned up their ownership conflicts and the game on the field. Instead, the National League jettisoned, with little compensation, the three denuded franchises and Washington, leaving an eight-team circuit for the 1900 season.

Against this backdrop, Ban Johnson cultivated his Western League to be the exact opposite of the Nationals. Byron Bancroft Johnson grew up in an upper-middle-class household in Cincinnati, where his father was a distinguished teacher and school administrator, serving a term as president of the Ohio Teachers Association. His home was austere and dedicated to education. Young Johnson inherited his father's driven, self-righteous personality, but not his love of study. Against his parents' wishes, he pursued baseball and boxing instead. The five-foot eleven-inch, 180-pound Johnson proved quite a fighter, though he never really developed as a ballplayer. After a year in college and another in law school, he quit to join the *Cincinnati Commercial-Gazette* newspaper and make his own way in the world. He established himself quickly as a sports reporter, even feuding with the pompous Cincinnati Reds owner, John Brush.

Despite the grudge with Brush, Johnson became friends with Cincinnati's manager, Charles Comiskey. Comiskey, whose contract expired after the 1894 season, was interested in landing a franchise in a newly forming Minor League. He invited Johnson along to the kickoff meeting. "The meeting Comiskey told me about was in Indianapolis," Johnson recalled. "I attended and went back to Cincinnati with the title of president, secretary and treasurer of the Western League. Actually I was president, secretary, and treasurer of nothing. My salary was to be $2,500 a year. I intended to continue with my newspaper work, which by this time I had learned to love."[6]

Johnson quickly realized that he loved running and building a baseball league more than just about anything else. He worked hard to clean up the umpire baiting and general hooliganism that had become commonplace in most other leagues. Johnson likewise proved his leadership in a showdown with Brush, who also owned the Indianapolis franchise in the Western League. Brush hoped to oust him as league president, but Johnson had earned the loyalty of the other owners through his tough leadership. Brush's attempted coup failed, and soon thereafter he sold his interest in the Indianapolis club. Meanwhile, Johnson smartly recognized the weaknesses and vulnerability of the National League, and when it contracted to only eight teams for 1900 he saw his opening.

Ban Johnson renamed his league the American League and placed a team in Cleveland, one of the now-vacated National League cities. Comiskey, who owned the St. Paul franchise, transferred his team to Chicago, in direct competition with the National League's Cubs. Although the American League was still technically a Minor League in 1900, Johnson clearly had designs on higher status. At the same time, a number of baseball men, including John McGraw, Cap Anson, and *Sporting Life* editor Francis Richter, were working to organize

American League president Ban Johnson, here seen at his desk in 1910, was the most powerful man in baseball at the time of the Federal League. (Courtesy of the Library of Congress)

a new American Association. The anarchic National League misread the relative threats. It may not have fought Comiskey's move to Chicago as forcefully as it should have because many National owners viewed the new American Association as the greater threat; they saw the American League move to Chicago as further fortifying that city against a possible American Association team there.

In 1901 Johnson moved daringly. He shifted several of the American League's franchises to the large East Coast cities of Boston, Philadelphia, Baltimore, and Washington, the latter two of which had been abandoned by the Nationals. To stock their teams with Major League–quality talent, Johnson

and his owners targeted established National Leaguers. They respected existing contracts but aggressively pursued those players whose contracts had expired and who were thus controlled solely by the reserve clause. The National
League, which had spent much of the last decade abusing its monopoly with
the players—extremely low salaries and punitive fines for petty offenses—had
earned little loyalty. Many stars eagerly defected for higher salaries and seemingly more enlightened management.

Johnson recognized that, more than determination and smarts, he needed
money, and lots of it. The huge salary increases required to induce stars to jump
leagues were only a portion of the start-up costs. To be a new Major League, the
American League also needed Major League–quality ballparks in which to play,
and in many cities this obligated the owners to buy sites and construct stadiums.
Fortunately, in this era ballparks were usually built of wood, quick to erect, and
relatively inexpensive (typically less than $50,000). Nevertheless, the costs were
well beyond the means of many Minor League owners.

Whether by foresight or luck, Johnson had addressed this obstacle on the eve
of challenging the Nationals. In 1899 he had met young Charles Somers, heir to
a coal fortune and bitten by the baseball bug. With a couple of partners, including John Kilfoyle, Somers met with Johnson, who convinced the group to buy
the Grand Rapids franchise in his Western League. "A little later the American
League was launched," recalled Somers. "Ban Johnson saw the opportunity for
bringing into existence a second Major League. Ban was a tireless worker and a
great idealist. He had long dreamed of this proposition and he came to me with
his plans. I knew Johnson was a good, honest man and a square shooter. He
needed money for his venture and I supplied it."[7]

Did he ever. Somers probably provided close to $1 million in both direct
support and loans. He essentially bankrolled four clubs: he owned the Cleveland
franchise outright, provided capital to Philadelphia principal owner Ben Shibe
and minority owner/manager Connie Mack, owned the majority of the Boston
franchise behind front men Harry Killilea and manager Jimmy Collins, and advanced funds to Charles Comiskey in Chicago.

As the third driving force behind the new league, Comiskey became one of
the American League's most powerful owners. Born on the old West Side of
Chicago, Comiskey's father, nicknamed "Honest John," was described in the
Sporting News as one of the "interesting characters" of Chicago's early days. Active in municipal politics, the elder Comiskey was an alderman for twelve years,
a county clerk, and an assistant county treasurer. Comiskey's mother, whom he
often called his best friend, died when he was still a youngster.

Bombastic Chicago White Sox owner Charles Comiskey was one of the American League's most powerful owners. (Courtesy of the Library of Congress)

In 1882 Comiskey put in with the National League's first competitor when he joined the upstart American Association as a player. He played first base for the Browns for several years and advanced the techniques used to play the position. One of the first to play off the bag at first base, he also helped originate the strategy of having the pitcher cover first on ground balls to the right side of the infield. Comiskey became the team's full-time manager at the end of his third season and led the Browns to four straight American Association pennants. No stranger to new leagues and always looking for a better opportunity, he jumped to the Players League in 1890, signing to manage his hometown Chicago club for $8,000, a large salary for the time. Comiskey later said the Players League was destined to fail because it "wasn't constructed along the right lines." He had long thought about owning a baseball franchise and eagerly joined Johnson's venture when the opportunity presented itself.[8]

A complex personality, Comiskey understood politics and promotion. Shortly after his return to Chicago, he purchased a large hunting lodge in Wisconsin, called Woodland Bards. He used this estate to entertain many of his friends and Chicago celebrities. Before the Black Sox scandal nearly twenty years later, Comiskey could claim to be one of the most popular men in Chicago, and his sympathetic press treatment owed much to including sportswriters on his guest lists. Baseball would make Comiskey an extremely wealthy man, and he would later be held up as a model of how much money could be made in the game.

The inner circle of Ban Johnson's merry band of challengers consisted of relatively young men who fought well-established business interests in an era that celebrated business success. In 1901 Johnson and Mack were only thirty-eight-years old, and Somers was thirty-two; at forty-one Comiskey was the old man. Johnson also enlisted John McGraw, star third baseman of the National League's Baltimore Orioles and later the club's manager just before its contraction, to head the new Baltimore franchise. Johnson's key lieutenants in the battle, many from poor backgrounds, had spent their whole lives in baseball. In a time when baseball was still emerging as big business, smart, determined ex-players could maneuver into ownership. A handful of them, led by Johnson, were now challenging an entrenched status quo.[9]

In defense the National League once again looked to the courts to enforce its contracts. After star second baseman Napoleon Lajoie jumped from the Phillies to the crosstown Philadelphia Athletics in 1901, the Phillies sued in Pennsylvania state court to prevent the move. In this instance the court ruled in favor of the Phillies and enjoined Lajoie from playing for the Athletics. Significantly, Lajoie's contract did not have the standard, ambiguous reserve language. It limited the reserve to three years and defined the next year's salary amount. Considering these specifics, the court ruled the reserve clause binding. But Ban Johnson outmaneuvered the Phillies. He reassigned Lajoie to the league's Cleveland franchise, and the Ohio court refused to enforce the injunction against Lajoie. To avoid being charged with violating the Pennsylvania court's order, Lajoie avoided traveling to Philadelphia whenever his team played the Athletics.

Andrew Freedman, owner of the National's New York Giants and reportedly one of the most obnoxious men ever to own a ballclub, had another plan to derail the new league. After scheming with Brush and McGraw, who had become disenchanted under Johnson's stricter discipline, Freedman induced McGraw to jump to his Giants as the team's manager. Freedman, Brush, and confidants followed up by purchasing a controlling interest in the Baltimore Orioles and simply releasing many of its best players. McGraw then signed them for the Giants. It required quick maneuvering by Johnson to regain control of the Baltimore franchise by American League–friendly owners and restock it with players from the other American League teams to keep it afloat.

The National League continued its self-destructive pattern of the preceding decade as Brush and Freedman unleashed their schemes on their own league as well. Rather than regroup with a united front to confront the upstarts, the owners split into two warring factions. After the 1901 season Brush and Freedman proposed a revised league ownership structure. In this era of trusts on the national scene, where one ownership entity would attempt to control an entire industry, Brush felt he could do the same in baseball. Rather than own individual teams, a single trust would control the entire league. As instigator of the plan and owner of the league's most profitable franchise, Freedman would receive the largest ownership share, 30 percent. His three co-conspirators, Brush in Cincinnati and the owners of St. Louis and Boston, would receive 12 percent each; the remaining 34 percent would be apportioned among the remaining four owners. This proposal bitterly divided the league at a moment when unity was paramount. The four excluded owners retaliated and eventually prevented the implementation of Freedman's scheme. But an atmosphere of extreme distrust made the National League's monopoly over big-league baseball all the more tenuous. His trust proposal defeated, Freedman decided he'd had enough and sold the Giants to Brush, who in turn sold the Cincinnati Reds. Had Brush and Freedman been able to push through their plan, professional sports leagues in America might look very different today.

In response to McGraw's raid and the National League's tactics, Johnson was now determined to invade New York. Having retaken control of the Baltimore franchise, he decided to move it to America's largest city. Baltimore investors, led by baseball enthusiast Judge Harry Goldman and Sydney Frank, still owned a 49 percent minority interest but couldn't prevent the move and settled for a buyout of their position. For the second time in five years, Baltimore had lost a big-league team to the New York area.[10]

Locating a new team in New York City was not a simple proposition. By the late nineteenth century many cities were governed by a hybrid political organization that was less than fully democratic. From colonial times urban government had generally been disorganized, and it now faced the population explosion of the late nineteenth century. A whole range of new infrastructure was needed; new immigrants from abroad and migrants from farm life needed social services, and many could vote to express their desires. Into this urban government vacuum stepped political party organizations, often called "machines," run by "bosses." They doled out favors to businessmen competing for construction projects and other municipal licenses, arranged city jobs for their supporters, and addressed many of the needs of working-class ethnic communities. The new urban machines were notoriously corrupt but often remained in control of city politics for years with the support of the voters and a frequently corrupt judiciary. The most celebrated of these organizations, a Democratic political machine dubbed Tammany Hall, controlled New York City for many years. Despite corruption, at some level the urban machines provided services that the older, more unwieldy governmental structures were initially incapable of delivering.[11]

Freedman used his connections with Tammany to block the few available suitable sites for a new ballpark in New York City. To gain control of a site, Johnson needed to line up some well-connected Tammanyites of his own to purchase the franchise. Fortunately for Johnson, he was friends with sportswriter Joe Vila, one of New York's better-connected personalities. Vila introduced Johnson to Frank Farrell, boss of much of the city's high-end, illegal gambling and an associate of Tammany's Big Tim Sullivan. Farrell jumped at the chance to own a big-league ballclub in New York and put up $25,000 as a good-faith deposit. To be his silent partner—at least initially—Farrell brought in Big Bill Devery, a shady former police chief who had escaped conviction despite two indictments. Even with their Tammany connections, however, Farrell and Devery could do no better than a marginal site just west of Broadway between 165th and 168th Streets, at the far north end of Manhattan. Nevertheless, Johnson had few real alternatives and agreed to sell Farrell and Devery the franchise rights for $18,000. To strengthen the club, Johnson also arranged for Chicago pitcher-manager Clark Griffith to join the New York club. Despite Johnson's efforts, with its out-of-the-way ballpark and limited success on the ball field, the New York Yankees (then called the Highlanders) could not challenge the popularity of the Giants. Farrell quickly became the face of ownership, and, interestingly, over time his press became more sympathetic, concentrating on baseball rather than his gambling connections. He was now a "sportsman," not a "gambler."[12]

By mid-1902 the National League magnates recognized the staying power of the Americans and were feeling the financial pinch. Now they were amenable to accepting the American League as an equal, and a compromise peace agreement seemed feasible. Brush remained the key obstacle to a settlement. Brash and obstinate, the American League's invasion of New York provided Brush

Yankees co-owner Frank Farrell, shown here in his box resting his head on his hand, was one of New York's most notorious Tammany-connected gambling bosses. (Courtesy of the Library of Congress)

additional motivation to obstruct any peace feelers. The new Cincinnati owners, however, who did not compete directly with an American League team, wanted an agreement, and team president Garry Herrmann quickly assumed a lead role in the negotiations.

It's difficult to imagine someone whose personality less resembled his photographs than Garry Herrmann. In images of him, Herrmann, born to two

German immigrants in 1859, appears austere and severe. His large mustache curled down at the ends of his mouth, giving him a perpetual frown. In fact, though, Herrmann was one of the flashiest dressers and biggest spenders in town. Later, as head of the National Commission, Herrmann commanded a large expense account, which he lavished on sportswriters and fellow owners. "He would attend each World Series and each major league meeting with his entourage often starting out at one small table," the writer Lee Allen recalled. "But as more and more of his friends would appear, Garry would wave them to sit down. One table after another would be added until Garry's party occupied almost the entire barroom. His very presence caused a chain reaction of mirth and good fellowship that was all-inclusive. And Garry always paid the tab."[13]

Herrmann entered Cincinnati political life as a young man—at twenty-three he won election to the board of education. A natural for politics—sociable, shrewd, and an excellent organizer—Herrmann eventually became the right-hand man of Republican boss George Cox. Supported by the wealthy Fleischmann brothers, Max and Julius, Cox's political machine controlled much of Cincinnati at the turn of the century. Herrmann, one of the few machine politicians to earn his pay, ran important city departments with some success. While head of the water works, he directed a complete overhaul of the municipal water system.

In the summer of 1902, when Herrmann, in partnership with Cox and the Fleischmanns, purchased the Reds from Brush for $146,000, a huge amount for the time, it was met with enthusiasm throughout the city. The team would finally be in the hands of local, wealthy, civic-minded owners. Despite his lack of baseball experience—none of the other three had any either—the group named Herrmann president and chief operating partner.

Herrmann could not have picked a more turbulent year to jump into baseball. The battle with the upstart American League was in full swing, and the divided factions within the National League were disorganized in their defense. After the 1902 season, with Freedman out of the picture and Brush alone in his desire to continue the fight, the Nationals, with Herrmann as a lead negotiator, agreed to a truce granting the American League Major League status. In 1903 the two big leagues and the Minors signed off on the National Agreement, creating and setting forth the rules and regulations for what came to be called Organized Baseball.

The new organizational structure, with the American and National leagues at the top and the Minor Leagues below, required an oversight body. For this purpose the owners created the National Commission, a three-person group

*Cincinnati Reds owner and National Commission chairman Garry Herrmann
was a man whose outgoing personality belied the stern expression with which
he always seemed to be photographed. (Courtesy of the Library of Congress)*

which included the league presidents—Ban Johnson, the driving force behind
the American League; Harry Pulliam, the recently elected president of the National League; and Herrmann. For the third and often deciding vote, the owners
wanted someone associated with baseball, but with the still latent hostility between the leagues, both sides were leery of selecting someone associated with the
other. The two leagues turned to Herrmann as the perfect compromise choice.
Despite his affiliation with the National League, Herrmann was acceptable to
Johnson because of their friendship from Johnson's time in Cincinnati and the
pragmatic way he helped arrange the peace agreement between the leagues.

   With the settlement behind them, the two leagues began a more or less
friendly rivalry. The National League continued to govern itself as a mostly
dysfunctional democracy, purposely maintaining its president principally as a
figurehead, his authority typically limited to overseeing the umpires and disci-
plinary issues. On important league matters the owners generally ignored the
league president and bickered among themselves to reach a resolution. Conversely, Johnson ran the American League as a constitutional monarchy. Most
of the owners were beholden to him for their franchises and often for financial

support, which came through Somers. With its better organization and leadership, the American League thrived during its first decade of existence and soon overtook the Nationals in attendance.

During these years Herrmann spent most of his summers casting the deciding vote on numerous baseball disputes, some with important implications and some on minor personnel matters. He disappointed and angered many in baseball since nearly every decision he made had at least one loser. But most felt that Herrmann carried out his responsibilities with a surprising deftness. "I'd be willing to take every one of Mr. Herrmann's findings to the Supreme Court of the United States, and I don't believe he'd be reversed in any case," wrote an admittedly not unbiased John Bruce, a Cincinnati attorney and secretary of the National Commission. "He has been eminently fair and from a judicial point of view his decisions rank as models."[14]

TIMELINE OF BASEBALL MILESTONES LEADING TO THE FEDERAL LEAGUE

1871   America's first professional sports league, the National Association of Professional Baseball Players, is formed and lasts five seasons.

1876   The National League, the first professional sports league run on modern principles, begins play.

1879   After the season the National League secretly initiates the "reserve clause," effectively binding the top players to their teams indefinitely by restricting their ability to become free agents at the expiration of their contract. By 1887 the reserve clause had fully evolved to include nearly everyone on the team and was written into all player contracts.

1882   The American Association is launched as a second Major League in competition with the National League.

1883   The National League and American Association reach a truce in which they agree to respect each other's reserve lists and territorial rights.

1884   The Union Association begins operation, hoping to compete as a third Major League. It folds after just one season.

1885   John Montgomery Ward organizes the first real baseball players union, the Brotherhood of Professional Baseball Players.

1890   The players, disgruntled with their treatment by Major League owners, form the Players League. Most of the top National League stars defect to the new league, but the league folds after only one season.

1891   The American Association, unhappy with the distribution of players after the demise of the Players League, abrogates its agreement with the National League.

1892   The American Association, having suffered in full competition with the National League, agree to a merger. Four teams join the National League and four teams are contracted out of existence, resulting in one twelve-team Major League.

1894   Ban Johnson takes over the presidency of the reorganized Western League, a Midwest-based Minor League.

1899   After the season the National League contracts four of its teams, leaving just one eight-team Major League.

1900   Ban Johnson, sensing an opportunity, renames his Western League the American League and moves the St. Paul franchise to Chicago.

1901   Johnson declares his American League a Major League, moves several franchises to larger Eastern cities, and refuses to honor the National League's reserve clause, signing many of its stars.

1903   In September a new peace agreement recognizes the American League as a second Major League. In this National Agreement the Majors and Minors officially recognize each other's reserved players, territorial rights, and the hierarchy of the Majors and Minors. The structure ratified by this agreement becomes known as Organized Baseball.

1908   The Minor Leagues just below the Majors in the baseball hierarchy— the Eastern League, the American Association (a new Minor League unrelated to the nineteenth century version), and the Pacific Coast League—begin agitating for an elevated status.

1911   For 1912, the Eastern League renames itself the International League.

1912   The United States League begins operating in a number of larger cities already home to a Major League team. Although not competing as a Major League, because the United States League is not a party to the National Agreement, it is considered an "outlaw" league by Organized Baseball. The league disbands after only two months.

2

Rumblings

With the end of the war between the National and American leagues, and the signing of the National Agreement that incorporated the Minors, baseball appeared to have reached a stable equilibrium. Each league generally accepted its place in the revised hierarchy; territorial restrictions were agreed upon, and Organized Baseball's control over the players was reasserted. As strife receded, business prospered. In 1907, four years after the peace agreement, baseball attendance exceeded 6 million fans for the first time, an average of just over 377,000 per team. Two years later attendance averaged more than 450,000 per team, with profits up commensurately. By comparison, in 1899, the last year of the twelve-team National League, attendance had averaged only 212,000.

In 1910 America was a much different place than it had been in 1871, when the National Association had first organized. The population of the United States had exploded from 38.6 million in 1870 to 92.2 million in 1910. The American economy was growing even faster. The gross domestic product of the United States—the economy's total output of goods and services—swelled from $98 billion in 1870 to $517 billion in 1913. Other countries were also growing over the second half of the nineteenth century as the industrial revolution gathered steam; but the American experience was exceptional. The United States made up only 8.8 percent of the world economy in 1870 and was still slightly smaller than Great Britain; by 1913 it accounted for 18.9 percent and was more than twice as large as any other economy in the world.[1] For Americans this changing world offered both incredible possibilities and fearsome consequences. For some, the new, mostly unregulated economy, presented an opportunity to join the middle class or even assemble a large fortune; it relegated others, particularly new immigrants, to ghastly working conditions. The labor historian Melvyn Dubofsky describes the era as a "time of chaos."[2]

With the explosion of the national economy, the nature of work and business changed. Great corporations evolved to take advantage of new efficiencies of industrialization. The ability to create a monopoly offered further incentives for large conglomerates to consolidate. Amid the laissez-faire attitudes of the late nineteenth century, the government did little to curtail these arrangements. Although Congress passed the Sherman Antitrust Act in 1890 to limit the more egregious of these mergers, the law was applied only sporadically and with little effect. It was only in the early 1900s, as Progressives reacted against squalid working conditions and huge industrial concerns, that President Theodore Roosevelt began to enforce anti-trust legislation with vigor.

Baseball was subject to the same influences as other American businesses: concerns over trusts and monopolies as large companies consolidated into huge conglomerates; new competition as entrepreneurs or other companies believed they could make a better product or make an existing one more efficiently; the introduction of professional management as companies became too big for their owners to run; and continuing labor unrest over low salaries and unfair work rules. Baseball's owners used their resources and influence to maintain their monopoly and exclude potential competitors. They also had the reserve clause to control players, a method effective only to the degree that they maintained their monopoly. Only in the area of professional management did baseball continue to lag behind the rest of American business.

Organized Baseball first began to experience the pressure of trust-busting in 1912. In March, Illinois congressman Thomas Gallagher proposed a special committee to encourage the Department of Justice to investigate Organized Baseball. Gallagher accused the club owners of presuming "to control the baseball game, its officials announcing daily through the press dictates of a governing commission, how competition is stifled, territory and games apportioned, prices fixed which millions must pay to witness the sport, how men are enslaved and forced to accept salaries and terms or be forever barred from playing."[3]

The National Commission proved its political smarts by simultaneously dismissing the more trivial complaints and appearing to welcome an investigation. "There is no baseball trust and can never be," asserted Garry Herrmann. "Different prices are charged in different cities. There can be an investigation at any time without any objection from the National Commission." Ban Johnson added, "We would be glad to have an investigation. There is no baseball trust and competition is not stifled. Any one who desires is welcome to get into the game."[4] They needn't have worried. Congress had little interest in pursuing Gallagher's initiative. Most saw little reason to investigate what they felt was simply a sport and, more important, little political advantage in attacking an American institution like baseball.

In early 1913, however, Gallagher found allies in Georgia's congressional delegation. Georgia's favorite son Ty Cobb was involved in a bitter contract dispute with Detroit Tigers owner Frank Navin, who told Cobb, "You'll play at my price or not at all."[5] "What I understand exists cannot exist legally," countered Georgia senator Hoke Smith.[6] Representative Thomas Hardwick, from Cobb's home district, threatened to renew the push for an investigation of baseball. The renewed congressional interest surely influenced Detroit to settle with Cobb more quickly and for a higher salary than the team had originally contemplated. After Cobb signed his new contract, the Georgia congressional contingent quickly lost interest in baseball's anti-trust status and moved on to other concerns. Gallagher continued to press his case for an investigation throughout the summer, meeting with several disgruntled baseball executives. Once again, however, he failed to generate much interest from his colleagues, and his proposal soon died in committee.

On the player front, baseball also appeared to be in full control. Because of its unique characteristics and the specialized skills of its players, baseball quickly hit upon a powerful deterrent to potential competitors—the blacklist. Unlike in other industries where skilled laborers could move to a company in a similar industry, a blacklisted baseball player had no such option. Thus most players were quite careful about engaging in any activity that might get them declared ineligible by Organized Baseball. To dampen competition, the club owners used this threat against any player who jumped his contract or reserve clause to sign with a team outside of Organized Baseball.

Nevertheless, three new leagues hoped to gain traction in the first few years after the 1903 National Agreement. An independent team in Hoboken, New Jersey, formed in 1904 to play Sunday exhibitions against New York–area clubs. To stock themselves with the best available talent, the Hoboken club signed some players on the reserve lists of Organized Baseball clubs. The National Commission quickly ostracized the new team and its players by forbidding any team within Organized Baseball to play Hoboken, which now harbored ineligible players. A year later the Tri-State League, with teams located in Alabama, Georgia, and Tennessee, attempted to organize independently using players under reserve to Organized Baseball clubs. Once again the National Commission reacted quickly, declaring that any player joining the new league would be declared permanently ineligible. The Tri-State League soon capitulated and was allowed to join Organized Baseball. Another league, the California, tried to organize independently in 1907 and suffered the same fate as the Tri-State; it too was soon assimilated into Organized Baseball. Players who had jumped to the California League were not removed from the ineligible list until 1912.

As baseball prospered, new competition was inevitable. The Chicago Cubs netted roughly $100,000 per year and the White Sox even more. Baseball's most profitable franchise, the Giants, earned at least $500,000 from 1906 through 1910, and probably more over the next several years.[7] In 1910 the well-connected sportswriter Sam Crane estimated profits for a mythical New York baseball franchise. He arrived at an annual profit of $200,000 based on revenues of $382,000 and operating expenses of $182,000, as detailed in table 2.1.[8]

Table 2.1.

Players salaries	$75,000
President's salary	$25,000
Secretary and assistant salary	$8,000
Rent of ballpark	$20,000
Employees	$5,000
Southern training trip	$8,000
Traveling expenses (hotels, trains, etc.)	$12,000
Incidentals	$5,000
Losses by postponements	$24,000
Total	*$182,000*

A confirming article several years later reported that in 1911 or 1912 the Giants netted $144,000, though $74,000 of that profit was directly related to their appearance in the World Series.[9] In other words, without qualifying for the Series the Giants would have netted closer to $70,000. In fact, only the top two or three most profitable teams in any given year would have made as much as $200,000. Taking in $382,000 in revenue would have been nearly impossible for all but the highest-grossing teams. At this time, well before radio, television, and merchandising revenue, nearly all dollars came from ticket sales. Concessions and advertising provided only nominal additional revenues. All teams had the same basic ticket price structure: bleacher seats, 25 cents; pavilion, 50 cents; grandstand, 75 cents; reserved seats, $1.00; box seats, $1.25 or more in some parks. Teams split the first 50 cents of a ticket price evenly with the visiting club and kept all revenue above 50 cents. Thus, on a 75-cent ticket the visiting team would receive 25 cents and the home team 50 cents. Assuming home and road attendance of 450,000 and an average ticket price of, say, 70 cents (there were generally a few more bleacher and pavilion tickets sold than reserved and box seats) results in revenue of $315,000, still enough for a healthy profit.[10]

Expenses also varied significantly by team. Many clubs had a lower payroll and paid a lower salary to the team president, but they also may have had a higher ballpark rent. And teams would have had to pay some sort of return to their investors. A relatively typical 6 percent rate on a total capitalization of $300,000 represents another $18,000 that would have been owed—but not necessarily paid in bad times—to the owners. Still, the clubs were making significant profits relative to their earlier franchise values.

As profits increased, baseball's magnates also benefited from exploding franchise values. For the first couple of years after the 1903 peace agreement, team values increased, but clubs generally still traded for less than $150,000. By the end of the decade, however, franchise prices were well above this postsettlement level. The hapless Boston Braves franchise sold for $187,000; no other team sold for below $200,000 and most were significantly higher. A half-interest in the crosstown rival Red Sox sold in 1912 for $150,000; one year later the same interest went for $200,000. In 1909 the Phillies sold for $350,000; in 1913 the Reds were valued at $450,000 for tax purposes, and the Detroit Tigers at $650,000 one year later.[11]

With the explosion in baseball profits and franchise values, outsiders sensed an opportunity to make money. And with a rapidly increasing urban population, more teams could be supported. From the end of the Civil War, much of America's growth had been produced by millions of new immigrants, most of them from Europe. These "huddled masses" swarmed to America's cities in ever increasing numbers, searching for a better life. In 1881 more than 669,000 immigrated to the United States, the first year of more than 460,000. The next quarter-century saw new records: nearly 790,000 in 1882, more than 800,000 in 1903, and finally over 1 million in 1905. By 1914 annual immigration ran at roughly 1.2 million. These new immigrants were joined by rural Americans leaving farms for better opportunities in urban America. As the new tools of the industrial revolution transformed farming, millions of farm workers were no longer needed to work the fields.[12]

If one lumps New York and Brooklyn together—Brooklyn was not officially annexed into New York until 1898—the United States in 1870 had only three cities of more than 300,000: New York, Philadelphia, and St. Louis, and only the first two exceeded 400,000. Over the next forty years, as America experienced unprecedented growth and urbanization, the nation's cities absorbed a disproportionate amount of this growth. Of the population in 1870, 28.7 million (74.3

percent) were classified as rural and 9.9 million (25.7 percent) urban. Over the next forty years urban America more than quadrupled to 42.1 million residents, accounting for more than 45 percent of the U.S population. Of particular interest for the story of Major League sports, there were now eighteen cities with more than 300,000 people and eleven with more than 400,000. In reality the increase was even more dramatic. Until around 1870 the concept of metropolitan areas was not really relevant because most cities were expanding within their existing municipal boundaries or annexing small neighboring towns. But as cities began growing beyond their boundaries in the late nineteenth century, the census introduced a definition of "metropolitan districts." First applied to the census in 1910, fifteen metropolitan areas had populations in excess of 400,000.

In his award-winning novel *The Magnificent Ambersons*, Booth Tarkington captures the spirit of this new urbanization:

> New faces appeared at the dances of the winter; new faces had been appearing everywhere for that matter, and familiar ones were disappearing, merged in the increasing crowd, or gone forever and missed a little and not for long; for the town was growing and changing as it never had grown and changed before.
>
> It was heaving up in the middle incredibly; it was spreading incredibly; and as it heaved and spread, it befouled itself and darkened its sky. Its boundary was mere shapelessness on the run; a raw, new house would appear on a country road; four or five others would presently be built at intervals between it and the outskirts of the town; the country road would turn into an asphalt street with a brick-faced drugstore and framed grocery at the corner; then bungalows and six-room cottages would swiftly speckle the green spaces—and a farm had become a suburb which would immediately shoot out other suburbs into the country, on one side, and on the other join itself solidly to the city. . . .
>
> But the great change was in the citizenry itself. What was left of the patriotic old-stock generation that had fought the Civil War, and subsequently controlled politics, had become venerable and was little heeded. The descendants of the pioneers and early settlers were merging into the new crowd, becoming a part of it, little to be distinguished from it. What happened to Boston and to Broadway happened in degree to the Midland city; the old stock became less and less typical, and of the grown people who called the place home, less than a third had been born in it. [Tarkington's Midland city was modeled on his hometown of Indianapolis, a city whose population exploded from 48,244 in 1870 to 339,105 fifty years later.]

Moreover, as Tarkington wrote, "A new spirit of citizenship had already sharply defined itself. It was idealistic, and its ideals were expressed in the new kind of young men in business downtown. They were optimists—optimists to the point of belligerence—their motto being 'Boost! Don't Knock!' And they were hustlers, believing in hustling and in honesty because both paid. They loved their city and worked for it with a plutonic energy which was always ardently vocal." Possessed of these dual characteristics of civic pride and a keen interest in new ways to make money, these new urban citizens made ideal potential investors for the men looking to establish new baseball teams.

For the 1912 season two new leagues hoped to reap the potential profits in baseball. They were not simply small regional circuits but included some of the country's largest cities, many of which already boasted Major League teams. John Powers's Columbian League was to include Cleveland, St. Louis, and Chicago. Powers, the founder of the class D Wisconsin League, did not expect to compete directly for players on reserve lists. Nevertheless, he recognized that he would face stiff resistance from the "baseball trust." When St. Louis backer Otto Stifel begged off in March, Powers suspended his plans.[13]

William Witman, a onetime manager in the Pennsylvania State League, lined up a coterie of mostly undercapitalized entrepreneurs and their partners to launch the United States League. It began play on May 1, 1912, with teams in New York, Washington, Reading (Witman's hometown), Richmond, Chicago, Cincinnati, Pittsburgh, and Cleveland. Opening Day attracted ample curious crowds, and with teams in Major League cities, the United States League threw a brief scare into Organized Baseball. By the end of the month, however, it was clear that the venture had failed. One postmortem in the *Sporting News* concluded that the league "bit off more than it can chew with a major league circuit for an organization of class B minor league strength."[14] Still, the undertaking underscored the conviction of many businessmen that Organized Baseball had not yet shuttered all barriers to entry.

Later in the summer two Pittsburgh businessmen, William McCullough, recently president of the Pittsburgh team in the defunct United States League, and Marshall Henderson, hoped to bring still another team to that city. McCullough had earlier broached the possibility of relocating the struggling Jersey City franchise to Pittsburgh with Ed Barrow, president of the class AA International League, one step below the Majors. In July Barrow and McCullough called on Pittsburgh Pirates owner Barney Dreyfuss to beg permission to share his territory. Not surprisingly, Dreyfuss refused. (This was not quite as preposterous a request as it sounds. Games would be staggered so that both teams would not play home games on the same day.) McCullough then carried the appeal to Garry Herrmann, who, according to McCullough, "agreed to get the sanction of

other magnates to the selling of the [Jersey City] franchise [to Pittsburgh investors who would then move the team] provided that another independent league
was not formed."[15] Dreyfuss, however, remained adamant, and other owners
respected his territorial rights.

Despite having filed for bankruptcy in June 1912 after the failure of the
United States League, Witman hoped to resurrect it in 1913. He put together
an eight-team grouping of Baltimore, Brooklyn, Lynchburg, New York, Newark, Philadelphia, Reading, and Washington, most of which played in substan-
dard venues. The season opened on May 10, 1913, to sparse crowds and folded
just three days later as several of the home teams failed to pay the $75 gate
guarantee to the visitors. As the clubs disbanded, players were left stranded
throughout the circuit.

Outsiders weren't the only ones who felt that baseball had room to readjust
its structure. The highest classification (Double-A) Minor Leagues were also
becoming increasingly unhappy with their status. Their dissatisfaction was
directed mainly at the section of the National Agreement that provided for
a player draft, which allowed teams to select players from teams in a lower
classification. The exact rules varied over the years, but typically teams could
draft from teams one or two levels below and lose up to one or two players to
the leagues above. The Majors, of course, sat at the top of the food chain and
could draft players from the highest Minor Leagues. Teams selecting players
would pay a draft price to the club from which they selected the player. For
example, the cost to a Major League club for drafting a player from a class AA
league team was $2,500.

Many of the best players who moved from the Minors to the Majors did so
through some sort of direct cash transaction, sometimes involving players as
well, but not via the draft. Although few top players came through the draft, its
very threat provided incentive for the top Minor Leagues to sell their best players
to the Major Leagues rather than hang onto them and lose them later for nothing
more than the draft price.

Based on their perspective, each level of Organized Baseball had a different
opinion about the desirability of the draft. The Major Leagues liked it because
theoretically it gave their clubs access to the best Minor League talent. To a large
degree the draft defined what it meant to be "Major," the ultimate destina-
tion for all the best players. The lowest Minor League levels tolerated the draft
because it provided a systematic way for them to earn money by having their
players advance. Because players in the lower Minors were typically less skilled

and less widely scouted, fewer opportunities existed to sell them for large sums. An organized draft gave these clubs a profitable outlet for maturing players. The draft also offered players ready to advance to the next level a systematic and institutionalized procedure for doing so.

On the other hand, the highest-classification Minor Leagues fervently and consistently fought against the draft. These clubs had long chafed at the fact that the Majors could effectively force them to release their players. For these leagues, the draft reduced the prices they could command from the Major Leagues for their best players and prevented those Minor League owners who wanted to retain their best players from doing so (though the draft did offer these teams an opportunity to restock their talent by drafting from the lower Minors). What's more, many of these owners operated in large cities and liked to think of themselves, their teams, and their cities as being near Major League. Tarkington's citizens demanded a higher status for their growing cities.

After the 1908 season two of the top Minor Leagues, the Eastern League (later to rename itself the International League) and the American Association (no relation to the Major League American Association of the nineteenth century or to the aborted version around the turn of the century), threatened to withdraw from the National Agreement if certain demands were not met. Most important, the high Minors wanted to limit the rights of the Major Leagues to "option" players to the Minors with an attendant right to repurchase them as a way of circumventing the "no-farming" rules—those regulations restricting the ability of Major League teams to keep contractual control of players in the Minors— and eliminate the draft. After several months of contentious meetings, the two leagues were granted some of their requests, but the draft remained in effect. The American Association, in particular, remained unhappy. In 1911 it presented two key proposals: that only one player per year could be drafted from its teams by the Majors, and that it have a representative on the National Commission. Both proposals were sternly rejected. To somewhat mollify the American Association and the International League, the 1908 accord was ratified officially after the 1911 season, and the two leagues along with the Pacific Coast League were moved into a newly created AA (or Double-A) classification.[16]

Despite low operating costs, an independent Minor League was not a highly profitable operation. Much of a club's profit came from its ability to sell players to higher leagues. A league outside of Organized Baseball did not have this option and had to support itself solely from gate receipts. Nevertheless, John Powers did not give up his desire to start a new league. In 1913 he successfully talked St. Louis brewer and machine politician Otto Stifel into owning a franchise in his hometown and also helping cover some of the league's start-up costs. Of the local giant brewery and competitor, Anheuser-Busch, Stifel would remark, "They make beer for the world. I try to make beer for a part of the good people of St. Louis." With the brewery business he inherited from his father, Stifel succeeded in making himself a wealthy man. A young-looking fifty-year-old with "iron gray hair" and "piercing eyes," Stifel looked like the Teutonic businessmen he emulated. He celebrated his German heritage and the beer business: "The German people all drink beer, and the German people are the greatest nation in the world."[17] Stifel had also worked himself into a prominent behind-the-scenes role as a political bigwig in local government. As a key mover in the Republican Party, he was reported to have "been instrumental in the election of several mayors of St. Louis."

Stifel recruited a number of local businessmen to join him in establishing a new baseball franchise. Calling themselves the "Thousand Dollar Club," each of the fourteen members anted up $1,000. Like the majority of baseball owners elsewhere, most were upper-middle class civic boosters without the vast wealth of leading American industrialists. When one member nominated Otto Stifel to be president, he hoped to force the wealthy brewer to increase his investment, saying, "Of course it is understood that our president shall have a larger interest than any of the common members." Stifel was perfectly happy to lead the group but was not about to be railroaded into funding more than his fair share: "Gentlemen, I am conscious of the honor you wish to confer upon me, but I think you are too generous."[18] The group of investors eventually worked out a plan of operation, leaving Stifel in charge.

On March 8, 1913, in Indianapolis, Powers officially incorporated his new organization, which he named the Federal League. He quickly secured additional franchises in Chicago, Cleveland, Pittsburgh, and Indianapolis. None of these teams was particularly well capitalized, and all played in second-rate ballparks. Luna Park, an amusement park principally owned by Fred Bramley, acquired the Cleveland franchise primarily to add another attraction to its venue. Indianapolis was also backed principally by the promoters of an amusement park. William McCullough and Marshall Henderson were the driving forces behind the capitalization of the Pittsburgh franchise. Powers and several associates controlled the Chicago club. Each franchise paid in $10,000 to join to league.

The Federal League's relatively small Midwestern footprint made for manageable travel costs, but the league needed a sixth team and targeted Cincinnati, a good fit for the geography. "All the cities are in with their money now except

Cincinnati," read one ownership solicitation letter to poultry processor William Graves. "I imagine that it will take that [$10,000] to properly finance the scheme in that City."[19] But Graves never signed on, and Powers traveled to Cincinnati to find backing for the club. Although investors could be found, lining up a ballpark site was another matter. Herrmann and Cox controlled much of the city's governing machinery and blocked access to suitable sites. Powers settled on Covington, a wide-open suburb across the river in Kentucky that "provided protected vice and entertainment for the larger city."[20] The stockholders quickly found a site on which to build a 4,200 seat stadium and hired ex-Major League star hurler Sam Leever to manage the team. Other teams also signed well-known ex-Major Leaguers to manage. Cy Young went to Cleveland, where he had starred as a pitcher several years earlier. Pittsburgh signed Deacon Phillippe, a mainstay of the Pirates' championship pitching staff early in the century. Bill Phillips, a former Cincinnati catcher, was hired to manage in nearby Indianapolis.

The newly minted Federals had little desire to challenge Organized Baseball directly. Mostly the teams signed top local semi-pro players, mixing in some aging former Major Leaguers and journeyman Minor League veterans. To keep costs in check, the owners agreed to a monthly cap of $3,000 per team for player salaries.[21] The expected caliber of play can be inferred from the class AA International League, which had a $6,000 monthly cap.[22]

The sporting press generally dismissed the new circuit, though several writers, particularly Hugh Fullerton in Chicago, offered support. "I am convinced that the majority of the newspaper boys will either help or not knock," Fullerton wrote to Powers. "The trouble will be to convince them that it is on the square and legitimate. . . . I do not look for active support from the American League, but felt certain from talking with [Charles] Comiskey and [Ban] Johnson that they will not offer any active objection. . . . Johnson thinks there is room for more clubs."[23] After further discussing the future of the league, Powers went so far as to offer the presidency to Fullerton, which the reporter declined.[24] Unfortunately for the Federals, Fullerton misjudged Johnson's reaction to the new competitor.

Chicago opened the season to a moderately disappointing crowd of 2,000 at DePaul University's little athletic field on Belden Avenue. The windows of a nearby university building had to be screened against foul balls. Throughout the league, public reception was uneven. But moderate success in a few cities made some men in Organized Baseball a little anxious. "If they are drawing people with the kind of players they have, and not much back of them, it strikes me that during the coming fall and winter they might be able to get substantial backing," wrote Minor League general manager Bob Quinn prophetically.[25] "If they do, they will be able to go out and get ball players. . . . You know the American League was sneezed at when it started, and while it takes considerably more money now than it did then, to run baseball and get plants [ballparks], there is always a chance that someone else may accomplish what others have," Quinn wrote to Ban Johnson. "A little attention to the matter now might save a lot of trouble later on."[26]

Robert Hedges in St. Louis was also concerned. "The Federal League in St. Louis is getting an equal part with the two major leagues in so far as newspaper publicity is concerned," he wrote Johnson, though he added, "They are getting no patronage. Have no classy ball players. Their park is situated in an inaccessible place. They are not making any money in St. Louis." Overall, "they are not dangerous right now, but I cannot tell how soon they will get a foot hold."[27] Johnson, nevertheless, dismissed the upstarts: "From my observations, I hardly think the Federal can last until the first of July."

In some cities the league was clearly struggling. By the end of the season Pittsburgh was drawing only a couple of hundred fans per game. William Kerr, the lead contractor for the little ballpark which had been built the previous year for the Pittsburgh club in the United States League, was still waiting to be paid in mid-1913. Accordingly, he foreclosed on his mechanics lien and took charge of the money-losing ballclub. Kerr was not a baseball operator, so he relied on McCullough to run the operation and recoup some of his losses. Kerr was not wealthy by the standards of Major League baseball ownership, and the $24,000 he was still owed on the ballpark represented a real hardship.[28]

In Cleveland the Federal team "has not attracted sufficient interest this spring to be worthy of any notice on our part," wrote Indians vice president Ernest Barnard to Johnson. "Their weekday attendance varies from one hundred to two hundred and there is no way of telling how many of these are paid and how many are free. . . . The Cleveland newspapers refused to take the Federal League seriously this spring . . . the promoters of the organization approached the afternoon newspapers and offered to stand the expense of installing telephones at the Federal Park so that the afternoon papers could carry a box score. The afternoon papers refused to do this even in the face of their offer to stand all the expense. . . . We feel reasonably sure that the present Federal League Outlaw club will be the last effort of anyone to introduce outlaw baseball into Cleveland for several years."[29]

Indianapolis attorney Edward E. Gates was fighting a similar battle against Western Union on behalf of the Federals. The company refused to carry Federal League scores on its ticker service, despite the willingness of the league to cover the costs. Gates hoped to force Western Union to recognize the league's results

Federal League attorney Edward Gates represented the new league in their most important legal battles. (Courtesy of the Dennis Goldstein Collection)

by complaining to the Interstate Commerce Commission that Western Union was violating its duties under the Hepburn Act, which held telegraph companies to be "common carriers."[30]

One of Indianapolis's leading citizens, Gates came from a family that boasted some of Indiana's first settlers. His grandfather had settled in the state in the early nineteenth century, and though the family never became truly wealthy, Gates's father made a comfortable living in the wholesale grocery business. Born in Indianapolis in 1871 and educated at the best schools locally, after his secondary schooling the family sent Gates east to Yale College, where he graduated in 1891. He continued his studies at New York Law School and in 1895 earned a degree from Indiana Law School. After a brief sojourn with the Indianapolis Field Artillery during the Spanish-American War, Gates settled into life as one of Indianapolis's most prominent attorneys. He made his mark locally in 1906 when he represented the Indianapolis Freight Bureau before the Interstate Commerce Commission. Neighboring cities had been offering discounts to the railroads to the detriment of Indianapolis-based shippers, and Gates won a decision in favor of his hometown. When the Federal League came along, Gates seized the opportunity to bring Major League baseball to Indianapolis. As the most prominent and successful lawyer among the owners, he quickly assumed a leading role in shaping the league's legal strategy.[31]

In June, Organized Baseball angered Gates and his fellow owners when they signed two players from the Hoofeds. The Federals had scrupulously avoided a confrontation by refraining from signing players under contract with Organized

Baseball. No doubt this posture was mainly for self-preservation, avoiding a battle they could not win at the moment. Organized Baseball paid little attention to the nuances of the Federal League's position and showed its disdain for the upstarts by grabbing players as they pleased.

By August, Ban Johnson had changed his tune somewhat. "The Federal League at this period cannot create any anxiety among club owners of the Major Leagues. This is not true, however, of the minor organizations," he wrote to Herrmann. Specifically, he noted that "the Federals had made considerable progress at Indianapolis and Kansas City [where the Covington franchise had shifted]."[32] Roughly fifteen backers had agreed to secure the Kansas City franchise and sign a lease for a ballpark site. To backstop the lease, angel investor Stifel told the landlord he would cover any shortfall in rental payments.[33] A few days later Johnson added, "It appears to me that they will be able to 'tide over' their first year. This in itself will be regarded as a marked achievement and will give the Federals much prestige. [Next year], with new parks and better locations, they will be a menace to some, and a positive blight to many of the leagues of the National Association [the Minors]."[34]

To help American Association teams immediately, Johnson proposed possible player transfers that skirted the legality of player rights under the waiver rules. Before a Major League club could send a player to the Minor Leagues (or a Minor League team could send a player to a team in a lower league classification), he needed to clear waivers. That is, he was made available to all the other clubs in his current league, and if any team claimed him he would go to that team for a small fee. There was one exception, however—if a player was claimed on waivers, his original team could withdraw the waivers and retain the player. The system did not always work as advertised. Gentlemen's agreements often led to Major League owners passing on a player who might have benefited them, with the expectation of reciprocity at some later date. In this particular instance, Johnson suggested, "Indianapolis and Kansas City must receive their help from the clubs in the Major Leagues with whom they have been in close touch. It is claimed that Mr. Murphy, of the Chicago National League Club, and Mr. Dreyfuss, of Pittsburgh, will be willing to render some assistance to these clubs, provided they can secure waivers on certain players. It is distinctly understood that these men are not to be surrendered permanently, but are only for temporary use."[35] Johnson also planned to influence the press. "I think it advisable that the Commission should inspire editorials in the Sporting Life and News to the effect that all players who violate the reserve clause of their contractual obligations will be punished in a manner similar to those who joined the California outlaw organization [i.e., blacklisted]."[36]

Despite modest successes, the Federal League owners were unhappy with Powers. They had little patience for some of his more bizarre decisions, the lack of press coverage, and an inability to get their game results into the newspapers in a timely manner. "President Powers of the Federal League sprung something on us Thursday night when he declared Monday's game between Indianapolis and Pittsburgh thrown out of the standings because an umpire made a bad decision at first base," wrote the *Indianapolis Star* on June 7. "Never before has a league hired an umpire and then because he erred in judgment as to whether a base runner was safe or out, thrown the game out of the standings. It's a bad move."[37] In July the dissatisfaction came to a head when Powers rescheduled one of Chicago's games with Pittsburgh to his hometown of Sheffield, Illinois. The Chicago ownership rebuffed him, refusing to shift a home game to a tiny town in central Illinois.

On Saturday evening, August 2, Federal League officials held a secret meeting in Indianapolis to review the season to date and consider the future. While no definitive conclusions were reached, the owners "decided to expand next season upon an independent basis and several plans toward that end were discussed."[38] The owners permitted Horace Fogel, recently expelled from Organized Baseball and claiming to represent potential investors in New York, Baltimore, and Philadelphia, to make a presentation. He proposed creating a ten-team league with two divisions. The owners also planned to look at possible expansion to Milwaukee, Detroit, or back to Cincinnati. Most important, they fired Powers, technically granting him a leave of absence, and installed a new interim president.

"A big rangy Chicago businessman,"[39] Long Jim Gilmore was looking for his life's next adventure. After growing up in Chicago, the six-foot-three Gilmore joined the army for the Spanish-American War when his father told him, "I fought in the Civil War. So did three of my brothers. You are my only unmarried son. Go to War." Gilmore lived a wide variety of experiences in the military: he spent time in Cuba, suffered through a debilitating bout of malaria, and was a commissary sergeant in the Philippines. Upon his discharge Gilmore resumed his prewar job as a coal salesman, at which he proved highly adept. He was a "good free off-hand talker, a good leader, a well-preserved man who would make a success, say in the railroad business."[40] Another admirer of his sales skills noted that "Gilmore could not only convince you the moon is made of green cheese, but he could sell you a slice of it."[41] His success at sales led him to the presidency of the Kernchen Company, a manufacturer of ventilators and ventilating engines.

In the summer of 1913 the thirty-seven-year-old Gilmore was playing golf with his friend Eugene Pike, an investor in the Chicago Federal League franchise.

Federal League president James Gilmore was an energetic proponent of his new league who didn't know when to keep his mouth shut. (Courtesy of the Library of Congress)

For their round the two were joined by E. C. Racey, who also happened to be treasurer of the team. Pike and Racey admitted to Gilmore that the club was losing money but invited him to invest in this new league in large Midwestern cities that could compete with Organized Baseball. Over the next few weeks, as Gilmore contemplated the opportunity, he not only decided that the Chicago investment could work but also that if he were to invest, he wanted an active role in running the league. Gilmore and his associate Charles Williams agreed to take an ownership interest in the team in exchange for assuming their share of the liabilities, mostly player salaries over the remainder of the season, which came to about $14,000. At the league's August 2 meeting Gilmore maneuvered himself into the presidency, though technically only on an interim basis.

Organized Baseball quickly picked up the new buzz coming from the Federals. The Indians' Barnard wrote to Johnson on August 4, "There seems to be so much activity on the part of the Federal League officials lately that it is possible that some of the promoters, of this organization, may have courage enough to gamble on a larger scale next season."[42] He was right. The Federals held another secret meeting in Indianapolis on August 26 and came to an understanding that they would vie for Major League status the next season, an aspiration that would require Major League–caliber ballplayers and ballparks. The successful bid for

Major League status by the American League only thirteen years earlier offered both a legitimate expectation and a blueprint for success.

At this point, however, all such plans were no more than wishful thinking; the Federal League had neither the wealthy owners nor the playing venues to support such aspirations. Most of the owners recognized their limitations, and the league did not issue an official statement, only leaking their intentions to the press. They also discussed bringing in a dynamic, baseball-connected president. In early September the Federals offered the presidency to an unnamed well-known sports reporter—most likely Hugh Fullerton again—but he declined after discussing the matter confidentially with Ban Johnson.[43] It was not an auspicious start to their drive for Major League status. The Federals had semi-publicly declared their intentions but had neither the resources nor the baseball connections to challenge interests as entrenched as Organized Baseball's. Nevertheless, they were convinced it was time to confront the existing order as a self-proclaimed Major League circuit.

3

Going Major

On October 14, 1913, St. Louis team president Edward Steininger made it official: "We are going to invade the majors and we will take some of their players, too. We are going to begin in St. Louis. . . . We have every reason to believe we will secure what players we choose to take into our organization."[1] One day later the first Major Leaguer of any consequence, St. Louis Browns first baseman and manager George Stovall, fired from his skipper role late in the year after a stormy season—including a suspension for spitting tobacco juice on an umpire—announced he was considering jumping to Kansas City in the new league. Several days later he did just that, suggesting he would lure several other Major Leaguers with him. Browns owner Robert Hedges ran a notoriously low-paying organization, and Stovall believed that most players would show him little allegiance. Known for his temper and competitive sprit, at thirty-five Stovall could still play, and looked forward to revenge on his old owner and the manager appointed to his old position, the now-legendary Branch Rickey.

The Federal League owners met again in Indianapolis on November 2, where they admitted Baltimore and Buffalo, two of the largest U.S. cities without Major League baseball. As the nation's ninth-largest metropolitan area, Baltimore in particular represented a real opportunity for a profitable franchise. Many of its leading citizens believed Baltimore to be Major League and were willing to back it up with their checkbooks. Judge Harry Goldman led a group of roughly six hundred Baltimoreans who raised $164,000 to capitalize the franchise. Goldman lured local hero Ned Hanlon, manager of the great Orioles National League clubs of the 1890s, to run the team. By this time a wealthy Baltimore business-

Ned Hanlon was a key Baltfeds investor and nineteenth-century Hall of Fame manager for Baltimore's stellar 1890s National League team. (Courtesy of the Library of Congress)

man in his own right, Hanlon also controlled an excellent site for a ballpark. Another key investor, Carrol Rasin, was the son of Isaac Freeman Rasin, the onetime boss of Baltimore's Democratic political machine.

In Buffalo, Dick Carroll, a former Minor League pitcher (with one Major League start), sourced much of the new club's capital from Canadian businessman Thomas Duggan. Local real estate developer Walter Mullen put up a significant share as did businessman William Robertson. Mullen was named president and Carroll business manager. With Baltimore and Buffalo signed on, the Federal League had officially settled on seven of its eventual eight franchises: Baltimore, Buffalo, Chicago, Indianapolis, Kansas City, Pittsburgh, and St. Louis.

The league's owners were dissatisfied with the Cleveland situation, chiefly because of an inability to secure a location for an adequate ballpark. Gilmore considered Toronto an attractive alternative and later brought in Bernard Hepburn, a Canadian member of parliament from Toronto, to present his case to the Federal League owners. Gilmore strongly supported Hepburn, whose group controlled an excellent ballpark site and had arranged ample financial backing.

Fred Bramley, owner of the Cleveland Federal League franchise in 1913, also made his case for remaining in the league. Despite the active opposition of Cleveland Indians owner Charles Somers, who tried to block access to suitable stadium sites, Bramley claimed to have gained control of a site at East 76th Street and Lexington Avenue. To bolster his case, he brought blueprints, highlighting his planned stadium. Bramley also claimed to have sufficient funding. Ultimately the league's owners sided with their president and selected Hepburn and Toronto. The announcement stunned Bramley, who couldn't believe his former colleagues would vote against him.[2]

Bramley refused to surrender. He convinced Gilmore and two league owners to come to Cleveland to view a site he had optioned for $1,000 per week. The officials liked the site but already had a full eight-team league. Moreover, the cost estimate for the site and ballpark construction came to roughly $600,000, an amount well above what Bramley could raise. To put the onus on the onetime Cleveland owner, the Federal Leaguers told Bramley he could purchase Kansas City's franchise for $60,000. But Bramley had little interest in paying for a franchise when he felt he rightfully owned one. Moreover, there was no certainty that the Federals could have delivered; Kansas City would not have given up its franchise without a court battle. In the end, an angry Bramley faded away, and Kansas City kept its team.[3]

Hepburn and Bramley were not the only ones looking to get into Major League baseball at a discount from the cost of an existing big-league franchise. As the Federal League solidified, Gilmore received inquiries from cities throughout the country. Potential owners in Boston, Providence, and Cincinnati submitted applications for a Federal League franchise, though most were well short of the necessary funding.[4]

The Federals also considered rule changes to increase offense in this dead-ball era, though none were implemented: installing a designated hitter for the pitcher, using a double foul line so that hard-hit balls past third base that fell just a little foul would not be counted as strikes, and issuing a walk after three balls instead of four.[5]

To maintain control over their teams, the Federal League technically owned the franchises, then leased them to the team's "owners." In Organized Baseball the owners themselves owned the franchises, subject to the leagues' bylaws and other agreements. The Federals hoped their organizational structure would give the league office more control over individual franchises. In practice, though, this was really form over function: the Federal League's president and key owners did not materially exercise any more control over their league's franchises than did those in Organized Baseball.

Despite advances by the Federals, Organized Baseball remained dismissive, at least publicly. "I know the clubs lost something like $15,000 each during their 1913 season," huffed the owner of Kansas City's (Minor League) American Association team. "I believe that if I were to offer $100,000 for the league, lock, stock and barrel, my money would be gobbled up in an instant, and the club owners would be glad of the chance to come out with their losses paid."[6]

Privately Organized Baseball remained complacent as well. As of mid-December 1913 the Federals had made little progress attracting players, and Hedges seemed to have held on to his supposedly disgruntled Browns players that Stovall expected to pilfer. "As far as my information goes, they have made absolutely no progress," Ban Johnson wrote to Herrmann, presumably unaware that Stovall was actually making inroads with his ex-teammates. "Otto Stifel, of St. Louis, has made an effort to get fifteen men to subscribe $5,000 apiece to start the Federals in that city for 1914. He has met with poor success."[7] Hedges added, "If the Federal League was such a good proposition, and Mr. Stifel such a rich man, why divide it up? From a reliable source I learn that Mr. Stifel's share of the losses last year was $18,000. Otto is evidently trying to raise money to reimburse himself for the losses of last year. When that is accomplished, he will say goodbye to the Federals."

Both Organized Baseball and the Federals recognized the importance of deep-pocketed owners. And the pool of potential candidates was surprisingly limited. While the wealthiest Americans such as the Vanderbilts, Rockefellers, Astors, and Carnegies were worth tens of millions of dollars, rapid economic growth at the close of the nineteenth century led to a highly skewed distribution of income. At the turn of the twentieth century there were about four thousand millionaires in the entire country. As the economy continued to grow over the first decade of the twentieth century, this number surely increased but still left only a modest pool of capitalists from which to draw baseball owners. The upper crust of American society initially shunned baseball ownership. Nevertheless, a huge secondary pool of potential owners existed: local upper-middle-class professionals and businessmen who could form investment syndicates to own a ballclub. Most syndicates included or were led by local politicians or those well connected to them, such as trolley company executives and building contractors. A syndicate would typically name its largest investor or most baseball-knowledgeable man as team president.[8]

With the Federals now on the scene, in late 1913 Johnson reorganized the American League's Boston franchise, one of baseball's most undercapitalized. The team had been run by Robert McRoy, onetime American League secretary and Johnson confidant, and James McAleer, a former Major League player. Two years earlier Johnson had presumably helped finance their purchase of half the team's stock. Now, with Federal League competition looming, Johnson turned to Joseph Lannin, a self-made real estate magnate from Quebec, maneuvering the transfer of the McRoy/McAleer half of the team to Lannin for $200,000 while McAleer was on an around-the-world baseball tour.[9]

With rumors swirling around the rejuvenated Federal League, the National Commission decided to get out in front of the story and publicly state the case for Organized Baseball. After consultation with Johnson and National League president Thomas Lynch, Herrmann presented the Commission's official stance on November 12 before the Minor League convention at the Virginia Hotel in Columbus, Ohio. He began by emphasizing the elevated standing, profitability, and peacefulness of Organized Baseball—with more than a little exaggeration.

> The game today is on a higher plane than ever before; your patronage has not only increased in numbers but in tone as well; the deportment of the players on the field shows a marked and steady improvement in recent years; the construction of new and modern plants has been pleasing to the patrons, resulting in more substantial and willing support on their part.
>
> The fear that existed among players when the National Agreement was first adopted and the Commission created, that it was for the purpose of reducing or limiting salaries, has been entirely eliminated. Salaries today are greater than ever before. Baseball litigation in the civil courts is a thing of the past. Club owners and players have been placed on equal footing. Neither is at an advantage or disadvantage in the case of any dispute.

Herrmann also took the opportunity to posture regarding the reinvigorated players union (which will be explored further in the next chapter):

> Concerted action by the players with all due regards to all other interests will, in our judgment, contribute materially to the betterment of baseball. But in formulating their demands and insisting on concessions, the privileges of patrons and rights of those financing the clubs, must be accorded adequate recognition. . . . The Commission is also firmly of the opinion that the best results can be secured if the Fraternity [the new players union] at such conferences is represented by a

committee consisting of the players themselves rather than by one, even if an officer of the organization, who is not directly connected with the game as a player, and this applies particularly to the President of the Fraternity [David Fultz] at the present time.

Herrmann continued at some length to criticize Fultz for his tactics, particularly his public complaints against the owners in the press. He then offered the Commission's thoughts on the new competition. "The Commission has never gone on record with reference to its attitude to either of these two leagues," Herrmann said regarding the defunct United States League and the Federal League, "but we will do so now with reference to the latter."

In typical Herrmann fashion, as with the Players Fraternity, he began by appearing to accept its legitimacy. "Baseball is not, cannot and will not be confined to those leagues, clubs or players who operate under the National Agreement [Organized Baseball]. The game is open to all. . . . College players, semi-pro players, free agents, and the boys on the lot, when entering the profession can cast their lot within or without Organized Baseball."

But because of the reserve clause, Herrmann made it clear that the players were not free to jump to teams outside Organized Baseball. "In former years there existed doubt with reference to the reservation clause in the player's contract, it being contended and probably correctly so, that it was not an equitable arrangement. This condition has now been changed. A player signing a contract containing the reservation clause is compensated for his action whether he is reserved or not. . . . For those players who do not respect their obligations there will be no place in organized baseball either now or in the future, and the same thing applies to the club owner as well."[10] Most of the owners would admit that the reserve clause was of dubious legality, despite a technical rewording of the contract language. They recognized, however, the power of the implied threat of banishment from Organized Baseball.

On Saturday, November 28, Federal League owners met in Pittsburgh to rally themselves to pursue players controlled by Organized Baseball under the reserve clause.[11] In the key session, club presidents banished everyone but Ned Hanlon of the Baltimore club, who gave them a pep talk on the signing of players from Organized Ball. Every player on the St. Louis American League team and the St. Paul American Association team, he told them, was ready to sign with the Federals. Hanlon had even brought player emissaries from these teams to testify to their interest. When he heard of the meeting, Pittsburgh Pirates owner Barney

Dreyfuss remarked that "Ned Hanlon seems to be the Moses they are looking for to lead them out of the wilderness."[12]

Despite Hanlon's motivational speech, Gilmore astutely realized that he needed more rich, high-profile owners to compete with the Major Leagues. Baltimore, Buffalo, Indianapolis, and Kansas City were owned by large groups of local stockholders. Kansas City had recently received a financial boost from the clothing merchant S. S. Gordon, now the team's largest shareholder; his associate, attorney Charles Madison, assumed control of the franchise. On the positive side, the large ownership base gave these teams a true community foundation, and their presidents were politically well-connected, upper-middle-class businessmen and civic boosters. But none of these ownership entities had the wherewithal for a drawn-out battle against Organized Baseball with all its financial and institutional resources.

The Indianapolis club, for example, planned to raise much of its capital through a stock offering. In this era before the creation of the Securities and Exchange Commission, one could make almost any claim in the offering. The prospectus put out by Indianapolis claimed that the club would probably earn $100,000 in 1914.[13] It also highlighted the fact that Charles Comiskey, the wealthy owner of the Chicago White Sox, had started in Organized Baseball with little more than what he earned as a player. The offering went on to point out that the current environment was even more favorable for baseball than when the American League started. In fact, in 1913 Indianapolis had lost $12,000 despite winning the pennant. "I just want to report to you that while the hotbed of the Federal League is Indianapolis," Johnson heard from one of his sources there, "I want to go on record as saying it is also financially the weakest. The entire staff of officers, in my opinion, cannot borrow $5,000 in this city without high-class collateral. I am a director in one of the largest banks of Indianapolis, and I believe I know what I am writing about."[14]

Indianapolis was not unique. In all the Federal League's cities, with the possible exception of St. Louis, the teams were trying to raise capital through stock subscriptions to the general public. In Pittsburgh efforts lagged. As of early January the club was at least $25,000 short of the capital necessary to fund the team, and the league had given it a deadline of February 1 or possible forfeit of the franchise. Contractor and part-owner William Kerr was still owed $35,000 from 1913 and was demanding to be paid out of any money raised.[15]

In St. Louis, which had endured small but real losses in 1913, the "Thousand Dollar Club" members had lost their initial investment. To compete head to head with the Majors in 1914, a much larger financial commitment was clearly necessary. All but a few investors dropped out, but Philip De Catesby Ball, a local magnate who had made his fortune developing refrigerated storage facilities, joined Stifel in the restructured ownership. Unlike owners in other Federal League cities, the Stifel-Ball team had the financial wherewithal, local connections, and commitment to winning to destabilize the undercapitalized American and National League owners in St. Louis.

Despite his aristocratic name, Philip De Catesby Ball had risen from humble beginnings. Ball's mother liked the idea of naming her son after a great uncle and commodore in the United States Navy, Ap Catesby Jones. Since she didn't like the sound of "Ap," she used the more patrician sounding "De." Born in Keokuk, Iowa, in 1864, Ball and family moved to Texas, where his father, an engineer, was building an ice plant. As a fourteen-year-old Ball found his first job assisting a team of surveyors. Over the next several years he traveled the middle of the country on surveying jobs and occasionally helped his father build ice plants as a junior engineer. While living in Shreveport, Louisiana, he played catcher on a local baseball team. He showed some promise, but any hope for a further career was cut short when his left hand was almost severed in a fight.

After finishing an ice plant in Paducah, Kentucky, Ball's father gave Philip $500 to travel to the Cotton Exhibition in New Orleans. En route Ball stopped in

Two of the Federal League's most important movers and shakers were President James Gilmore and Chifeds owner Charles Weeghman. (Courtesy of the Library of Congress)

Shreveport to see an old girlfriend. He and her brother hooked up to enjoy the night life, and young Ball lost his money gambling and drinking: "I was cleaned out of all except a 10-cent chip in my pocket." He was forced to ask his father for $20 so he could get home. Ball eventually saved some money and settled in St. Louis in 1890. He bought out his father's business, the Ice & Cold Machine Co., for $20,000, and his father retired to California. Ball had learned the business in his years assisting on the plants and later recognized the transformational importance of refrigeration. Over the next several decades he built the business into a multimillion-dollar enterprise. The plainspoken Ball—"he frequently said things he regretted afterward"—was generally regarded as a fair but tough businessman. He believed in and generally lived by the axiom that "honesty is the best policy." When asked his most important decision, Ball replied, "Picking out a fine woman for a wife."[16]

Stifel and Ball in St. Louis represented the first truly wealthy investors in a Federal League franchise. The league clearly needed others. In particular Gilmore wanted strong, aggressive ownership for its largest market, Chicago. He succeeded in attracting Charlie Weeghman, a popular, wealthy, and well-connected local businessman. Weeghman owned a string of restaurants around Chicago, mostly self-service lunch counters—what passed for fast food at the time. Typical of a restaurateur, he was an aggressive marketer and glad-hander. He knew almost everyone in town, and his friends included many movers and shakers with less than stellar reputations, men like gambler Monte Tennes (later implicated in the 1919 Black Sox scandal) and Mayor Big Bill Thompson.

After schooling in Indiana, Weeghman had arrived in Chicago around the time of the World's Columbian Exposition in 1893 with just a few dollars and looking for the big time. He got a job in King's restaurant, a popular establishment for the late-night crowd. At King's he learned the restaurant business and married Bessie Webb, one of the cashiers. When he struck out on his own several years later, his wife became a valuable partner in the business by managing many of the day-to-day details that Weeghman couldn't be bothered with. By the time Gilmore came calling, the Weeghmans had a string of twelve restaurants, the best of which cleared more than $50,000 in profits annually, along with some other business interests.[17]

"Now, Weeghman," Gilmore proposed, "I have a fine business opening for you, but we need more financial resources. We are going to reorganize the club with a capitalization of $50,000. If you will take $26,000 worth of stock, that will give you control of the club."

"Are you sure $50,000 will be enough to finance this thing?" Weeghman asked. "Won't there be any other expenses that crop up when the club gets under way that will be likely to cost a lot of money?"

"Oh no," Gilmore assured him, "all we want is $50,000. There won't be any other expenses. That will be all the money we shall require."[18]

After making the investment, Weeghman quickly realized that his initial instinct had been correct and that the club needed much more than $50,000. To help with the burden, Weeghman approached his friend William Walker, a local fish merchant. The two men and their wives had been friends for years; Walker supplied fish for Weeghman's restaurants. The two had also recently purchased a small theater together. Like Weeghman, Walker was a baseball enthusiast and self-made man, and when Weeghman outlined the proposition, Walker agreed it sounded attractive. He bought in and stayed mostly in the background, letting the suave, more outgoing Weeghman remain the front man.

Ball and Weeghman represented real successes for the Federals, but the question remained: Would it be enough? While Gilmore and several league syndicates struggled to raise moneyed investors, Ban Johnson offered a cautionary note. Johnson, of course, was opposed to competition from a new league, but he had been through these wars before on the side of the newcomer. "I cannot see how the Federals can expect to make much progress," Johnson observed. "You see, they must build new ballparks, which will require a hefty outlay. Then, again, they must have a lot of money to induce star players to go with them. I do not know whether each Federal League club has put up a $25,000 guarantee, but if the money has been posted, what does it amount to? It will require many times that sum to put the Federal League on a sound basis."[19] Johnson was pretty much on the mark. At this point, in early December 1913, Gilmore was still working on Weeghman, and only two Federal franchises, St. Louis and Baltimore, had anything resembling stable, well-capitalized ownership.

Albert Spalding, another baseball executive who had seen several baseball wars in his many years in the game, understood what the Federals were up against: "I read the other day that the Federal League had $10,000,000 with which to fight the two major leagues. In January $10,000,000 is equal to about $500,000 in July. Inexperienced men who are ready to furnish money to start this movement have been told of the future in glowing terms, but when the time comes to pay salaries and other expenses in June, with gate receipts dwindling, they may find that they have been deceived."[20]

Gilmore may have been new to baseball, but he appreciated the difficulties he faced and understood that to succeed each of his clubs needed even more than just ballplayers and wealthy owners. They also required ballparks and well-connected managers. To project a big-league atmosphere the teams needed to move beyond the rinky-dink ballparks most had played in during 1913. One of Gilmore's greatest achievements was in prevailing upon the league's owners to invest the large sums necessary to acquire prime sites and construct new ballparks.

Unlike a decade earlier, when the upstart American League could build and compete with relatively inexpensive wooden ballparks, most big league teams now played in a new generation of steel-and-concrete stadiums. These new ballparks were the result of new fire codes and baseball's increased prosperity. Beginning with the opening of Philadelphia's Shibe Park in 1909, many more facilities quickly followed so that by 1914 big-league fans expected a new, modern ballpark experience. These new stadiums had much greater capacities and made an architectural statement emphasizing the permanence and majesty of the game. The owners also hoped these new structures would increase their profits and prestige, placing them among the cream of American society that had so far generally ignored baseball. Most of these ballparks would survive, with some modification, for another half-century, until teams deserted them for new cities in the 1950s and the arrival of multipurpose stadiums in the 1960s.[21]

Not only would the costs of building new ballparks be potentially prohibitive, but each Federal League franchise also had to battle entrenched interests to gain control of a site and acquire the necessary building permits. In Buffalo the team could not even begin construction of its $130,000 steel-and-wood ballpark until March 18. Nevertheless, the twenty-thousand-seat ballpark was ready by Opening Day, May 11.[22]

In Baltimore, Ned Hanlon controlled a site directly across the street from the Federals' International League rivals. The team leased Hanlon's site and spent $82,649 to build a quality concrete, steel, and wood stadium. Indianapolis president Ed Krause found a site just blocks from downtown. When it appeared that Krause was set to build a wooden grandstand, however, James McGill, owner of the Indianapolis Indians of the American Association, asserted that city ordinances required that the new stadium be built of steel and concrete. In all these cases the Federals had little time to fight ordinance interpretations in court; they needed these stadiums ready in just a couple of months. In the end Ed Krause, Edward Gates, and the Indianapolis ownership spent more than $100,000 to acquire the site and build the twenty-thousand-seat Federal League Park.[23]

St. Louis team president Ed Steininger gained control of Handlan's Park, a private site in a residential neighborhood south of the two competing Major League venues. At the time the location seemed pretty good—it was "within fifteen minutes of any place in town"[24]—but by the end of the season the team's owners were complaining that it was too far removed from regular travel patterns. Steininger had signed a three-year lease for $10,000 per year that contained a purchase option for $250,000, a huge amount for the time. As a local contractor who was well connected to local politicians, Steininger managed to skirt some of the fire codes on his third application by calling his grandstand temporary. Even with this exemption, Steininger needed to build a mostly steel-and-wood structure but wrung the costs down to roughly $75,000, testifying to Stifel and Steininger's influence with the municipal authorities.[25]

Only in Kansas City and Pittsburgh were there preexisting stadiums the Federals could assume. Kansas City team president Charles Madison lined up Gordon and Koppel Field, the twelve-thousand-seat park named for two local merchants and located along Brush Creek. Unfortunately, this venue was far from Major League quality and little better than many Minor League parks.

In Pittsburgh, Kerr and McCullough arranged for the use of Exposition Park, home to the Pirates until the opening of their new stadium, Forbes Field, in 1909. The ballpark was of the older wooden variety, but the Federals expanded it to seat sixteen thousand. Late in the 1914 season when Gilmore attended a Pirates game at Forbes Field, located about three miles from downtown, he was overheard complaining that it was a better location than the Exposition Park site across the Allegheny River. This may have been so, but Pittsburgh baseball fans had spent many years watching quality baseball at Exposition Park and could easily have found their way back.[26]

The Pittfeds site was controlled by the B&O Railroad, and the team agreed to lease it around the first of the year. In late January Pirates owner Barney Dreyfuss explored leasing the site himself to prevent the Federals from playing there, but he was too late.[27] One baseball executive claimed that Dreyfuss was not sufficiently vigilant in blocking this site from the Federals: "The egotism and vanity of some club-owners and the fact that everybody seemed to be sleeping at the switch last winter, made it possible for the Federal League to start; it would have been easy for Dreyfuss for instance to prevent the Federal entry into smoketown, but excuses himself now by putting the blame on the B&O R.R."[28]

In fact, Dreyfuss followed the activities of the Federals more closely than almost any other Major League owner. Like many owners, he was not independently wealthy and spent most of his adult life acquiring the resources and making the contacts necessary to control a Major League baseball team. His path to baseball began at nineteen when he immigrated to America to join his cousins' distillery business in Paducah, Kentucky. Told by a doctor that he needed to get outside more, Dreyfuss began organizing baseball matches, using the distillery workers

National Commission chairman Garry Herrmann and Pittsburgh Pirates
owner Barney Dreyfuss, one of the National League's most involved owners.
(Courtesy of the Library of Congress)

as players. As the distillery grew, the family decided to move its headquarters to
Louisville, home of the American Association Colonels. Dreyfuss bought a small
piece of the team, which joined the National League in 1892. Over the next several
years he continued to increase his stock in the team until by the mid-1890s he
had gained control of the franchise. When the National League consolidated from
twelve to eight franchises for 1900, Dreyfuss was at risk of having his Louisville
club contracted. With help from John Brush, he purchased a controlling interest in
the Pirates and transferred most of the best players from Louisville to Pittsburgh.[29]
Dreyfuss outlined his philosophy of player acquisition: "In the baseball business an
owner must act quickly and secretly. He does not have time to consult a board of
directors. He must act on the jump and talk afterward."[30] The combined Pirates/
Colonels club proved the best team of the early twentieth century, winning three
consecutive pennants from 1901 through 1903. Along with the Cubs and Giants,
the Pirates dominated the National League in the early years of the century: from
1901 through 1913 those three teams won every pennant.

Diminutive, stubborn, and a stickler for detail, Dreyfuss proved a valuable
but annoying voice in the National League's backrooms. "His fellow club owners often accused him of being arbitrary, unreasonable and obstinate," sportswriter Fred Lieb remembered. "Barney, you're like a bulldog. You get a hold of

something you never let go," Charles Ebbets once told him. "He was one of the game's greatest and most far-seeing club owners," Lieb concluded. "If, when in a moment of anger or peeve, he occasionally did a small thing, his vision was wide and his heart and keen mind were always on the better side of baseball."[31]

Gilmore and his owners also recognized that having well-known, popular managers, like Joe Tinker, could help create legitimacy for their league in the minds of the fans. More important, respected managers would be important ambassadors for recruiting Major League players. Of the existing teams, only pennant-winning Indianapolis kept their 1913 manager, Bill Phillips. With Gilmore's input, Mullen and Carroll hired Larry Schlafly as Buffalo's manager soon after being awarded their franchise. Schlafly had played briefly in the Majors several years earlier and for part of 1913 managed Jersey City in the International League. He reportedly left his job because Jersey City's owners meddled with his handling of the club. Part of Schlafly's pitch to Gilmore and the Buffalo backers was that he knew of "more than 30 players, many of them big leaguers, who were willing to sign Buffalo contracts."[32] Kansas City had earlier signed George Stovall to manage for similar reasons.

Buffeds manager Larry Schlafly was one of the Federal League's most aggressive recruiters. (Courtesy of the Library of Congress)

Baltimore initially targeted the New York Giants' popular, feisty third base-man Buck Herzog, who was disgruntled with manager John McGraw. Herzog was on the verge of accepting the position when McGraw traded him to Cincinnati to keep him in Organized Baseball. With the option of a better Major League opportunity, Herzog's salary demands became so exorbitant that Baltimore backed off. Hanlon next approached Wilbert Robinson, whom he had managed with on the old Orioles in the 1890s and who now coached for McGraw. Robinson liked the idea of returning to Baltimore and reportedly agreed to terms. McGraw, however, again beat his old manager Hanlon to the punch. He convinced Brooklyn owner Charles Ebbets to hire Robinson as manager of the Dodgers. Robinson, with a chance to manage in the Major Leagues, broke off his dealings with Hanlon. With his many contacts throughout baseball and solid backing from ownership, Hanlon still had several attractive options. In early January he finally landed Philadelphia Phillies second baseman Otto Knabe to manage the new Terrapins. "The Baltimore stockholders treated me very liberally, and I can't lose out," Knabe said. "I have half my money now."[33] The Federals would find this a vexing issue going forward; because of the players' very real fear that the league would not succeed, many demanded a significant portion of their salary up front.

Also in early January, Pittsburgh secretary William McCullough announced that the Pittfeds had signed well-respected veteran outfielder Jimmy Sheckard to manage the club. Under pressure from Organized Baseball, Sheckard soon changed his mind and backed out—a surprisingly poor misreading of his value and surely the result of poor advice. Sheckard, who had been waived in 1913 before being claimed by the Reds, accepted a demotion to the Double-A American Association in 1914 and never again played in the Majors. Pittsburgh settled on Doc Gessler, a former American League outfielder now practicing medicine.[34]

Stifel grabbed Mordecai "Three Finger" Brown, one of the National League's best-known pitchers, to manage in St. Louis. Brown, a longtime friend of Tinker's, could have been the poster child for so many players feeling little loyalty to their clubs. From 1904 to 1911 Brown led the Cubs to four pennants as one of baseball's best pitchers. In the spring of 1912 the thirty-five-year-old signed a three-year contract calling for $5,500 per year. Brown also made a side agreement with owner Charles Murphy for an additional $1,500 each year.

In midseason 1912 Brown injured his knee sliding into second base and could not pitch during the second half. Murphy canceled the contract and demoted him to the Minor League Louisville club in which he (Murphy) owned an interest. At Louisville, Brown's new salary called for only $300 per month. At the time

Murphy's move was within the club's rights as long as no team claimed Brown on waivers. The standard contract had two big outs for the club: (1) if a player was incapacitated by injury for a period of fifteen days or more his contract could be canceled, and (2) in any event a club could release a player upon ten days written notice. (By 1914, under competition from the Federal League, many clubs began removing these clauses from player contracts.)

Fortunately for Brown, in 1913 his old Cubs teammate and then Reds manager Joe Tinker believed he could still pitch and rescued him from Louisville. Cincinnati president Garry Herrmann agreed to a restructured $6,000 total pay package with $1,000 deferred until the end of the season.[35] When the time came, however, Herrmann refused to pay this final installment. Brown believed Herrmann was holding back in an effort "to coerce [him] into signing [for 1914] . . . at a reduced salary."[36] In fairness to Herrmann, the contract put the final $1,000 payment at Tinker's discretion, and Herrmann claimed he never heard from Tinker on the matter. In any case, Brown happily joined the new league when the opportunity arose in December. Once Herrmann learned that Brown had joined the Federals, he futilely offered up the $1,000 payment as an inducement to lure him back.

As the Federal League's owners hired higher-profile managers during November and December 1913, both the owners and their new skippers set about recruiting Major League ballplayers. On the surface there was no shortage of disgruntled players. Many intuitively understood they were paid less than fair value, and many had been treated high-handedly by their clubs and harbored strong resentments. Organized Baseball naturally considered these players technically still bound to their existing teams by the reserve clause in their contracts, though most legal authorities did not consider the clause legally binding. As the anti-trust pressure first rose on Organized Baseball during 1912, the owners had changed the wording of the reserve clause in the uniform players' contract. For 1913 the contract stipulated that 75 percent of the player's pay was for his services and 25 percent for agreeing to be reserved for the following season. Of course, the player's pay didn't actually change; the owners simply changed the contract to show that some of the compensation was for agreeing to the reserve clause. For 1914 this standard language was again altered so that the percentage allocations were left blank and filled in by the club. This new language did not change the opinion of most legal authorities toward the legitimacy of the reserve clause but it did provide Major League baseball owners with one more argument when threatening players who were looking to sign elsewhere.[37]

Major League baseball players at the time earned more than most salaried men in America, though not excessively so. On the eve of the Federal League an average starting position player or pitcher made roughly $3,000 per year; the top salary was $12,000, earned by Ty Cobb. By comparison, according to a contemporary article, in 1905 the United States Steel Corporation had 168,205 employees on salary as opposed to those considered wage earners. "Of these, 122,690 receive salaries of $800 or less; 43,987 receive salaries ranging between $800 and $2,500; 1,308 receive salaries ranging from $2,500 to $5,000; 156 receive salaries ranging from $5,000 to $10,000; 51 are paid salaries ranging from $10,000 to $20,000, and 13 are paid salaries of $20,000 or more."[38] This total surely included a number of women, who would have been relegated to the lowest end of the salary distribution. Even so, the vast majority of male employees earned less than $2,500 per year. Wage earners made even less; in 1905 the average annual pay in manufacturing was around $560. As another point of comparison, the average postal employee did a little better, earning roughly $935 per year. After a relatively stagnant 1890s, income grew over the decade between 1905 and 1914, so that earnings would have been higher by the latter year. Historical data for wage earners suggests growth in the range of 20 percent for the decade; imputing similar growth to salaries seems a reasonable assumption.[39]

With open checkbooks and high expectations, in late December and early January the Federal League owners, managers, and other agents approached nearly every unsigned big-league player. Hoping to make a big splash, Gilmore wired Ty Cobb a five-year contract offer at $15,000 per year (including the first year paid in advance), which would have been the biggest contract in baseball history. Cobb parlayed this offer into a salary increase with his existing team, the Detroit Tigers. As the Federals soon discovered to their dismay, many players reacted similarly.[40]

George Stovall, because of his early jump to the Federals, became one of the league's first and most energetic recruiters. As early as November he began methodically tracking his former charges in St. Louis. Relatively quickly he lined up pitcher George Baumgardner, catcher Sam Agnew, and outfielder Gus Williams, some of the first players of consequence to throw in with the new league. The Browns immediately threatened a court challenge to the signings. All concerned recognized the potential impact of a court ruling: "Baseball men say the Baumgardner case is crucial for the Federal League," reported the *Chicago Tribune*.[41] Stovall ignored the legal threats—leaving any legal complications to Gilmore, Gates, and Madison—and hastened out to California to try to sign players from the class AA Pacific Coast League and Major Leaguers residing on the West Coast.

Buffalo manager Larry Schlafly went after several players he thought disgruntled, starting with Cleveland's top pitchers. Cleveland owner Charles Somers's years as the financial angel of the American League were long behind him, and he had fallen on hard times. His coal empire was overleveraged and struggling to meet the demands of his bankers. On December 20 Schlafly traveled to Cleveland to meet with Cy Falkenberg, the Indians top hurler. Falkenberg liked what he heard and agreed to go with Schlafly to Chicago to meet with Gilmore and Weeghman, who would further sell him on the new league. Falkenberg persuaded teammate George Kahler to come along, and also telephoned Fred Blanding at his home near Detroit to meet them in Chicago. At the meeting Gilmore made a convincing case for the Federals and signed all three: Falkenberg signed with Indianapolis for three years at $7,000 per year, including $5,000 paid in advance; Blanding signed with Kansas City for three years at $5,800 per year, including $2,500 up front; and for his efforts Schlafly got Kahler for three years at $3,350 per year with a $2,500 advance.[42]

Joe Tinker also proved a tireless ambassador for the new league. In his pursuit of ballplayers Tinker was aided by Weeghman's enthusiasm and the fact that Gilmore's office was located in Chicago. On January 9 Weeghman marked the next key Federal League player seizure by announcing the pilfering of four noteworthy Major Leaguers: catcher Bill Killefer and pitcher Ad Brennan from the Phillies, pitcher Gene Packard from the Reds, and pitcher King Cole, recently acquired by the Yankees from the Minors. To convince these players of the staying power of the new league, all were signed to three-year contracts.

Tinker also signed infielder Rollie Zeider away from the Yankees. Zeider would have remained in Organized Baseball, but New York refused to meet his demand of a $5,000 salary and an opportunity to play third base. Soon thereafter, Tinker signed two Pirates, catcher Mike Simon and pitcher Claude Hendrix, along with Yankees spitball pitcher Russ Ford. In several of Tinker's signings, he was not acting solely for the Chifeds, but often as an agent for the entire Federal League. Although Tinker never revealed this specifically, reporters understood that Ford could end up elsewhere with the league.[43]

Meanwhile, Pittsburgh successfully landed St. Louis Cardinals center fielder Rebel Oakes. The Pittfeds offered a $1,300 raise over the Cardinals' offer and guaranteed the contract for three years. Cardinals scout Bob Connery thought he had secured Oakes in early January when he met with the outfielder in Shreveport, Louisiana. They discussed a contract and the forthcoming season but did not agree to a salary, and Connery also insisted the contract include a clause banning the "excessive use of intoxicating liquors." For the extra money and no such social limitations,

Pittfeds player-manager Rebel Oakes became one of the Federals' most dogged recruiters. (Courtesy of the Dennis Goldstein Collection)

Oakes signed with the Pittfeds, who in his honor became known as the Rebels. They also signed disgruntled hurler Howie Camnitz, who had spent nearly his entire career with their cross-town rivals and remained popular in Pittsburgh. He had been one of the mainstays for the Pirates during their 1909 World Series Championship season but had slumped since. In late 1913 the Pirates unloaded him in a trade to the Phillies; over the 1913 season as a whole Camnitz lost twenty games.[44]

Sloufeds manager Mordecai Brown targeted several former teammates on the Cubs. To secure a shortstop he traveled to the home of Al Bridwell in Portsmouth, Ohio, where he signed his man. Brown also landed starting Chicago outfielder Ward Miller. While helping his owners recruit players, Gilmore was also trying to stock the Toronto franchise as its backers tried to put together an ownership group. Gilmore signed veteran third baseman Bill Bradley from the Toronto International League club to manage the Toronto Federal League team.

Bradley had spent a number of years as the American League's best third base-man but hadn't played in the Majors since 1910.[45]

Most of all, the Federals concentrated their player efforts on the Philadelphia Phillies, where new owner William Baker was out of his depth. Baker had only just taken over the club upon the death of William Locke, himself a short-term owner. For many years a Pittsburgh sportswriter and then a minority owner and team secretary for the Pirates, Locke had been a well-liked, intelligent baseball man. Upon his death in 1913, the team's directors elevated his cousin Baker to the presidency, a move that—other than a fluke pennant in 1915 orchestrated by new manager Pat Moran—doomed the Phillies to years of futility. Baker inherited a promising team but turned out to be the worst sort of owner, a man with little actual interest in the game, limited capital, and an unwillingness to ask for advice. As one newspaper later observed after his death, "Mr. Baker was intensely jealous of his position and the rights of owners in the National League. He was disinclined to accept counsel from subordinates and perhaps carried that quality too far. At times he lost the value of good advice as he was unwilling to share the operation of baseball with experienced baseball men."

Overmatched Philadelphia Phillies owner William Baker and his wife. (Courtesy of the Library of Congress)

Before taking over the ballclub Baker had spent several years as New York City police commissioner. One of Gotham's relatively honest politicians during the Progressive Era, Baker had begun his working life in Pittsburgh as a clerk in a railway freight department. Eventually he served as private secretary to the industrialist William Shinn, whom he followed to New York. Baker later became private secretary to Bird Coler, an unsuccessful candidate for governor in 1902 and the state controller. Baker also spent time in Coler's banking and brokerage firm and built up connections within the New York financial and industrial hierarchy. With his many contacts, he helped Locke raise the necessary funds to purchase the Phillies. Once in charge he became one of baseball's cheapest owners.[46]

One of Baker's first orders of business was to re-sign several star players for 1914. To secure Tom Seaton, one of the National League's top pitchers, Baker sent him a contact on January 13: "Enclosed find copy of contract for season 1914 for $4,000 with an additional $500 as stated in the contract, which if you do as well as you did last year will not be difficult to earn. This is an increase of 50 percent what you were getting for 1913."

"Will not sign for less than $5,000 and the same bonus," Seaton telegraphed business manager Bill Shettsline.

"Will give you $4,500 and same bonus two year contract," Baker wired back.

"Wired my terms to Shettsline and they were not accepted so cannot see how I can be of any service to the Phila. Club," Seaton wired manager Red Dooin.

"Accept terms your wire to Shettsline Jan. 18th, $5,000 and same bonus as contract sent you," Baker replied.

"Make bonus $1,000 and will accept two year contract," Seaton pushed.

"Accept your terms," Baker responded on January 22.

"Having agreed to terms kindly send your signed contract immediately," followed up a nervous Baker on February 7.

"Please explain by wire whether my bonus calls for 35 full games," Seaton wired back.

The club wired back that Baker was out of town for a couple of days. On February 13 he wired, "Club not crippled. Everybody came to terms but Brennan. . . . Terms offered by you January 22 and accepted by us same day will have to stand." Baker neglected to note that key performers Knabe, Killefer, Camnitz, and possibly shortstop Mickey Doolan were jumping to the Federal League.

Three days later Seaton dropped his bombshell: "Am on my way to sign with Feds. If I sign with Philadelphia it will be for $7,500 per year for three years. . . . This stands until tomorrow Tuesday noon."

Upon receiving this news, Baker wired Seaton to tell him they intended to hold him to the apparent agreement created by the January 22 wire. Baker also contacted Gilmore directly: "Understand pitcher Seaton . . . to sign Federal contract. We accepted Seaton's terms middle of January and will take every legal step possible to protect ourselves."[47]

By this point Gilmore and his owners and managers were no longer sympathetic to the Major League owners' complaints over the contractual technicalities of its targeted players. The Federals were having more difficulty than originally anticipated in signing Major League players, who were rightly skeptical of the long-term viability of the new league and afraid of being blackballed from their chosen profession. Many used offers from the Federals to leverage large raises from their existing teams. Mordecai Brown, for example, went hard after Chicago first baseman Vic Saier, reportedly offering $18,000 for three years, but the Cubs responded with an offer of their own and kept him in the National League.[48]

Baltimore manager Otto Knabe offered slugging outfielder Gavvy Cravath, another of Baker's Phillies, a two-year contract for $12,000 with $4,000 up front as a signing bonus. Pittsburgh's Gessler and Indianapolis's Phillips also wired Cravath asking for his terms. Cravath reported these advances to Baker, writing that he was tempted to jump but preferred to stay in Philadelphia if Baker would meet his terms: a salary of $5,200 plus a $500 bonus. This was a surprisingly modest request from the man who had led the league in home runs in 1913, and Baker knew enough to keep him: "Your terms accepted: am forwarding contract." "The salary is not as much as the Federals offered," Cravath told the press, "but I am better satisfied to take $5,700 in the Nationals than a lot more in the Federals."[49]

Both Tinker and Knabe pursued Cincinnati hurler George "Chief" Johnson (at the time almost every Native American ballplayer was nicknamed "Chief"). Johnson was seriously considering the new league when he received a call from Reds teammate Heinie Groh. Groh strongly recommended he meet with owner Garry Herrmann before doing anything rash. Herrmann tried to scare Johnson away from the Federals, insisting that "the Federal League had no ballparks, was not financially responsible, and would not last until the opening of the season."[50] On the strength of this warning, Johnson rebuffed both Tinker and Knabe and re-signed with Cincinnati. In similar fashion, Hanlon believed he had convinced Pirates third baseman Mike Mowrey to join the Baltfeds but soon learned otherwise.

Tinker, trying to put the best possible face on their situation, bragged about another source of talent:

> There are any number of players of the Minor Leagues who are anxious to come with us, and by the way, did you ever think what our organization will do to the Minors? They make a lot of money every year selling players to the Majors, and those players have to go where they are sold and accept what is offered them. Now, when one of those clubs sells a star to the Majors, nothing can prevent us from taking that player for nothing, and we'll get a lot of them simply because instead of paying money to the magnates for them we'll give that money to the players themselves.[51]

During December 1913 and January 1914 the Federals challenged the Major Leagues head-to-head for players, ballpark sites, and media attention. In this initial confrontation the established Major Leagues proved much more aggressive and resilient than the Federals foresaw, leaving them disappointed and disillusioned. They had fallen well short of their expected Major League player signings, and those they landed cost significantly more than anticipated. Still, this was only the beginning of the campaign, and the Federals hoped that with a continued aggressive approach they could open the season with affordable Major League–quality rosters. What's more, the players were once again forming a union, a potentially valuable ally in the battle against the entrenched interests and restrictive player-control rules of Organized Baseball.

4

A Real Players Union

At the close of the nineteenth century many American industrial workers labored in appalling conditions. In response they formed unions, giving them the ability to act collectively and gain greater negotiating leverage. Almost from the start, labor unions in America diverged in two directions. The more radical unions and socialists such as the Industrial Workers of the World believed that laborers could achieve reasonable working conditions only through a complete rearrangement of the existing economic order. The other philosophy, later embodied by Samuel Gompers and the American Federation of Labor, concentrated on material improvements—particularly wages and hours—and disdained many of the larger moralistic and societal reforms. At this more conservative end of trade unionism, union leadership believed in a strong central union authority that negotiated within the framework of the existing economic order.

Never subject to the ghastly conditions of factories, by the late 1880s ballplayers nonetheless toiled in an environment that today seems callous and unfair. Their frustration first manifested itself with the founding of the Brotherhood of Professional Baseball Players, a radical union that hoped to restore to players some of the control they had enjoyed before the reserve clause. Led by New York shortstop John Montgomery Ward and with the backing of wealthy businessmen, the players formed their own league to challenge the established Major Leagues. As noted earlier, though many of baseball's best players jumped to the Players League, it failed after just one season, and Organized Baseball's owners soon reestablished their dominance over the players.

In mid-1900, as Ban Johnson schemed to bring Major League status to his American League and rumblings of a new Major League American Association roiled the waters, the players again organized a union. This version was much less radical than the first. Players still hoped to revamp the player-control rules but had little interest in overturning the existing baseball structure. Chicago Cubs pitcher Clark Griffith was elected vice president of the new Protective Association of Professional Baseball Players—an ironic choice given his later anti-union attitude as a Major League owner. The players recognized that the coming turmoil could give them additional leverage with the owners, some of whom might even see an advantage in allying with the players against rival leagues. The National League generally remained haughty and dismissed the union, but Ban Johnson courted the organization, listened sympathetically to its demands, and lured its players. Unfortunately for the players, when the two leagues declared a truce two years later, Johnson quickly lost interest in the welfare of the players. Having won higher salaries during the struggle and now facing a uniformly hostile front from the owners, the Protective Association quickly faded.

The absence of a union did not indicate that the players were more content, only that there was no organizing catalyst to face down a determined group of owners. That catalyst, however, appeared in May 1912 when Ty Cobb jumped into the stands and attacked a disabled fan who had been heckling him. Ban

Players Fraternity leader Dave Fultz caused the baseball owners nearly as much consternation as the Federal League. (Courtesy of the Library of Congress)

Johnson suspended Cobb, leading to a spontaneous Detroit Tigers player strike in his support. Based on this apparent solidarity and a general sense of player dissatisfaction, in September a man named Dave Fultz officially organized the Players Fraternity.

Few men had a background less compatible with a career as a ballplayer and union organizer than Fultz. At a time when most players were immigrants or first-generation Americans, Fultz's great-great-grandfather, John Morton, had been a signer of the Declaration of Independence. At a time when few Southerners played Major League baseball, Fultz came from Staunton, Virginia, where his father was mayor. At a time when most players had never been to college, Fultz had graduated from Brown and earned a law degree.[1]

Several teams aggressively pursued Fultz upon his graduation from Brown, where he starred in both baseball and football. He signed with owner Colonel Rogers of the Philadelphia Phillies for $2,400, then the legal limit for the National League (though often exceeded under the table). After an inauspicious debut over the second half of the 1898 season, Fultz was offered only $1,200 for 1899. When he balked, he soon learned the reality of baseball salary negotiation. Rogers "explained" that $1,200 of his previous year's salary had, in fact, been a signing bonus, so that his actual salary remained the same. "There was nothing in the original contract to that effect," Fultz noted. "I remember going out of Rogers' office and saying to myself, 'My gorry, is that what we ballplayers are up against?'"[2] Rogers ended up releasing the unhappy outfielder, who signed with the Baltimore Orioles. Fultz experienced more of the capriciousness of baseball after the season when he found himself without a job after the Orioles were contracted out of existence. In 1900 manager Connie Mack picked him up for his Milwaukee club in the American League, still a Minor League. When Mack moved on to become the new Philadelphia Athletics manager in 1901 in the newly declared Major League, he brought Fultz with him. A speedy center fielder, Fultz finished in the top ten in stolen bases four times. His best season was 1902 when he hit .302, stole a career-high forty-four bases, and led the league in runs scored. After the season Ban Johnson directed Fultz's sale to New York as he tried to strengthen his Gotham franchise to compete with the Giants. Fultz's career came to a premature end on September 30, 1905, in a horrific collision with shortstop Kid Elberfeld while chasing a fly ball. Fultz broke his jaw, suffered a broken nose, and injured an eye. He was carried off the field to a hospital, where he remained for several days. After spending the next six months with a splint on his jaw, Fultz officially retired from baseball, concentrating on his law career.

Although he decided to take up the cause of the players, Fultz had little interest in overturning the existing order. While he clearly recognized the unfair working rules under which ballplayers labored, particularly at the Minor League level, organizing them to improve their lot was the extent of his intentions. Unlike the Brotherhood two decades earlier, Fultz simply wanted to help the players achieve a measure of control over their own contracts; he did not wish to create a new league or otherwise challenge the position of the owners. He could, however, occasionally lapse into bouts of moralizing, once lecturing the players not to buy cars.[3]

Thirty years later Fultz recalled his accomplishments and the need for an organized players union. His remarks reflected his generally conservative approach and sense of justice: "The Fraternity which I headed from 1912 to the World War was not a trade union. It was merely a professional solidarity which the men had asked me to organize for the purpose of abolishing a lot of abuses. They no longer exist. They won't crop up again. The ballplayers of 1912 weren't getting fair play. They can have no such complaint today. For one thing, Judge Landis is fair to the men and makes the club owners toe the mark."[4] Fultz's reflections at age sixty-nine clearly undersold his actions when he led the Fraternity. He needed an aggressive posture to force the owners to negotiate, including occasionally threatening a strike.

Throughout 1913 Fultz continued to recruit players and press the National Commission to correct some of the owners' more extreme actions. Late in the year, as anxiety over the Federal League's impact grew, Fultz astutely pushed his agenda. He sent a list of seventeen demands to the National Commission. Not surprisingly, the owners stalled. With the Federal League chasing their players, they did not wish openly to oppose the union, but like owners and bosses in other industries, the baseball magnates were hostile to unionism and organized player action. Fultz kept pushing, however, and as the Federal League made inroads during December the owners began to rethink their position. They clearly hoped that any goodwill they could earn with the players and the union would benefit them in the upcoming battle with the new league. And some of the arbitrary actions by individual owners—particularly in the Minors—were so egregious that many felt some minimal redress was in order; they were simply reluctant to have them appear to be achieved through an organized players union.

Organized Baseball finally agreed to meet with a delegation of players at the National Commission's annual meeting in Cincinnati. The conclave at the Hotel Sinton on January 8, 1914, drew roughly 150 baseball dignitaries. As the banquet

room filled up for the 11:30 a.m. opening, the Commission members—
Herrmann, Johnson, and recently elected National League president John
Tener—and their staff assumed the head table. They were joined by a select
contingent of Minor League executives. The principal owners of fourteen of
the sixteen Major League teams along with other team officers and a large
collection of Minor League owners sat anxiously in the audience. To their
pleasant surprise, the press was allowed in the meeting and eagerly awaited the
proceedings. Finally, the players had a six-man delegation. Led by Fultz, the
key players included Boston Red Sox pitcher Ray Collins, a college graduate;
Brooklyn Dodgers pitcher Ed Reulbach, a lawyer; and Brooklyn Dodgers first
baseman Jake Daubert, a leader in the union movement.

With pleasantries out of the way, Herrmann opened the proceedings by
declaring that the Commission would be happy to hear the players' requests,
consider the matter privately, and respond to the players at a later date. Fultz and
the players objected strenuously: Herrmann and his Commission had had two
months to review their grievances, and it was time for action. Herrmann probably never really planned to push this proposal—after all, with nearly everyone
associated with Organized Baseball in the ballroom, he had to have been prepared for a full negotiation of the grievances. He next tried to marginalize Fultz
by calling on Reulbach to state the case for the players. The owners had long
recognized that the players would be a much less formidable force without their
leader. Hence they often rather disingenuously argued that they would be happy
to negotiate with the players but not with an "outsider." By calling on Reulbach,
Herrmann hoped to put the players, rather than Fultz, at the forefront of the
negotiations. Reulbach, however, had been well coached and deferred to Fultz,
advising that their union leader would be doing all the negotiating.

To understand the player-owner relationship of the time, it is worth reviewing Fultz's seventeen demands. Many of these were already in force at the Major
League level but were regularly violated by some Minor League owners.

1. A released player may sign with any club immediately, but his new contract
   will begin with the expiration of the ten-day period. (When Major League
   players were released during the season they had to be given ten days' notice,
   essentially allowing them an additional ten days of salary.)
2. Minor League players shall receive ten days' notice before they can be unconditionally released.
3. When a player is transferred he shall be subject to all the terms of his contract. (Typically, if a player was sent to a lower league, even in midseason, his

salary would be cut accordingly. The union wanted the player to retain his contractual salary.)

4. A player transferred shall be notified in writing.
5. A player shall be notified of his unconditional release in writing.
6. A player shall receive a copy of his contract.
7. All written agreements shall be mutually binding.
8. Clubs shall furnish uniforms at their expense.
9. All clubs shall pay traveling expenses during spring training. (Some struggling Minor League clubs did not pay player expenses to spring training.)
10. Players not tendered contracts after the forty-five-day probationary period shall be free agents.
11. Players shall be free agents after ten years in the Major Leagues.
12. If a player has been in the Major Leagues or Double-A Minor Leagues for twelve years and no team desires his services (i.e., he is unclaimed on waivers), he shall become a free agent.
13. Waivers shall not be withdrawn. (The Players Fraternity wanted to end this option of withdrawing waivers; they wanted a player to be able to go to the club that claimed him and most desired his services.)
14. Fined or suspended players shall be notified in writing.
15. No player shall be discriminated against because of his Fraternity connection.
16. All parks will be equipped with a center-field blank wall painted green. (This was to give batters better visibility of pitched balls. In this pre-batting-helmet era, beanings often led to serious injury.)
17. A complex, five-paragraph section addressing the waiver rules with the intent of making it more difficult to force a player to a lower level if any other team at his existing level wanted him.

Once the negotiations got under way at the National Commission's annual meeting, the owners quickly agreed to the more innocuous demands. At 3 p.m. items 2, 3, 7, 11, 12, 13, and 17 were still outstanding, and the Commission cleared the room of sportswriters and other outsiders and went into executive session. Regarding number 2, Fultz and the players settled for five days' notice for class AA and class A players and none for the lower Minor Leagues. As to number 3, the players withdrew their demand under intense pressure from the Minor League owners. They did persuade the National Commission to agree to review more egregious salary cuts if appealed by a player.

Number 7 was modified slightly to prohibit side agreements outside the contract. Numbers 11 and 12 were granted in form only; the club could continue to reserve the player after his contract expired if they so chose. The owners merely agreed that if a longtime veteran who met the service time requirement was waived and not claimed, he would become a free agent (as opposed to being eligible to be sent to a lower classification). As to number 13, the owners did not agree to make waivers irrevocable.

Finally, much of the debate surrounded the waiver rule demands of number 17. The final compromise was that players would be offered sequentially to lower leagues. For example, a Major League player who cleared waivers (i.e., no other Major League team claimed him) must first clear Double-A waivers before he could be exposed to being claimed by a Single-A club.

The Players Fraternity's list of demands did not include the removal of either the reserve clause or the ten-day clause (allowing the unconditional release of a player on ten days' notice) from the standard contract. The new agreement left both provisions untouched. Fultz did not so much wish to change the structure of baseball as to reform its most egregious abuses. He was surprisingly ambivalent toward the Federal League and believed that generally siding with Organized Baseball would earn the union goodwill. For as long as the Federals were around, this was probably a reasonable assumption. In any case, a more militant stance against the reserve clause would have been counterproductive. The owners were not about to give up this hook into the players, particularly with the emergence of the Federals, and the players were in no way sufficiently well organized or motivated to push this issue through collective action.[5]

With the final document, henceforth dubbed the Cincinnati Agreement, agreed to, the entire party, including the sportswriters, retired to a celebration in the hotel ballroom. As befitting the occasion, many dignitaries made toasts to the various attendees. Fultz, who could not stay for the celebration, was the butt of Ban Johnson's remarks. Even at this moment of apparent peace, Johnson could not resist minimizing the absent Fultz. The various grievances, Johnson remarked, could have been "easily and readily adjusted had it not been for the lawyer-president of the Fraternity, David Fultz."[6]

Fultz's accomplishment cannot be overstated. The owners of both the Major and Minor Leagues had long been hostile to granting even the most basic rights to the players, much less treating them as equals and engaging with a collective bargaining unit. Of course, extenuating circumstances were operating to Fultz's advantage. Most important, the challenge from the Federal League made Organized Baseball more willing to negotiate. The goodwill generated with the players could be used as another bargaining chip in the competition for players. Second, particularly at the Minor League level, some of the treatment of players in viola-

tion of their contracts had become so deplorable that many Major League owners actually wanted to see them reined in. Regardless of circumstances, however,
Fultz not only prevailed upon Organized Baseball to deal with his Fraternity, but
he actually got them to recognize the union and sign an agreement.

Unfortunately for the Federals, Fultz believed the players union would soon
enjoy a mutually respectful accommodation with Organized Baseball. While he
would continue to fight for players' rights when he felt a man had been wronged,
he hoped to maintain a cordial relationship with Major League owners. As the
owners had hoped when they consented to the Cincinnati Agreement and recognized the union, Fultz generally ignored the new league and did not encourage
players to disregard the reserve clause and jump to the Federals. The upstarts
would need to succeed without any support from the new players union.

5

The Battle for Chicago

Chicago remained the key. As America's second-largest city, it had the population to support a third Major League team, particularly since the Cubs played in an old wooden park on the West Side and the fans resented the club's frugal, less than fan-friendly ownership. Chifeds owner Charles Weeghman recognized that the most logical spot to locate a ball team was on the city's North Side. Chicago had a population of around 2.2 million in 1914, roughly 800,000 of them on the North Side, a population larger than any other city in America, excepting New York and Philadelphia, and now accessible by two branches of the "L," Chicago's commuter trains. If Weeghman could tap into this market, he felt he could create a valuable baseball franchise.

Weeghman's preferred site had long been identified as a potential ballpark location. In 1909, chafing at their second-class status to the Major Leagues, two American Association owners, Minneapolis's Mike Cantillon and Milwaukee's Charles Havenor, had purchased a site on Chicago's North Side with hope of locating an American Association team there. Not surprisingly, White Sox owner Charles Comiskey, whose team played on the South Side, and Cubs owner Charles Murphy had no intention of allowing another team into Chicago. Once it realized the intensity of the opposition, and unwilling to risk an open breach with the Major Leagues, the American Association backed off. But Cantillon and Havenor never lost the desire to enter Chicago. Over the next couple of years Cantillon and his brother-in-law Edmund Archambault bought out Havenor's interest.

Cantillon's site offered a perfect solution for Weeghman. Cantillon was tiring of the financial burden of carrying the site and, in light of his league's recent

One of baseball's most despised owners, Chicago Cubs owner Charles Murphy was forced out of baseball at the start of the Federal League war. (Courtesy of the National Baseball Hall of Fame Library, Cooperstown, New York)

squabbles with Major League owners over the draft, felt no particular allegiance to the Chicago Major League clubs. As a backup, in case Cantillon succumbed to pressure from the Major League owners, Weeghman secured an option on the old White Sox Park, only four blocks away from Comiskey Park, the team's grand new facility. Competing against the popular White Sox with an inferior ballpark would surely have failed, but fortunately it wasn't needed. Weeghman negotiated a ninety-nine-year lease with Cantillon, calling for $16,000 per year for the first ten years, $18,000 per year after that, and a $30,000 down payment.[1]

Weeghman still needed one more strip of land adjacent to the site to build his intended stadium. Fortunately, the parcel was owned by a friend of Weeghman's—he knew just about everyone in the city—and he initially believed acquiring it would not be a problem. But he would have an anxious moment or two:

> I had been assured of getting it [the strip of land], but had neglected to close the deal. About a week ago this friend of mine was approached by some unknown man and offered $25,000 in cash for that bit of ground. . . . I knew Organized Baseball was behind the offer. . . . The prospective buyer asked for time to close the deal and

agreed to pay the $25,000 on Saturday afternoon at 4:30 o'clock or lose his chance to buy. Well, no one showed up at 4:30 Saturday afternoon with the $25,000. . . . [I] felt much better when the time expired and the option had not been taken up.[2]

An agent for Organized Baseball later offered $40,000, but it was too late.[3] With this strip of land now under his control as well, Weeghman could finally start construction.

Organized Baseball was not about to concede Chicago without a fight. Cubs owner Charles Murphy, in particular, was working desperately to keep a third team out of Chicago. In early January he called a fellow National League owner, Brooklyn's Charles Ebbets, asking him to come to Chicago immediately. Murphy believed he had worked out a deal with Weeghman, his partner William Walker, and their star shortstop and manager, Joe Tinker, to induce them to quit the Federals. Without the Chicago franchise, it was highly unlikely the league could expand beyond its 1913 fringe status.

Under Murphy's arrangement, the Chicago trio would abandon the outlaws for $60,000: Brooklyn would get Tinker back by paying him $32,500 in salary and bonus over the next five years, and Weeghman and Walker would receive $27,500, which would be funded by the Major League baseball owners. Because Ebbets owned Organized Baseball's rights to Tinker and would be responsible for paying the $32,500, he needed to sign off on any deal. Once in Chicago, Ebbets huddled with Murphy, Tinker, and James McGill to solidify the agreement. McGill, the new owner of the Indianapolis Indians franchise in the American Association, was included because the settlement would also allow the Federal League's Indianapolis backers to buy into his club. Although annoyed at Tinker's high price, Ebbets nonetheless wanted the star shortstop and recognized the benefits of blocking the new league. He also passed along details of the agreement to American League president Ban Johnson. "Everything was done in a rush and, of course, in strictest confidence," Murphy wrote in his characteristic bluster. "No one must talk. We must ACT. If anyone talks he is a LIAR. This would, no doubt, kill this Federal League movement for 1914, and J.T. [Joe Tinker] says, forever."[4]

Weeghman and his partner, William Walker, were disappointed by the relatively few players and little money lined up by the other Federal League owners. They were considering Murphy's proposal and ready to quit if their fellow owners couldn't demonstrate the wherewithal to challenge the Major Leagues. By mid-January each Federal League team was supposed to have signed at least five

Major League players and a manager. The fact that several had not yet done so could provide the Chicago owners cover for bolting the league. Murphy and the Major League owners expected Weeghman and Walker to accept their offer and announce their abandonment of the Federal League.

In a separate overture, an intermediary approached Weeghman regarding the possibility of his buying the American League's St. Louis Browns if he would quit the new league. Weeghman quickly dismissed this option—he wanted a team in Chicago and could not even confirm that the proposition on the Browns came from an agent of Organized Baseball.[5]

When Federal League owners heard rumors of Weeghman's impending desertion, they knew they needed to reel him back in quickly. Gilmore called a league meeting for Saturday, January 17, in Chicago, where Weeghman's fellow owners cornered him regarding his intentions. In response, Weeghman complained bitterly about the lack of solid Major Leaguers they had signed and ridiculed the idea of a Toronto franchise. Each Federal League owner, Weeghman felt, had agreed to "forfeit $25,000 if it failed to pay $40,000 for five Major League players."[6] None of the teams had come close to this kind of success with Major Leaguers, and Weeghman was rightfully concerned about the success of his league without them. The other owners eventually calmed Weeghman and convinced him they could still successfully lure Major League ballplayers. After the meeting Weeghman said he was back in the fold and told the press he was satisfied that his fellow owners had "show[n] me some money and players."[7]

For one thing, the self-made Weeghman hankered to get into baseball. He had spent a boatload of money putting a team together and wanted more than simply a small payoff if he were to fade away. He didn't have to wait long for another, more attractive proposition. On January 22 he met with American Association president Thomas Chivington and Cleveland Indians owner Charles Somers. The American Association, a Minor League just one step below the Majors, feared competing with the Federals in two of their announced markets, Indianapolis and Kansas City. The top Minor Leagues rightfully worried that their fans, who naturally believed their city to be "Major League," would desert their Minor League club for the putatively Major League Federals. Accordingly, they were looking for ways to short-circuit the new league before it opened. Somers and Chivington hoped to wrest Weeghman from the Federals by offering him an American Association team in Chicago. At least some Major League owners appeared willing to allow another team in Chicago if it would stop the new league. And fortunately for Chivington, he had leverage thorough Cantillon's landlord relationship with Weeghman.

Pushed by the financially strapped Somers, Johnson and the American League agreed that granting an American Association team to Weeghman in Chicago was a small price to pay for eliminating the challenge of a third Major League. Technically, Weeghman was to buy the St. Paul franchise and transfer the club to the ballpark he hoped to build on Chicago's North Side. Apparently Johnson, who still ran his league in dictatorial fashion, received sufficient support from his owners and did not subject his approval to a formal vote. His prompt support of the scheme was all the more remarkable because Charles Comiskey was on an around-the-world baseball trip and unavailable for consultation. Comiskey's South Siders would have been less affected by a team in the Lakeview district than the Cubs, but Comiskey, one of the American League's most powerful owners, would almost surely have opposed the move.[8]

Despite his public assurances to the contrary, Weeghman secretly indicated to Johnson that he would jump to the American Association if the Major League owners acted quickly. The season was fast approaching, and Weeghman remained under tremendous pressure from his fellow Federal League owners to remain loyal. He was also working feverishly to get a ballpark constructed and assemble a team. Meanwhile, the National League scrambled to set up a phone tree for a quick vote on the proposition. On January 23 Pittsburgh owner Barney Dreyfuss called several National League owners with the following message: "Information has just reached me that the Chicago Federal League man is ready to abandon that league and join hands with the American Association, placing a club in the North Side of Chicago. The American Association is ready to approve this. . . . Understand all American League Clubs are in favor of this scheme." Seven of the eight National League owners indicated approval, the exception being Charles Murphy, who adamantly refused to allow another team in Chicago. Although technically a majority vote would have been sufficient for approval, once a couple of National League owners realized that Murphy was opposed they withdrew their affirmative votes. The owners felt that a team should have veto rights over its own territory. Part of this stance was purely selfish; the men wanted the same courtesy shown to them on issues within their geographic area. Murphy's effective veto scuttled the plan to detach Weeghman from the Federals.[9]

Weeghman, though, remained unsatisfied with his league's progress. In late January he sent his attorney on a tour of the Federal League's Eastern cities to determine their progress in establishing ballparks and creating local interest. To get his own direct read on the situation in these cities and make sure their teams were preparing adequately for the season, Gilmore scheduled his own trip in the attorney's footsteps. In Toronto and Buffalo Weeghman's emissary found little movement, though in Baltimore the contract for the new grounds happened to be signed the day he arrived. Meanwhile, Gilmore stopped in Pittsburgh to meet with that franchise's undercapitalized owners. Gilmore rightfully feared a negative report back to Weeghman.[10]

When Gilmore returned on February 7 he walked right into another crisis meeting, as Weeghman was again threatening to bolt. His attorney's report had further solidified Weeghman's skepticism of the Federals' staying power, and he remained dissatisfied with his fellow owners' lack of progress. Several Major League owners, sensing another opportunity and angry with Murphy for derailing the American Association plan, had reportedly told Weeghman he could buy the Cubs for $400,000. In the midst of a raucous meeting, Sloufeds owner Phil Ball seized the floor. "We've got the opportunity of a lifetime, but some of you fellows seem to think too much of your bankroll," Ball chided the less aggressive owners in support of Weeghman. He also pleaded with Weeghman: "If you'll have a little patience things will come out all right for us." Ball then turned back to the other owners: "We seem to be up against a rather tough proposition—but we all knew that when we got into this thing. Some of you fellows seem to be showing the 'white feather.' Well, it's up to you to show your mettle. You've sunk a big bunch of money into this venture. Sink some more—you can't expect to win out in a big business enterprise against well-entrenched competition unless you are willing to back up that proposition to the limit of your wad. Get busy. Don't be short sports. Don't be tightwads. Loosen up—and we'll come out with flying colors."[11] Ball's challenge to their manhood seemed to strike home. The owners publicly rallied around Ball's comments and pledged fealty to their new league.

By 1914 Charles Murphy had long been the bane of his fellow baseball owners. A onetime Cincinnati sportswriter and editor, Murphy became a press agent for the New York Giants in the early 1900s. In 1905 he purchased a controlling interest in the Chicago Cubs for $105,000, borrowing most of the purchase price from his former publisher in Cincinnati, Charles Taft, the half-brother of future President William H. Taft and the husband of heiress Anne Sinton. Murphy's purchase of the Cubs proved a tremendously lucrative venture. In 1906, when the team won the pennant, profits were estimated at $165,000. Over the next several years annual profits generally exceeded $100,000. With his portion of these profits Murphy repaid his loan to Taft, who retained a small ownership stake in the franchise. Murphy's and Taft's interest in the Cubs illustrates one of the National League's normally hidden conflicts of interest. Although the league had supposedly eliminated ownership in multiple franchises after their disastrous experience in the late 1890s, Taft and Murphy held a generally unacknowledged interest in the Philadelphia Phillies, and Mrs. Taft held the ground lease on the Phillies ballpark site.[12]

Obnoxious and pompous, Murphy soon incurred the enmity of the other owners and his team's fans. He caused a ruckus soon after buying the team when he apparently colluded in allowing a large proportion of the Cubs World Series tickets to fall into the hands of scalpers. The National Commission rarely chastised owners but after a short investigation felt it necessary to reprove the Cubs for their handling of the tickets. Murphy further earned the public's wrath for his callous treatment of some of his star players. Late in the 1912 season, with manager Frank Chance, the "Peerless Leader," recovering from surgery to relieve a blood clot in his brain, Murphy declared that the Cubs had failed to win the pennant because of lax discipline and too much drinking by the players. The next season, he announced, he would include clauses in their contracts restricting their alcoholic intake. When Chance loudly and publicly defended his players, Murphy refused to back down. Chance returned to take the helm for the celebrated postseason Chicago city championship series versus the White Sox, and the Cubs lost the deciding Game Seven 16–0. Using this debacle for his excuse, Murphy fired his popular manager and installed second baseman Johnny Evers as his new skipper.[13]

Murphy also annoyed several owners with his loud and continuous criticism of National League president Thomas Lynch. Philadelphia Phillies president Horace Fogel, an ally of Murphy's and Taft's, had also made public accusations against Lynch for supposed umpire biases. Over the second half of 1912, while chastising his players, Murphy ratcheted up his provocations by publicly questioning the honesty of the pennant race. He claimed that the New York Giants could not win the championship "without undue assistance from other teams," implying that some teams might purposely let up against the Giants. Murphy went on to suggest that such assistance might have come from St. Louis Cardinals manager Roger Bresnahan, a longtime friend of Giants manager John McGraw. At the end of September, in a letter covertly instigated by Murphy, Fogel publicly charged that the Giants had received "favorable decisions" from the umpires, and that without this help they would not have won the pennant.[14]

For the National League owners, this was the last straw. They hauled Fogel before a tribunal and expelled him from baseball. Several wanted to force out Murphy as well. As majority owner of the Cubs, however, Murphy was a more challenging target. To avoid the unpleasant and uncertain task of trying to boot Murphy, the owners, including National Commission chairman Garry Herrmann, grudgingly accepted an apology.

Shortly thereafter, Herrmann reached a handshake deal with Murphy and Cubs manager Johnny Evers to acquire Joe Tinker to be the Cincinnati Reds player-manager. The three agreed to meet the next morning at 10:30 to sign the necessary papers. Murphy never showed and called off the deal. Although he later landed Tinker, Herrmann must have rued his lack of resolve in pushing for Murphy's banishment when the momentum was there.[15]

Now, fewer than two years later and under the threat of a new Major League, Murphy's refusal to allow an American Association franchise in Chicago and the consequent missed opportunity of stopping the Federal League incensed his fellow owners. A catalyst for his removal emerged when Murphy clumsily fired player-manager Johnny Evers during the 1913 National League meetings in New York. One of Chicago's most popular sports heroes, Evers was one year into a five-year contract. He had reportedly been flirting with the Federal League, and Murphy saw a chance to get out from under Evers's expensive contract. Evers had signed two contracts, one as a player and one as a manager. He thought he was signing an ironclad five-year deal, but in fact Murphy outwitted him. The manager contract had a rider that attached it to the "ten-day" clause in the player contract—the clause that allowed a team to terminate a player's contract at any time with just ten days' notice.[16]

The Major League owners were furious at Evers's firing. To that point the Federal League had signed only a few name players, and Murphy was now effectively offering up one of the National League's biggest stars on a platter. As the Major Leagues feared, the Federals responded quickly, offering Evers a three-year contract at $15,000 per year with a year's salary paid in advance. Once Murphy realized the storm he had unleashed, he tried to rescind Evers's firing and trade him to the Boston Braves. Evers demanded that he be declared a free agent to sign with whomever he chose.

The National League owners had learned from their Tinker debacle and responded quickly. They orchestrated Evers's transfer to Boston and arranged for a $25,000 bonus and a four-year $10,000-per-year salary from owner James Gaffney. Although he claimed he could have received more from the Federals, Evers happily accepted the move to Boston and became one of the highest-paid players in baseball.[17]

American League president Ban Johnson, who had wanted to expel Murphy as far back as the scalping scandal in 1908, publicly lambasted him now but cloaked his denunciation as sympathy for Evers. "To discharge him five days before the [spring] training trip and after he had made practically all arrangements for this work," Johnson said, "seems cruel and uncalled for," later adding his main objective: "The American League has become tired of the blunders of this man, and for the good of baseball I think a change in the ownership of the Cubs is necessary. . . . The American League is determined to purge baseball of persons within the ranks who are enemies of the sport."[18]

National League owners were also finally resolved to purge Murphy from their ranks. Murphy, however, remained defiant. He attacked Johnson: "The Cubs are not going to be sold. I'm in baseball to stay, and no —— —— —— is going to force me out of the game. I am not going to stand for Ban Johnson's methods, any longer, either. I am going to sue him for conspiracy and slander right away."[19]

Despite no definitive mechanism in the bylaws to remove recalcitrant owners, the National League was not without leverage. Several National League owners publicly floated a plan in which they would withdraw five teams—Cincinnati, Pittsburgh, Philadelphia, New York, and Boston—from the league and combine with the three best-capitalized Federal League teams—Chicago, St. Louis, and Baltimore—to form a new National League.[20] This scheme represented a surprisingly drastic measure and needed the support of all five owners. At least one, Harry Hempstead in New York, remained problematic. In addition, Brooklyn and St. Louis would never have accepted this new arrangement without a fight. Such an extreme proposal was never more than a threat made out of frustration, but it demonstrated how polarizing Murphy had become.

More important, Taft still owned a piece of the Cubs and was tiring of constant bad publicity. He had little interest in taking an active ownership in baseball, but at a meeting in Cincinnati on February 21 league president John Tener and Cubs minority owner Harry Ackerland finally convinced him of the need to rid themselves of Murphy. With Taft's support, pushing Murphy out would not be quite as complicated. Taft agreed, and after the meeting he called Murphy. To the relief of the baseball owners, Murphy backed off his legal threats and Taft negotiated a buyout for $503,500.[21]

Despite the announced sale, some owners remained skeptical of the exact nature of the transfer. Taft and Murphy were longtime friends and business associates. Taft did little to reassure his fellow magnates when he named William Hale Thompson, Murphy's confidant and former assistant, to a prominent role with the team. Nevertheless, the National League owners felt they had satisfactorily addressed the crisis. True, they had not mortally wounded the Federals by severing Weeghman and the Chicago franchise from their ranks, but they had prevented Evers from jumping and eliminated the Murphy problem.

The Chicago Cubs franchise remained one of the National League's most valuable. Once Taft had the team, Johnson took another shot at trying to wean

Weeghman from the Federals by trying to arrange the sale of the Cubs from Taft to Weeghman for $503,500, Taft's acquisition cost. This idea, however, didn't take. Shortly thereafter, a local investment group reportedly bid $750,000 for the Cubs. With the Federals about to open on the North Side, it is unlikely this huge offer was legitimate. Moreover, it is hard to imagine Taft turning it down.[22]

Now that Weeghman had his site, he still needed a stadium. And time was running short. To start the project, he hired architect Zachary Davis Taylor, who had designed Comiskey Park, called the "finest ball park in the United States" by the *Reach Guide*. Weeghman had little time to spare and did not need a palace; he needed a good, functional ballpark in less than two months. Moreover, his Federal League adventure was beginning to cost more than even his readjusted expectations. "When this thing started, we sat down and figured out we could sign a ball team and have a nice, modest little park for an expenditure of $50,000. We're in $125,000 already [including $40,000 in salary advances to players], and we haven't started work on our grandstand. Walter and myself will each have $125,000 invested by the time the season opens."[23] This may even have been a low estimate: the construction contract for the ballpark came to $219,000.[24]

Amid great fanfare, ground was broken on March 4, leaving fewer than seven weeks until Opening Day on April 23. Organized Baseball's owners and lawyers searched for legal loopholes and used political pressure to prevent its construction but were not optimistic regarding their chances. Weeghman's connections obviously smoothed the process. When the contractor violated a city ordinance by building an eight-foot brick fence, the inspectors did not require its removal. A potentially project-delaying strike by the Teamsters lasted only three days. (The team rewarded the man who helped settle the strike with a season ticket.)[25] Organized Baseball had some hope, however, of blocking necessary neighborhood approvals by having agents lobby the nearby residents. Weeghman and other Chifeds employees, though, used season tickets as currency to reward and influence neighbors and politicians, offering them to many of the neighbors who signed petitions in favor of the new ballpark.[26]

Despite some tense moments, the stadium was ready by Opening Day. Even so, Weeghman was not yet in the clear. The *Chicago Tribune* reported:

> [T]he consent of nearly 1,000 more property owners in the neighborhood must be obtained before the Feds will be secure in their new park. Apparently every one within 1,000 feet, or nearly three blocks, of the park must have his say in the matter, whereas the Feds believed that only property owners immediately across

from the four sides of the park need be consulted. It was said Chifed agents were canvassing the district last night for the needed signatures [no doubt armed with season tickets]. A permit for today's game [Opening Day] has been secured from the city officials, but the necessary consent of two-thirds of the neighbors must be obtained before Monday, so the rumor goes.[27]

Someone from Organized Baseball likely dug up the offending ordinance and brought it to the attention of city officials. Whether by offering season tickets and the promise of their own North Side ball team or simply by using political influence at city hall, the Chifeds sidestepped this final obstacle. On April 23 Weeghman Park, today better known as Wrigley Field, opened for its first Major League baseball game.

While struggling to sign Major Leaguers and keep Weeghman in the fold, Gilmore bought his league some staying power in Toronto. In early February he had crossed the border to line up a stadium site and settle the franchise's ownership with a politically well-connected group he had assembled, one willing to invest roughly $125,000. Serendipitously, Gilmore was introduced to Robert Ward, visiting friends in Toronto, by a friend of Ward's son. Gilmore knew a golden goose when he met one, and called Ward the next day to ask for an audience. Ward, a longtime baseball enthusiast, agreed to meet. Gilmore gave his best sales pitch, and Ward gave the response Gilmore wanted: "If you will put your cards on the table and things are as you represent them, I will go into this scheme with you."[28] At the time Gilmore may not have realized quite how much they would need Ward, but for Gilmore and the Federals, having an owner of enormous wealth who could backstop some of the weaker franchises would be critical.

Gilmore could not have found a better owner for his technically still homeless eighth and final franchise. Ward's family had come to America from Ireland and operated a small bakery business in Pittsburgh. The older family members joined the Union army during the Civil War, and at age eight young Robert began working in the family bakery. When he turned twenty-one his father told him it was time he started his own business, so Robert and a partner bought a small grocery store. Five years later the two decided to part ways, and Ward accepted a buyout. In this era of rough-and-tumble capitalism, aggressive, smart young men could start a business with relatively little capital. Many start-ups, of course, failed, but some grew spectacularly. Ward used his small nest egg to buy back into the industry he grew up in, purchasing his own small bakery.[29]

Ward's hard work and genius quickly built his small business into one of the largest in Pittsburgh. Much of the growth could be attributed to two innovations. First, Ward recognized that some of the coarser grades of flour could make a more affordable loaf of bread for the poor. Second, and more important, he tapped into some of the food safety concerns of the age. In this era of the early industrialization of food processing and production, hygiene problems were rampant. Ward promoted the safety of his product under the slogan, "Bread from Baker to Consumer, untouched by the Human Hand."[30] With his emphasis on advertising—a business strategy that became more important in the new world of mass production—Ward became the leading producer of a product that the public wanted. Beyond simply offering an outlet for his love of baseball, Ward saw a Major League baseball team as a wonderful advertising vehicle. In naming his club the "Tip-Tops," after his bread, Ward looked at the ball team as an extension of his baking empire. He was joined in his business and in his baseball venture by his brother George, son William, and George's son Walter. George was a "dignified sort of man," but his playboy son enjoyed the night life and soon began to take advantage of the additional perks that came to a baseball owner.

Ward offered the new league more than just money. He was an astute businessman, and in launching a new operation he understood the importance of making an immediate splash. When Ward invaded the New York bread market he did not start small and strategically build market share. "We invested two million dollars in our New York venture before we turned a wheel or gained the market for a single loaf of bread," Ward later recalled. "The day we started our great plants we loaded a hundred wagons with bread and sent them out, instructing our salesmen to give the bread away as samples. The next day we sent them out again, this time to sell the bread. They have been selling bread ever since."[31]

For a man who built a huge industrial enterprise during an era of emerging capitalism, Ward had earned a reputation of unsurpassed integrity. An observant Methodist, he would later prompt resentment among his fellow owners by refusing to allow his team to play on Sunday. At a time when some states and municipalities still banned baseball on the Christian Sabbath, owners were anxious to cash in on big Sunday crowds in those locations where it was permitted.

When Ward agreed to take a franchise in the new league, its location had not been officially decided upon. Baltimore's Ned Hanlon, constantly in contact with Gilmore as they worked to strengthen the league, convinced the Wards that they should locate their team in Brooklyn. He still resented Brooklyn Dodgers owner Charles Ebbets because of a power struggle he had lost to Ebbets years earlier. Hanlon believed that a well-heeled Brooklyn owner could effectively compete with the capital-constrained Ebbets.[32]

Ebbets would not be an easy mark. He was a Brooklyn politician who had spent nearly his entire adult life with the Dodgers and had finally achieved his lifelong dream in 1905 when he wrested full control of the team. He was not about to surrender the territory willingly. Ebbets had come of age in New York during the raw capitalist era of the late 1870s and early 1880s. As a young man he had wanted to be an architect, so he joined a firm where he could work as a draftsman. New York was booming during this postwar period, and Ebbets had the opportunity to work on high-profile projects. He soon abandoned the design profession, however, to go into book sales, where he printed and sold cheap novels.[33]

One of baseball's cheapest owners, Brooklyn Dodgers owner Charles Ebbets was highly active behind the scenes in National League politics. (Courtesy of the Library of Congress)

Tiring of books, in 1883 the twenty-three-year-old Ebbets joined the Brooklyn baseball club, then in the Inter-State Association, as a jack-of-all-trades in the office. He sold tickets and scorecards, acted as bookkeeper and clerk, and generally kept the office running. After seven years of service, Ebbets acquired a small ownership interest. In 1898, though still a minority stockholder, he gained effective control of the franchise. When the National League consolidated a year later, the Baltimore and Brooklyn franchises were merged into Brooklyn. Owners Ferdinand Abell, Harry von der Horst, and Ebbets believed they could make much more money with a championship team in Brooklyn than in Baltimore, where profits had been disappointing. In the new ownership structure Abell, Brooklyn's principal owner, held a 40 percent share; Harry von der Horst, Baltimore's principal owner, 40 percent; Ebbets, 10 percent; and Baltimore manager Ned Hanlon, 10 percent. Baltimore had been one of the great teams of the mid-1890s, and with all this talent now in Brooklyn, the team won the pennant in both 1899 and 1900.

Hanlon and Ebbets clashed from the start. Both were in their early forties, and both wanted control of the team. As the club lost players to the upstart American League in 1901, the team's won-lost record and profits dropped, and von der Horst and Abell began to lose interest, aggravating the direct interaction between Ebbets and Hanlon. As team president, Ebbets technically had veto power over Hanlon's decisions. Practically, however, Hanlon, who earned $10,000 to Ebbets's $4,000 and was one of baseball's most respected leaders, acted as the de facto general manager. Over the next couple of years, though, the wily Ebbets began to exert his influence and gain control over major decisions. To Hanlon's consternation, Ebbets, considered one of the cheapest owners in the league, was unable and unwilling to spend money for players.[34]

When von der Horst fell on hard financial times, Ebbets and Hanlon both vied for his shares and ultimate control of the franchise. Hanlon, who had turned down more lucrative managing offers over the years, believed von der Horst, his longtime boss and friend, owed him first shot at his shares. With von der Horst's shares under his control, Hanlon probably intended to move the team back to Baltimore. But Ebbets outmaneuvered him. He convinced von der Horst to sell to an Ebbets-friendly investor and, like several years earlier, soon regained effective control. Disappointed and betrayed, Hanlon had one card left to play. He filed suit against the team, charging that Ebbets had actually been receiving a salary of $10,000 in violation of team rules. He also claimed that the directors did not notify the secretary of state of its annual meeting, thus invalidating the election and putting the runners-up, including Abell and Hanlon, into elected positions. Ebbets shrewdly used the opportunity to gain full control of the team. He convinced Abell to sell him his 40 percent share for $20,000 (with only $500 down). Without Abell's support, Hanlon was forced out, receiving $10,000 for his 10 percent interest. Ebbets and Brooklyn had the Dodgers. Hanlon eventually returned to Baltimore and acquired a Minor League franchise before selling it to Jack Dunn in 1909.[35]

Once Ward had settled on Brooklyn for his Federal League franchise, Hanlon helped the new Tip-Tops owners gain the use of Washington Park, the home of the Dodgers until 1912. The Dodgers had just moved into their new steel-and-concrete structure at Ebbets Field, leaving their old wooden ball grounds unused by Major League baseball. To bring the stadium up to code, Brooklyn's politicians and city inspectors forced the Wards to rebuild Washington Park at a cost in excess of $200,000. When it reopened in 1914 the stadium had a capacity of 14,750: 1,600 box seats at $1.25, 3,200 reserved seats at $1.00, 6,000 seats at 75 cents, 2,600 covered seats at 50 cents, and 1,350 seats in centerfield at 25 cents. Architect Corry Comstock made one big mistake in the design of the stadium: he located the stands too close to the field. Only twelve to fifteen feet from the foul lines, the tiny foul territory caused nearly all foul balls to end up with the spectators. At the time fans were not allowed to keep foul balls (Weeghman would introduce this practice several years later), leading to a tacky atmosphere as team officials constantly wrestled balls away from fans. Apparently this flawed design was due to a desire to get the fans closer to the field and also to protect a portion of Fourth Avenue for the construction of apartment buildings.[36]

To help run the ballclub, Ward hired John Montgomery Ward (no relation) as business manager. A great player in the nineteenth century, Ward had been the driving force behind establishing the Players League in 1890 and had long been an advocate for player rights. After many years in the game, John Montgomery Ward had recently settled down to a life in private practice as an attorney. But the challenge of a new league and the opportunity to work for a franchise with well-heeled owners lured him back to his first love. He was also friendly with new National League president John Tener from his days in the Players League and may have hoped this connection could help smooth the new league's relationship with Organized Baseball.

Brooklyn also wanted a field manager with more name appeal than Bill Bradley, tentatively lined up by Gilmore during his trip to Canada. Gilmore subsequently thought he had convinced Jake Stahl, a veteran first baseman and skipper of the 1912 Red Sox, recently retired, to become manager of the Tip-Tops. Stahl, however, had just begun working for a bank, and the bank's executives refused to allow him to manage a ballclub while on the job. In defending his decision to decline the Brooklyn job, Stahl cryptically declared that "he was not influenced in his decision by the threats of Ban Johnson to expose him and force him out of baseball, asserting there was nothing in his past that he was afraid to have made public."[37] After Stahl's rebuff, Ward circled back to Bradley, signing him for three years at $5,700 per year, a shockingly large amount for a washed-up third baseman.[38]

With the Wards committed in Brooklyn, the eight-team Federal League circuit was complete. While not quite representing the population base of the two established Major Leagues (as table 5.1 indicates), the Federals could claim a respectable effective population in their markets.

Table 5.1.   Market Population Comparison (1910 Census)

City	NL	AL	FL
New York (1)	2,762,522	2,762,522	
Brooklyn (n/a)	1,634,351		1,634,351
Chicago (2)	2,446,921	2,446,921	2,446,921
Philadelphia (3)	1,972,342	1,972,342	
Boston (4)	1,520,470	1,520,470	
Pittsburgh (5)	1,042,855		1,042,855
St. Louis (6)	828,733	828,733	828,733
Baltimore (8)			658,715
Cleveland (9)		613,270	
Cincinnati (10)	563,804		
Detroit (12)		500,982	
Buffalo (13)			488,661
Washington (17)		367,869	
Kansas City (19)			340,446
Indianapolis (23)			237,783
Effective Population	6,121,959	5,701,673	4,156,093

Notes
*All population counts are for metropolitan areas except for New York and Brooklyn.
**Metropolitan population rank in parentheses.
***New York population is for Manhattan and Bronx (the entire New York area metropolitan population was 6,474,568).
****"Effective Population" adjusts for cities with more than one team by dividing the metropolitan population by the number of Major League teams.

With a full circuit and one of America's richest industrialists on board, Gilmore knew he had enhanced his league's staying power. Moreover, Weeghman had not deserted the Federals and was instead an enthusiastic free-spender in America's second-largest city with the league's best ballpark. Gilmore could look with certainty toward Opening Day. One key question, however, remained: Could the Federals stock their teams with Major League–quality players?

6

Organized Baseball Responds

Organized Baseball would not make it easy for the Federals. Their owners disparaged the Federal League's chances of long-term survival and reminded the players that they would be unable to return to Organized Baseball when the Federals inevitably collapsed. Players who signed with the Federals were immediately contacted by representatives from their former team and usually offered significant salary increases to return.

Bill Killefer was one of the first to cave in to the pressure from Organized Baseball. Less than two weeks after his announced signing with the Chifeds, Killefer re-signed for three years with the Phillies. At first Killefer denied having signed with the Federals, but Charlie Weeghman refuted his assertion by producing the contract. In fact, Killefer's three-year contract with the Chifeds called for a total of $17,500, of which $500 was advanced as a bonus. To lure him back, the Phillies gave him $19,500 over three years, a huge increase over his $3,200 salary in 1913.[1]

The Federal League's leadership was unprepared for the speed and scope of the response by Organized Baseball. These were seasoned businessmen and under no illusion that Organized Baseball would welcome them. But they generally believed, naively as it turned out, that if they played by what they considered fair rules, Organized Baseball would reciprocate. The key component of this approach was that the Federals adopted a hands-off attitude toward those players actually under a Major League contract; they targeted only players whose contracts had expired and thus were controlled only by the reserve clause. The Federals expected that Organized Baseball would give the same respect to their contracts.

Regarding Killefer, the shocked Weeghman responded first with bewilderment, then bluster: "I can't understand the report. I have the signed contract of Killefer in my possession."[2] Shortly thereafter, once he realized that Killefer had reneged, he added, "If Organized Baseball starts taking players we have signed, I will start the same thing, and I'll have Christy Mathewson and Ty Cobb and some more of them playing for me on the north side, because I'll give them more money than anybody else."[3] Joe Tinker refused to believe the established leagues could recapture their players: "Organized ball knows it has no legal right to sign our ballplayers. It merely wants to tie them up so they can't play with us."[4] Even with the evidence before them, Weeghman and Tinker continued to hold out hope that Killefer would honor his contract and report to spring training. When the club finally left for Shreveport, Louisiana, on March 8, though, their new catcher was nowhere in sight.

Weeghman and Tinker also lost pitcher King Cole back to Organized Baseball. When Cole first received notice from New York Yankees owner Frank Farrell that they had drafted him from Columbus, he demanded a salary of $3,300. The Yankees acquiesced to Cole's request in writing on January 2.[5] Cole, however, reconsidered his salary demands and contacted Gilmore, and the two quickly came to terms at a higher salary. To avoid any appearance of impropriety, Gilmore told Cole, "Now to avoid any trouble we will date these contracts December 30th, 1913."[6] In fact, the contract was signed on January 3.

When, after agreeing to Cole's salary request, the Yankees didn't hear back from him, they naturally grew anxious and followed up forcefully. "We hereby notify you that our acceptance of your offer effected a contract binding in law," Yankees owner Frank Farrell wrote to his wayward pitcher.[7] He also dispatched scout Arthur Irwin to Chicago to bring Cole back for a little reindoctrination. After consulting with his attorney, Cole realized he was now committed to two contracts and in a sticky legal situation. Under the combined pressure of the New York owners, his attorney, and the press, Cole publicly renounced his Federal League contract and officially signed the $3,300 contract with the Yankees.[8] The whole process proved highly embarrassing to Weeghman and Gilmore, who were publicly exposed for backdating the contract.

In Cleveland, Charles Somers recognized that the loss of George Kahler, Fred Blanding, and Cy Falkenberg would devastate his Indians pitching staff. Once he learned that they had signed with the Federals, he enlisted the help of Ban Johnson and continued to pursue them. After a couple of weeks of threats and promises of higher pay, Somers and Johnson finally convinced Kahler and Blanding to return to Cleveland. When local sportswriters realized that Falkenberg, the best of the three, was also wavering, they printed the rumor of his defection. Alerted to Falkenberg's vacillations, the Federals put on a full-court press. Disregarding any specific team affiliations, they dispatched Buffalo director Dick Carroll to baby-sit Falkenberg and keep an eye on any agents sent from Organized Baseball. Seeking reinforcements, Carroll called in Buffalo manager Larry Schlafly and Baltimore manager Otto Knabe. The latter brought $10,000 as an advance on Falkenberg's contract, and Indianapolis further agreed to pay the expenses of his wife and two children traveling to spring training.[9]

Meanwhile, Brooklyn's Charles Ebbets had not given up on Tinker, one of the Federal League's most stalwart proponents. On January 26 Ebbets sent a letter to Tinker agreeing to Tinker's earlier demand for a three-year contract at $7,500 per year. By this point, however, Tinker was fully committed to the new league and turned Ebbets down.[10]

St. Louis Browns owner Robert Hedges also had no intention of letting his players get away. Like many baseball owners of the time, Hedges came from a poor background and had worked himself into upper-middle-class society. Born on a Missouri farm near Kansas City, when Hedges was ten his father died, and the family moved into town. After coming of age, Hedges eventually made his way to Hamilton, Ohio, near Cincinnati, where he started a carriage manufacturing company. He sold out in 1900 for a substantial profit, just as automobiles were first becoming available. While in Cincinnati the handsome Hedges became something of a man about town, marrying an attractive socialite and becoming friends with Ban Johnson. When Johnson needed an owner for his American League team in St. Louis, he turned to Hedges, who, with a couple of partners, purchased the team for $50,000. During their first dozen years the Browns were unsuccessful on the field but profitable nonetheless. Hedges had a knack for uncovering talented Minor Leaguers, many of whom he hastily resold to other Major League teams. He was also a frequent violator of the rule limiting control of Minor League players by Major League teams, often engaging in illegal handshake agreements with Minor League owners. Shrewd but generous, Hedges was rumored to have had a falling out with Johnson as the Federal League battle neared (which Hedges later denied). Regardless of his personal animosities, Johnson supported any owner in his battle with the hated upstarts. Hedges enlisted Johnson's help to pressure outfielder Gus Williams and pitcher George Baumgardner to return to the Browns after having jumped. Under the combined assault, both players rejoined the Browns in time for spring training.[11]

To prevent fringe Major Leaguers from jumping to the Federals instead of accepting a possible demotion to the Minors, for 1914 both Major Leagues

Undercapitalized St. Louis Browns owner Robert Hedges aggressively pursued his players considering the Federal League. (Courtesy of the Library of Congress)

suspended the twenty-five-man roster limit, allowing teams to carry as many ballplayers as they wished. Although it helped keep these players in Organized Baseball, paying all of them big-league salaries was an extremely expensive proposition for the clubs.[12]

On February 12 the National Commission voted to make the blacklist official, banning every player who "fails to report to his club on the opening day of the season." Surprisingly, the Players Fraternity backed this move and ruled that any player barred from Organized Baseball would also be automatically suspended from the union. In general, player representative Dave Fultz felt it best not to antagonize the owners over the reserve clause. He carefully avoided taking a formal position on the rule, refusing to support it but also usually refusing to advise players on its validity. Fultz did, however, take a stand on contract jumping and agreed to suspend players who jumped a signed contract.[13]

To encourage players to return to Organized Baseball before the season started, the blacklist applied only to players who actually appeared in a game with the Federals. The National Commission decided that "all players who signed with the reconstituted Federal League would be permitted to return to Organized Baseball, provided they reported previous to the opening of the season of the League of which they are member."[14] Regarding players who jumped from Minor League teams to the Federals in 1913, the National Commission regarded this as purely a Minor League matter.

In February the Commission sent a bulletin to all teams outlining new guidelines and regulations designed to combat the upstarts. The Commission advised the clubs to sign as quickly as possible all players not under contract and held only by the reserve clause. Toward this end, the bulletin included a sample letter to be sent to all players informing them that jumpers would be banned from Organized Baseball for at least three years. The teams were also given talking points for publicly addressing potential anti-trust and contractual complications: "Club owners are cautioned against claiming exclusive rights to territory and are counseled to make it plain to newspaper interviewers that Organized Baseball is not a trust or monopoly," and "The sanctity of contracts and reservations must be respected and that a disregard of these obligations will result in chaotic conditions, which will impair public confidence in the game's integrity."

The memo also defined the status of players who jumped:

As the [Federal] league was regarded as an independent organization last season, deserting players during 1913 may be recalled by their respective clubs. . . . The Federal League is now declared an outlaw league by the Commission and will be treated as such in the future, although formal promulgation of its status will not be made. Club owners are cautioned against discussing the matter except among themselves. Players, who have signed with that league for 1914 . . . and do not report . . . before the beginning of the coming championship race [i.e., the start of the season], will not be eligible for service in Organized Baseball at any time or under any circumstances except on special application to the Commission and by its permission. Club owners should, therefore, make special efforts to have their deserting players sign contracts at once and report by the first day of the major league pennant races *without regards to their having signed Federal League contracts* [my italics].

In other words, Organized Baseball would not respect Federal League contracts; the reserve clause was binding, and players who signed with the Federals had violated an existing contract and were still legally bound to their Organized Baseball team. Furthermore, teams were instructed to try to sign players to two-year contracts so as to limit the number of unsigned players potentially available to the Federals after the 1914 season.

The Commission also ruled that "in all cases in which a player deserts to the Federal League, the financial loss shall be borne by the club having title to services at the time he jumps." To help clubs that competed head to head with the Federals, the bulletin suggested that "in disposing of surplus players, Major League clubs should give preference to Double-A clubs in cities in which there is Federal League opposition." To further aid the Minors, the Commission agreed to allow Minor League teams, most of which operated under a salary cap, to exceed their limit until further notice. The Commission also hoped to control litigation with the new league by declaring that "under no circumstances should a club commence court proceedings against a Federal League club over a player or on any other issue without consulting the Commission and securing its approval."[15]

As the Major Leagues went about recapturing many of the players the Federals thought they had successfully lured away, Gilmore still imagined a grudging accommodation with Organized Baseball could be arranged. Although full of bluster, he certainly recognized the advantages the established Major Leagues held over his newcomers. Ban Johnson disparaged the new league both publicly and in private, but Gilmore believed that if he could just make his case in person, Johnson might be willing to enter into some sort of détente. Gilmore's brother Charles was an acquaintance of Johnson's. When Charles first approached the American League president about a meeting with his brother, Johnson replied that "their interests were so wide apart it would probably be advisable not to meet him."[16] But Charles persisted, and Johnson reluctantly agreed. On February 16 the two met at the Automobile Club in Chicago.

"Mr. Johnson, I am here to tell you two or three things and make a suggestion or two," Gilmore told him. "The first one is that we are in this game to stay, and we have got sufficient funds to carry it on. Secondly, we do not desire to have any ball player breach a contract, and if you will recognize contracts of ball players signed by the Federal League, valid or invalid, we will do likewise. We do not care to affiliate with you, but will continue as an independent organization, but if you endeavor to get ball players to breach our contracts and we do likewise, the ballplayers and the lawyers will get all the money, and furthermore interest in the game will lag."

"Gilmore, you are in a fight," Johnson responded, "and my advice is to get all the ball players you can. I believe, Gilmore, that there is one very serious proposition you are overlooking, and that is what disposition you are going to make of ball players who are of no value to you. [The Federals had no established Minor Leagues where they could send excess players.]"

"That is a subject we have given considerable thought to and are competent to handle when the time comes," Gilmore responded. He then returned to his main point, the respect for player contracts. "What do you think of my suggestion?"

"It is a very good suggestion," Johnson agreed.

"How far will you go?"

"Will you attend a conference with Mr. Herrmann, Mr. Tener, and myself?"

"Eliminate Herrmann," Gilmore told him, "and I will be glad to confer with you as the head of the American League and Mr. Tener as the head of the National League, as I have full authority to make such arrangements as I want, and I presume that you have similar authority."[17]

According to Gilmore, the meeting ended with Johnson driving him over to the Chicago Athletic Club and promising to call the next day after conferring with Tener.

In a letter to Herrmann that shows him at his most perceptive, Johnson summed up his thoughts on the meeting:

> From the drift of the conversation, I was convinced that the Federals are experiencing much difficulty in the matter of signing the players of Organized Ball. . . . He [Gilmore] intimated that an immediate fight would be made for the services of Killefer and Kirkpatrick. No reference was made to the American League players, and I assume that he has no positive knowledge of the desertions that have returned to our organization. . . . I told him I would communicate with Governor Tener on this point. This I have not done. Both organizations [the American and National Leagues] have decided on a course in this matter, and a conference would only be "wising up" the opposition. Mr. Gilmore has a most absurd idea of the amount of money to be made in baseball. He did say, however, that he was sorry that he had entered the baseball field, and that some of his colleagues felt the same way.[18]

When Blanding jumped back to Organized Baseball in late February, just days after Gilmore's meeting with Johnson, Gilmore pushed for a follow-up meeting but Johnson ignored him.[19] Gilmore's frustration boiled over. He believed that the Federals had acted honorably. Blanding became at least the fourth signed player whom Major League baseball had enticed to return to the fold. "If our contracts are no good, their contracts are no good," Gilmore vowed on March 3, "and a player can disregard a contract with a club in Organized Ball as easily as he can in ours. . . . If the American and National Leagues ignore our contracts and fail to appreciate the spirit of sportsmanship we have shown, we will start the biggest of baseball wars."[20]

As Gilmore fumed, Ban Johnson, in an interview printed in the *New York Evening Sun* on March 5, 1914, blasted not only the Federals but also National League owners for an apparent willingness to negotiate with the new league:

I don't favor these confabs. If the idea is to bring about a peaceful settlement of the present trouble in baseball the American League will put a stop to all negotiations. There can be no peace until the Federal league has been exterminated. Put it as strongly as you can that we will fight these pirates to a finish. There will be no quarter.

Yes, I've heard that peacemakers are at work, but they are wasting their time. The American League will tolerate no such interference . . . and we will refuse to take part in any peace confabs.

This Federal league movement is taken too seriously, why, the whole thing is a joke. They are holding a meeting once a week to keep from falling to pieces. Quote me as saying that the Federals have no money in Buffalo, Indianapolis, and Pittsburgh. They have no ballparks in any of their cities, except an amateur field in Kansas City and a ramshackle affair in Pittsburgh. There are some wooden bleachers put up on Hanlon's Park in Baltimore, I believe.

We hear from day to day that the Feds have millions behind them. If that is true they ought to build half million dollar stadium[s] in a few weeks. But getting down to brass tacks, they have neither grounds nor players that amount to anything.

When the list of players is finally announced the baseball public will realize what a bluff these fellows have been putting up. They have many unknown players, taken off the lots, and a bunch of Bush Leaguers with a sprinkling of big fellows. But the American League will not lose more than 10 men.

Blanding has gone back to the Clevelands. Yes, it is true that he was induced to sign with the Federals first, but he belonged to Somers, and we will take his case to the courts. We are going to cut and slash right and left from now on. We intend to show up the four flushers and the bluffers in the proper light.

I haven't answered Gilmore's telegram relating to tampering with players. I do not intend to answer. Gilmore knows little or nothing about baseball, so why waste time over him? If the National League sells the club [Chicago Cubs] to Weeghman and the Cardinals to Stifel that will not concern me. I know nothing about it, but I doubt very much if Weeghman would be willing to put up much money. Just say in *The Evening Sun* once more that we are going to fight the Federals until they have been counted out.[21]

Gilmore offered two concrete ripostes to Johnson's diatribe. In Pittsburgh he had finally lined up significant backing for the franchise. The new president, Edward Gwinner, son of a wealthy contractor and bank president, had been brought in by Corry Comstock, Robert Ward's architect and engineer for his bakery facilities. Comstock purchased a minority interest in the club and became the team's vice president. With the solidifying of the Pittsburgh franchise, the Federals lined up quite well financially versus Organized Baseball. Brooklyn was owned by one of baseball's wealthiest men. Chicago, St. Louis, and Pittsburgh were all owned by partnerships headed by men wealthier than many Major League owners. Baltimore and Buffalo were well capitalized through local stock offerings to many upper-middle-class investors and run by fairly wealthy, well-connected local leaders with large investments. Indianapolis and Kansas City were similarly structured but less well capitalized.

Second, Gilmore and the Federal League had a fresh pool of unsigned players to target. After the 1913 season, New York Giants manager John McGraw and Chicago White Sox owner Charles Comiskey had organized an around-the-world baseball tour. The party included two teams, nominally the Giants and White Sox but in fact made up of a number of Major League players from various teams, who played a series of exhibitions literally around the world. Starting in Cincinnati on October 18, the two teams played across America until they reached Seattle. After heading up to Vancouver, the expedition journeyed across the Pacific to Japan, Asia, and Australia. From Australia the tour went through the Suez Canal to Cairo and then to several European destinations and finally to England.

On Friday, March 6, the world travelers at last returned to New York on the *Lusitania*, a luxury liner whose sinking a year later by German torpedoes would become an international incident. Important for our story, several of the returning players had not yet signed contracts for 1914. Gilmore publicly announced that the league would target eight of them, most prominently Boston's great center fielder Tris Speaker and Detroit's star right fielder Sam Crawford. Speaker had long been an outspoken critic of the owners' heavy-handed treatment and seemed a logical candidate for the new league.

Several days before their ship was due to arrive in New York, Gilmore sent telegrams to the players advising them that the Federals would be waiting to present them with huge salary offers when they landed. He put together an impressive welcoming committee of Federal League owners and managers to meet the players at the docks and induce them to sign contracts before their Major League teams could get to them: Brooklyn owners George and Walter Ward; managers Mordecai Brown, George Stovall, Larry Schlafly, and Otto Knabe; St. Louis owner Otto Stifel; Baltimore mainstay Ned Hanlon; and league attorney Edward Gates from Indianapolis. Gilmore, Gates, and most of the group planned to ride out to the returning liner on a "revenue cutter," a customs ship that met incoming ships before they docked. Gilmore's highly public blustering that the Federals would sign the returning ballplayers, however, was a tactical mistake. With ample warning, the Major League baseball owners prepared a counterstrike.

Boston Braves owner James Gaffney, connected to New York's Tammany Hall political machine, thwarted Gilmore's plan. Gaffney had grown up on the Lower East Side and became another late-nineteenth-century self-made New Yorker. A onetime policeman, he was elected a New York alderman with the help of the Tammany political machine. Through his Tammany contacts Gaffney made his fortune as a building and excavating contractor. As he worked his way up the machine ladder, he became a close confidant and backer of Tammany boss Charles F. Murphy (no relation to the Cubs owner).

In 1913 New York governor William Sulzer was impeached for misusing campaign contributions. Sulzer charged that Murphy was behind the impeachment because Sulzer had defied him on several issues—most importantly when Murphy wanted Gaffney appointed state highway commissioner. "I will wreck your administration," Sulzer claimed Murphy threatened. "It's Gaffney or war."[22] In his defense, Gaffney produced a press article quoting Sulzer: "he [Gaffney] was the right kind of man for this commission." He then attacked Sulzer: "It is no satisfaction to me to convince any one that Sulzer deliberately falsifies every time he discusses this matter [illegally appropriating the campaign funds]. He had his chance to deny what there was against him and the only defense he put up was 'My wife did it.' Any one who will do that will lie about anything."[23] Despite raucous press coverage over the next few months, Gaffney suffered no serious setback from the incident.

Gaffney had first become involved in big-league baseball in 1911, almost as an afterthought, when William Russell, leader of the Boston Braves (then called the Rustlers) ownership syndicate, suffered from failing health. Ned Hanlon, sensing an opportunity to purchase the franchise and move it to Baltimore, offered $169,000, well above what Russell's group had paid but low for the time. Russell rejected the offer. When he died later that year, his estate put the team up for sale.

John Montgomery Ward, now a New York lawyer, longed to join the Major League ownership fraternity after all his years fighting them. For $5,000 he secured a short-term option to purchase the Boston franchise and went searching for backers. With time running out he approached Gaffney. Gaffney recognized a bargain when he saw one, and with a third partner, Gaffney and Ward purchased the team for only $187,000. Ward expected that Gaffney, a baseball novice, would remain a silent money partner while he ran the operation. Gaffney had other ideas, and the two powerful personalities could not jointly operate the team. By mid-1913 Gaffney had forced Ward out and bought his small ownership interest.[24]

Gaffney generally remained quiet at league meetings but operated effectively behind the scenes. He quickly tired of the "long-winded" Ebbets and the "argumentative" Baker. He intuitively understood that key decisions were typically made outside of formal meetings. "No members ever were converted from opinions previously held," Gaffney stated. "But I suppose that every man thinks it his duty to shine somewhere, and all of his talk is saved for this occasion."[25]

Now, with the *Lusitania* bringing players home from the around-the-world tour, Gaffney used his influence to commandeer the revenue ships for use by representatives of Organized Baseball, stranding the Federals dockside. With this head start, the baseball magnates could try to re-sign their players before the Federals could get to them. Several of the players recognized their bargaining position and refused to sign immediately; they knew the Federals were waiting. To further hamper the Federals, at least one credible source reported that "East Side gunmen" were recruited to keep them away from the docks.

The Federals quickly devised a backup plan. They rented a suite of rooms at the nearby Knickerbocker Hotel to entertain the players. To get the players to the hotel, the Federals enlisted several agents—unknown to the supposed gunmen—to obtain dock passes and meet the players as they came down the gangplank. The Federal League managers had all signed a number of small cards, which the agents then discreetly handed to the players as they left the ship, often by slipping them to the players as they shook hands. Many players showed up at the hotel to hear the Federals' pitch, including at least four of the targeted tourists: Tris Speaker, Mickey Doolan, Lee Magee, and Steve Evans.[26]

Mordecai Brown and several cohorts met with Magee in one of the suites, offering a large salary increase. Magee surprisingly declined, believing he would be traded. "Fellows, I'm for the Federal League heart and soul," Magee told them, "but I'm pretty certain of being traded to New York [the 1913 National League pennant winner], and if I get a chance to play in the World's Series I will value that pretty highly. McGraw is after me and promised to put through a trade for me if I do not jump."[27]

Speaker, too, was highly tempted. The Wards laid out a certified check for two years' salary along with two $500 bills as a signing bonus. Speaker longingly fingered the check and money but eventually left without signing. "For God's sake, men," he told the Wards, "take this money away or I'll fall. I promised on my word of honor that I would give [Boston Red Sox owner Joe] Lannin a chance before I signed up."[28] Denied Speaker, the Wards were determined not to come away empty-handed and turned their focus to Evans. It cost them a large bonus—Evans was reportedly flourishing three $1,000 bills around New York that evening—but Brooklyn got a legitimate Major League outfielder.[29]

Hanlon and Knabe went hard after Mickey Doolan, Knabe's unhappy keystone partner in Philadelphia. In 1908 and 1909 Doolan was paid an extra $600 per year as team captain, an important and labor-intensive role at the time. Red Dooin became player-manager in 1911 and took the team captaincy duties as well. The Phillies therefore reduced Doolan's bonus pay to only $100 per year. While this naturally disappointed Doolan, what really peeved him was that the team refused even to pay this reduced amount in 1911 and 1912, and he could only squeeze it out of Baker in 1913 once the owner realized that the Federal League was coming after his players. For 1914 Doolan apparently agreed to, but did not sign, a contract with Baker calling for $4,600, a raise over his 1913 salary of $3,500.[30] When Hanlon offered a three-year contract at $6,000 per year, he eagerly signed with Baltimore.[31] At the banquet celebrating the players' return, Baker and Doolan got into a shouting match after Baker challenged his ex-shortstop's manhood.

In the end, the Federals were disappointed. Despite all their planning and scheming, of the eight targeted ballplayers they landed only two, Evans and Doolan, and neither was a star of the caliber of Speaker or Crawford. The real beneficiaries of all the competition were the players. Salaries of all eight rose dramatically. Speaker signed for two years at $15,000 per season (reported at the time to be as high as $18,000), a large increase over his 1913 salary of $9,000 and one of the highest in baseball. Detroit owner Frank Navin boosted Crawford's pay from roughly $5,000 to $7,500 while Magee received a new three-year contract at around $6,000 per season.

Stovall managed to evade Organized Baseball's thugs and make it down to the docks. He hoped to sign another of his old St. Louis players, pitcher Walter Leverenz. Stovall briefly buttonholed Leverenz and whispered something to the pitcher just before Browns owner Robert Hedges could reach him. Leverenz, who made $2,100 in 1913, told a nervous Hedges that Stovall had just offered him $6,000. Hedges and the hurler settled on a nice raise, and Leverenz remained in Organized Baseball.

In the aftermath of the signing flurry, National League owners Baker and Gaffney arranged a meeting with Gilmore and Gates. Both hoped they could talk Gilmore into allowing a couple of pitchers to return to Organized Baseball. Baker wanted Tom Seaton back, and Gaffney thought he should be allowed to keep Jack Quinn, another Federal signing. Baker and Gaffney claimed that their respective hurlers had agreed to terms before being lured away by the Federals and therefore were not really available. "If you gentlemen want to play fair," Gilmore responded, "I am willing to. Killefer belongs to us by reason of signing a contract with us and accepting advance money. There is no need of further talk unless you want to turn over Killefer and avoid an injunction suit."[32] Not surprisingly, Baker had no intention of surrendering Killefer to the Federals, and the meeting soon broke up.

Frustrated by Johnson's diatribe and the Federals' relative failure at the docks, Gilmore repeated his earlier threats. The Federal League's owners would now target all players in Organized Baseball, he declared, even those already under contract. "It's war to the end," Gilmore announced. "We will show the public that the Federal League is not a piker and that Ban Johnson of the American League is a four-flusher. We have not violated any confidences. We have been clean and above board in our efforts to secure the services of players who are not under contract. We have not made any overtures to players under contract, but as long as one of our players who is under contract to one of our clubs has been 'lifted,' we are perfectly justified in going after players who are under contract to the clubs of Organized Baseball."[33] Gilmore now sanctioned the targeting of any players under a contract that contained the potentially invalidating "ten-day" clause.

As noted earlier, the standard Major League contract contained a provision that allowed a team to release a player on ten days' notice. Because the player could not also terminate the contract on such notice, many legal scholars believed the agreement lacked mutuality, a key component for a valid contract. Gates and other attorneys who had reviewed this matter for the Federals maintained that the ten-day clause made the Major League contract vulnerable.

Johnson and several American League owners had recognized for some time that the ten-day clause could cause them legal trouble. On December 19, 1913, Johnson had sent a letter to Herrmann suggesting that they remove the clause from the standard contract. Johnson pointed out that the clause did not benefit the clubs commensurate with the ill feeling and possible legal ramifications it created. Some of the clubs, mostly in the American League, did indeed begin to remove the ten-day clause from key player contracts.

If the Federals would now target players under contract, a whole new group of potential signings came within their sights. Gilmore convinced new Pittsburgh owners Gwinner and Comstock to send ex-Pirate and recent recruit Howie Camnitz to the Pirates training site in Hot Springs, Arkansas, to troll for players. In particular, Camnitz targeted pitcher George McQuillan and second baseman Jim Viox. He met with both on March 20 at the Eastman Hotel in Hot Springs and offered each a $5,000 salary to jump to the Federals; both were under contract and turned him down. Pirates owner Barney Dreyfuss probably overreacted by asking the Arkansas state court for an injunction against Camnitz's approaches to his players. Dreyfuss may have been encouraged to try the courts by a recent injunction that Boston Braves manager and Georgia native George Stallings had won in a Georgia court on March 18, enjoining Federal League agents from attempting to lure away players under contract with the Braves.[34]

Ban Johnson understood the cost and potential danger of such insignificant court rulings. He feared "the cross petition filed by Camnitz and others at Hot Springs, requiring the Pittsburgh club to produce their contracts in court." The last thing Organized Baseball wanted was a public airing of player salaries. At the time, player salaries were generally kept secret. Disclosure that numerous paychecks were well below the occasionally leaked figures would have been a public relations disaster for Organized Baseball. In response to Dreyfuss's court filing, Johnson sent a scathing letter to Herrmann. "It caused me much anxiety," Johnson wrote, "when I found that Organized Baseball had been forced into an issue of this sort in a distant court, and under conditions I deemed highly unfavorable. All Major League club owners and the National Association [the Minors], had been specifically notified that no court proceedings were to be instituted without the consent and knowledge of the National Commission."[35] In fact, the court ruled for Dreyfuss and enjoined Camnitz from approaching Pirate players.

Johnson's fears were well founded, however, as the Pirates salaries for McQuillan and Viox were revealed to be only $3,600 and $2,500 respectively, well below the expectations of many observers.[36] Only solid legal work by Dreyfuss's attorneys prevented additional Pittsburgh contracts from being made public. Johnson recognized the hollowness of the legal victory: "The restraining order issued against the Federal League agents could have no substantial value [it applied only to the state of Arkansas], and I am surprised that some of the National League clubs should have resorted to such a course."[37] Moreover, Camnitz's threat was probably overstated. An alcoholic who had probably fallen off the wagon, Camnitz "had been drunk all week and was constantly in the hands of some persons of bad repute."[38]

Most important, and clearly justifying Johnson's concerns, Judge J. P. Henderson had parenthetically added to his opinion that he would have declared the standard Organized Baseball contract void had the issue been raised by a player, mainly because of the existence of the ten-day clause. Like many legal authorities, Henderson believed the contract lacked mutuality. Dreyfuss's impatience to use the courts to bar Camnitz had brought the contract issue to the forefront. In response to Judge Henderson's ruling, several more Major League teams began removing the clause from their contracts.

George Stovall also hoped to capture some Major League players. Fully empowered by Kansas City's communal ownership to make player acquisitions, Stovall continued to believe he could lure some of his old Browns charges to Kansas City. Despite his previous setbacks, Stovall hastened to St. Petersburg, where the Browns were training. Over a whirlwind day and a half on March 10 and 11, he sat in the stands and taunted Browns executives by flashing rolls of bills and calling to the players. During his stay in Florida, he met or otherwise communicated with most of the Browns in an attempt to entice them to the Packers. Stovall signed no players on the trip but expectantly laid the groundwork for landing several at a later date.

That later date occurred in late March during a popular preseason series between the Browns and Cardinals. Stovall and team president Charles Madison took up residence at the Beers Hotel in St. Louis and met with various players both at the hotel and at the players' residences. The duo offered three-year contracts to four key players: catcher Sam Agnew, $5,000 per year; pitcher Earl Hamilton, $7,000 per year; outfielder Clarence Walker, $4,500 per year; and outfielder Burt Shotton, $5,000 per year. Including Williams and Baumgardner, whom Stovall threatened with court actions if they did not return, Stovall and Madison hoped to secure a total of six of Hedges's key performers. But once again the Federals came up short. In the end the carrot-and-stick response from Organized Baseball—big raises from the Browns, fear of being blacklisted, and worry over the claimed invalidity of the ten-day clause—prevented all but Hamilton from signing.[39]

Even the Hamilton victory was short-lived. Stovall had signed Hamilton, after a brief courtship, at his apartment. When he went to Hamilton's room, the pitcher and his roommate, Clarence Walker, were making breakfast. Stovall sauntered in with a sack of cash and laid four $1,000 bills on the kitchen table.

"We'll give you this $4,000 and a three-years contract for $21,000," Stovall told Hamilton. "Will you join us?"

Hamilton, just starting the second year of a three-year contract that paid him a total of $10,000, had never seen so much money in his life. Nevertheless, he kept his wits about him. "Make it $5,000 in advance," Hamilton responded, "and I'll sign the contract right now."

Stovall resisted the additional request; after all, he was already offering a young, unproven pitcher a huge salary. But Hamilton held firm; no doubt the sack of cash suggested that Stovall might be willing to part with more. Stovall eventually gave in and put another $1,000 bill on the table: "Now will you sign?"

When Hamilton received a further assurance that his new contract would be guaranteed, he grabbed the money and signed.[40]

Initially taken by surprise when Stovall signed one of his players already under contract, Browns owner Robert Hedges responded quickly and smartly. He traveled to Hamilton's family home in Oswego, Kansas, to meet with the pitcher's father. Hedges convinced Mr. Hamilton that his son had made a mistake in jumping his contract and expressed his willingness to raise the pitcher's salary. Hamilton's father agreed to call his son home for a conference. To secure his leave from the Kawfeds, Hamilton told Stovall that he was homesick, and the manager approved a short trip home. When Hamilton arrived, his father and Hedges gave him the hard sell, and the pitcher caved in to their combined pressure. Now back in the fold, Hamilton was quickly spirited off to Detroit to join the rest of the Browns on their road trip. "I can go out and get these ballplayers," Stovall lamented when he learned of the defection, "but I can't chain 'em down."[41] The Federals refused to give up quietly. Out of understandable frustration, Madison filed a $25,000 lawsuit against Hamilton for breach of contract and threatened Williams and Baumgardner with $10,000 suits. The Federals eventually decided not to pursue the cases against Williams and Baumgardner, and Hamilton's attorneys dragged his case out, shifting venues at least once, before the lawsuit eventually faded.

Gilmore himself joined the renewed advance on Major League players. At the beginning of March he wired Christy Mathewson, the National League's most venerated hurler, an offer of $65,000 over three years—which would have made him the highest-paid player in baseball—to pitch and manage the Brookfeds. Mathewson spurned the huge offer, instead signing for a nice raise with the New York Giants. Cubs president Charles Thomas complained of an April assault by the Federals on his players. Gilmore met with Larry Cheney; other representatives made offers to Fred Mollwitz, James Lavender, Heinie Zimmerman, Jimmy Archer, and Frank Schulte. None were successful.[42]

Like the Federals, the Majors planned to stake out the spring training camps of their adversaries to recapture their players. Philadelphia's William Baker had not given up on recovering pitchers Tom Seaton and Ad Brennan. His success with

Killefer convinced him that with a combination of the carrot and stick he could induce them to jump back. Accordingly, Baker dispatched team secretary Billy Shettsline to Shreveport to re-recruit his two ex-hurlers. Shettsline slipped into Shreveport, where the Chifeds were training, and registered at an out-of-the-way hotel. He then called Seaton and Brennan to arrange a private meeting to make his pitch. The two ex-Phillies, however, still harbored strong resentments and contrived to have the meeting at the Hotel Youree where the team was staying. When Shettsline showed up, he was ambushed in the lobby by Tinker while about a hundred players, guests, and writers looked on.

"You have a large crowd around you, I see," Shettsline deadpanned.

"Yes, and we'll have the crowd around us all season, too," Tinker boasted. "The public likes to see the ballplayer get what's coming to him and that's why the Federal League exists. We are going to pay the players some real money— money they are worth, and we are going to treat them right."

Shettsline refused to back down. "Why, the players surely have prospered under Organized Ball and have been treated all right."

"You think they have?" shot back Tinker, calling attention to a grievance with a personal resonance. "What did the Philadelphia club do to keep Tom Seaton last season? Didn't it keep a telegram away from him in Chicago, a message asking him to come home at once because his wife was dangerously ill? They kept that message away from him and made him pitch a game that afternoon and probably miss two or three trains for home."

"Yes," Seaton piped in, "and you had the telegram before noon."

Shettsline claimed to know nothing of the incident.

"Didn't you make Killefer miss several days of the season last year because you refused to pay him the measly little $250 that had been promised him and which he had coming, and didn't he have to quit the team later in the season in order to get the money?"

Shettsline claimed not to know anything about this incident either.

Tinker continued his diatribe, pouring out a long list of grievances against Organized Baseball and the National Commission. Other players chimed in with their own grievances until eventually the shell-shocked Shettsline retreated in the company of a few sportswriters.

Shettsline defended his trip to Shreveport by telling the reporters that Seaton had agreed to terms with the Phillies by telegram before signing with the Federals. "But it looks," concluded Shettsline, wryly stating the obvious, "that he's satisfied here and wants to stay."[43]

Seaton's travails were not quite over, however. He had originally signed with Tinker for $7,500. When the Wards joined the league, Gilmore convinced Weeghman to "trade" Seaton to Brooklyn to give the Wards a more competitive team. Seaton, not surprisingly, balked at the proposed move. He had signed with Chicago not only for the increase in pay but also because fellow Phillie and close friend Ad Brennan had also signed with the Chifeds. Furthermore, their wives were good friends, and Seaton's wife was the sister of White Sox first baseman Jack Fournier. After two weeks of public embarrassment for the Federals as this proposed move played out in the press, Ward solved the issue with his check-book. He increased Seaton's pay by another $1,000 and agreed to pay the costs of having Seaton's wife travel on all road trips. Seaton furthermore received the unique promise that if the Federals were ever taken into Organized Baseball or the Brooklyn team folded, he would revert to Chicago.[44]

Two Major League owners proposed "continuous baseball" to counter the new league. To discourage the Federals from reinvading Cleveland, Indians owner Charles Somers, who also owned the Toledo team in the American Associa-tion, shifted that franchise to Cleveland for the 1914 season. The Minor League team would play in Cleveland's League Park when the Indians were on the road. Somers hoped that staging baseball competition every day during the summer would keep the Federals away.

Brooklyn Dodgers owner Charles Ebbets proposed a similar strategy: moving the unprofitable Jersey City International League franchise to Brooklyn. Ebbets did not own the Jersey City team, but he hoped to sell the team's owner on the benefits of playing in Ebbets Field. He might have succeeded, but as one of base-ball's cheapest owners he also wanted to charge the Jersey City owner an inflated rent. Not surprisingly, Jersey City declined the offer. Ebbets next proposed mov-ing in the Newark International League franchise, which Ebbets controlled. The Jersey City franchise would then relocate to Newark, viewed as a better baseball location. This scheme died as well when Ebbets exorbitantly demanded $50,000 from Jersey City for the Newark territory and use of the stadium.[45]

The Minor Leagues fought back too. In February the Double-A leagues pe-titioned Major League owners to exempt them from the Major-Minor League draft for one year. They had been pushing a draft exemption for some time; now the Federal League competition brought new urgency to the matter. The Minors had some expectation of success and pushed the issue to a vote at the February 11 American League meeting, but the league voted six to two against the proposal.[46]

The American Association responded to this snub by working out a secret accord with the Federal League. The two leagues agreed that they would not aggressively pursue each other's players, and on March 14, 1914, the American Association officially codified this accord: "Whereas the Federal League has not signed any players under contract to the American Association to date—Therefore be it resolved that it is the opinion of the meeting that the American Association should refrain from signing any players under contract to the Federal League so long as the Federal League does not sign any players under contract to the American Association."[47]

The Minors also threatened lawsuits. Minor League manager Gene McCann refused to surrender his players to the new league. McCann managed New London in the class B Eastern Association and lost two players to Brooklyn, both of whom were fringe Major Leaguers he had just purchased from Major League teams. McCann had spent good money to acquire the two players and had no desire to see his investment lost to the Federals. At this time Brooklyn owner Robert Ward, one of the more upstanding owners in baseball, would not take players under contract to another team. McCann knew of his position, and traveled south to confront Ward at his spring training site.[48]

Much to the players' dismay, Ward released them back to McCann. A novice to the game and surprisingly trusting for a man who had built a huge industrial conglomerate, Ward began to pour out his baseball troubles to McCann. "Ward said that he had gone into baseball for the advertising there is in it; that he was not familiar with all the angles of the game, and that he found he needed advice—good advice," McCann later told Ban Johnson.[49] Of course, Ward had longtime baseball man John Montgomery Ward as team secretary, but for some reason he never leaned on him as he might have. Robert Ward then asked McCann if he could make a deal for some of McCann's players. Aside from the question of why Ward would want a bunch of class B ballplayers, the question testifies to Ward's naiveté relative to the hostility of Organized Baseball. A surprised McCann responded that "such a proposition was entirely out of the question."

"Mr. Ward, you say you need advice," McCann said to him. "There is only one thing for you to do, for you will soon learn that you cannot live in the Federal League. Why don't you buy a franchise in the International League?"

"I am quite willing to do that," Ward told him, "but I would like to have the Pittsburgh Federal League club taken care of."

Nothing ever came of this potential opening. Either Ward was just venting and had no real interest in deserting his colleagues, or no one in Organized Baseball followed up aggressively. Tener in particular was dismissive of this potential opportunity to deprive the Federals of their richest backer, telling Herrmann, "I learned of the proposition to give Ward an International franchise in Brooklyn but realize the whole matter was preliminary, and under the stress of the present situation it could hardly be brought about forthwith."[50]

In its campaign against the Federals, Organized Baseball also used the press to powerful effect. It had cultivated reporters for many years and now could count on the support of most. In Major League cities with a Federal League competitor, most papers sided with the established league over the upstarts. *Sporting Life* treated the Federals surprisingly well, but the *Sporting News* overwhelmingly favored the existing Major Leagues. In fact, *Sporting News* publisher Charles Spink saw an opportunity to augment his status with Organized Baseball and complained to Johnson and Tener that he wasn't receiving the proper recognition for his stance. He whined that while rival weekly *Sporting Life* received $400 from National League clubs for publishing their schedules, the *Sporting News* received nothing despite treating Organized Baseball much more favorably. "We have fought the Federal League as much as possible, and have even done all that is in our power to keep it down," despite the fact that this editorial position had not increased circulation. Spink went on to complain, "We also note that whenever the subject of a money consideration is taken up with the Commission, whatever they agreed to pay the *Sporting News*, even reluctantly, *Sporting Life* comes in for the same amount, indicating that someone always protects the *Life*'s interests." In spite of Spink's protests, it does not appear that the Commission changed its posture relative to the two weekly sporting papers.[51]

In the natural subterfuge that baseball executives engaged in with the press, John Montgomery Ward, typically one of baseball's more press-savvy executives, carelessly alienated one of baseball's most influential sportswriters. He gave Joe Vila of the *New York Evening Sun* the story that "John M. Ward is somewhat exercised by the repeated assertion that he is identified with the Federal League in putting clubs into New York and Brooklyn next year."[52] Vila quoted Ward's denial. In fact, at the time Ward released this information to the press, he was already deeply involved with the Brooklyn team. Once Vila realized he had been lied to, he turned against the Federal League, telling Yankees owner Frank Farrell that he "intended to roast the Federal League from hell to breakfast hereafter." Vila was quite close to the owners of Major League baseball and would never have sympathized with the upstarts anyway, but Ward's early attempt at exploitation of the egotistical Vila, for little obvious benefit, certainly accelerated and deepened his hostility to the new venture.

Despite all the press devoted to the player battles, the Federals clearly failed to make significant inroads into the big leagues. They had landed only four Major League players with more than 400 at bats in 1913: the Phillies keystone combination of Mickey Doolan and Otto Knabe, Cubs shortstop Al Bridwell, and Pittsburgh outfielder Rebel Oakes. In fairness, they did make a few other important signings, including Tinker (382 at bats in 1913), Steve Evans, and a couple of catchers. The Federals had a little more success with pitchers: in total they signed ten who had thrown more than 190 innings in 1913. Here too the Phillies suffered the most, losing three of the defecting hurlers. Crediting the Federals with sixteen significant jumpers adds up to only two per team. Several American League teams were barely affected. As opposed to his decimated cross-town rival, Connie Mack lost no Major Leaguers from his Athletics roster. On the positive side, as Opening Day approached the Federals' pursuit of players—though largely unsuccessful—had dominated the sports pages for four months.

Most of the Federal League's players came from the Minors. Ban Johnson's right-hand man, Robert McRoy, prepared an internal analysis of the Federal League rosters in mid-May, based on which Organized Baseball club controlled each player's rights. He identified a total of 186 signed players in the Federal League (just over 23 per team). Of these, fifty came from the Major Leagues—other than those noted above, most were fringe big leaguers—seventy came from the high Minors (classes AA and A), forty from the low Minors (classes B and below), and twenty-six were true free agents, meaning they were not currently associated with Organized Baseball. This last category consisted chiefly of Minor League journeymen but would also have included local amateurs. Clearly the Federal League had not staffed its teams with a bounty of Major Leaguers. But perception was at least as important as reality. Could the Federals convince their fans that this was indeed a Major League or would soon become one, and could they win enough court cases to hold onto the players they had landed?

7

The Season Opens: On the Field and in the Courts

As consolation for the loss of Bill Killefer back to the Phillies, the Federals saw an opportunity to force the courts to invalidate Organized Baseball's reserve clause. League attorney Edward Gates and President Jim Gilmore enlightened the public on the Federals' perceived no-lose position: If the Federals won the case, then they would get Killefer back and not have to worry about Organized Baseball re-recruiting their players. If the Federals lost and Killefer was allowed to remain with the Phillies, the court would have in effect declared baseball contracts (like the one Killefer signed with the Chifeds) to be nonbinding, and the Federals could go out and sign any player they wanted regardless of his contract status.[1] Organized Baseball recognized the significance of the case as well. Warily, they had purposely not used the courts to restrain players held only by the reserve clause. Ban Johnson in particular believed it unlikely that any court would uphold its validity. But until or unless it was declared nonbinding in court, the owners could claim it was in full force and effect when negotiating with the players.

On March 20, 1914, Gates filed suit in United States District Court in Grand Rapids, Michigan, on behalf of Chicago owners Charles Weeghman and William Walker. He asked for a temporary restraining order to prevent Killefer from playing on any team other than the Chifeds. Gates hoped that a victory in federal court would provide a precedent applicable throughout the country as opposed to only the state in which he filed. To help with the litigation, he brought in a prominent Grand Rapids attorney, the son of a former local district judge.

Organized Baseball tapped George Wharton Pepper to organize its defense. A blue-blooded Philadelphian born on Walnut Street in 1867, Pepper was

George Wharton Pepper was the lead attorney for Organized Baseball's most important legal victories and later a U.S. senator. (Courtesy of the Library of Congress)

descended from prominent Philadelphia families on both his mother's and father's sides. Nevertheless, his upbringing was far from spoiled. His father died when he was only five years old from the effect of a wartime injury. Because of poor eyesight, Pepper could not attend school, and his mother educated him at home. She also gave him a "deep interest in literature and in language as a vehicle of thought." "I suppose a cynical onlooker would say that I then and there became a narrow little Episcopalian," Pepper later remarked on the intensity of the religious portion of his mother's schooling. "If so, later experience sufficed to widen my horizon."[2]

As he matured, Pepper's eyesight improved, and he gained admittance to the University of Pennsylvania. There he seemed determined to catch up on all the things he had missed out on at home: he excelled in sports, became a leader in student government, played a lead role in a school production of a Greek play, and was editor-in-chief of the school newspaper. After graduation he stayed on to attend law school, where he received several honors. Upon completion of his law degree, he joined a prestigious Philadelphia law firm. Pepper later returned to his alma mater as a law professor and earned recognition as a brilliant constitutional and corporate law scholar. When the Phillies needed an attorney to defend the Killefer case, they could not have chosen better than Pepper. A great mind with thespian experience, he was the perfect choice to argue a contract law case in a front of a judge or jury.

Federal Judge Clarence Sessions heard the case on Saturday, April 4, 1914, in his courtroom in Grand Rapids. In a key evidentiary victory for Pepper, he convinced Sessions that after the 1913 season Philadelphia had approached Killefer and offered a raise, and that Killefer had verbally agreed to play for the team in 1914. Sessions often interrupted Gates's presentation with questions on this aspect of the case. On April 10 Sessions gave his ruling. In it he posed two questions he had considered: "First, are the provisions of the 1913 contract between [Killefer and the Phillies], relative to the reservation of the player for the succeeding season, valid and enforceable, and second, are the plaintiffs by their own conduct barred from seeking relief in a court of equity?"

On the first point Sessions ruled against the reserve clause: "The leading authorities, with possibly one exception, are agreed . . . such contracts are lacking in the necessary qualities of definiteness, certainty, and mutuality." Sessions went on, however, to offer an out: "The principle embodied in the maxim, 'He who comes into equity must come with clean hands,' is a cardinal one," adding that "any willful act in regard to the matter in litigation, which would be condemned by and pronounced wrongful by honest and fair-minded men, will be sufficient to make the hands of the applicant unclean." Sessions concluded that the Federal Leaguers, "knowing that the defendant, Killefer, had a moral, if not legal, obligation to furnish his services to the Philadelphia Club for the season of 1914, they sent for him, and by offering him a longer term of employment and a much larger compensation induced him to repudiate his obligation to his employer." Sessions denied the request for injunction.[3]

Organized Baseball could not have been happier. Not only did the Phillies get to keep Killefer, but, more important, a federal judge had also thrown some ambiguity into the nonenforceability of the reserve clause. Weeghman bitterly understood this turn of events: "If the reserve clause is not valid, why did we come into court with 'unclean hands'? I cannot understand such a decision."[4] The Federals did find one small rope to cling to: like Judge Henderson in the Howie Camnitz case, Sessions expressed concern over the ten-day clause.

"[Killefer's contract] lacks mutuality," Sessions wrote, "because the Philadelphia Club may terminate it at any time upon 10 days' notice while the other party has no such option and is bound during the entire contract period."[5] Gates seized on this passage, which received surprisingly little notice at the time, to declare satisfaction with the result because the court had held that "the reserve clause of the 1913 contract of the Philadelphia club is absolutely unenforceable and that the contract is void for lack of mutuality on account of the ten days' clause therein contained."[6] Of course, trying to claim "clean hands" when inducing a player to jump his contract because of the lack of mutuality was a problem that remained unaddressed by Gates. In any case, the Federals' true dissatisfaction with the decision became public several weeks later when they filed an appeal.

The Killefer decision prompted some Major League owners to become more aggressive in the courts. After receiving no satisfaction from Gilmore and Gates six weeks earlier, Boston Braves owner James Gaffney now responded to the loss of pitcher John Quinn, Baltimore's Opening Day starter, by filing a $25,000 lawsuit against the Federals. He accused Otto Knabe and Ned Hanlon of enticing Quinn after he had already agreed to terms with Boston, even if he had not actually signed. Nothing much ever came of this suit as the National Commission recognized that it was not a strong case—an unexecuted acceptance of a contract—on which to try the validity of the reserve clause. To eliminate the willy-nilly filing of lawsuits by disgruntled owners, the National Commission reemphasized in late April that no club should initiate any lawsuit unless cleared by the Commission to do so.

The Federals resumed the offensive shortly after the Killefer ruling. With the blessing of Gilmore and Gates, Kansas City owner Charles Madison traveled to Cincinnati to pick off two reportedly disgruntled Reds, Cuban outfielder Armando Marsans and pitcher George "Chief" Johnson. Johnson believed he had been unjustly fined for being out of shape; the real cause of his lack of conditioning was tonsillitis and influenza, contracted after he was forced to pitch exhibition games in wet weather. The Federals had been secretly informed of the players' discontent by the recently fired Reds clubhouse boy. Tinker promised the attendant a job with the Chifeds if he could help induce any of the Reds to jump.[7]

On April 20 Madison met with both players in his room at the swanky Hotel Sinton in Cincinnati, hoping to entice them to the Kawfeds. He told them that their contracts were invalid due to the ten-day clause and offered significantly more money. Marsans declined, but Chief Johnson, making only $3,200, seemed intrigued. Madison offered a three-year contract calling for $5,000 per year and punctuated his sales pitch by laying twenty-five $100 bills on the table as an advance against Johnson's salary. He then paused, looked at Johnson, and laid

*Pitcher George "Chief" Johnson
was the subject of a crucial 1914
midseason court case. (Courtesy
of the Dennis Goldstein Collection)*

down another five. Johnson was sold. Madison paid his hotel bill, and the two took off that evening by train for Kansas City.

Organized Baseball had little choice but to return to the courts. Even Ban Johnson, generally against testing their contract clauses in court, recognized that they could not let players violate existing contracts. Accordingly, with Chief Johnson scheduled to pitch his first game in Chicago's home opener on April 23, the National Commission called a meeting in Chicago. Both Commission chairman Garry Herrmann and National League secretary John Heydler (on John Tener's behalf) grabbed a train in time to have an earlier meeting on April 22. The three agreed they needed to stop Chief Johnson as a matter of principle, though Herrmann, in his awkward dual role as Commission chairman and Cincinnati's president, acknowledged that Johnson might not be worth the legal fees it would take to get him back. With the Commission on board, the lawyers for the Cincinnati club asked for a temporary injunction in Cook County Superior Court to prevent Johnson from pitching for Kansas City just hours before he was scheduled to start. Judge Charles Foell gave the Reds everything they asked for: he granted two injunctions, one against Johnson performing with the Kawfeds and another banning the team from tampering with any other Cincinnati ballplayers.

The day's legal proceedings finished as farce and testified to just how contentious the battle was becoming. With the injunction in hand, the Reds sent deputy sheriffs to Weeghman Park, where the throng was cheering on the Chifeds against the Packers in the first game ever played at the field. The officers arrived shortly after the game had started, and at the end of the second inning they served Johnson with legal papers prohibiting him from playing with the Federals. The Kawfeds had little choice but to remove Johnson and send out a substitute to begin the third inning, a move they smoothly pulled off as though nothing untoward had occurred. But in the bigger picture this was a huge blow to the Federals: they lost a key Major League defector, and the legality of the ten-day clause remained undetermined. When Foell refused to lift the injunction several days later, the Federal League had little choice but to fight the injunction at a full hearing. Initial arguments, including Chief Johnson's affidavit, were introduced on May 5, after which the hearing was continued to May 14.[8]

Some Organized Baseball owners also saw an opportunity to strike at the Feds through their Baltimore club. A week or so before Baltimore's home opener, several of its players had second thoughts about the new league. Four who had defected from Rochester in the International League approached Rochester owner C. T. Chapin and offered to rejoin his team if he would reimburse them for the bonuses they had received from Baltimore. Chapin, in a vindictive mood, refused to take them back and give them bonuses. A number of parties within Organized Baseball, however, saw a real opportunity to deal a blow to the Terrapins on the eve of their season. They pressured Chapin, arguing that for a relatively small outlay he could embarrass the Baltimore Federals. But Chapin held out, and Baltimore's season opened without a hitch.[9]

Despite their uneven record in court and disparagement by Organized Baseball, the first few weeks of the 1914 season were a heady time for the Federals. The league

Once again a Major League city, Opening Day in Baltimore drew a huge crowd of enthusiastic fans. (Courtesy of the National Baseball Hall of Fame Library, Cooperstown, New York)

opened on Monday, April 13, in Baltimore, a day before the Major Leagues began their regular season. Gilmore and his owners could not have hoped for a better reception. The game began amid great fanfare and roughly 27,000 fans. Probably the one Federal city most desperate for Major League baseball, Baltimore quickly embraced its new franchise. To compete with the Federals' home opener, the city's International League club (the Orioles) scheduled an exhibition game against the New York Giants, at the time baseball's most venerated franchise. Orioles owner Jack Dunn, a longtime Minor League baseball operator, received a foretaste of the coming season when the Giants game drew only 1,000 fans. Over the next couple of weeks Baltimoreans continued to express their strong preference for the Federals. On April 21, Opening Day for Dunn's team, the Internationals drew 619 fans; the Baltfeds played to 3,085. Two days later the Federals drew 2,574 versus only 62 for Dunn's club; unfortunately for Dunn, on days with a competing Baltfeds game, crowds of fewer than 100 were not uncommon.[10]

The Major Leagues opened with full slates in both leagues on April 14. The four American League games drew 90,000 fans, an average of 22,500. Chicago, perennially among the league leaders in attendance, paced the league with 25,000. The National League fared not as well, playing to only 63,000 in the four games, an average of just under 16,000. The home opener for the Pittfeds, the only Federal League opener on April 14, drew 20,000 fans, quite a decent showing in comparison to the established Major Leagues.[11]

On Thursday, April 16, two more Federal League teams began their seasons. The Sloufeds opened before 14,000 to 16,000 fans, not bad for a three-team town, and more than either the Browns or the Cardinals. Over the next few games, however, the Sloufeds attracted about 1,500 fans per game, well below expectations. As many feared, St. Louis was probably too small to support three major teams, and all would struggle mightily at the gate during the season. Across the state, Kansas City reportedly drew 9,000 to its small, outdated ballpark. The spectators included many local celebrities, team investors, and others let in on free passes.[12]

On Thursday, April 23, two more Federal League teams opened at home. In Indianapolis the team drew 16,000, a promising crowd for Major League baseball's smallest metropolitan area. In Chicago, Weeghman put on a huge gala for Opening Day and attracted 21,000 fans to his 18,000-seat ballpark. Many fans purchased standing-room-only tickets for the grandstand, and seats were placed on the field to handle an additional 2,000. While the White Sox opened well, the Chifeds were clearly affecting the Cubs, who struggled in their West Side ballpark. On a beautiful Sunday, April 26, the Cubs drew only 6,819 fans.[13] The next day, another with fine weather, the Cubs game had to be postponed because the grounds were wet. Visiting team owner Barney Dreyfuss complained that "such tactics not only make the Chicago Club unpopular in their own league, but even more unpopular with the Chicago public, who are being fooled into going out to the grounds on a good day, only to find the 'No Game' sign up."[14] New Cubs president Charles Thomas continued to operate the club in the same high-handed manner as that of his friend and predecessor, Charles Murphy. On the two days following the canceled game, the Cubs drew only 1,159 and 714 fans.

The final two Federal League clubs opened at home on Monday, May 11. Amazingly, the Wards had rebuilt their ballpark in Brooklyn. The team drew a capacity crowd of roughly 15,000 but did not sell out the extra seats placed on the field for the hoped-for overflow crowd. Buffalo attracted about 14,000 in terrible weather; all its seats, except for the bleachers, were sold out in advance. Business manager Dick Carroll felt that with good weather the team would have drawn close to 20,000.[15] With all the difficulties faced by the new league, the fact that the teams had ballparks ready by Opening Day ranks as an impressive accomplishment and surprised many in Organized Baseball. Opening all their games on time and, for the most part, in acceptable Major League–quality ballparks, helped offset the Federals' failure to field many recognizable Major Leaguers, at least initially, in the minds of many fans.

The strong Federal League openings caught the attention of the players too. Star New York Giants hurler Christy Mathewson wrote under his own byline in a syndicated newspaper column:

> The new organization has made a profound impression on the ballplayers lately, especially since the opening of the league in Baltimore across the street from where the Giants were meeting the Baltimore International Leaguers. . . . A holiday was made of the occasion in Baltimore and the governor of Maryland attended. . . . If the Feds can keep this sort of an attendance pace for any length of time they are going to convince the ballplayers that they really have a Major League. Many of the stars in the big leagues have been holding off until the Feds got underway before believing that the new organization is liable to stick. A lot of them will listen to offers for next season if the present showing holds up. Of course the attendance at the start may be simply the result of the curiosity of the fans to what the new league will do and may not be any true indication of how far the league will go. As I have said before, I don't think the league has the ballplayers to carry it through the season with the patronage necessary for success in these days of high salaries. However, if the Feds make it this year it is going to be easier for them to pick up real stars next winter. You would be surprised at the sensible players in this busi-

Brookfeds Opening Day at Washington Park: the Federals never drew as well as hoped in Brooklyn. (Courtesy of the Michael Mumby Collection)

ness who are beginning to take the Federal League seriously. I know one man who has been on a club that has taken three world's championships who made this remark to me recently: "If the Federal League makes me an offer next fall like the one it did last spring I'm going to consider it a long time. If I don't take it, I'll worry somebody anyway."[16]

Mathewson's caution of an attendance decline was well founded. Federal League figures began to fall after the first several weeks, particularly in the cities—excepting Chicago—that competed with Major League teams. The two teams competing with the American Association generally outdrew their Double-A rivals nearly two to one over the first part of the season. Association team president James McGill admitted as much in Indianapolis. For a midseason example, on July 4 the Hoosiers attracted 6,000 versus 2,900 by the American Association club. In Kansas City on Friday, May 1, the Packers reportedly drew 2,000, as opposed to only 700 for the Association team, though the figures for both teams may have been exaggerated.[17]

All the attendance figures appearing in the newspapers need to be considered with more than a little skepticism. Team executives on both sides generally inflated attendance announcements as part of the propaganda war to promote their success. To counter the Federals' exaggerated attendance, Organized Baseball hired "clockers," typically private detectives armed with mechanical counters, also called clockers, to count attendance at nearly all Federal League games in 1914. These counts were significantly below anything trumpeted by the Federals. Owners would often use this information to refute Federal League attendance claims, and after Opening Day the Federals generally stopped releasing any attendance figures. The clockers' estimates, however, were often understated. Because they tried to physically count all the patrons as they entered, or went into the ballpark to count them, they often arrived at less than true attendance. Their counting method clearly had a number of limitations. It is difficult to tally a large group of people even in the best of circumstances, but with people milling about inside or outside a ballpark, it becomes almost impossible. Moreover, many Federal League fans entered on "passes." A large proportion of these would have been distributed as part of a promotion or complimentary ticket scheme to help bolster interest. Organized Baseball conveniently dismissed these fans as having entered for free and thus discounted them from their attendance estimate. In fact, some of these passes were part of a season package (equivalent to a season ticket today) that patrons would have paid for; other passes might have been given in exchange for services rendered to the club.

Over the first couple of weeks Federal League games were relatively high-scoring affairs. In response, the Chicago club moved its left-field fence back to 327 feet to reduce home runs. More important, at the end of April the league introduced a new baseball that reportedly reduced the resiliency of the ball by 15 percent. The league shipped 60 of these new balls to each club. Even so, the ball remained livelier than that used in the Major Leagues. Barney Dreyfuss later cut open a Federal League ball and found a two-ounce rubber center, which he claimed improved the hitting stats of the Federal Leaguers. The Federals may have been remiss not to celebrate their higher-scoring games. Rather than deaden the ball early, the league might have continued to lure fans with a slightly different brand of baseball. Instead of trying to be a clone of the existing Majors, the Federals could have set themselves apart in a way that might have enhanced fan appeal.[18]

Almost all neutral observers agreed that the quality of play and umpiring in the Federal League was well below that of the Major Leagues, and both sides recognized this disparity. To achieve parity on the field and in the mind of the public, the Federals continued to stake their hopes on landing additional players. Buffalo targeted two young Washington players, pitcher Jim Shaw and second baseman Joe Gedeon. Early in the season Buffalo manager Schlafly sent both telegrams asking what it would take for them to jump. When both turned him down, he sent former player Tom Fleming to follow the team from Washington to Boston to New York to try to persuade them. As Shaw and Gedeon began to waffle, the Federals turned up the heat. Ward and Gilmore met with the two personally, but ultimately to no avail. Despite nearly three months of heavy pressure and personal contact, neither player came to terms with the new league.[19]

Each Federal League manager naturally went after players who were most dissatisfied and those he knew best, typically players on the team the manager had just left. For a Federal League manager, pursuing Major League players was part of his job description. Early in the season the Pittfeds replaced manager Doc Gessler with Rebel Oakes. Oakes immediately went after St. Louis Cardinals players Dots Miller, Slim Sallee, and Dan Griner. Once Cardinals president Schuyler Britton realized what was happening, he agreed to remove the ten-day clause from these players' contracts. All three stayed with the Cardinals.[20]

Gilmore understood that while losing out on these players represented a setback, landing a true star player or two would instantly change the competitive landscape. He convinced the Wards to take the lead in this pursuit, and they aggressively pursued Walter Johnson, the American League's best and most popular pitcher. In May, Tinker had met with Johnson while in Washington for an exhibition game. "The Federal League looks good to me," Johnson told him, "and I will do business with you next year if you will pay me more money than Washington offers."[21]

The Federals kept the pressure on Johnson. In June, while the star was on a road trip to New York, Ward arranged for Johnson to come to his home where he could plug his Tip-Tops squad and the league. Ward reportedly offered a three-year contract for $25,000 per season, the largest offer ever made to a ballplayer. Johnson almost signed with Brooklyn but pulled back at the last instant. He decided instead to use the overtures from the Federals to see how well he could leverage the Senators. Clark Griffith, Washington's manager and minority owner, told Johnson that he could offer $16,000 per year on a five-year contract or $18,000 per year for two. Griffith's promise of a new long-term contract was enough to keep Johnson with Organized Baseball. Later, after discussing the matter with team president and largest stockholder Ben Minor, Griffith backed off a five-year commitment but did not revisit the salary amounts.[22]

The Wards did not sit still after losing out on Johnson. Walter Ward traveled to Chicago to see Athletics second baseman Eddie Collins, one of the American League's best players. The two met for dinner after a game at Comiskey Park. According to Collins, who declined to be specific, Ward offered at least $25,000 per year. Shortly thereafter, Gilmore arranged a follow-up meeting with the waffling Collins but at the last minute had to cancel. Whether Gilmore's absence made a difference remains unknowable, but in any case the Feds once again struck out. Collins, though tempted, elected to remain in Organized Baseball and signed a new five-year contract with Philadelphia for a huge raise to $11,500 per season. According to another report, when asked what he wanted Collins demanded a three-year contract for $80,000, $20,000 as a cash advance, and the remaining $60,000 to be deposited in a bank account, a request so outlandish that it likely represented a diplomatic way of declining.[23]

To undermine their new competitors, Organized Baseball's owners continued to work tirelessly to deny the Federals star players and disparaged the league and its prospects at every opportunity. They also could be underhanded. Ban Johnson engaged a private detective to infiltrate the Chifeds and report on their activities. The operative found employment with the Federal League club by posing as a landscape specialist and was hired to direct the landscaping and site work around the ballpark. On April 14 he reported that Tinker told him Cubs outfielder Jimmy Archer and pitcher George Pearce were considering jumping. In the same report the operative mentioned that a Cubs employee in charge of selling bleacher seats was providing attendance figures to a friend of his with the Federals. The following day, the operative forwarded two letters he purloined from the trainer's private office, addressed to Tinker and recommending a Seattle-based player.

Charles Murphy also seemed to be spending quite a bit of time around the Federal League park, despite rumors of his continued interest in the Cubs. The operative reported that many around the team felt that Murphy wanted to join the Chifeds, replacing business manager Charles Williams, but that he worried about the league's prospects because of lower than anticipated attendance among the Eastern teams. The informer further reported that many within the Federal League were sweating the outcome of the Chief Johnson case. If contracts with the ten-day clause were held to be valid, landing players would become much more difficult.

Based on further conversations with Murphy, the operative learned that Weeghman was still trying to persuade Ty Cobb to jump to the Chifeds. According to Murphy, Weeghman was offering $25,000 per season, though Cobb was already tied to Detroit with a new $15,000 contract he had just signed in March.[24]

By mid-May the reports from Johnson's informer made it clear that the Federals were growing nervous. Murphy told him that Weeghman was "getting more crazy every day," and that "if he don't quit spending money he will go broke." At a dinner with the operative and Murphy, Tinker's friend Abe Jacobs remarked that "he would starve if he depended on the Federal League for a living." Murphy further speculated that the National League would buy the Cubs from Taft and sell the team to Weeghman, and that without Chicago the Federal League would fold. Murphy eventually realized that no opportunity existed for him with the Chifeds, and he stopped hanging around the team.[25]

Edward Gates and his legal team remained convinced they would eventually prevail at the full hearing of the Chief Johnson case in front of Judge Foell. In anticipation of their eventual victory, the Federals scheduled a large-scale raid on the Major League's most vulnerable teams. Ball and Stifel lined up four or five players on the St. Louis Cardinals, including hurlers Slim Sallee and Bill Doak. In Buffalo, Dick Carroll targeted pitching star Ray Caldwell and Al Schulz, also a pitcher, of the Yankees plus star first baseman Hal Chase of the White Sox. Pittsburgh and St. Louis were on the verge of corralling several players mainly due to a serendipitous travel arrangement. On a road trip to St. Louis, the Pittfeds found themselves at the same hotel as the Cincinnati Reds. Manager Rebel Oakes pounced on the Reds, and as the players compared salaries the Federal League began to look more attractive. When he realized what was afoot, Sloufeds manager Mordecai Brown hustled over to the hotel to help with the recruitment. Roughly seven players, including Armando Marsans, Dave Davenport, Rube Benton, and Tom Clarke, agreed to join the Pittsburgh and St. Louis Federal League clubs.[26] In total, the Federals may have enlisted close to twenty Major Leaguers to jump. Gilmore and his owners were practically giddy at the opportunity to strike a major blow for their league.

But there was one hitch: These players were already under contract to Major League teams and had little interest in jeopardizing their future if their contracts were enforceable. Many of the players thus delayed and refused to commit until Foell's decision in the Chief Johnson case, now scheduled for early June. Surprisingly, the Federal League teams did not press the players to commit unconditionally. Whether due to overconfidence or simply lack of a sense of urgency, the Federals were betting heavily on the decision of a Cook County judge. Yet Foell had already twice ruled in favor of the Reds in this case, and his demeanor appeared much more sympathetic to Organized Baseball than to the upstarts.

On June 6 Foell ruled resoundingly for Cincinnati, upholding his injunction prohibiting Chief Johnson from playing on any other team. The judge did not find the existence of the ten-day clause sufficient to allow the player to terminate his contract. He noted that Johnson had voluntarily signed his 1914 contract, which called for a higher salary. Moreover, players had long been signing contracts with this provision, and Foell could not see players continuing to do so if they found it objectionable. Of course, the counterargument was that without an alternative for their services, the players had no real choice, but Foell saw it otherwise.

In other circumstances this decision would not have been particularly devastating. Technically a ruling by a county judge in such a case could not be enforced outside the jurisdiction. Ban Johnson had used such a loophole in 1901 to retain star second baseman Napoleon Lajoie when a Pennsylvania judge ruled he could not play for anyone but the National League's Philadelphia Phillies. Gilmore recognized that he had this alternative, but for the time being he elected not to pursue it. Gilmore planned to appeal the decision and "did not want to show disrespect to the court or to prejudice Johnson's case."[27] In fact, Foell's decision became one of the key turning points in the confrontation between the leagues. After the decision, nearly all of the players so patiently lined up by the Federals chose to stay with their Major League teams. A defection of twenty or so Major League players to the new league in June would have provided a huge lift and swung momentum to the Federals.

Some of the Federal League recruiters had advised the prospective jumping players to give their employer ten days' notice before signing their new contracts, as a way of emphasizing that the ten-day clause needed to be mutual. Several of these notices arrived right around the time Foell rendered his decision. Thus, in several cases, the Major League owners had some sense of the impending desertions. One newspaper printed the conversation between a star Yankees pitcher (presumably Ray Caldwell) and manager Frank Chance, no doubt embellished a little by a writer sympathetic to the team. When owner Frank Farrell received notice from Caldwell that his pitcher was quitting to join the Federals, Farrell dispatched Chance to talk sense into him.

"So you want a new contract," Chance demanded of his pitcher.

"Well, guess a fellow can go home if he wants to, can't he?"

"Do you want to go home? Well, if you do, I'll pay your transportation out of my own pocket. What's the fare?"

"Well, I want a new contract," admitted the pitcher.

"A new contract! What for? Haven't you been treated right by the club?"

"I ain't got no kick there."

"Has your work for me justified any more salary than you've been getting?"

"Don't know as it has," the pitcher responded meekly.

"Do you not think you have been paid more than you are really worth? Come now, tell me the truth."

"I guess maybe you're right there. But a fellow ought to be able to go home if he wants to."

"Go to—go home; the quicker the better for this club. And take along any of the rest of the fellows who feel the same way. I want to tell you right now that if you stick around here you're going to earn a little more of that salary that you acknowledge is too much. If you don't care to try to earn it, beat it while your shoes are still good."

That evening Judge Foell announced his decision. Caldwell called Chance on the phone and in a shaky voice told him he liked playing for the Yankees after all. "Boss," he said, "I guess I don't care to see the old folks after all. I'd like to pitch against Walter Johnson tomorrow."[28]

Despite Foell's ruling in the Johnson case, a few players, most notably Davenport and Marsans from the Reds and Chase from the White Sox, chose to risk a jump anyway. The two Reds had given Herrmann their ten-day notice in early June and joined the Sloufeds. Marsans, who had signed a three-year contract with the Reds during the off-season, quickly realized he had signed too cheaply and protested to Cincinnati manager Buck Herzog. The manager, a gruff, headstrong, and demanding leader, showed little sympathy for the regal Marsans. An open hostility soon developed between the two, and Marsans in particular resented the demeaning attitude and treatment he received from Herzog. Their simmering feud came to a head at a game in late May in which Marsans was tossed by the umpire for disputing a call. Herzog faulted Marsans for the ejection; Marsans felt his manager should have backed him up. In any case, the ensuing confrontation between player and manager led to Herzog suspending Marsans until he publicly apologized to the team. For Marsans the timing was convenient. He slipped off to St. Louis with Ball and Stifel, who put him up at the American Hotel under guard—to prevent agents from Organized Baseball from changing his mind—as they waited for the ten-day-notice period to expire. On Sunday, June 14, Marsans debuted with the Terriers, and just after midnight he signed a three-year contract with St. Louis for $21,000.

Once again Herrmann and the Major League owners would not allow a player to defect from what they believed to be a valid contract. While the baseball stakes would not be as high as in the Johnson case—there was no mass exodus prearranged to jump with Marsans—the legal stakes would be even higher. Because Marsans was not an American citizen, Herrmann would have to ask for his injunction in federal court. Any verdict on the validity of the Major League baseball contract would have a wide-ranging effect throughout the country.

It did not take long for the Reds to assemble their legal machinery. On June 18 Marsans was served notice by a federal marshal that an injunction application had been filed. The hearing for the temporary injunction took place four days later in federal court in St. Paul, Minnesota, before Judge W. H. Sanborn. As this was only a preliminary hearing, the presentation of evidence and arguments lasted only a day. Sanborn, not surprisingly, was unwilling to invalidate baseball contracts on such a limited body of evidence. He did, however, go a little further than he needed to that evening and granted the Reds the requested injunction while parroting Organized Baseball's position:

> [The team and player had] a contract to employ him for certain specified periods at a fixed compensation on the condition that it should have the right to discharge him upon ten days' notice, and the defendant accepted that offer in writing. This made a valid and binding contract, especially after the defendant entered upon the performance of the contract and received compensation. . . . It is a settled rule of law that where a person agrees to render services that are unique and extraordinary, and which may not be rendered by another, and has made a negative covenant in his agreement whereby he promises not to render services to others, the court may issue an injunction to prevent him from violating the negative covenant.

Sanborn offered one sop to the Sloufeds by requiring the Reds to post a $13,000 bond to cover any damages that ultimately might accrue to St. Louis as a result of the injunction.[29]

Unlike the other players involved in injunctive rulings, Marsans had no intention of complying. "At all events I will never play in Cincinnati again," Marsans declared.[30] This suited St. Louis as well. They agreed that as long as Marsans refused to return to the Reds, they would pay his salary, even if he could not play for them. One interesting side effect of the injunction was that in contraposition to the proclaimed blacklist, Herrmann had to acknowledge publicly his willingness to welcome Marsans back.

The decision in the Killefer appeal was released shortly thereafter. Gates still believed that the Feds would win on appeal for both substantive and more personal reasons. Substantively, he had been shocked when Judge Sessions implied that the reserve clause placed at least some obligation on the player to bargain with the team. On a personal level, the son of one of the three appellate judges was a Federal League lawyer. Although the judge recused himself, Gates hoped this relationship would at least remove some of the bias against the so-called outlaws. It was not to be. On June 30 the United States Circuit Court of Appeals affirmed the Killefer decision.

June had been an unmitigated legal disaster for the Federals. Judge Foell's decision had stopped short their planned mass player defection. Now a federal judge in St. Paul had likewise validated the Major League baseball contract, and the U.S. Court of Appeals for the Sixth Circuit had implied that the reserve clause did in fact suggest a burden on the player to negotiate with his previous team. The Federals had little choice but to appeal Sanborn's injunction to a full hearing; there was no way they could allow such a decision to stand. The court initially set a hearing for July 8, well within a time frame that would allow the Federals room for further 1914 raids. But the hearing was first postponed until July 30 and later into the fall to accommodate the criminal cases on the court's docket.

The Federals finally received some good news on July 16 when the Appellate Court of Illinois reversed Foell and nullified the injunction prohibiting Chief Johnson from playing for the Kawfeds. The court specifically ruled that the "provision that the club may give the players ten day written notice to end all its liabilities under the contract . . . is so wanting in mutuality . . . that the complainant cannot, therefore, enjoin a breach of the negative covenant of the player."[31] With this decision Johnson could finally join the Federals and resume his pitching career. But it was too late to salvage the Federals' June strategy. The decision was not nearly as important as the fact that the Federals had missed the chance for a mass exodus.

Nor did the decision end Chief Johnson's legal saga. Much to the consternation of Ban Johnson, who had little interest in the cost of pursuing noncritical state court injunctions, Barney Dreyfuss talked Herrmann into filing for an injunction in Pittsburgh to prevent Chief Johnson from playing for Kansas City. The Allegheny County judge ordered a temporary injunction, but, as Ban Johnson expected, Madison simply ignored the injunction, and Chief Johnson continued to pitch for Kansas City except when the team traveled to Pittsburgh. Gates filed in the same county to enjoin Cincinnati from continuing to pursue the case against Johnson.

Organized Baseball was also challenging the defection of Hal Chase, who had jumped from the White Sox to the Buffeds in June for a $2,000 increase in salary. One of baseball's best first baseman, Chase was also one its great troublemakers. He often feuded with his manager and several years later, in the wake of the Black Sox scandal, he was unofficially banished from baseball for his gambling involvement. Despite his reputation, at the time Chase was a star and a valuable addition to the Federals. To keep Organized Baseball at bay as long as possible, the Federals orchestrated Chase's defection. He debuted for Buffalo in Chicago on Sunday, June 21, so that no travel was involved. As with Marsans, with the courts closed on Sunday the Major League team could not secure an injunction. After the game Chase skipped town before the White Sox attorneys could get into court on Monday morning. The Chicago club chased after him. Comiskey, National Commission attorney Ellis Kinkead, and Ban Johnson's private secretary Robert McRoy all set out by train for Buffalo.

Business manager Dick Carroll wanted a big splash for his new signing. He trumpeted that Thursday, June 25, was Hal Chase Day and widely publicized the event. The challenge would be getting Chase back to Buffalo and out of sight for four days so he could appear at the ballpark on June 25 before being served with papers enjoining him from playing. When Chase arrived in Buffalo, Carroll and owner William Robertson met him at the train and spirited him by car to another train that took him to Niagara-on-the-Lake in Canada and away from the jurisdiction of U.S. courts. On Wednesday Carroll and two private detectives drove Chase to a waiting motorboat that carried him to Grand Island, in the Niagara River on the New York side of the border. Chase spent the night at an inn guarded by the detectives. On Thursday morning he again traveled by motorboat to the U.S. mainland, where another automobile met him and took him to the Century Club in Buffalo. From there, Chase was taken to the office of private detective Tommy O'Grady, where he changed into "feminine clothes" (though for propriety's sake the team later denied this). To smuggle Chase into the stadium they brought him into the toolshed, where he changed into his uniform and remained out of sight. To make sure the sheriff could not serve Chase before he appeared in the game, the home team Buffeds batted first. With leadoff hitter Frank Delahanty at bat, Chase came out of the toolshed and to a loud ovation made his way to the dugout and the on-deck circle. When he finally made it to the plate, he struck out. After the Buffeds' half-inning ended, Chase took his spot at first base without interruption. But that was it. When he came in from the field, McRoy and the law enforcement officers were there to serve him the injunction papers, cutting short Chase's Buffalo debut.[32]

The attorneys argued their positions in front of Judge Herbert Bissell on July 9 and 10. The Buffeds brought in Gates and another Federal League attorney, Keene Addington. This time Gates and his legal team won a resounding victory. On July 21 Bissell ruled that although baseball was not interstate trade and therefore not subject to the Sherman Act, the ten-day clause lacked mutuality. "This court will not assist in enforcing an agreement which is a part of a general plan having for its object the maintenance of a monopoly, interference with the personal liberty of a citizen and the control of his free right to labor wherever and for whom he pleases; and will not extend its aid to further the purposes and practices of an unlawful combination. . . . The motion to vacate the preliminary injunction . . . is therefore granted."[33] Chase was free to play with the Buffeds.

Over a period of five days in late July the Federals had won two court cases. Their impact, however, should not be overstated. The cost of fighting every injunction in every possible locality was prohibitive. The lengthy time lag also discouraged players from jumping contracts. At least a month was typically required to get a court to rule after the preliminary injunction was served. Even then there was no certainty that the court would find for the player. What's more, the Major Leagues were finally taking Ban Johnson's advice and pulling the ten-day clause from contracts. The owners often paid the players a small bonus to re-sign a new contract without it. The Federals had little to show for a summer of costly maneuvering, and as the Majors restructured their player contracts, opportunities for large in-season player raids dried up. Gilmore, Weeghman, Ward, and company would have to maintain fan enthusiasm over the second half of the season with the players they had.

8

The Struggle Continues

By the early summer of 1914, as turnstiles slowed and the player grab came to naught, the Federal magnates realized that their situation was much worse than anticipated. Visions of joining the profitable Major League fraternity dissipated amid red ink and lost court cases. In the early months of the season they had brought in only one marquee player, Hal Chase. Only in Baltimore and Chicago could the league be considered a success, and even there the teams were losing money. St. Louis and Pittsburgh were not drawing well but at least had wealthy backing. Brooklyn fell well short of its hoped-for attendance, though the Wards, the wealthiest owners in baseball, could absorb the losses. Because they actively discouraged unionization at their bakeries, the Wards also suffered from occasional labor boycotts at ballparks both at home and on the road. Kansas City, Indianapolis, and Buffalo had capitalized their franchises with stock sales, and as their losses rapidly exceeded initial projections, reserves dwindled quickly with little prospect for additional funding.[1]

Chicago, the Federals' flagship franchise, was drawing fans but not covering expenses, and Weeghman was clearly feeling the pinch. He reportedly borrowed $100,000 from meatpacking mogul J. Ogden Armour, a supplier to Weeghman's restaurants. Weeghman also borrowed heavily against his Chifeds stock from the Fort Dearborn Bank in Chicago. Cubs president Charles Thomas, who passed this information along to Garry Herrmann, snidely added that another large depositor withdrew his money when he learned of this loan. (In these days before the FDIC, deposits were not insured, and bank failures were a regular occurrence and a hazard of doing business.)[2]

The Federals' frustration occasionally turned to bluster. Travis Hoke, a young statistician associated with the Browns and their manager Branch Rickey, found himself in Cafferata's Cafeteria in St. Louis in June one evening around 10 p.m. He recognized a group of Federal Leaguers—Phil Ball, Otto Stifel, Mordecai Brown, Jim Gilmore, Armando Marsans, and several others—and found a seat nearby where he could eavesdrop on the conversation. Hoke noted that they may have been eating but in any case were clearly drinking.

"I'm going to put 'em out of business," Stifel boasted. The others did not look quite so enthusiastic.

As Ball got up to leave, he called Brown over for some confidential advice. "Fight 'em, Miner, fight the umpires," he breathed in Brown's ear. After repeating this maxim several times, Ball continued, "Fighting the umpires is what the fans like, especially our fans." "Which may be true," Hoke cleverly commented when relaying the conversation to Ban Johnson.

Willis Johnston, business manager of the Sloufeds and a former newspaper reporter, recognized Hoke and pointed him out to Stifel. "Sit down, Miner. Run along, Phil," Stifel prodded. But Ball was good and drunk and continued to lecture Brown on the importance of fighting umpires. Finally, Stifel demanded that Ball "Shut up and sit down."

"Go to hell," Ball shouted. When the waiters and guests turned to stare at the outburst, Ball finally left.

As to the rest of the party, "Marsans looked sleepy. Johnston looked sick. Stifel looked drunk. The waiters and attendant satellites [the other hangers-on at the table] looked happy. Gilmore did not."

"I'm going to put 'em out of business," Stifel repeated.[3]

They may not have been putting the Major Leagues out of business, but the Double-A International League was on the ropes. In Baltimore, Jack Dunn was in particular trouble, and he knew it. His Double-A International League club was all but being ignored by the city and the press. As residents of the eighth-largest metropolitan area in the country, Baltimore's baseball fans felt slighted that they no longer had a Major League team. Twenty years earlier the Baltimore National League franchise had won three consecutive pennants, and the city had later been a charter member of the American League. Many still resented the loss of their American League team to New York after the 1902 season.

Ned Hanlon's early success with the Baltfeds threatened Dunn's lifelong dream, one he had finally realized when in 1909 he purchased the Orioles from Hanlon. Dunn had begun his Major League baseball career in 1897 as a pitcher with the Brooklyn Dodgers and later played for Hanlon. After his arm lost effectiveness, Dunn reinvented himself as a utility infielder and played several more years in the Majors, including three in New York for John McGraw's Giants. A shrewd, fierce competitor, Dunn had learned much playing for Hanlon and McGraw, two of the era's best managers. According to Fred Lieb, he "had the same Irish terrier truculence that got McGraw into so many arguments," but also, like McGraw, "he was a master strategist and had a remarkable sense for recognizing talent in the rough."[4] In 1907, when Hanlon wanted a new manager for his Minor League Baltimore club, he turned to Dunn. Two years later, in another example of sharp, strong-minded ballplayers moving into management, Dunn bought the Minor League Orioles from Hanlon for $70,000. Under Dunn's ownership the Orioles were consistently respectable but could never win the International League flag. More ominously, Dunn still owed Hanlon $4,000 on the original purchase.

As the Baltimore baseball season unfolded, rumors of Dunn's distress surfaced almost immediately. By late April he was forced to declare publicly that he was not going out of business. But behind the scenes he was begging for help. He enlisted his friend Connie Mack, minority owner and manager of the Philadelphia Athletics, to make his case to Ban Johnson. Dunn complained to Mack that he could not make his June 4 payroll; he had borrowed $7,500 and the bank would lend no more. Complicating the request were rumors of an under-the-table relationship between Dunn and Mack, with the latter often getting first shot at Dunn's best players. Nevertheless, Johnson recognized the seriousness of the situation and, after getting Mack's word that he did not have an ownership interest in the Orioles, passed along Mack's concerns to the rest of the Commission.[5]

To compete with the Federals, Dunn had put together a stellar Minor League team. He was paying relatively high salaries for top talent, further cutting into his team's profitability. By midseason Dunn's squad was well out in front of the league, making his struggles at the gate all the more galling. He claimed to have lost $20,000 over the first half of the season, a considerable amount for a Minor League operator without outside means. To muddle through the season, Dunn weighed a couple of strategies. One option was to move the team out of Baltimore; interests in Richmond, Virginia, had offered $62,500 for a 49 percent share of the club if Dunn would transfer the team there. Alternatively, as befitting a first-place club in the high Minors, Dunn had a number of players with significant value to Major League teams. White Sox owner Charles Comiskey, for one, had reputedly offered $60,000 for his top five position players and Babe Ruth (then a pitcher).[6]

From Organized Baseball's standpoint, neither of these options was particularly appealing. The former would require a negotiation and possible payment to the Virginia League for invading their territory. More important, it would represent the abandonment of the Minor League's largest market to the Federals. The latter option would strip the International League's best team, a tacit admission that it could not compete with the Federals.

The rest of the International League was struggling as well. Only three of the league's eight clubs had owners with anything resembling deep pockets. Buffalo, the other International League team competing directly with the Federals and the nation's thirteenth-largest metropolitan area, was being pummeled at the gate. In Montreal the International League players were so disgusted with their poor attendance that they sent a delegation to petition owner Sam Lichtenhein to trade them or sell the club. Later they warned they might go on strike if the franchise were not transferred. Newark president Charles Ebbets Jr. had to borrow $2,000 from his father to meet payroll.[7]

Vying for relief, International League president Ed Barrow petitioned the National Commission for assistance. He asked either for financial aid to help keep Baltimore and Buffalo afloat or "to exempt International League players from the draft. . . . The Federal League has far outdrawn us in both Buffalo and Baltimore. . . . The sole reason for this is that a majority of the fans look upon the International as a Minor League and the Federals as a Major League. . . . The sporting writers in Buffalo and Baltimore have repeatedly stated that if our players were not subject to the draft, they would consider the International League to be just as much entitled to a Major League rating as the Federal League."[8] The National Commission acknowledged that the situation had become critical and agreed to meet with a delegation from the International League to work out a relief plan. Herrmann, Johnson, and Tener traveled to New York's Waldorf-Astoria Hotel for a conference with Barrow, Dunn, and three representatives from the Toronto International League team.

The International League contingent was surprisingly successful and received provisional support from the Commission for designation as a third Major League under the Organized Baseball umbrella. American League president Ban Johnson may also have been peeved at several of the owners in the American Association over that league's secret accord with the Federals. In mid-June he had begun to suspect something when he learned from a newspaper friend in Buffalo that Gilmore had sent the Buffalo club instructions not to sign any American Association ballplayers. Any new league that involved restructuring the high

Minors would create winners and losers, devaluing those franchises left out. After the meeting Ban Johnson announced:

> There will be a third Major League, and I think it will be a good thing for the peace of Organized Baseball. It is true that the Commission has not formally ratified the new project. But that is only a question of formality. We will now see how far the Federal League can go against real Major League opposition on every hand. Let me tell you the new circuit will soon prove its merits over the so-called class of Gilmore's league.[9]

Barrow recognized the power of this announcement and told Herrmann soon after the meeting, "I have it on good authority that the real 'men behind' the Federal League were worried more by the 'third Major League' story than by anything else the Commission had done."[10]

A couple of scenarios were discussed. The principal scheme involved peeling off the four strongest markets from the International League—Baltimore, Buffalo, Toronto, and Newark—and merging them into a new league with four clubs from the American Association, most likely Indianapolis, Cleveland/Toledo, Milwaukee, and a choice of Minneapolis, Louisville, or Columbus. The remaining franchises in the two class AA leagues would then be formed into a new Minor League. An alternative proposal would offer "continuous baseball" in all the Major League cities. In this permutation, Baltimore, Buffalo, and Toronto would be joined by other International League and American Association franchises, which would transfer into the one-team Major League cities of Detroit, Cincinnati, Pittsburgh, Cleveland, and Washington.[11]

The "continuous baseball" scheme never really had any chance of success. No Major League owner would voluntarily permit another Major League club in his city unless and until conditions grew much more dire. In any event, the International's hope to become a third Major League died quickly over the next few days. Most Major League owners had little interest in adding another Major League to the already fierce competition for fans and players. Furthermore, the American Association had little interest in the proposal. Indianapolis and Kansas City had both fared tolerably, and the secret, nominal truce with the Federals on player signings prevented the sort of desperation that would lead to a willingness to dissolve their league. In retrospect, it is unlikely that the third Major League option was ever feasible. While the International League was clearly in serious trouble, the Major Leagues, and even the American Association, had not yet reached the point where they were willing to dilute their monopoly.

Despite the failure of the third Major League scheme, some help was forth-coming. The National Commission decided to raise $25,000, partly to aid the International League and partly to pay for the rising legal costs of all the player battles. The Commission agreed to provide a loan to the International League and assume the obligations of the Buffalo franchise. Unfortunately, many Major League clubs, particularly those in the National League, could not meet this ob-ligation immediately, "owing to prevailing conditions, some of [whom] owe the treasury an unusually large amount for assessments and baseballs."[12] Because of the urgency of the matter, Johnson gave Barrow a personal check for $3,219 as an emergency loan to keep Buffalo afloat. The Commission also agreed to let Dunn sell his players, provided he promised to keep his team in Baltimore through the end of the season.[13]

In a last-ditch effort to keep Dunn from dumping his players, his fellow In-ternational League owners offered Dunn a loan of $3,000.[14] Dunn rebuffed the deal and sold six of his players, including Babe Ruth, to three different Major League teams for a total of around $40,000.[15] Barrow demanded that a portion of that purchase price be deposited with the league as security until Dunn formally promised he would finish out the season and not fold or move his team. The National Commission backed Barrow—much to Dunn's consternation—and Dunn eventually agreed in writing that he would finish the season in Baltimore. His first-place team dropped quickly in the standings after the player sales. He defended his decision as his attendance problems reached absurd proportions, highlighted by two games in early July when he drew only twenty-nine paying fans on a Friday and twenty on Saturday.[16]

In the end, the National Commission lent the International League $18,719: $13,219 went to Buffalo, $2,500 to the ailing Jersey City franchise, and $3,000 re-mained for future contingencies, of which there would be many. For one season at least, Herrmann, Johnson, and Tener had organized effective relief for one of the top Minor Leagues and prevented Organized Baseball from surrendering any of its cities to the Federals.

With Dunn struggling to finish the season, Ned Hanlon saw a possible exit strategy for his Federal League team. According to New York sportswriter Joe Vila, Hanlon had become so concerned about the future of the Federal League that he entered into secret negotiations with Barrow to get his Baltimore fran-chise into the International League. Hanlon suggested to Barrow that when Dunn finally was forced to sell his team, Hanlon and the Baltimore Federal owners would buy it and merge the Federal League franchise into it. Johnson put enough stock in Vila's credibility that he sent the article on to Herrmann. As to the future of the International League, Hanlon reportedly favored Barrow's backup plan to the third Major League scheme, which entailed moving the Jersey City and Montreal franchises to Pittsburgh and Brooklyn. According to Vila, if the National Commission also abolished the draft, as the International League wanted, the league in effect "will be a new major league circuit."[17]

The players union too looked to enhance its position. In July, Brooklyn owner Charles Ebbets waived Clarence Kraft, who, when unclaimed by all other Major League teams, was assigned to Newark in the Double-A International League. Brooklyn had drafted Kraft from the Southern League, lost him on waivers to the Boston Braves, and recently reacquired him. Nashville, in the lower Single-A Southern League, asserted it had a prior claim on Kraft in the event he was returned to the Minors. In addition to playing in a lower classification, Kraft's assignment to Nashville would result in a $150 pay reduction. Kraft protested to the National Commission, arguing that the Cincinnati Agreement stipulated that a player should be allowed to play in the highest securable league. The Commission ruled in favor of Nashville, whereupon Kraft appealed to Players Fraternity president Dave Fultz for support. In fairness to the Commission, the fine print of the agreement between the Majors and Minors included a clause that a player drafted directly from Single-A by the Majors needed to be offered back to that league first—this was the situation with Kraft. Fultz and the players, however, believed that as part of the Cincinnati Agreement there had been a tacit understanding that this Single-A prerogative had been relinquished.

In any event, Fultz sensed this was a good case with which to cement the relevance and authority of the Fraternity. Threatening an open break with baseball, Fultz warned that unless the Kraft ruling was reversed, all players in the Fraternity would strike. Johnson perceived an opportunity to break the union and looked forward to a confrontation. He consulted with Barrow and National League president John Tener to plan a course of action. This was primarily a National League issue, however, and Tener, Herrmann, and Ebbets chose to defuse the situation instead. They brokered a compromise in which Ebbets (whose son owned the Newark club) paid Nashville $2,500 for the rights to Kraft. In this first crucial confrontation since the Cincinnati Agreement, Organized Baseball, though believing it was in the right, backed down. Unfortunately for the players, Fultz learned the wrong lesson—that he could threaten the owners and they would yield. The magnates, especially Johnson, would never again be beaten by Fultz.

In the wake of the Kraft case, Julius Fleischmann sent a letter of support to Herrmann. Although a significant minority wanted to fight the union, "I did not agree. I am for a fight if a fight can get you anything, but just at the present time it is my sincere belief that we have got enough fight on our hands without courting any further trouble. A fight such as was threatened on account of the Kraft case, would have been pie for the Federal League. This talk of Johnson's about closing the season, all that is more or less of a joke. . . . If the season were closed or even a strike was projected, it would be an advantage given to the Federal League that would never be overcome. Just at the present time we have got to swallow our pride."

The last three paragraphs of Fleischmann's letter contained some shrewd analysis, in relation not just to the baseball battles of the time but also to business conflict in general:

> This Federal League fight is not going to last forever; no business fight ever does. The Federal League is either going to be licked or eventually has got to be considered in connection with Organized Baseball. I am of the opinion that they are going to be licked, but I have seen a good many business fights where the underdog did not always come out entirely to the bad at the end.
>
> Once the Federal League fight is out of the way, then we can deal with the Players' Association, or whatever they call themselves, as the situation may warrant, but we do not want that fight just now.
>
> When one fellow is hitting you in the face and another one is kicking you in the back, it is very difficult to determine whether you want to put your face or your back against the wall. In either case you are liable to make a mistake because they are both apt to attack the part that is exposed.[18]

While the Majors struggled to rein in the Minors and the players, Gilmore continued his efforts on behalf of the Federals. He traveled to New York to raise additional funds but achieved little. He also had agents examining other possible markets. In Cleveland he "organized a crowd of one hundred men—claiming that they are to put in $5,000 apiece to put a club here."[19] The Federals also gave some thought to peeling a Minor League away from Organized Baseball. The midseason replacement of Mordecai Brown with Fielder Jones as manager of the Sloufeds led to all sorts of speculation. Most recently, Jones had been based in Portland, Oregon, as president of the Northwestern League, and his signing fed rumors that he would line up his former league to affiliate with the Federals. In fact, Jones was not particularly well liked or active as league president, and the league's owners had little interest in aligning themselves with Jones or the Federals.[20]

The Federals also worked to better promote their league. For one, they bailed out Ernest Lanigan's publication *The Base Ball World*, which was about to go under, and distributed the publication free after the August 16 game in Chicago.[21] The Pittfeds reduced prices in the grandstand from 75 to 50 cents and in the bleachers to 25 cents.[22]

Organized Baseball offered no respite; they continued to search for ways to undermine the newcomers. In June, St. Louis Browns owner Robert Hedges engaged the Thiel Detective Service to investigate the Sloufeds financial situation. The operative learned from confidential conversations that the team was in dire financial straits and days away from having a lien filed against the ballpark. The club had paid the Spuck Iron and Foundry Company, which erected the ironwork for the stands, only $5,000 of the $17,000 invoice. With little expectation of receiving the balance, the company threatened to place a lien on the property. Stifel and Ball, the two wealthiest investors backing the club, had little desire to fund this shortfall. According to the agent, Stifel was "known to be thoroughly disgusted and apparently desperate in his efforts to find some kind of an opening where he can at least save a portion of the money he has sunk into the Federal Park. . . . He has expressed himself repeatedly to intimate friends that he is ready to throw up the sponge."[23] Thiel recommended to Hedges that he find an angel investor to pay off the iron contractor, assume the lien position, and commence foreclosure proceedings against the club, forcing them out of the ballpark—an interesting suggestion that Hedges never chose to implement. Most likely, Ball came up with the necessary funds in exchange for a portion of Stifel's ownership interest.

In Indianapolis a couple of attorneys for the Federal League club who were owed money approached Herrmann though intermediaries, offering to force the franchise into receivership if Organized Baseball would guarantee to cover any portion of their fee they did not receive through the bankruptcy proceedings. Herrmann was naturally intrigued by this opportunity to bankrupt one of the Federal League's franchises and sent the proposal on to the Commission's attorney, Ellis Kinkead, for advice. Kinkead advised Herrmann to stay as far away as possible from the proposition. He pointed out the huge conflict of interest in an attorney acting against the best interests of his client. In fact, he doubted the legitimacy of the offer. By entering into such an agreement, he cautioned, Organized Baseball could be setting itself up for its own legal difficulties. Kinkead emphasized how difficult it would be for the attorneys to force the team into bankruptcy over their legal fees.

Organized Baseball was also examining the Buffeds ownership situation. When Dick Carroll acquired the rights to the Buffalo franchise in November 1913 he did so on behalf of Thomas Duggan, who put up the initial deposit. To capitalize the franchise the Buffalo club issued common and preferred stock at a 7 percent dividend. The club needed to raise $100,000 in preferred stock and agreed that if it couldn't, it would refund the investors' money. As an incentive, the club offered one share of common stock for every two shares of preferred stock purchased. When the stock sale stalled out at $62,500, Gilmore and the league stepped in and agreed to make Carroll and the Buffalo club a loan for the remainder. As security, the league demanded that much of the club's stock be assigned to the league until the loan was paid off. Upon review, Duggan learned that some of this stock was rightfully his, and he spent much of the season trying to regain control of his ownership share. By the end of the season he was furious with Carroll and the league. He had put up significant funds and was being stonewalled by Carroll and Gilmore in receiving his fair share of the stock, which at that point amounted to roughly a one-third ownership position.

When James McCaffrey, owner of the International League's Toronto franchise, learned of this situation, he worked through an attorney friend to secure copies of the correspondence material to the controversy. McCaffrey then engaged another attorney to review the documents with an eye toward Organized Baseball working with Duggan to gain a controlling interest in the franchise. After sifting through the information, the lawyer concluded that pursuing the matter offered little benefit. "There is plenty of material for a lawsuit," wrote attorney W. N. Ferguson, "but there is nothing on which to make an investment, because even if you got the whole $77,500 of stock [the amount of Duggan's interest] you would still be a minority stockholder, and you know what that means. If I were in Duggan's place, however, and had my investment, I would commence an action in the State of New York against Gilmore, Mullen, Carroll, the Federal League, and the Buffalo Club."[24]

In St. Louis, Indianapolis, and Buffalo, Organized Baseball looked hard to disrupt Federal League ownership but could never quite find the right angle. The Federal League's supporters were not without their own tricks. A Dr. Thomas V. Thomas wrote to all Major League clubs asking for club stationery with which to decorate the rooms of his hunting and camping club. Ever vigilant and suspicious, Barney Dreyfuss recognized the handwriting as that of Tom Fleming, an old ballplayer turned scout, now working as a Federal League agent. Dreyfuss passed his discovery on to Herrmann, alerting him to the ploy. Nothing apparently ever came of Fleming's maneuver; he was most likely operating on his own initiative. But it did highlight the level of subterfuge each side was willing to employ for even the slightest advantage.

As the battle continued, Robert Ward bared his thoughts to Jim Price, a New York sportsman, before a game on August 8. A close friend of Ban Johnson's, Price had gained prominence as a sportswriter and editor and is generally credited with introducing the name "Yankees" for New York's American League team. He later moved on to other ventures, including an ownership interest in a Minor League team, an unsuccessful run for president of the International League, and a stint as a New York state boxing commissioner. In what was clearly represented to be an off-the-record conversation, Price asked Ward about the Federal League's plans for 1915.

"Why, we're going on," Ward told him. "Did you ever hear anybody intimate to the contrary?"

Price told him that he had, but that his source was the newspapers. He further asked Ward if the league was "prepared to go on and lose as much money next year as it has lost this year."

"Certainly," Ward responded. "We didn't figure we would make any money this year, and we don't think we will make money next year, but we do believe we will be all right in our third year, and that we will begin then to get back some of the money we have lost."

Price asked if all the owners felt the same way. "Six of them do," Ward answered. "We think that $50,000 apiece will cover our losses next year. What's that amount to? Practically nothing, when it is considered that we are establishing a Major League and getting a firm foothold in the baseball world."

When Price asked Ward to name the six optimistic owners, Ward demurred, explaining there would be changes in the circuit for 1915.

"About two weeks ago you told me," Price continued, "that Kansas City will not be in your league next year. Does that still hold good?"

"Yes."

"What about St. Louis?"

"St. Louis had a bad year. We think this was due to the good showing of the American and National League teams there. But St. Louis will stick. Stifel has said so. Gilmore told me this."

"Did you ask Gilmore when he was here recently, if he made a statement in Pittsburgh that the Federal League would put clubs in Detroit, Cincinnati, and Cleveland next year?"

"I did. He said he never made such a statement. That was only another one of the fool things that get in the papers about our league. I hear some funny things myself occasionally. Why, only this week I was told that Barney Dreyfuss has lost so much money this season that he is getting ready to quit."

"Who told you that story?"

"A man from Pittsburgh."

"Do you believe it?"

"No, I don't believe it, but I heard it just the same."

"What about the park over the Pennsylvania Railroad tracks in New York?" Price asked, regarding the potential move of a Federal League team to New York. "Is there anything new about that matter?"

"Well, I had a letter from them about a week ago, asking what I was going to do about it, and I replied that I was not prepared at this time to give a definite answer."

"Mr. Ward, you are too good a man to be identified with an outlaw league," Price suggested. "This is not only my opinion, but I have heard Organized Baseball men say the same thing."

"I am glad to hear you say that. I have always tried to be on the level. I have never signed a player who was under contract to another club, and won't do so. To those men in Organized Baseball, whoever they are, who think well of me, I feel grateful. But it seems that Organized Baseball and the Federal League can't get along together. They won't recognize us, although they ought to."

"What do you want them to do?"

"Well, for one thing, we ought to get together on the schedules. I am a believer in continuous ball. There should not be any conflicting dates in Brooklyn, or Pittsburgh, or Buffalo. It would be easier for everybody if there were no conflicts. Of course, we can wait until the other leagues get out their schedules, and then draft ours, but it would help matters if we worked together at the same time."

This conversation ended as the game began. Price bid Ward goodbye, and he called back, "Come and see me again, Mr. Price. I'll talk to you any time."[25]

John Montgomery Ward, on the other hand, had lost some of his fire for the battle as the season drew to a close. Brooklyn was not drawing fans, and his role had been marginalized by the active participation of the Wards. Accordingly, John Montgomery Ward announced his retirement from the Tip-

Tops organization and a return to his law practice. Before leaving the stage, however, he offered his perspective on the state of the baseball war. He saw no prospect for peace between the leagues: the Majors would not accommodate the Federals as a Major League, and the Federals would never agree to reconstitute themselves as a Minor League or amalgamate their teams within the existing Minors. Ward also defended the Federal League, both practically and morally: "One trouble is that Organized Baseball fails utterly to appreciate the financial strength of the Federals. By a cheap system of espionage and 'clocking' they have assured themselves that most of the Federals are losing money . . . and therefore they will quit. This, however, does not give sufficient credit to the courage and business sense of the men who have already invested upwards of $2,000,000." Another mistake of Organized Baseball, as Ward saw it, "is in starting with the assumption that it owns the national game as well as the players and that therefore the Federals are trying to rob it of its property. When we recall the language of this State in a recent decision, the effrontery of this attitude on the part of Organized Baseball becomes disagreeably apparent." Ward closed with cautious optimism: "The circuit of the Federal League doubtless requires some change, but there is ample opportunity to bring this about."[26]

As the season wound down, Jim Gilmore hoped to score additional public relations points. On September 15 he sent a letter to John Tener challenging the World Series winner to play the Federal League champion. Not surprisingly, he was ignored. In Indianapolis the public and press were clamoring for a postseason series between the Federal and International League teams. President James McGill of the American Association's Indianapolis team wanted to play the series, winner to take all the gate receipts. He asked the National Commission for its permission to play the series or at least not punish the players if they played without official sanction. Johnson and Tener quickly sent their refusals to Herrmann. Any series with the outlaws would provide the legitimacy that Organized Baseball was working desperately to deny.

After Indianapolis won the Federal League pennant, they petitioned the National Commission to join in the World Series. Indianapolis Hoosiers secretary James Ross sent a letter on October 9 to Herrmann, Johnson, Tener, Ben Shibe of the American League champion Athletics, and James Gaffney of the National League champion Braves, challenging the winner of the World Series to a contest for the "World's Championship." Of course, he received no reply. Ironically, Rube Foster, manager of the American Giants, the country's best black baseball team, challenged Weeghman's Chifeds to a postseason tournament. Given the racial atmosphere of the era, Weeghman remained as silent to Foster as Organized Baseball had been to Gilmore.[27]

This did not quite end the postseason possibilities. Indianapolis Hoofeds star pitcher Earl Moseley revealed that the Indianapolis team was held together through the end of the World Series at some cost to the club. According to Moseley, the Philadelphia Athletics players had, in the event that they won the World Series, agreed to play a series against the Hoofeds. If the National Commission and Philadelphia owners Ben Shibe and Connie Mack attempted to stop the games, Moseley claimed that the Philadelphia players were ready to jump en masse to the new league. Unfortunately, history was spared this pandemonium when the Athletics fell to the Braves in the World Series. *Sporting Life* considered Moseley's revelation "a peculiar story, but it has a pretty good ring to it at that." Bitter at the dalliances between his players and the Federals, Mack broke up his pennant-winning team over the next couple of years. His anger and disappointment seemed much too vitriolic to be caused solely by the players' natural interest in using the Federals to achieve higher pay. While it seems unlikely that the entire team would have agreed to such a scheme, it is certainly possible that a number of the underpaid Athletics were ready to play or jump.[28]

Under pressure from the Federals, Major League baseball attendance nosedived in 1914, from an average of 401,000 per team in 1913 to 278,000 in 1914, a decline of more than 30 percent. The hit was especially severe in the National League, where attendance fell by nearly 41 percent to only 213,000 per team. At the time, Major League teams averaged somewhere around $140,000 in operating expenses. Assuming a 70-cent average ticket price, a team would need about 200,000 in attendance to break even, and five of the sixteen Major League teams fell short of this mark. The Chicago Cubs, in an intraleague memo, complained that their net profit fell from $100,000 on attendance of 419,000 in 1913 to $20,000 on attendance of 202,516 in 1914.

Federal League attendance figures remain murky. Gilmore bragged that the Federals played to 1.6 million fans in total (200,000 per team), but this seems wildly exaggerated, and he did not break down the attendance for each team. Organized Baseball's teams tracked attendance for the Federals based on their "clockers." New York owner Harry Hempstead collated the figures sent to the National Commission office to calculate an estimate of Federal League patronage. He also took into consideration missing games and, in several instances, free admissions. When the season ended, the Commission released Hempstead's team-by-team Federal League attendance summary to the press. In total, he claimed the Federals drew only 786,000 paid patrons (98,000 per team), fewer than half of Gilmore's announced total.

The results varied dramatically by team. Weeghman reported that his Chifeds played to 312,000 versus the 200,729 released by Organized Baseball. In Buffalo the team announced attendance of 180,000, well above the 71,255 claimed by the clockers. The best sense of the level of attendance may be gleaned from some actual Kansas City attendance figures obtained by James McGill, president of the Indianapolis American Association club, covering the first 51 games. A comparison with the clocked figures shows the actual attendance in Kansas City was roughly 87,450, a full 34 percent above Organized Baseball's estimate. This seems reasonable given the difficulties of counting all the patrons in a ballpark, the natural bias of Organized Baseball, and the likely overestimation of the number of fans entering free through the press gate. Applying the 34 percent factor to the clockers' overall numbers results in total Federal League attendance of 1.053 million (an average of 132,000 per team).

In this era before radio, television, and licensing revenue, all the Federal League's revenue needed to come from their million or so patrons, and 132,000 fans per team would not have been enough for these teams to break even, much less show a profit. Ball later admitted he lost $88,000 in 1914. Baltimore's financial records are available through one of the later court cases and offer insight into the finances of the new league. As table 8.1 shows, the Baltfeds lost $36,892 on revenues of $86,572 and expenses of $123,465, of which player salaries accounted for $72,467. As the third highest-drawing team with a relatively modest payroll and few ballpark-related costs beyond ground rent, Baltimore's deficit probably fell toward the lower end of the losses suffered by the Federal League's clubs.

Attendance estimates may also be tested against these known revenue figures. For example, Hempstead estimated 124,072 patrons for Baltimore; increasing this by 34 percent results in an estimated attendance of 166,256. Assuming a 60-cent average ticket price—slightly lower than the Major League average—with approximately 25 cents going to the visiting team, 35 cents went to the home team. Thus home revenues under these assumptions would total $58,189; actual home revenues came to $59,501. Using a similar calculation for the team on the road, where Baltimore would have played to approximately 126,755 fans, suggests road revenues of $31,688. In fact, the Baltfeds took in $20,301 from their road games; perhaps they didn't get a full 25 cents on road admissions as teams lowered ticket prices late in the season, or perhaps Baltimore didn't draw on the road as well as some of the other higher-profile teams such as Chicago and St. Louis.[29]

Table 8.1. Baltimore Financial Results, 1914

Receipts		
Home	59,500.63	
Road	20,302.79	
Season tickets	400.90	
Concessions	6,084.00	
Miscellaneous	284.16	
		86,572.48
Expenses		
Player salaries	72,466.83	
Player bonuses	6,083.33	
Traveling expenses	17,566.53	
Rent	4,410.00	
Interest	101.67	
Federal League assessment*	5,550.00	
Other expenses	17,286.43	
		123,464.79
Net Profit		*(36,892.31)*

*Not paid

Civic ownership of half of the Federal League clubs led to further problems for the Feds. Investors in Buffalo, Baltimore, Indianapolis, and Kansas City had generally purchased their interest in the form of preferred stock, with the funds used to acquire a ballpark and cover start-up costs. These investors all wanted a return on their money, but now they were being told they would have to pony up more money to fund operating deficits. Most had little inclination to increase their investment. Thus it fell on the wealthier owners, principally Robert Ward, to loan these franchises operating capital.

Early on Ward had induced some of his business associates to invest with him in the Federal League. Canadian flour tycoon Charles Herendeen, a business associate and personal friend, had helped back Federal League clubs to the tune of roughly $135,000. By the end of the year, however, Herendeen had had enough and was looking "for some avenue of escape."[30] Ward and the other wealthier Federal League owners were similarly inclined; they had suffered huge losses and were financially supporting the weaker franchises. While they had both the money and the will to slug it out for another year, they recognized that the financial bleeding was not slowing. They desperately hoped to reach some sort of accord with Organized Baseball.

9

A Possible Settlement

Throughout the summer of 1914, Minneapolis Millers owner Mike Cantillon remained in touch with his tenant, Charlie Weeghman. Cantillon and Weeghman each considered himself a dealmaker and often discussed the various goings-on in baseball and the condition of the Federal League. From their conversations arose all sorts of ideas as to how to end the struggle between the Federals and Organized Baseball. As Cantillon talked baseball with his fellow American Association owners, he would have mentioned his discussions with Weeghman. At some point Louisville owner O. H. Wathan passed the nature of these conversations along to Garry Herrmann. Sensing an opportunity, Herrmann wrote to Cantillon asking his opinion of Weeghman's thoughts about a possible settlement.[1]

Cantillon responded on August 19 that he thought Weeghman could be weaned from the Federal League. Weeghman, Robert Ward in Brooklyn, and Phil Ball in St. Louis were the league's three wealthiest owners and were also helping bankroll several other teams. Cantillon told Herrmann that "if Brooklyn was taken care of in some way in the East . . . Weeghman could be gotten in the AA [American Association]. He is interested in both Kansas City and Indianapolis [American Association cities], and can pretty near break the league alone."[2] Shortly thereafter, Ban Johnson confidant Robert McRoy contradicted Cantillon, telling Herrmann that after being "Major League" and with all his sacrifices during the year, Weeghman would never "be satisfied with an American Association franchise."[3] Nevertheless, Herrmann continued to push Cantillon to see what settlement terms might be available.

With Herrmann's encouragement, at the end of August Cantillon traveled to Chicago, and on Wednesday, September 2, he met with Weeghman and Jim Gilmore at the latter's office. Gilmore asked Cantillon, "Are you talking for yourself or with authority?" Cantillon responded that he had conferred with the two other Double-A leagues, the Pacific Coast League and the International League. Cantillon also made sure to distance himself from official representation by saying that the National Commission was not actively seeking an agreement but that it had given him permission to discuss the situation. The trio then discussed amalgamating the Federals into the high Minors, whereupon Gilmore asked about the possible elimination of the draft, something Cantillon would have desired as much as the Federals. Cantillon knew his Major League owners and responded that it would be highly unlikely.

Cantillon believed he had negotiated the outline of a deal with the Federals. He followed up with a long letter to Herrmann summarizing the key points that he claimed Weeghman, Gilmore, and the Federals would settle for:

1. The Brooklyn and Pittsburgh Federal League clubs would be given franchises in the International League. The Federal League clubs in Baltimore and Buffalo would be allowed either to buy the existing International League clubs in those cities or to be bought out by them. The Federal League clubs in Indianapolis and Kansas City would be allowed either to buy the existing American Association clubs in those cities or to be bought out by them.
2. The Chicago Federal League team would be given a franchise in the American Association in Chicago.
3. The St. Louis Federal League club would be left out of the settlement; the Federal League would "take care of the St. Louis people in their own way."
4. One of the high Minor Leagues would be given the Federal League name.
5. The draft would be eliminated. As noted earlier, the high Minor Leagues had long chafed at the Major League–Minor League draft, which allowed the Major Leagues to cherry-pick their players. The end of the draft would significantly raise the status of the high Minor Leagues; Cantillon would have pushed for this with or without the Federals.

Cantillon concluded that since this was the first proposal from the Federals, they were almost certainly willing to accept less. He felt that if the Majors wanted a settlement, one was possible. Publicly, Gilmore continued to insist that the Federal League was "Major League first, last, and always."[4]

Herrmann, much more of a conciliator than a hard-nosed negotiator, liked the proposal and passed the letter along to his two partners on the National Commission, Tener and Johnson. Both told him to be careful, that the Federals were in trouble and that Organized Baseball should not be too open about jumping into negotiations. When Johnson routed the letter to his league owners, most had a similar reaction. Joseph Lannin of the Red Sox responded that he thought Cantillon rather than the Federals was responsible for much of the content of the letter. Herrmann disagreed; he believed much of what Cantillon reported really did originate with the Federals.[5]

In general, the Major League owners believed they were winning the battle and "of the opinion that a satisfactory settlement of the baseball situation cannot be secured at the present time." Herrmann dutifully passed this message along to Cantillon. With something like 80 percent of the players signed through the 1915 season and the ten-day clause eliminated from most contracts, the Majors felt well positioned to fight for another season. Nonetheless, Herrmann remained eager for a settlement. He sensed that something could be worked out along the lines Cantillon mentioned, but he needed the Federals to make the first move. "Of course," Herrmann responded to Cantillon, "if the Federal League people would come to the National Commission, or some other authorized authority, and take the initiative in the matter looking towards a condition which might involve the absorption of that League, the same to be treated in a confidential way, something might be brought about that might be satisfactory to all concerned after a general conference on the subject."[6]

On September 14 Herrmann sent a confidential eleven page memo to his fellow commissioners summarizing the state of baseball. He made three seminal points:

1. The Federal League most severely impacted the high Minor Leagues.
2. With most Major Leaguers under contract for 1915 and the dwindling enthusiasm of Weeghman and Robert Ward to bankroll the league, the Federals would increasingly concentrate their raids on the high Minors for players.
3. The Federal League hurt the Major Leagues in many ways: driving up salaries; damaging interest in many markets; and creating an environment in which the Players Fraternity could thrive.[7]

Herrmann itemized how the consolidation of the Federal League with the American Association and the International League along the lines outlined by Cantillon would solve the problems he identified. The high Minors would be saved; Major League competition would be eliminated; and without the threat of a rival league, the players would become "tractable." The Federal League players, officially blacklisted from returning to the Major Leagues, could remain with their Federal League team in the high Minors. Many other owners agreed with Herrmann's assessment of the risk from the players union. Dreyfuss encapsulated this opinion: "The fraternity is far the greater menace, but cannot be fought successfully with the other League in existence."[8]

As part of Herrmann's campaign, he reiterated to Ban Johnson, one of the staunchest proponents of a fight to the finish, that he believed Cantillon's letter accurately reflected the desire of the Federals to settle, and their terms. To confirm his understanding, Herrmann met with Cantillon in his Cincinnati office when Cantillon was traveling thorough that city on his way to his farm in Hickman, Kentucky. Cantillon responded to Herrmann's cross-examination regarding the genuineness of the representations in his letter "in a positive way" and even proposed meeting with Herrmann and Weeghman to prove it. Herrmann gained further confidence in Cantillon's estimates when he heard from Cantillon's brother Joe that Weeghman was late on the ground rent for his ballpark.[9]

Others were also engaged in back-channel negotiations. During the season International League president Ed Barrow and C. T. Chapin, owner of that league's Rochester franchise, approached William Ward, Robert Ward's son, who was living in Rochester. Barrow suggested a meeting with the senior Ward, intimating an "interesting proposition." At first Ward did not respond, but late in the season, with the league's financial losses escalating—for which Ward was footing much of the bill—he reconsidered. When approached by New York sportsman Jim Price to broker a meeting, the senior Ward responded that he would be happy to meet "anyone who has any business with me."[10]

Barrow hoped to keep this meeting secret and proposed to meet Ward alone. But due in part to the Federals' desperation, and in part because of his loyalty to the league, Ward summoned Federal League president Jim Gilmore, Baltimore director Ned Hanlon, and Pittfeds president Ed Gwinner to the meeting. Just before it was to occur, Price called it off, claiming Barrow was out of town. Most likely, Barrow did not feel he had sufficient authority to enter into a full-scale negotiation with half the Federal League.[11]

Weeghman was also engaged in conversations with other members of Organized Baseball. In late September he traveled to New York to meet with his fellow Federal owners. Brookfeds business manager John Montgomery Ward arranged a short, clandestine meeting between Weeghman and Boston Red Sox owner Joe

Lannin in Garden City, New York. Lannin told Weeghman, "You are licked and had better throw up the sponge." Weeghman laughed and responded that they were far from licked. The two men traded pleasantries, with Lannin noting that the Majors had "about all the men signed up for next year that they cared about," but acknowledging that salaries had grown too high. Weeghman had to cut the meeting short to catch his train back to Chicago. Lannin felt the Federals were trying to set the stage for a follow-on meeting with more substance.[12]

These various peace negotiations left Gilmore in an awkward position. As president of a putative Major League and often in the news, Gilmore liked the salary and prestige of his job. His wealthiest owners—Weeghman, Ball, and Ward—however, were obviously tiring of the battle and would welcome a settlement. Ball's St. Louis partner, Otto Stifel, another of the league's well-heeled backers, declared publicly that "he did not propose to throw away any more money into a lost cause," and that he was unable to find an investor to buy out his stock.[13] Gilmore recognized his owners were losing interest and tried to stay in front of the negotiations by publicly announcing that the league was willing to make peace at "fair and honorable terms" but were "not standing on the doorstep, hat in hand."[14] The next day the Federal League office—surely a euphemism for Gilmore himself—released a statement that Gilmore had met in New York with Lannin, Cleveland owner Charles Somers, Philadelphia Phillies owner William Baker, and Boston Braves owner James Gaffney. Gilmore was probably embellishing the short meeting between Weeghman and Lannin, but with this pronouncement he foolishly overplayed his hand. Over the next few days the Major League owners he mentioned could categorically deny the story and further ridicule Gilmore's league.[15]

Along with Weeghman, Robert Ward was the key Federal League owner huddling with Organized Baseball's representatives. A mutual friend of both Ward and Edward Walsh, a minority owner of the Washington Senators, called Ward to arrange a meeting in Washington. Because he feared that traveling to a meeting could be misconstrued by the press as an act of desperation, Ward declined. Both men were interested in getting together, however, and met at the Hotel Belmont in Philadelphia the day before the World Series opened. Walsh confided to Ward and his brother George that the Senators (and Walsh personally) were losing a lot of money, and that he was trying to arrange a settlement conference in Boston during the World Series. Ward, under the impression that Ban Johnson would attend, agreed.[16]

On October 12, Ward went to the Fenway Park office before Game Three between the Athletics and the Braves, ostensibly to pick up his tickets. There he encountered Joe Lannin. After a brief conversation, the two agreed to meet later that evening at the Hotel Lenox. Ward, disappointed that neither Johnson nor any other Major League executive was on hand, said he wished to purchase an Eastern Major League franchise, particularly in New York. He told Lannin that he believed the other Federal League owners (except Weeghman, who was negotiating for the Cubs) would accept Minor League franchises, but that they all needed to be taken care of. Lannin replied that he felt the purchase of the Yankees might be arranged.[17]

Later that month, Ward followed up by phone with Lannin: "Do you still think the New York American League franchise could be purchased?"

"Yes, I do," Lannin told him.

"How much money would it take to proceed?" Ward asked.

"I don't know, but I suppose in the neighborhood of half a million dollars. And there is a possibility that one or two of the franchises of the National League clubs of eastern cities could be purchased, but I can't be sure."

Ward, wanting to get Lannin more directly involved in the negotiations, asked, "Can you call and see me to discuss further?"

"No. I don't have authority to continue negotiations," Lannin replied. He was not particularly affected by the Federals and had no desire to land in the middle of talks.[18]

Cantillon and the Federal League owners also sought to arrange meetings with key Major League baseball executives. Cantillon sent around a series of telegrams trying to organize a meeting for the day after the final game of the World Series. According to Cantillon, he spoke with Weeghman, telling him, "If you are on board with what we agreed to in Chicago [the main points of his letter to Herrmann] we can meet Herrmann in New York."[19] Weeghman asked to have Johnson and Tener present as well, but Organized Baseball's leaders were unwilling to allow the presence of the entire Commission to imbue the meeting with such significance.

Cantillon ultimately scheduled the meeting for Ward's office in New York. He lined up a host of Federals: Weeghman, Weeghman's partner William Walker, Gilmore, and Ward. The Major League owners, fearful of a trap coordinated by the Federals to make it appear as if the Majors were actively pursuing settlement negotiations, were reluctant to appear. In the end they agreed that only Herrmann should attend. This would give them an opportunity to hear the Federals' proposal without appearing overeager.

On October 14 Weeghman called Herrmann to confirm the meeting for later that day. Herrmann asked that Weeghman come directly to his hotel room at the Waldorf. He was a busy man. At that moment he was with commission secretary A. J. Flanner, a longtime sportswriter, in his main room. New York Giants owner Harry Hempstead and some other executives were in his small bedroom, and he was waiting for a committee of Elks from Bedford City, Virginia. When Weeghman arrived, Herrmann was meeting with the Elks. After he finished, Herrmann joined Weeghman in the parlor to discuss the status of negotiations in private.

Herrmann opened by invoking the Elks: "Mr. Weeghman, you are an Elk. I am Past Grand Exalted of the Order, which no doubt you are aware of." After Weeghman acknowledged that he was, Herrmann bound them to secrecy, the conversation to be "man to man and not to be repeated to a single person in case nothing comes of it." (As it happens, we know the details of this meeting only because Herrmann related them in a letter to Johnson.) Weeghman stated that Cantillon told him at their September 1 meeting that he "represented or would act" for Organized Baseball. (This was probably not true—it was contradicted by both Cantillion and Gilmore.) Herrmann denied that Cantillon had such authority and then said, "Well, it does not make much difference how the meeting came about, what I am anxious to know is whether or not the proposition as submitted to us as coming from the Federal League was authentic or not." Weeghman naturally then asked what was submitted.

Herrmann summarized the key issues: the Federal League was ready to go out of business; the league would be absorbed by the American Association and the International League, and franchises in these high Minors would be placed in Chicago, Brooklyn, and Pittsburgh.

Weeghman responded, "That is ridiculous. That cannot be brought about at this time. Our situation has been bad as you know, but we are ready to continue the fight. I will say this to you, however, Mr. Herrmann, that we would be ready to fix matters along reasonable lines conditioned that two things can be brought about—We want a major league club in New York or Boston. We understand that the New York Americans or possibly the Boston Nationals are for sale and we would be ready to take up with either proposition, but preferably New York. In addition to that we are ready to purchase the Cubs, if they can be secured at a reasonable price, or else we would be ready to take Mr. Taft in with us if some amicable arrangement could be made." In other words, Weeghman was selling out the league. If Ward could buy either the Yankees or Braves and Weeghman the Cubs, the Federals would be without their wealthiest backer (Ward) and flagship franchise (Chicago), and some sort of settlement involving amalgamation into the Minor Leagues could then be imposed on the remaining Federal League teams.

Herrmann, taken somewhat aback, replied that purchasing these two clubs was something he "could not talk about; knew nothing of and had never heard it discussed." He then asked again whether Cantillon's letter had been authorized by the Federals, and Weeghman again told him "no." The two chatted a bit more, and Weeghman then left on good terms with a comment that he might call back before Herrmann left New York.

Weeghman knew Taft was in New York and called to see if he would meet to discuss the sale of the Cubs. Taft was surprisingly willing to head right over to Weeghman's hotel. Less than half an hour later, Weeghman called to tell Herrmann he had just met with Taft, who was willing to sell the club. Herrmann came away from the meeting and Weeghman's follow-up phone call with the clear impression that "the Ward Brothers, possibly Weeghman and Walker, are looking out for themselves. If they could purchase a major league club, I suppose the entire controversy could be adjusted quickly."[20]

Ban Johnson, the stubborn, dictatorial president of the American League, leaked news of the Herrmann-Weeghman meeting to the press, insinuating that Weeghman had requested the meeting when he sent "his card up to Mr. Herrmann and asked for an interview." (This was clearly not correct; the meeting had been prearranged by Cantillon.) Weeghman responded in the press by claiming that Herrmann had called him to New York. This spat quickly blew over, but it made clear how fragile the negotiations were and how the press reacted to isolated details. The partial information appearing in the papers hampered the negotiations by causing the various parties to worry about their own reputations. Gilmore, in fact, made an extraordinary admission to the press: "In the course of the next few months I may have to tell many lies. If I could avoid it, I would, but there are some things that must be kept quiet, and in order to insure secrecy it is very often necessary to stretch the truth a little. I hate to do it, but there are times when the truth is not apt to be practicable."[21]

On October 23 the Federal Leaguers held their first substantial postseason conference. A lot of tough talk and defiance came out of the meeting, but the key Federal League backers continued talking with Herrmann and other Major League owners behind the scenes. Over the next week Herrmann and Weeghman remained in contact, holding a key meeting on Saturday, October 31, at the Congress Hotel in Chicago. Afterward Herrmann clearly believed the two had come to an understanding.

Federal League officials 1914: top row: Charles Weeghman (Chicago), Walter Ward (Brooklyn), Corry Comstock (Pittsburgh); middle row: L. Edwin Goldman (Baltimore), Robert Ward (Brooklyn), Ed Steininger (St. Louis), James Gilmore (league president), George Ward (Brooklyn), George Schleunes (Baltimore), William Walker (Chicago), William Robertson (Buffalo); bottom row: Ed Krause (Indianapolis), Phil Ball (St. Louis), Harry Goldman (Baltimore), Walter Mullen (Buffalo), Lloyd Rickart (league secretary), Ned Hanlon (Baltimore), Edward Gates (Indianapolis and league attorney), John George (Indianapolis), Dick Carroll (Buffalo). (Courtesy of the Library of Congress)

On November 3 Herrmann sent telegrams to all the National League owners (and a long letter to Ban Johnson) asking them to approve a settlement with the Federals "along the lines of admission on their part that a third major league was a failure; the purchase of one or more major league clubs, if they can be secured; a re-arrangement of some of their other clubs in the International and American Association . . . with the understanding that nothing definite or conclusive is to be done without the approval of the National League."[22] Herrmann believed he had worked out the rough framework of a deal with Weeghman and wanted the National League owners to bless it so he could wrap up the details. The purchase of the Major League clubs by the Federals was anticipated to be Weeghman purchasing the Cubs from owner Charles Taft, who was eager to get out of baseball, and Ward purchasing the Yankees from Frank Farrell and William Devery, two of baseball's shadier owners.

After a little cajoling, all the owners responded to Herrmann affirmatively. Only Harry Hempstead of the Giants threw a small wrench in the plan. The

Yankees shared the Polo Grounds, the Giants ballpark, which was controlled by Hempstead. Hempstead refused to allow a team purchased by Federal League owners to share the stadium. Any other buyer would be all right, but "Mr. Ward and his associates who cost baseball so much cannot endeavor to recover their losses by playing on the New York Polo Grounds."[23] A second obstacle to the Wards' purchase of the Yankees was the American League's posturing that they wanted no Federal League owners in their league. Ban Johnson believed the Federals were on the rocks and was much less interested in settling than Herrmann and the National League owners. Most American League owners wanted an agreement, but Johnson chose to remain noncommittal.

Within baseball, most officials believed that peace was at hand. The Minor League owners met for their annual meeting in Omaha on November 10 amid concern over their future and the future structure of Organized Baseball—of the forty leagues that had begun the 1914 season, only twenty-nine would be around for 1915. To make sure the Minors stayed loyal to the existing Organized Baseball structure, Herrmann and Johnson successfully lobbied the event: in one of their first orders of business the Minors pledged continued fealty to the existing arrangement that ceded nearly all authority to the Majors. After making this pledge, however, many talked about the impending peace agreement. Barrow went so far as to outline the new arrangement for his International League: Jersey City would move to the Brooklyn Federal League ballpark (this club would cease to exist when the Wards bought the Yankees); the Federals in Baltimore and Buffalo would consolidate with the International League teams; and the Montreal team would be moved to the Pittsburgh Federals' ballpark.[24]

Even as Barrow was explaining these measures, however, things were beginning to unravel. On Monday, November 9, Weeghman brought Ward and William Robertson, Buffalo's managing partner, to a meeting with Herrmann. Robertson still harbored dreams of Major League baseball for Buffalo and "spoke of a peace agreement, which, however, would necessitate recognition of a third Major League."[25] This was clearly a nonstarter. The Majors were happy to amalgamate the Federals into the high Minors and sell the richest Federal League owners two franchises they would just as soon change ownership of anyway. But they were not about to recognize a third Major League unless the pressure grew much, much worse. When Herrmann and Weeghman met again on Thursday, Weeghman asked about the possible purchase of the St. Louis Cardinals by Ball. This was certainly feasible, as the Brittons were struggling financially and probably willing to sell, but adding a third club to the potential agreement at this late date further suggested that all was far from settled.

Buffeds president William Robertson, one of the key Federal League owners unwilling to settle for any compromise peace that would put the Buffeds in a Minor League. (Courtesy of the Library of Congress)

Weeghman was also finally realizing that the varied interests in his outlaw league might not coincide with his own. He had fully expected that by arranging Major League franchises for the three wealthiest backers of his league, he could persuade the others to see the merits of amalgamating into the high Minors. But the ownership in Indianapolis, Baltimore, Buffalo, and Kansas City consisted of numerous smaller stockholders who believed their city was "Major League." Even though they had suffered large financial losses, they were not yet willing to throw in the towel. These men continued to press Weeghman, and because he had not completed his purchase of the Cubs, he could not use his defection as a hammer on the more recalcitrant owners. As a follow-up to his last meeting, Weeghman's fellow owners effectively pulled him out of the lead negotiating position. Gilmore and Robertson, however, completely misread the Major League owners, who were unwilling to settle on anything but the original terms. They expectantly proposed a negotiating summit between Gilmore, Ward, and Robertson on the Federal side and the full National Commission (Herrmann, Johnson, and Tener) on the other. This met with frustration from Herrmann and silence from everyone else. One final meeting occurred on November 13 between Hermann and Weeghman, Ward, and Robertson. The latter two had come west on the inflated hope that the Majors were willing to convene a true peace summit. When Robertson added that all the Federals still had Major League aspirations, Herrmann knew a comprehensive settlement would not happen.[26]

Without Weeghman, Ward, and Ball the Federal League could not have continued the fight, but Ward and Ball, at least, were not yet willing to abandon their fellow owners. Weeghman, on the other hand, told Herrmann confidentially that the Federal League clubs were required to meet certain conditions by November 28 and that several would not be able to do so. Assuming he could buy the Cubs, Weeghman would "jump the traces" and bolt the Federal League. Without Weeghman's Chicago franchise, the most successful in the circuit, it was unlikely the Federals could survive.[27]

Cubs owner Charles Taft was happy to sell, and he gave Weeghman a short-term option, presumably to press him to arrange his financing and equity partners. The price was never officially revealed, but Weeghman most likely received an option to purchase an interest in the club for roughly $150,000 and an option to purchase the rest at some later date for a price in the neighborhood of $600,000.[28] On November 17 Weeghman asked for an extension to December 1, but Taft refused and pulled the team off the market. Weeghman may have been having some difficulty raising the money—hence the request for an extension— but the main reason for Taft's pulling the deal was the reemergence of Charles Murphy, the thorn whom the owners thought they had rid themselves of back in February.

Murphy still owned the West Side Grounds where the Cubs played, and he had no desire to lose his paying tenant. Upon purchase of the franchise, Weeghman intended to amalgamate the two teams—his Federals and the Cubs—and move the team to his new ballpark on the North Side. But Murphy had leverage. When Taft bought him out in February, he had put very little money down. Murphy had accepted 52 percent of the club's stock as collateral for the balance of the $450,000 owed on the purchase price. Therefore, unless Weeghman could finance the entire purchase and pay Murphy off—highly improbable on such short notice—Murphy effectively held a veto over the sale of the franchise.[29] Many of the owners, as well as Johnson, who knew just about everything going on in baseball and hated Murphy, were apparently unaware of his stake and angered by Murphy's ongoing influence. Murphy happily revealed his continuing claim on the franchise to the press, which naturally played up the fact that he had not actually been ousted despite the claims of the owners. Meanwhile, they publicly denied Murphy's continued control and privately wrote to one another in dismay—"cannot some way be found to muzzle our friend Murphy?"[30]

Now that peace appeared out of reach, Ban Johnson could renew his belligerent attack on the Federals, leaking to the press that the deal had fallen through because Weeghman couldn't raise $150,000. In fact, Weeghman almost surely could have raised the money if given another two weeks. While it is true he was late on his October 1 rent to Cantillon—the reason Johnson probably felt comfortable leaking his "information"—Weeghman quickly made the rent payment once the sale fell through. Herrmann went so far as to send Weeghman a letter denying he had leaked word of the failed financing and, to further distance himself from the debacle, added, "I do not know why Mr. Taft called off his deal with you. He did not consult with me before he did so."[31]

In retrospect, neither side had yet suffered enough to reach a settlement. The Major League owners would allow two or three of the wealthier Federal League owners to buy into their fraternity and amalgamate the rest into the high Minors, but that was the extent of their concession. This solution appealed to those Federal League owners permitted to buy into the Majors, but the stockholder-run teams in those cities without another Major League franchise understandably balked. They had little interest in a revamped Minor League club and believed they could stick it out for at least one more year. The wealthiest Federal League owners could have abandoned their comrades and forced an accommodation, but Robert Ward was as yet unwilling, and Weeghman unable.

10

Player Reinforcements

As the two antagonists danced and haggled over settlement terms, the fight for players continued. The Federals still hoped to capture talent from the Major Leagues despite the mixed messages they received from the courts. The Marsans case had been a bitter defeat, but the Chase decision and the ruling on Chief Johnson's appeal offered some hope that contracts with the ten-day clause were voidable. Equally important, though Organized Baseball had signed many of its stars through the 1915 season, talented players were still available. Throughout the second half of the 1914 season Federal League managers and executives began laying the groundwork for the coming off-season.

In mid-August 1914, Sloufeds owner Phil Ball and team president Edward Steininger traveled to Chicago to meet with catcher Roger Bresnahan. Well past his prime, Bresnahan remained a popular and charismatic personality. Tough and ornery, he had learned the game from John McGraw, the epitome of the win-at-all-costs attitude. Before coming to Chicago, Bresnahan had spent several years as the St. Louis Cardinals player-manager. Not surprisingly, given the prejudices of the time, Bresnahan soon had a falling out with the female owner, Mrs. Helene Britton, once she took over the team from her uncle.

Helene Britton never set out to be a baseball owner, but once it was thrust upon her, she proved more than willing to accept the challenge. On March 27, 1911, Stanley Robison had died, leaving most of his $400,000 estate to his niece Helene. Much to the chagrin of the traditionalist National League owners, Robison's estate included the hapless St. Louis Cardinals. Britton, only thirty-two when she inherited the team, initially wondered whether she really wanted it,

St. Louis Cardinals owner Helene Britton and her husband Schuyler. Britton was baseball's first female owner, and her fellow National League male owners often resented her involvement in league affairs. (Courtesy of the Library of Congress)

especially since she would be thrown among the older "tricky baseball men of that period," who clearly resented her membership in their fraternity. Britton had reportedly considered selling the franchise to Charles Weeghman—even back in 1911 Weeghman was thinking about getting into baseball—but she had a stubborn, rebellious streak and decided to hold on to it. To take active control of the club, she first had to sue the executor of the Robison estate to preclude him from assuming its voting rights. The first female owner, nearly a decade before women even had the right to vote for federal office, Britton struggled to be taken seriously by her fellow owners, the players, and the press, who nicknamed her "Lady Bee."[1]

Britton recognized that she needed a strong president. She initially hired construction executive Edward Steininger (the same Steininger who later became active with the Sloufeds). His short tenure led Britton to appoint her attorney as successor. She generally delegated operating decisions to her president but always attended league meetings and made sure she was in the celebratory owners' picture.

Britton's first season was surely her most enjoyable. The Cardinals remained in the thick of the pennant race well into the season before finishing fifth, their best showing in many years, and turned a profit of $165,000. In her exuberance Britton signed catcher-manager Bresnahan to a high-salaried five-year contract. When the team struggled in 1912, the hotheaded Bresnahan looked to place blame elsewhere, and Lady Bee proved an easy target. He had once offered $500,000 to purchase the team, only to find himself now bossed by a woman. He showed Britton little respect and berated her to her face. "No woman can tell me how to play a ball game," Bresnahan fumed.[2] He still wanted to buy the team and couldn't understand why a woman would want to hold on to it. Furthermore, like nearly all ballplayers of his time, he had little respect for a female owner and little patience for her appropriate and reasonable involvement in the team. After his outbursts, Britton had little choice but to fire Bresnahan despite his guaranteed salary; the final four years on his contract cost her a settlement of $20,000. Bresnahan eventually landed with the Cubs, who assumed a portion of his contract.

After the Bresnahan fiasco, for 1913 Lady Bee brought in Miller Huggins as manager and named her husband Schuyler Britton, an attorney working for a printing company, team president. A man who enjoyed his wife's money and the nightlife, Schuyler had little baseball knowledge, but he mingled well and would, albeit grudgingly, take direction from his wife. For the next several years, he nominally ran the team and was heavily involved in player salary negotiations and in blocking attempted incursions from the Federal League. His fellow owners tried to promote Schuyler as the face of the franchise to minimize Helene's involvement. Much to the owners' exasperation, however, Helene continued to claim her full rights as an owner.

Ball and Steininger now hoped to lure Bresnahan back to St. Louis for a huge payday. Ball offered a multiyear contract of $12,000 per year plus $25,000 worth of stock in the Sloufeds franchise and a $5,000 bonus. Ball further claimed to hold an option to purchase the Cardinals from Britton for $300,000, which may in fact have been true. In the event that Ball purchased the Cardinals, Bresnahan would be able to return to that team without the dreaded female owner. Ball and Steininger further added that if the Cardinals wouldn't sell, Ball and his politically connected partner, Otto Stifel, would force the issue by having a street cut thorough the team's ballpark. The St. Louis duo's bombast tempted but couldn't convince Bresnahan; he remained in Chicago.

Despite his refusal, the Federals did not give up on Bresnahan. On October 14, Game Seven of the postseason Chicago city series between the Cubs and White Sox, scheduled for Comiskey Park, was rained out. As the players milled about, an agent for the Federals met Bresnahan under the grandstand and told him to contact Gilmore. The Federals' president arranged to meet Bresnahan at the Chicago Athletic Club, where he told the player that Robert Ward wanted him in Brooklyn and was not afraid to pay up. Unlike Ball, Gilmore wouldn't take "no" for an answer and asked Bresnahan to name his price. Bresnahan named the highest, most absurd price he could think of: $50,000 over three years with $10,000 up front. Rather than laughing or angering, Gilmore told Bresnahan he would hear from him. The Federals needed recognizable stars if they were to challenge in 1915.

Not long thereafter, Gilmore convinced Bresnahan it would be worth his while to take an all-expenses-paid trip to New York to meet with Ward. Bresnahan happily accepted the invitation, fully understanding the intent: he stopped in Toledo to pick up his attorney. In New York, Ward offered a three-year contract for $50,000 with $5,000 up front and a small portion of the remaining $45,000 in stock. After consulting with his attorney, Bresnahan also demanded that Ward personally guarantee the contract, to which Ward agreed. The next morning Gilmore, George Ward, and Weeghman, who had traveled to New York to help his fellow Federals, showed up at Bresnahan's hotel room with a $5,000 check and the contract. Bresnahan begged off cryptically: "You don't want me, and we will call it off."[3]

Robert Ward remembered the denouement differently. The Federals would pursue only players who had the ten-day clause in their contracts, and before signing a player would require him to produce the contract so they could confirm its existence. Bresnahan claimed that his contract was locked in a safe deposit box in Toledo. Ward's brother George arranged to meet with Bresnahan in Chicago, where the player would produce his Cubs contract. When Ward finally met Bresnahan, he still did not produce the contract, and the Wards ended their discussions. Whichever story is accurate, another popular player had slipped through the fingers of the Federal Leaguers.[4]

A tactic often used by the Federals was to approach Major League players while they were visiting a Federal League city on a road trip. When the Pirates came to St. Louis on September 1 to begin a series against the Cardinals, Sloufeds manager Fielder Jones was ready. He sent pitcher Otis Crandall to the Planters Hotel to recruit young Pittsburgh pitcher Wilbur Cooper. The well-organized Federals even had Cooper's former Minor League teammate, Kawfeds pitcher Eugene Packard, in town for a series against the Sloufeds, accompany Crandall. The two persuaded Cooper to meet with Jones at the American Hotel and to bring second baseman Jim Viox along as another potential recruit. Jones claimed that both players told him they were not under contract for 1915; Pittsburgh owner Barney Dreyfuss disputed this version of events. In any event, Jones offered Viox $6,000 per year for two years with one year's salary to be paid in advance, and $5,500 per year, also for two years, to Cooper. Both declined.

The Federals continued their pursuit of both players throughout the fall. On September 25 player-manager Rebel Oakes buttonholed Cooper and tried to land him for the Pittfeds. Although he again declined, Cooper must have shown some interest because Pittfeds business manager William McCullough approached him on November 2, again to no avail. Oakes had more success with the Pirates' disgruntled star first baseman, Ed Konetchy, convincing him to move across town to the Pittfeds with a three-year contract for $22,500. The Rebels believed they had also finally lured Jim Viox away after nearly a year of intensive recruitment. Oakes, one of the more aggressive Federal League recruiters, likewise enticed Brooklyn pitcher Frank Allen to his club in time to start the team's final game on October 10.[5]

Buffeds manager Larry Schlafly also pursued Major League stars aggressively for his club. In September Buffalo finally landed Ray Caldwell from the Yankees. Caldwell left the club in mid-September for the Buffeds and a $2,500 advance. Manager Schlafly actually had some thought of getting him into a couple of games over the remainder of the season, but once in town the club realized they could not pitch him because he was under a binding contract with New York for the 1914 season. Schlafly also successfully lured another American League pitcher in October. Hugh Bedient had struggled with the Red Sox in 1914 after two strong seasons; he happily signed a two-year contract with Buffalo. Once they realized he had jumped, the Red Sox waived him to Providence in the International League to minimize the significance of his loss.[6]

Schlafly also secured Jack Dalton from Brooklyn after having pursued him all season. Sometime after Dalton's contract expired on October 7, Schlafly went to the player's home in Newark to ask what he wanted. Dalton responded with the most outrageous request he could think of for a journeyman player: a two-year contract for $16,000 with a $4,000 advance and a guarantee from a bonding company. Schlafly left and discussed the terms with team president William Robertson, and the two agreed to meet them. Robertson sent Dalton a telegram accepting his terms. The next day a shocked Dalton called Brooklyn scout Larry

Sutton with the news. Sutton persuaded Dalton to meet with him and sit down with owner Charles Ebbets. The naive ballplayer didn't understand all the legalities of contract law and sent Ebbets a letter telling him he was terminating his contract in ten days. Before going to the meeting, Dalton checked with Fultz's office to ask if the reserve clause was binding. Throughout the Federal League war, Fultz studiously avoided taking any position on this issue and was surprisingly unsupportive of players jumping to the Federals; he told Dalton he would go over the matter and get back to him. When Dalton met with Ebbets, the owner explained to him that the ten-day notice wasn't valid because his contract had expired, but the reserve clause was still in effect. He then read a letter from Organized Baseball's attorneys, John Galvin and Ellis Kinkead, emphasizing its legality as they saw it. The increase in pay was so tempting, however, that Dalton successfully resisted the pressure.[7]

Because of Ebbets's famous cheapness, the Federals believed that Brooklyn's players would be particularly susceptible to their offers. Besides Dalton, the Federals grabbed two others during the 1914 season. Chifeds manager Joe Tinker signed catcher William Fischer for Chicago, and, as noted, Oakes signed pitcher Frank Allen just in time to start one game for the Pittfeds.[8]

The Federals also overcame the pressure exerted on Cincinnati's backup shortstop, Marty Berghammer. Once Herrmann realized that he had lost Berghammer to the Pittfeds, he sent the shortstop a contract re-upping him under the reserve clause for $2,400, "trust[ing] that you sign this contract." A standard counterattack in these situations was to admonish the player that he was violating a legal and moral obligation and emphasize the legal standing of the reserve clause as interpreted by Organized Baseball. In the cover letter sent with the contract, Herrmann reminded Berghammer, "The United States Circuit Court of Appeals decided in Killefer's case that though he signed with the Federals he was under obligation to first negotiate with the Philadelphia Club with whom he had been under contract for the preceding season."[9]

The Cardinals, one of baseball's least prosperous clubs, haggled shamelessly with their players to force salaries as low as possible. Lee Magee had signed a two-year contact in March 1914 for $6,000 per year plus a 20 percent bonus should the team finish first, second, or third. Because of their surprising third-place showing, Magee picked up an extra $1,200. Nevertheless, Magee tested his value with the Federals. In December he called Schuyler Britton to tell him he was going to Chicago with Terrier manager Fielder Jones to meet Gilmore.

"I thought I would let you know," Magee told Britton as he wrapped up the conversation.

"We are not worrying about that because you are under contract with the St. Louis Club for 1915," Britton told him.

"Well, I just wanted to let you know that I was going to Chicago."[10]

In Chicago, Weeghman and Gilmore talked Magee into jumping, and Ward scooped him up to be the Brookfeds player-manager.

Pittsburgh's Oakes also targeted several of his old Cardinals teammates. In June 1914 he made overtures to young pitcher Pol Perritt and catcher Ivey Wingo, among others. Other Federal Leaguers pursued the Cardinals players as well, and as the season neared its conclusion these players began listening more closely to the Federals' enticements. In September Oakes's pursuit finally paid off, as the Federals surreptitiously signed Perritt and Wingo to three-year contracts that called for large increases over their 1914 salaries. Oakes secured Perritt, and Robertson and Schlafly landed Wingo for Buffalo.

Perritt explained:

All this summer I have received offers from Federal magnates. I refused to do business with them, because I expected the Cardinals to come forth with a proposition. They ignored me. [Manager Miller] Huggins did not seem anxious to sign me, and when the big opening came I didn't let it get away from me. When we reached Philadelphia on September 19, I received a long distance telephone call from [Pittfeds manager] Rebel Oakes. He asked me if I was open to sign with him, and if I would consider a proposition. I answered that I would talk with him. Then he told me that he would catch the Saturday night train and call upon me Sunday morning.

We arranged for our meeting in Philadelphia on the morning of September 20. Rebel didn't lose any time. We greeted each other in a hurry and he pulled out a contract. He told me to look it over. I did. I couldn't wait until he handed me the fountain pen, so I signed.

I feel that I played a fair hand with Huggins, Britton and the Cardinals. I signed a one-year contract with them and I served until my final day. My contract expired after the season, and I believe that I am free to go where I care to for 1915. They had their chance to hold me for 1915, but apparently did not consider me good enough in the middle of the season to sign me for next year, as they did several other players.[11]

Huggins disputed Perritt's account: "When I tried to sign Perritt, he told me that that he did not want to talk about signing until we returned to St. Louis. I wanted to come to terms then [on the road trip] and would have met any figure he would have named. After our little chat, in Boston, I called upon Polly again and asked him if we could get together. He again told me that he would rather wait until we came back home and then he would take the matter up with Mr. Britton. When we returned home, naturally I thought Polly would come to us. We were prepared to meet anything he named, but he 'crossed' us. He did not give us a chance to bid for him, and I know that he could have done as well with us as with the Federal League." Huggins may or may not have met Pittsburgh's offer, but it was clear that the Cardinals would submit market offers only under the most extreme duress.[12]

Wingo, a highly regarded young catcher who split the backstop duties with Frank Snyder, even more dramatically illustrates the Cardinals' attitude. As with Perritt, the Federals had pursued Wingo throughout the summer:

> Federal League agents have camped on my trail for months and months. I waited for the Cardinals to come after me, but they did not. Surely it wasn't my place to go to Huggins and Britton, and ask them if they wanted me! They did not break any speed records coming after me, so I decided that it was to my benefit to take the biggest bid. This came from Larry Schlafly of the Buffalo club. On several journeys through the east and even at home, Federal managers have given me offers.
>
> Joe Tinker wanted me; Madison over in Kansas City was after me; Oakes in Pittsburgh tried to get me; also Phillips in Indianapolis. When we were on the Eastern trip Schlafly telephoned me in New York. He asked me if I had signed with the Cardinals for 1915, and I replied that I had not. The Buffalo manager asked me where I could see him, and I told him that we would leave New York that night, which was September 29, for Pittsburgh. I told him we would be in Pittsburgh Tuesday morning, and that he could see me then. He met me, and we discussed the affair thoroughly. He showed me where I could make $21,000 in three years; I asked him if he would give me a bonus, and he informed me that if I would sign the contract he would hand me $3,000 and make the contract for $18,000 for three years. That was good enough for me. I couldn't turn it down, so I signed. I believe that I can make as much in three years as I could with the Cardinals in five years. Any young fellow would be foolish to turn down such a fabulous offer, especially at this stage of my career.

After Wingo signed his lucrative deal, he discussed his disappointing salary negotiations upon his return from the around-the-world baseball excursion the previous March:

> I met Mr. Britton when I landed. We talked about our 1914 contract. He made a suggestion, and I also came out with an idea. I asked Mr. Britton to give me a three-year contract for $15,000, $5,000 per season. He informed me that he would not sign me for more than one year. He even refused to give me $5,000. We compro-

mised on $4,500, but at that time I told him he made a mistake; that he should sign me for three years, but he only laughed. I consented and signed for 1914 at $4,500.

Before joining the squad at St. Augustine [for spring training], I went home. I found a letter from the Cardinals for 1914 enclosed. This contract called for a salary of $2,600 for 1914. I was informed in writing that it would be impossible for them to give me more than $2,600 and that if I did not care to sign for $2,600 I could remain in Georgia. Wasn't that funny? I had a laugh on them. No doubt this letter was written long before the Cardinals thought of the Federal League. Britton could have cinched me for three years. I was willing to sign for $15,000. Well, they won't miss me. They have a couple of good catchers, anyway.[13]

On the Monday after the conclusion of the season, the Cardinals executed a plan to quickly re-up all their unsigned players. Each unsigned player came to the team's Robison Field offices to collect two checks—one a final paycheck for the season, and one a bonus for finishing third—from treasurer Herman Seekamp. After receiving their checks, each player entered Britton's private office to sign his contract for 1915. When Perritt met with Britton, he excused himself, saying he would return in a few minutes to talk business. But after slamming the door on his way out, Perritt, already under contract with Pittsburgh, never returned.

A furious Britton stopped payment on the third-place bonus checks for Perritt ($600) and Wingo ($900). Britton justified his actions on the grounds that the players had a duty to negotiate with the team under the reserve clause in their contracts and had violated that obligation.[14] Robert Hedges, president of Organized Baseball's other team in St. Louis, became alarmed when Britton told him of his actions. He recognized the suspect legality of the clause and didn't care to provide any player with an easy set of facts to further challenge the clause in court. "As you know," Hedges complained, "the reserve clause in baseball is as important as the ten day clause. The two together constitute the real heart of our contracts and organized ball. The very best legal talent should be used in any fight, pertaining to the right of reservation."[15] After taking with Hedges, Britton recognized his relatively flimsy legal ground and its potential impact on larger issues, and asked for an endorsement from Garry Herrmann.

The National Commission, particularly Ban Johnson, knew better than to run up legal fees in a case as weak as Britton's. Johnson had been through these player wars before and understood that Organized Baseball had not truly lost anyone until he appeared in a regular season game with the Federals. Plenty of moral persuasion and financial incentive could be lavished on wayward players before that eventuality. "Personally, I do not favor the plan to push the cases now pending in the courts," Johnson wrote. "The funds are not available for any additional expense. There are outstanding obligations that have not been met, and it would be well to get our bearings before we proceed any further."[16] Johnson understood that Organized Baseball could reclaim many of the players without resorting to the courts and risking an adverse decision. It was all right to lose an occasional marginal player; let the Federals file the court challenges if they wished to reclaim the players who jumped back to Organized Baseball.

With the Federals concentrating on the National League's weaker franchises in their player raids, and with the collapse of peace negotiations, the senior circuit in particular fretted over the future. At its annual meeting at New York's Waldorf-Astoria, the National League, in an austerity move, voted to reinstitute a player limit for 1915, reducing its in-season roster size to twenty-one players. Several managers who carried the most players, including John McGraw of the highly profitable Giants, protested this decision. The American League also decided to reinstitute a roster limit, but it chose to return to the 1913 limit of twenty-five, still the standard today.[17] At a later New York meeting, National League owners discussed several other key issues, including the waiver rules. When Lady Bee formally addressed her fellow owners, it marked the first time a woman had taken an active part in league debate. The other owners rather condescendingly congratulated her on her familiarity with the draft and waiver rules.[18]

The Minor Leagues also worried in the wake of the failed peace agreement. International League president Ed Barrow and American Association president Tom Chivington continued to push for the elimination of the draft. The International League's situation had become so precarious that Barrow recommended drastic austerity measures, such as reducing roster sizes to only seventeen players, cutting the season to 140 games, eliminating spring training trips, and limiting the umpire staff to five or six men. The league also met with the National Commission for approval to transfer Jersey City to Syracuse and Baltimore to Richmond, though only the latter occurred.[19] The National Commission and Major League owners naturally sympathized with the plight of the Minor Leagues, and rumors abounded that the draft would be eliminated. Once again, however, the Minors could not mount a sufficiently compelling, or threatening, case.[20]

After their pursuits and signings during the fall of 1914, many Federal Leaguers grew increasingly optimistic. Unfortunately, several leading executives did not know when it was best to keep their mouths shut. Gilmore had many strengths, but he and others continually exaggerated the prospect of players ready to jump to the Federal League. This not only gave Organized Baseball advance warning of likely defectors, it also raised unrealistic expectations among fans and writers. In late September 1914, when he was shown a list of players that included such stars as Walter Johnson, Red Dooin, Hans Lobert, and Sherry Magee, Brooklyn's Walter Ward (nephew of Robert) confirmed that "some of these men" had signed with the Federal League, but he refused to specify which ones.[21]

Of course, having players stump for the Federals was a little different. Their pronouncements could help convince other players of the viability of and support for the Federal League. In the fall of 1914 Tom Seaton confirmed the potential exodus of more Phillies to the Federals. "It's all off with the Phillies," he said. "Two or three members, including [star pitcher Grover] Alexander may be left behind when the Feds get through with them. I have information from the inside and know from personal experience how a greater part of the club stands toward the new league. I know manager Dooin is going to be deposed [he was] and when the change is made there is going to be trouble. Two veterans, Sherwood Magee and Hans Lobert, are after the position and each head a faction on the club. No matter which player is selected, the other will certainly leave the club for the feeling is bitter between the two sides."[22]

The Federals also targeted the Philadelphia Athletics. Manager and minority owner Connie Mack had fallen into a deep funk after his team lost to the Boston Braves in the 1914 World Series in four straight games—the first such sweep in the history of the fall classic. He blamed his players for not being sufficiently motivated and for being too enthralled by possible pay increases from the Federal League. No doubt he also had word of a possible mass defection to the Federals in the event his team won but was denied the opportunity to face Indianapolis in a playoff series. In his dark mood, Mack asked waivers on three of his veteran starting pitchers: Chief Bender, Eddie Plank, and Jack Coombs. Such waivers, for the purpose of releasing a player to another Major League team for the waiver price or sending a player to the Minor Leagues, were generally kept secret. But Detroit manager Hughie Jennings, who had feuded with Mack in the past, publicized his seemingly heartless move.

In early December 1914 the Federals pounced on a second wave of players, including Mack's pitchers. On December 2 Baltfeds treasurer Harry Goldman signed Eddie Plank in his hometown to a generic Federal League contract. Two days later Goldman went to Philadelphia to sign Chief Bender for two years at $7,500 per year, a huge increase for an aging hurler who had never made more than $4,000 with Mack. Coombs remained in Organized Baseball with the Brooklyn Dodgers.[23]

While Goldman was signing the two Athletics, Robert Ward was meeting with star New York Giants hurler Rube Marquard. The pitcher represented to Ward that his contract had expired and that he was effectively a free agent. To cover himself, Ward required Marquard to execute an affidavit attesting that he was no longer under contract with the Giants. Ward signed Marquard to a three-year contract calling for $10,000 for the first year, $12,000 for the second, and $15,000 for the third, plus a $1,500 bonus. The Federals appeared to be on a roll.

But they still longed for a true superstar. Consequently they stepped up their pressure on the best player available, Walter Johnson. Although Johnson had rebuffed them during the summer, he had clearly been willing to listen. And despite the promises he had extracted in June, Johnson had not yet been formally tied up by Washington.[24]

When the season ended, Phil Ball dispatched manager Fielder Jones to meet Johnson on the train as he traveled to his farm in Coffeyville, Kansas. Ball had authorized Jones to offer $20,000 per year on a two-year contract. Naturally tempted, Johnson declined subject to the anticipated offer—in the $16,000 to $18,000 range—from the Senators' Clark Griffith.[25] "I told him [Ball] it was a fine offer, but I didn't think I was in the market for the Federal League, as I thought Washington would make me an offer that I should accept."[26] After Johnson turned Ball down, Weeghman asked Ball if *he* could take a shot at Johnson; Ball had no objection, though in exchange for his permission he exacted the Federal League's rights to Eddie Plank.

Weeghman sent Tinker, the Federal's best spokesman, to Coffeyville to woo Johnson to the Chifeds. Tinker's timing was perfect. After Johnson returned to Coffeyville he received a contract in the mail from Senators owner Ben Minor. "He wrote to the effect that I was the lawful property of Washington; that the best figure they could make me now was $12,500 [he had earned $12,000 in 1914], and that if I did not accept this figure they would renew their old contract according to the option [the reserve clause]."[27] Minor, who composed this letter after the collapse of the peace talks, must have believed the Federal League was about to fold, and that without competition from the Federals he saw no reason to honor Griffith's proposals and offer Johnson a significant increase. No other explanation makes sense for sending such an insulting letter to his star pitcher.

Johnson, quite naturally, was offended at both the substance and tone of Minor's letter. When Tinker showed up on December 3, it took the two only twenty minutes to agree to a three-year contract at $17,500 per year with a $6,000 advance. Later that day, Johnson received a cable from Griffith, telling him to ignore the letter from Minor. He had managed to talk some sense into the Senators owner. "If I had received that letter in the morning, instead of the afternoon,"

Johnson recalled, "I would have at least put off signing with the Federal League until he had had a chance to state his case. But as things were, they were settled, I thought, so far as I was concerned."[28]

With the signing of Johnson, the Federals could barely contain their glee. "Please say this for me," bragged Gilmore, "that within two or three days we will have all the Major League material that we can use."[29] "Plank," declared Ball, "was the first star to jump. Next day it was Johnson. Marquard followed and on Saturday it was Bender. This will continue each day for at least two weeks."[30] One of those days was to include star Athletics third baseman Frank "Home Run" Baker. Plank and Bender were past their prime and no longer really stars, but both eventually ended up in the Hall of Fame, and one can't blame Ball for touting their defection. Johnson and Baker, on the other hand, were among baseball's best players.

To highlight the success of the fall campaign, in early December Ball's club released a list of players who had signed with the Federals for 1915. Gwinner and Oakes had landed two regular pitchers, Frank Allen and Pol Perritt, plus Konetchy. In addition, and not on the list, Pittsburgh had lined up St. Louis Browns third baseman Jimmy Austin, who signed soon after. Schlafly had seven new Major League regulars in Buffalo: pitchers Ray Collins, Bedient, and Caldwell, plus Wingo, Washington shortstop George McBride, White Sox outfielder Ping Bodie, and Brooklyn outfielder Jack Dalton (not yet officially identified). In addition to Marquard, the Wards had signed Lee Magee and Jim Viox for Brooklyn. On top of their coup with Johnson, Weeghman and Tinker signed Cleveland hurler Rip Hagerman. Baltimore could boast Bender and another defecting Phillie, Dode Paskert. Ball thought he had persuaded Phillies third baseman Hans Lobert to come join the Federals, and St. Louis was allocated Eddie Plank. The Federals did not advertise any new players on the financially struggling franchises in Kansas City and Indianapolis, which faced only Minor League competition. All in all, this represented quite a haul for the Federals. They had apparently captured eight regular pitchers and ten position players, and it was only early December. Once again, the Federals could not resist trumpeting their successes, offering the opposition much-needed intelligence when secrecy was advisable.[31]

Once more Organized Baseball countered swiftly and effectively. Some of these identified players, such as McBride, had not yet technically signed with the Federals and could be pressured and financially motivated to stay with the Major Leagues. The others, who were already signed, were subjected to a more systematic, aggressive response. The American League had no intention of letting

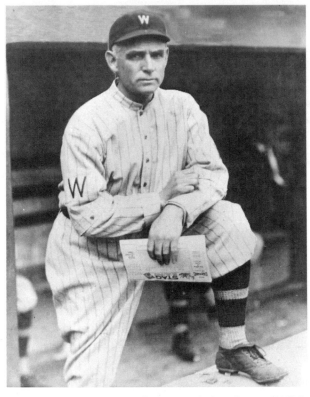

Washington Senators manager and minority owner Clark Griffith, who hoped to prevent star pitcher Walter Johnson from jumping to the Federal League. (Author's collection)

Walter Johnson get away. His situation was certainly not settled as far as Griffith was concerned. After a couple of days of bluster, during which he minimized the loss, Griffith changed his tune and resolved to recapture Johnson. He recruited Pirates manager Fred Clarke, a fellow Kansan, to visit Johnson and pressure him into returning to Organized Baseball. Playing on Johnson's sense of obligation, Clarke persuaded the pitcher to meet with Griffith.[32]

Meanwhile, the news that Johnson had signed with the Federals shocked Organized Baseball, which had grown complacent in the few weeks after the collapse of peace negotiations. At the American League meeting in New York on December 8, Ban Johnson and American League owners worked to blunt the Federals' momentum. Connie Mack, an old friend of Ban Johnson's, was looking to cash in on several of his star players before they jumped to the Federal League for more money. His second baseman, Eddie Collins, still only twenty-seven years old, was one of baseball's half-dozen greatest stars. Deftly handling two problems at once, Ban Johnson, who still exerted a surprising level of control over his league's franchises, engineered the sale of Collins to the White Sox. He first discussed the sale with the prospective new Yankees owners, Jacob Ruppert and Tillinghast Huston, as a way to bolster the flagging New York club. "Ban Johnson suggested we take Eddie Collins," Huston recalled, "but at the same time we didn't even own the New York club and there was a good deal to do [closing on the purchase of the team] before we could map out any comprehensive campaign for the future."[33] Johnson then turned to his old friend Charles Comiskey, who leaped at the chance to get a player of Collins's caliber. Johnson thus deftly strengthened Chicago's American League squad to compete with Weeghman's team and found a willing buyer for Mack's most valuable player. One of the few American League owners who could afford Collins, Comiskey paid $50,000 to the Athletics, the highest price ever paid for a player to that point. He further agreed to a five-year $75,000 contract plus a $10,000 signing bonus with his new second baseman. Collins also extracted a $5,000 check from Ban Johnson, who had promised the inducement when he was trying to get Collins to agree to move to the White Sox.[34]

While Ban Johnson was helping Mack stay afloat financially, Griffith traveled to meet with Walter Johnson. Calling on his skills of persuasion and his role as Johnson's manager and mentor, Griffith told Johnson that "he had worked hard and invested all his money in trying to make Washington a winner . . . he said that he didn't deserve any such treatment from me, as he had always done well by me."[35] Griffith also highlighted all the negatives of jumping to the Federals, including public perception and the blacklist. Minor had not given Griffith permission to raise his offer, so Griffith had to apply all the moral persuasion and threats of dire consequences he could muster. After a long, grueling meeting, Griffith convinced Johnson to return to Washington for the $12,500 previously offered, including a $6,000 advance, and promised he would get Johnson a better contract the following season.[36] "The mistake he [Johnson] made," Sloufeds manager Fielder Jones remarked, "was to consent to meet Griff and his lawyers without having some of his own friends along with him. It is almost a certainty any man's will would be broken in the course of a nine-hour conference closeted with seven men opposing him."[37] (Johnson later denied that any lawyers were present.) Griffith delivered on his promise, later signing Johnson to a five-year contract at $16,000 per year.[38]

Griffith still needed to find the $6,000 advance for Johnson that Weeghman had promised. He called the American League office in Chicago to see if Ban Johnson would pay it out of the American League funds. Johnson, who had just anted up $5,000 to help induce Collins to go to Chicago, and still angry with Minor for causing the debacle in the first place, refused to help. He asked Griffith to hold and put on Comiskey.

"Hello, what do you want?" demanded Comiskey.

"I want [$6,000]," Griffith told him.

"For what?"

"To pry Walter Johnson away from the Federal League."

"That's your problem, not mine," laughed Comiskey.

"Oh no, it isn't," replied Griffith, "it's your problem too."

"How do you figure that?"

"Well, you just bought Eddie Collins from the Athletics for $75,000 [*sic*], didn't you, Commy?"

"Yes."

"Well, then how would you like to see Walter Johnson playing for the Chicago Feds next season and drawing all those fans away from White Sox Park?"

"Holy smokes, how much did you say Johnson wants to stay in the American League?"

"[$6,000] will turn the trick."

"You'll have my check in the morning, Griff," Comiskey concluded.[39]

Shirley Povich's reconstruction of this conversation, likely based on Griffith's recollection, may not have been exact. After all, the sale of Collins was made as a consequence of Johnson's defection. But it does give flavor to the close relationship between these three men and how they reacted to the potential disaster of losing Walter Johnson.

Many of the players who signed with the Federals did not do so simply for more money but often because they were dissatisfied in their current situation: they may have developed an antagonistic relationship with their manager or teammates, a dislike for the city they were playing in, or a lack of trust with an owner. To reclaim disgruntled players who had already jumped and to hold on to those still waffling, Organized Baseball's owners engineered trades to the wealthier teams that could pay more and also offer a fresh environment.

After the Cardinals' Ivey Wingo signed with the Federals, Garry Herrmann, as Cincinnati's president, and Schuyler Britton got together to discuss a potential solution that would benefit both parties. They would swap disgruntled players. Herrmann felt that for the right price he could convince Wingo to defect back to the Major Leagues. With Britton's permission, Herrmann delegated Cincinnati manager Buck Herzog to handle Cincinnati's end of the bargain. With a little persuasion and a salary increase, Herzog was able to lure Wingo back. In exchange, Britton would receive Armando Marsans. But first they had to re-sign Marsans. In early January St. Louis manager Miller Huggins traveled to Cuba to meet with Marsans. He brought a new contract, told Marsans he would be traded to St. Louis if he signed, and assured him how much he wanted him with the Cardinals. Proud and fed up with Organized Baseball, Marsans declined Huggins's offer and stayed in Cuba, leaving the owners in an awkward situation. Wingo had signed with the Reds despite technically still being the property of the Cardinals. Because both teams wanted to keep Wingo in Organized Baseball, they eventually agreed to substitute young catcher Mike Gonzalez for Marsans, saving Wingo from the Federals.[40]

Manager John McGraw of baseball's most successful franchise, the New York Giants, saw an opportunity to use the appeal of the Federal League to strengthen his own squad. He traveled to Chicago to recruit Hans Lobert away from the Sloufeds; he then needed to work out a trade with Phillies owner William Baker, who still held rights to Lobert. Surprisingly, given his lack of negotiating leverage, Baker managed to extract a couple of pretty good players in return. Phil Ball defended the Federals' effort in trying to recruit Lobert. "How high did you want us to go? I first offered him $6,000, then boosted the price to $8,000. Finally, when McGraw cut in I offered to guarantee Lobert $25,000 for three years. Guess that's going some, isn't it? I know he's not getting that money in New York."[41]

McGraw also happily agreed to sign Pol Perritt. Once again he promised a player to be named later to St. Louis in exchange for Perritt's rights; once again McGraw also surrendered a pretty good ballplayer in Bob Bescher. With an opportunity to play for the National League's premier franchise and a raise, Perritt jumped back to Organized Baseball. James Gaffney of the World Champion Braves also used the potential defection of a disgruntled player to bolster his club. He agreed to take star outfielder Sherry Magee from Philadelphia for a couple of players to be named later. Again, Baker and new Phillies manager Pat Moran extracted at least one useful player in the transaction. (By the end of the 1915 National League season, Baker and Moran had turned the tables on the wealthier Giants and Braves. After an off-season in which they had been forced to trade several of their best players, the Phillies won the pennant, their first and the last they would win until 1950.)

Marquard, too, soon proved ephemeral for the Federals. The Giants pointed out that Marquard was not, in fact, a free agent. He was under a valid contract with New York for 1915 and not free to sign a contract with the Brookfeds. On July 22, 1914, Rube Marquard had re-signed with the Giants for 1915 and 1916. The contract called for $5,600 per season and struck the ten-day clause. The Wards put up a brave front for several days, but once they realized Marquard

Harry Hempstead was the owner of baseball's most profitable franchise, the New York Giants, which he inherited from his father-in-law. (Courtesy of the Library of Congress)

had lied in his affidavit, they backed off.[42] Several Major League owners also considered bringing new legal proceedings against the Federals. Giants owner Harry Hempstead in particular wanted to bring criminal conspiracy charges against the Wards because of their signing of Marquard.[43]

In one way, Hempstead was a luckier man than Schulyer Britton. When John Brush died in November 1912 he left a $3 million estate, which included the New York Giants baseball club. Although technically he left his holdings to his second wife and two daughters, Brush's will named Hempstead, who was married to Brush's daughter Eleanor, a trustee and gave him the authority to vote the team's stock. Hempstead, not his wife, controlled the team. A true blue blood, Hempstead was a descendant of John Alden, often credited with being the first person off the *Mayflower* at Plymouth Rock in 1620. Born in Philadelphia, Hempstead had graduated from Lafayette College in 1891 and married Eleanor in 1894. Eighteen years later he was running the Giants.

In 1913 Hempstead moved his family to New York from Indianapolis, where he had been managing Brush's department store operation. He also maintained a cordial relationship with McGraw, one of baseball's most popular and most difficult personalities, despite the fact that the manager had hoped to secure a larger role in the reorganization after Brush's death. Forty-four years old when he inherited the team, Hempstead enjoyed the prestige that came from running baseball's premier franchise, though he never really warmed to the task. "The only ones who really get any fun out of owning a major league team," he once grumbled, "are those who can afford to ride a hobby and care little about the cost."[44] In retrospect, his complaints seem self-serving; Hempstead was the president of baseball's most profitable team. Generally regarded as a quiet, competent businessman, he was not shy about expressing his opinions on league matters, often protecting the narrow interests of the Giants over larger considerations, much to the frustration of his fellow owners.

After reviewing Hempstead's request to sue the Brookfeds, Herrmann asked league attorney Ellis Kinkead to update a July 1914 report evaluating the advisability of bringing conspiracy charges against the Federal League. In his memo on July 19 Kinkead had written:

> We have been investigating . . . whether a suit could be brought on the grounds of conspiracy against the leaders of the Federal movement and in that proceeding injunction secured against their interfering between club owners and players. We have not found any close precedent but on principle we are inclined to believe that an action might be brought by all the clubs of the National League, or all the clubs of the American League, against such leaders of the Federal League as we can in good faith charge with conspiring to seduce players away from the clubs bringing the suit.
>
> If we can secure evidence that those whom we might make defendants have united and are threatening to continue to cooperate in seducing our players, the bill, we think, would be sustained.

In December, Kinkead updated his thinking:

> We think that if it is desired to bring such an action now it should be based upon what is being done or is about to be done or is threatened to be done by the Federal League people now or in the future, rather than to base it entirely upon anything that has been done in the past or is already completed. In other words, we must have some evidence of a present intent to continue these injurious activities and if we have such evidence we can then use the completed transactions of the past as tending to strengthen our charge of conspiracy.
>
> We think therefore, that one of the first things to be done is to have evidence of what has been done and what is being threatened now, furnished us in a compact and definite form.

You should understand, however, that in an action of this kind we are certain to be met with the defense which was presented in the Chase case in Buffalo and sustained by Judge Bissell in his opinion which you have, namely the claim that the plaintiff or plaintiffs are themselves parties to an unlawful, or at least an inequitable, contract such that a court of equity will not afford them relief in matters which are in any way connected with their association.

The National Commission took the memo under advisement and, with the recapture of Marquard, deferred any decision regarding a suit against the Federals. It did implement the first step recommended in the letter and asked each owner to document interference from the Federal Leaguers.

As in 1914, the speed and force of Organized Baseball's reaction to defecting players demoralized the Federal League's managers and executives. Oakes, watching nearly a year's worth of work go down the drain as his new recruits returned to the Major Leagues, confronted Perritt in a St. Louis bar. When the meeting escalated into a full-blown fistfight, Perritt knocked down his onetime prospective manager. In another incident at a bar in Cincinnati, Lee Magee and Herrmann nearly came to blows after Herrmann called the new Tip-Tops manager a "contract-jumper."

A couple of dispirited Federals hoped for a small public relations boost by including the fans in a team-naming exercise. Weeghman sponsored a contest to come up with a team name more inspiring than "Chifeds." He offered a season pass for the winning entry. Out of 350 proposals, Weeghman selected "Whales," turned in by one D. J. Eichoff of 1451 Hood Avenue.[45] Buffalo also wanted a team name more original than "Buffeds," and for 1915 decided to call themselves the "Blues."[46]

The Federals also settled on two more actions with potentially much greater impact. The owners commissioned each manager to sign at least one Major League star, regardless of cost.[47] This was easier said than done, of course, and testified to the player fallout from early December. The owners finally were beginning to appreciate the huge institutional advantages held by Organized Baseball. In a desperate and expensive roll of the dice, the Federals now decided to try to recast the baseball landscape through the federal courts.

11

Anti-trust Attack

The defections back to Organized Baseball surprised and dismayed Gilmore, Gates, and the Federal League's owners and managers. They could not believe that Organized Baseball could disclaim their Federal contracts with impunity and re-sign players who had been legitimately acquired, players who were tied to their Major League team only by the reserve clause, which was of dubious legality. Legal fees from the various court cases were running into the tens of thousands of dollars, and none had delivered the clear-cut, precedent-setting decision the Federals needed and believed was right.

The Federals had drawn up a more reasonable player contract, but the courts did not seem to care. While the new contract could not be described as player friendly, it did try to redress some of the players' key concerns. The Federals' reserve clause called for a 5 percent raise over the previous year's salary and required written notice by September 15. Thus the clause was definitive, precluded a pay cut, and needed to be invoked before the close of the previous season so that the player knew where he stood. The contract also allowed for free agency after ten years' service in the league. While the standard contract contained the ten-day clause, the clubs often did not include it, particularly in high-profile multiyear deals.

Despite this apparent advantage, the Federals needed a new, game-changing tactic to regain the initiative in the pursuit of players. Gilmore and his attorneys, Edward Gates and Keene Addington, were convinced that such an opportunity existed, particularly in light of recent anti-trust legislation. The new, strengthened anti-trust statutes followed from President Woodrow Wilson pushing his anti-trust reform agenda through Congress. After a decade or so of applying the Sherman Act, many reform-minded politicians recognized that a more detailed law would make the application of anti-trust statutes more fair and efficient. The result of Wilson's efforts was the Clayton Antitrust Act, passed by Congress and signed by the president in October 1914. The new law more specifically defined monopolistic practices and the control of markets by illegal combinations. Gates and Addington believed that with the recent enhancement of anti-trust law, they stood a good chance of persuading a court to rule once and for all that Organized Baseball acted as an illegal monopoly. Gilmore and the owners thus resolved to force a showdown with Organized Baseball in federal court.

Having decided on the anti-trust route, the Federals wanted a sympathetic judge, one who might not fully recognize the far-reaching impact of their re-quested remedies, or who hated monopolies enough not to care, or who would implement just enough of the law to give the Federals a better chance at survival. They identified their man in Chicago federal judge Kenesaw Mountain Landis, mainly based on his reputation as a "trust buster" who disliked big business and saw himself as the defender of the "little man." In one of his earlier anti-trust decisions, Landis had fined Standard Oil $29,240,000, the largest fine in Ameri-can history, though it was later overturned on appeal. The Federals also planned to introduce the testimony of some of Landis's beloved Cubs from their World Championship years, such as Joe Tinker and Mordecai Brown, highlighting vari-ous unfair actions perpetrated on them by Organized Baseball.[1]

Landis, however, was also vain, prone to displaying whim and personal bias, and a huge baseball fan, and thus, on the question to be presented, unpredict-able. The Federals clearly did not understand the judge's love for the game and did not recognize that it might translate into deference toward its existing structure. The Major Leagues, on the other hand, had some inkling of Landis's sympathies. On January 5, the same day the Federal League filed its suit, Herr-mann sent Washington manager Clark Griffith a letter inquiring about the ac-curacy of a story he had heard: that Landis had written to Walter Johnson at the time he jumped his contract, telling him that he was making a serious mistake. Team president Ben Minor replied that he did not know the specifics of any let-ter, but if Landis did write to Johnson, it would have been along friendly lines. "If this letter was written to Walter I can no doubt get possession of it," Griffith told Herrmann, "but I think it would be a big mistake to let it become publicly known that such a letter was written. I feel as though our interests are safe in Judge Landis's hands." Several days later Minor, probably after verifying the ex-istence of such correspondence, wrote to Herrmann, "With respect to the Walter

Judge Kenesaw Mountain Landis was the presiding judge over the Federal League's antitrust challenge and later commissioner of baseball. (Courtesy of the Library of Congress)

Johnson matter referred to in my letter, I would suggest in confidence that you speak to Mr. Bruce [the National Commission secretary] about it."[2]

In their complaint, Edward Gates and Keene Addington poured out all of their pent-up grievances. In federal court in Chicago on January 5, 1915, they charged Organized Baseball with numerous violations of law and demanded drastic remedies. For technical jurisdictional reasons, the sole complainant in the case was the Federal League, not the individual teams. The league charged that the National Agreement (essentially Organized Baseball's governing rules and regulations, and overseen by the National Commission), the American

League, the National League, and the National Association (the organizing body of the Minor Leagues) violated anti-trust laws because the resultant monopoly was a conspiracy against the public and against players subject to its terms and those wishing to enter professional baseball outside of Organized Baseball. The suit maintained that because baseball was interstate commerce, it was therefore subject to the United States anti-trust laws: "they are engaged in the buying, selling, exchanging, bartering, and dealing in players, and in converting players by means of the instrumentalities of commerce between and among the states."[3]

The complaint also charged that Organized Baseball had entered into a conspiracy to destroy the Federal League. The defendants unfairly broadcast that the Federal League was financially weak; threatened players who went to the new league with blacklisting; and maligned players in the new league as contract jumpers and outlaws. As evidence the Federal League lawyers cited the unlawful interference by Organized Baseball and related individuals in the cases of Chief Johnson, Hal Chase, Armando Marsans, William Fischer, Ed Konetchy, Ray Caldwell, Pol Perritt, Ivey Wingo, Pat O'Connor, Martin Berghammer, Hugh Bedient, Jimmy Austin, Frank Allen, Chief Bender, Eddie Plank, Rube Marquard, and Walter Johnson.

For remedies, the lawyers asked for pretty much everything, probably in the hope that they would be given something. They demanded that "the National Agreement and the rules and regulations of the National Commission [be] declared void; to have the defendants found to be a monopoly in violation of the antitrust law; to enjoin the defendants from attempting to destroy the business of the Federal League; from claiming that its constituent members were financially irresponsible; from blacklisting its players and calling them 'contract jumpers and outlaws'; to have all the contracts of the National and American Leagues declared void; to require the defendants to dismiss the suits against George W. Johnson, Harold H. Chase, Armando Marsans and Lee Magee; to enjoin the bringing of suits against the other players named above; [and] to have the amount of damages sustained by the Federal League determined and have a judgment for that amount."[4] Clearly, though many of these requested remedies were reasonable and just, together they would have thrown the existing baseball order into chaos, at least for the short term. Gates and his legal team specifically sought a preliminary injunction for their demands, which they expected would be followed up with a final ruling.

Organized Baseball again turned to George Wharton Pepper, hero of the Killefer case, for their defense. Pepper's response defended the substance of Organized Baseball's practices, but this was clearly a difficult argument to sustain. His main line of defense was that the anti-trust laws did not apply to baseball for two reasons: (1) baseball players were not engaged in commerce, and (2) baseball itself was not "interstate" commerce. Under the commerce clause of the Constitution, Congress was specifically granted the right to regulate interstate commerce. At the time, however, the courts often used a narrow interpretation of interstate commerce and exempted from congressional legislation commerce that was not self-evidently "among the several States." If baseball did not fall under the anti-trust laws, its actions were not subject to the laws' statutory restrictions.

The trial of *The Federal League of Professional Baseball Clubs v. The National League, the American League, et al.* opened on January 20, 1915, to a packed courtroom in Chicago. More than six hundred people jammed into a space designed for no more than two hundred, with another thousand turned away at the door. Many observers stayed in their seats over lunch to make sure they didn't lose their place. The court employed ten bailiffs to maintain order. Amid this spectacle, Landis was in his element.[5]

During four days of testimony, Landis made it clear that he viewed baseball as a game, not commerce.

"[Baseball] is not a commercial enterprise, it is not trade," Pepper argued at one point, "and if the contract for the players services is not a commercial contract, the exploitation of the contract cannot possibly be."

"I have such an impression, as the result of thirty years' observation," Landis replied. "I might as well be frank with you gentlemen about this. As the result of thirty years' observation of that thing that goes on out there [the game on the field], I am somewhat shocked to hear you call it labor. I do not say you are not right, speaking of the Clayton Law—"

"Certainly. I understand," Pepper agreed.

"I have not associated that thing that I have been looking at all this time as a thing that comes within the four corners of the words used by Congress in defining what should be considered an article of commerce," Landis added.

To conclude this portion of his argument, Pepper said, "So I leave with you, sir, the contention that we are not engaged in commerce or trade at all, even if you should be of the opinion that our service is not labor service; and that even if we are engaged in trade or commerce, we are not engaged in interstate commerce, but are engaged in matters of purely local concern."

Landis opened the final day of testimony by asking the Federal League's attorneys specifically what they wanted him to do: "Let me ask you before you go any further, just what you have in mind, if you get a restraining order in this case, that the provisions of that order should be? What do you think the court should now restrain on this preliminary hearing?"

"I understand that the bill of complaint in this case states in general terms all the relief that the pleader thinks he might be entitled to," Gates responded, "and also those things which are shown to be an emergency in the bill, and asking for a temporary injunction. What we are asking here is a temporary injunction restraining these defendants from harassing the plaintiff and its constituent members, and from tampering with, inducing or seeking to induce the players mentioned in the bill of complaint; and from instituting proceedings in diverse and various jurisdictions so close to the opening of the season that the plaintiff will be irreparably damaged before justice can be consummated, and preventing the plaintiff from being compelled to defend a multiplicity of suits. We are not asking that the defendants be stopped at this time from operating in the usual course of business."

"Of course," Landis rejoined, "I realize that on this application you gentlemen probably did not expect, if you obtained a restraining order, that the order would go to the length of your prayer [i.e., give the Federals everything they asked for]."

"No, sir, certainly not," Gates admitted.

"Now, I want to know just what you have in mind definitely; I want to know what it is."

"I think that it is embraced, practically, in the statement that I have just made," Gates responded.

Landis and the attorneys next engaged in a short discussion regarding Landis's jurisdiction. The judge was certainly willing to be convinced: "The court would not be displeased to see his jurisdiction clearly established, because this is a mighty attractive controversy that you gentlemen have brought in here; but I must see my jurisdiction very clearly established."

Late in the day, Landis expounded on his regard for the national pastime: "I think you gentlemen here all understand that a blow at this thing called baseball—both sides understand this perfectly—will be regarded by this court as a blow at a national institution. Therefore you need not spend any time on that phase of this subject."

Gates concluded his testimony by reiterating what the Federal League wanted from Landis immediately: (1) "restraining by suit or otherwise interference with the players specifically mentioned in our bill of complaint"; (2) "ordering the dismissal of all pending actions against players of the plaintiff and its constituent members"; and (3) "restraining the continuance of the various utterances charged in the bill as having been made against plaintiff and its constituent members or any of them." Gates also repeated his assertion that baseball was "as much within the Sherman Act and the Clayton Bill, as the control of commerce is by the Constitution of the United States given to Congress."

As the testimony concluded and the lawyers asked if there was anything further they could provide, Landis showed he had a sense of humor: "I will attempt to struggle along tomorrow without any legal authorities."[6]

At the conclusion of the trial, the outcome remained in doubt for both sides. The case was not as sure a thing as Organized Baseball had hoped. Landis obviously revered baseball as an institution and agreed that the activities of a baseball player were not commerce. But he also often sided with the underdog, in this case the players, and did not feel restrained by a narrow reading of the Constitution's commerce clause. The judge seemed torn on how to rule: he wished to eliminate some of the more egregious actions of Organized Baseball, but he feared dismantling its organizational structure if he ruled for the Federals.

The potential impact of a ruling in favor of the Federals led to all sorts of speculation by baseball executives. On a Saturday afternoon at the end of January, John Montgomery Ward found himself at the Hotel Imperial in New York with two executives from Organized Baseball and several reporters. Ward, who had recently left the Brookfeds to return to his law practice, remained a staunch defender of the Federal League. When challenged about the new league, he argued strongly in its defense, even going so far as to insist that another Major League could be on the horizon:

> The promoters of independent baseball are prepared to launch another circuit of major pretension and within the next season or two you will find the Federal champion pitted against this new rival in World's Series competition. I do not mean necessarily that the men who invested in James A. Gilmore's enterprise will back a fourth circuit, but they have influence and friends of means ready to furnish the wherewithal at a word's notice. There is no doubt in my mind that there is plenty of room for a fourth major league. . . . The success of the National and American Leagues following their war proved conclusively that continuous baseball [two teams in one city] has been a blessing to every city which attempted it. Enough cities of major league caliber are still open to continuous promotion to assure the success of a fourth major league.

As to the source of the talent, Ward maintained that "the country is swarming with good players. This was proved to my satisfaction by the Federal League last year."[7]

Like many of the owners, Ban Johnson began considering how to counter the Federals' suit, both legally and politically, and the overall impact of the anti-trust statutes. For a couple of reasons, Johnson did not think Herrmann was up to the task. For one thing, he began to suspect Herrmann's judgment. "I have a copy of the letter you sent [players union leader] Mr. Fultz," Johnson admonished Herrmann. "For many reasons I do not think it advisable to secure any support from that quarter. I thought you had been advised on this point."[8] Johnson also believed that as the sport matured Herrmann lacked the necessary gravitas, and that baseball needed a "prominent sportsman not connected with the business of baseball, preferably a lawyer" to head the National Commission.[9]

Pat Powers, a longtime Minor League baseball executive who was considering throwing in with the Federals, wrote to Herrmann in late January, sending along an article written by Fred Lieb in the *New York Press*. "The enclosed from the NY Press speaks for itself and I think there is something in it. The minors will lose their friend if you are deposed because you have always been willing to give and take. Johnson, on the other hand, has always wanted to take but never ready to give. Had you been supported two months ago in your efforts when there was a chance to get the Federals in line there would be peace in baseball today but Johnson got on his high horse and shouted with all his might—'Garry Herrmann is acting as an individual and not in behalf of the National Commission.'"[10] Lieb wrote that Johnson wanted a National Commission chairman not in any way connected with baseball but one who understood the game. Lieb agreed the Commission needed a stronger man and should add union leader Fultz to the Commission as well. He further speculated that Johnson fancied John Bruce, treasurer of the Commission and a minority owner of the St. Louis Browns, for the post.

From Powers's follow-up it was evident that Herrmann had weathered Johnson's displeasure, at least temporarily:

> Glad there is no truth to the report of your being deposed from the National Baseball Commission because with Tener and you on the Commission there is a chance of a peace settlement with the Feds. . . . Johnson will stick to you because he cannot help himself but those that sat at the table in the Grill Room of the Hotel Sinton that night last January and heard him wagging at you (Garry, you must give up the Presidency of the Cincinnati club or withdraw from the Commission) must doubt his sincerity now. With Tener supporting you in a diplomatic manner there may be a chance for peace [in] another year but with Johnson belittling the Feds there is no chance.[11]

In the immediate aftermath of the anti-trust trial, the Federals did manage to land two more Major Leaguers. Tinker signed outfielder Les Mann to a two-year contract for the Whales, and the Brookfeds signed pitcher Ed Reulbach, one of the National League's best several years earlier with the Cubs. By 1914 Reulbach was toiling for Brooklyn and clearly past his prime. He had been one of the leading organizers of the Players Fraternity and had advised Dodgers players how to maximize their salary leverage with owner Charles Ebbets. Ebbets finally tired of Reulbach's activism and waived him on November 21, and when no one claimed him, Reulbach was released on January 27. Fultz rebuked Brooklyn for this delay: "Reulbach was not notified that waivers had been asked or of the club's intention until January 27 of this year, three days before the club, by the rules of Organized Baseball, would have to either send him a contract or give him his release. On this day he was released unconditionally after all clubs had practically completed their rosters for the coming season." Now that he was a free agent, the Federals quickly snapped him up.[12]

Star outfielder Bennie Kauff, known as the Ty Cobb of the Federal League, hoped to jump to the New York Giants for a big payday. (Courtesy of the Michael Mumby Collection)

Any excitement over landing Reulbach and Mann, however, was short lived. When Jimmy Austin and Rip Hagerman returned to Organized Baseball in February, the Federals could do little more than hope that Judge Landis would come to their rescue. "The Federal League has a war fund of $100,000," Weeghman explained. "It was to be used only for emergencies but the emergency seems to be upon us. . . . I am going to Indianapolis at once to consult with our attorneys to see what if any steps can be taken . . . but it is doubtful if anything can be done in advance of the decision [in the Landis anti-trust case]."[13] Of the eighteen regulars identified as new Federal Leaguers in the heady days of early December, only six would open the season with the new league.

Not only were the Federals failing to sign new Major Leaguers, they were also in danger of losing the top stars they had. The Federal League's best player in 1914 had been Benny Kauff, a fast-living, fast-talking, fancy-dressing twenty-four-year-old dynamo in his first full year of Major League baseball. Often called the Ty Cobb of the Federal League for his batting skill and speed, in 1914 Kauff had led the league in runs, hits, doubles, batting average, and stolen bases. Indianapolis had originally secured Kauff in early 1914 by signing him away from their cross-town American Association rival. Now that his monster season had helped lead the Hoosiers to the pennant, teams in Organized Baseball began taking notice.

A signee from the Minor Leagues, Kauff had accepted a salary of $4,000 from the Hoofeds. In recognition of his strong season, in August Indianapolis extended his contract for three years, but without a raise. By the end of the season Kauff recognized that he had probably signed too cheaply and consulted with several attorneys to find an out in his contract. Although none could find a loophole, Kauff believed that one serendipitously arose when he was unilaterally reassigned from Indianapolis to the Brookfeds. New Brooklyn business manager Dick Carroll, aware of Kauff's restiveness, re-signed Kauff to a new $6,000 contract during spring training. When Carroll returned north, however, Robert Ward was furious that Carroll had raised Kauff's salary, and initially refused to countersign the contract. Carroll, who had jumped the troubled Buffalo franchise to replace John Montgomery Ward in Brooklyn, was off to an inauspicious debut with his new boss.[14]

Meanwhile, New York Giants manager John McGraw had been pursuing Kauff for some time. Despite the stated ban on Federal Leaguers returning to Major League baseball, during the World Series McGraw purportedly gained permission from the National Commission to pursue Kauff. As a sop to the

Minors, however, the Commission required the Giants to compensate the India-napolis American Association club, owner of Kauff's Organized Baseball rights, with $25,000.[15]

Kauff had been pursued all winter by Jack Hendricks, manager of Indianapo-lis's American Association team, as an agent for the Giants. With some apparent confusion now surrounding his contract status, Kauff saw an opportunity to defect to baseball's most prestigious team. He negotiated a three-year deal with McGraw for $10,000 per year and a $5,000 advance. At the request of the Giants, Kauff also executed an affidavit in which he denied he was under contract with Brooklyn. McGraw immediately introduced his new star into the lineup and scheduled him to play centerfield against the Boston Braves on April 29. Braves president James Gaffney objected to Kauff's presence; as a jumper from Orga-nized Baseball, Kauff was ineligible to play until officially reinstated. Umpire Ernest Quigley, however, ordered the Braves to take the field or risk forfeiting the game to the Giants. The other umpire, Malcolm Eason, got on the telephone with league president John Tener to discuss the situation. Tener agreed that Kauff was ineligible and couldn't play for the Giants. In the meantime, however, Quigley had further complicated the situation: he had forfeited the game to the Giants by the time Eason got off the phone. When McGraw realized that Tener had ruled against him, he rounded up owner Harry Hempstead for support. While numerous fans in the area gawked at the proceedings, the two confronted Gaffney. "Gaffney, you're the man responsible for forfeiting of the game," Mc-Graw yelled. "You're the one objecting to my playing Kauff. That's a fine way for you to repay the favors I have done for you. I'll get even. You can't make a fool of me and get away with it."[16] Gaffney pointed out the obvious: he did not wish to jeopardize the eligibility of any of his players by having them play with a blacklisted player, and he would not allow his team to play without the blessing of the league president.

The confused umpires ordered the game to begin without Kauff, though Mc-Graw insisted that it was now simply an exhibition and that the forfeit should stand. The Braves won 13–8, and at the end no one really knew who, if anyone, would get credit for a victory. The next day the National Commission met to resolve the situation. They ruled as expected: Boston won the game, and Kauff, as a contract jumper, could not apply for reinstatement until three years after the date of his defection. The Commission, though, sidestepped the full implications of this decision by ruling that since Kauff was under contract with the Federals, he was not eligible in any case. It turned out that Ward had eventually coun-tersigned the contract negotiated between Kauff and Carroll, so that Kauff was not, in fact, a free agent. Had Kauff truly been a free agent, Organized Baseball would have found itself on flimsy moral and legal grounds in voiding his Giants contract and denying reinstatement. The National Commission was highly strategic in its approach to defecting players. It managed over the course of the battle with the Federals to avoid a situation in which a free agent player (one held to his Federal League club only by the reserve clause) demanded to return to Organized Baseball.

When Robert Ward first heard that the Giants had signed Kauff, he was furious. One of baseball's more upstanding men, Ward scrupulously followed what he felt were the dictates of fair play. Players under valid contracts were off limits. Before he realized that the Giants were misled, he planned a full-scale counterattack, regardless of the cost. "If Kauff had played with the Giants that afternoon, eight Giants would have jumped into automobiles I had waiting outside the Polo Grounds and would now be with the Brooklyn Tip-Tops," business manager Dick Carroll claimed. "I went to the grounds armed with the contract Kauff had signed. The eight players who were about to jump to Brooklyn saw the contract. They concluded if that contract was not binding, no contract was."[17] Of course, one must view these boasts of possible defections with some skepticism. If it was so easy to attract players, the Federals would have been more successful over the winter. Nevertheless, with Ward's money and the lack of binding contracts, Ward and Carroll might have made a significant impact on the Giants.

An embittered Kauff dejectedly returned to the Tip-Tops. "It seems R. B. Ward had signed my contract submitted to him and calling for $6,000," Kauff defended himself, "although I had no knowledge that he had signed it."[18] Kauff also believed the Giants owed him the promised $5,000 advance. To enforce payment, Kauff hired as his attorney former Brooklyn business manager John Montgomery Ward, now back in private practice but still a thorn to Organized Baseball. Ward and Kauff sued the Giants for the money, which Kauff claimed solely depended on his execution of the Giants contract.

Holding on to Kauff was crucial, but the Federals needed to do more than simply defend the status quo. Regardless of Landis's ruling in the anti-trust case, Gilmore recognized that the Federals needed to strengthen their ownership ranks. Robert Ward and the league were bankrolling Kansas City and Indianapolis, Buffalo was struggling, and even Weeghman, despite league-leading attendance, was stressed. Several Major League teams were also feeling the pinch. To bolster their financial staying power, both sides hoped to add wealthy industrialists looking to get into baseball. Over the winter the antagonists battled not only for players but also for moneyed investors.

12

Owner Reinforcements

As the leagues battled for players over the winter of 1914–1915, Ban Johnson and Jim Gilmore both understood the importance of shoring up their league's weakest franchises, and both wanted the same man for New York: Jacob Ruppert. One of New York's most eligible bachelors, Ruppert ran his family's brewery operation and had accumulated a substantial fortune. Well dressed and at home in upper-class society, Ruppert occasionally lapsed into a German accent when agitated, despite his native birth. He also dabbled in exotic hobbies: he collected jade, Chinese porcelain, and oil paintings; for a time he kept a collection of small monkeys; and he raised St. Bernards. Like many of the upper class at the turn of the last century, he also raised and raced horses.

Popular, wealthy, and well connected to the German American community, Ruppert was a natural for politics. Late in the 1880s Tammany Hall tapped him to run for city council president, but they withdrew his candidacy due to various political machinations and miscalculations. The Democratic organization later sponsored him to run for U.S. Congress in 1898 in a generally Republican district. Ruppert won in a mild upset and served four terms. After eight years in Congress, he concentrated most of his energies, aside from his hobbies, on the brewery business. Ruppert had loved baseball since his youth. In 1914 he began talking to people in and around the game, inquiring about buying in. Both Gilmore and Ban Johnson remained in close touch with Ruppert, hoping to entice him into their leagues.

Johnson's mortal enemy, New York Giants manager John McGraw, may have inadvertently helped Johnson in his quest. McGraw was a close friend of

Tillinghast L'Hommedieu Huston, another wealthy investor looking to buy into baseball. An engineer by training, Huston had remained in Cuba after fighting in the Spanish-American War, and started an engineering and construction company. By 1914 he was a rich man, near the level of most baseball owners but well below Ruppert's fortune. Huston reportedly secured an option to purchase the Chicago Cubs for $600,000 in 1914 and planned to bring along his pal McGraw as manager and part-owner. McGraw initially expressed an interest but soon claimed he was tied to New York by his multiyear contract. In reality, he probably did not wish to leave New York and simply wanted an excuse so as not to embarrass his friend. Without McGraw on board, Huston allowed the option to lapse.

Ruppert and Huston did not know each other, but the baseball ownership fraternity was small, and once they met—probably through McGraw—the two agreed to join forces for the right opportunity. It was likely that McGraw first suggested that the New York Yankees might be available, and the two reluctantly agreed to look into what was generally regarded as one of baseball's most hapless teams. In Johnson's eyes, the Yankees were the perfect franchise for the duo. Ruppert was a well-connected New Yorker without too much Tammany baggage, and Frank Farrell and William Devery, always of suspect character, were out of money. As an inducement, Johnson convinced the American League's owners to make some decent players available to the Yankees if Ruppert and Huston were to gain control of the club.

Farrell, though, didn't really want to sell the Yankees. He liked all the perks that came with owning a Major League baseball team in New York. He dragged out the sale by lingering over minor contractual matters in the hope that something might change. What's more, the team's books were a mess, and Ruppert and Huston were more than a little leery about what they were getting into.

In late 1914, while Ruppert was reconsidering, Gilmore and Weeghman traveled to French Lick, Indiana, the resort community where Ruppert spent a portion of the winter. They hoped to tempt him into purchasing the Indianapolis franchise in the Federal League, which he would move to New York or its environs.

Once Ban Johnson realized how close the Federals were to landing Ruppert, he snapped back into action. Moreover, Farrell's partner, William Devery, who generally liked to stay behind the scenes, was ready to cash out. On Saturday, January 30, as negotiations remained stalled, Johnson had finally had enough of Farrell's procrastination. He put Farrell and Devery in one conference room, Ruppert and Huston in another, and trusted the lawyers to hammer out the final document. In the end the new owners closed on the team for roughly $460,000 and assumed $20,000 in debt.[1]

Gilmore could offer only sour grapes:

> Ban Johnson is the stumbling block in the way of peace. One word from him and the war would be over. National League magnates are hungering for a settlement, and American League club owners are also desirous of settling the fight; but Johnson has the Americans hypnotized and the Nationals are afraid of Big Ban.
>
> Col. Jake Ruppert is hooked to an awful lemon in New York. They've saddled a two-year Polo Ground lease on him, calling for a total cash outlay of $80,000. Col. Jake will have to sell a lot of beer to pay the freight.
>
> There never would have been a Federal League if we hadn't the best legal advice obtainable that the reserve rule, 10-day clause, and entire National Agreement were absolutely and unqualifiedly illegal.
>
> We'll be in New York—the Bronx—next year. That's where I wanted to locate Col. Jake Ruppert. . . . Kansas City has re-established its finances and will go to bat stronger than ever. We don't want [Ray] Caldwell back. He can stay with the Yanks. [Ivey] Wingo and [Walter] Johnson signed perfectly legal contracts. We'll get 'em back, or make 'em pay big damages.[2]

After several years pursuing other interests, Pat Powers longed to get back into baseball. Powers had been elected president of the Eastern League (the predecessor of the International) in 1893. In 1901 he added the presidency of the National Association, becoming the first leader of this revamped governing body of the Minor Leagues. After eighteen years of overseeing the Eastern League, many owners began to tire of his leadership; also, Powers had developed several outside interests that some owners feared blurred his focus. That December, during a contentious league meeting, Powers ignominiously lost his job as the Eastern League owners elected Ed Barrow by a five-to-three vote. The outcome infuriated Powers. He later sent Barrow a rambling, scathing letter, accusing him of running an underhanded campaign and, once in office, of bullying players and umpires.

While president of the Eastern League, Powers had befriended oilman Harry Sinclair and had tried to interest him in his various business ventures. Now out of baseball, Powers hoped to convince Sinclair to back him financially as he sought to acquire a Major League franchise. Powers could not have chosen better. Wealthier and younger than nearly all the other owners, Sinclair possessed the energy and wealth to fund a franchise. The son of a pharmacist, he had inherited the business as a twenty-one-year-old and earned a pharmacy degree from

Oil magnate Harry Sinclair bought into the Federal League in early 1915 and moved the Indianapolis franchise to Newark. Sinclair provided fresh capital to the Federal League when it was desperately needed. (Courtesy of the Library of Congress)

the University of Kansas. But Sinclair had little interest in life as a small-town druggist. He soon lost most of his money starting several other small enterprises before hitting on the oil business. Using money secured from investors and speculators, he organized many small companies to drill for oil. Relatively unremarkable physically but for "piercing blue eyes" and a "decisiveness of voice," Sinclair proved highly adept in his latest chosen field and became a multimillionaire with surprising speed. By 1907 he was the richest man in Kansas, and when Powers came calling four years later, Sinclair, now the namesake for Sinclair Oil, ran sixty-two oil companies and owned eight drilling rigs. "He was shrewd but hearty, tough but genial, a masterful trader, a hard-driving sportsman," recalled one colleague.[3]

Only thirty-seven when the Federal League first challenged Organized Baseball, Sinclair brought his strong, youthful personality to the fight. Another colleague remarked on his shrewdness and generosity: "Fearless to the point of recklessness, devoted to his friends, generous, lavish, but in all his daring speculations shrewd."[4] One of Sinclair's associates probably best summed up Sinclair's potential impact: "I don't know whether he will make or lose money, but before

Harry Sinclair is through he will write baseball history." One possibly apocryphal remark credited to Sinclair when he threw in with the Federals had him bragging that "he would like to have Colonel Ruppert and the other magnates of the two big leagues on a boat on the ocean and that he would throw overboard two dollars for every one thrown over by the other sixteen."[5]

In late 1913 Powers had worked to convince Sinclair to purchase the St. Louis Cardinals, rumored to be on the block, from Helene Britton. Her fellow National League owners wanted to get rid of the woman owner in their midst, and the team was struggling at the gate; but Britton remained ambivalent about selling. Sinclair also remained cautious, chiefly because he rightfully feared the Federal League adding a third "Major League" team in St. Louis. To convince Sinclair otherwise, Powers enlisted Pittsburgh owner Barney Dreyfuss to denigrate the Federal League's likelihood of success. In the end, however, Sinclair chose not to pursue the matter, and Powers was left to suffer another season outside the inner circle of baseball.[6]

Sinclair spent 1914 considering his baseball options. Wealthier than any owner in baseball (with the possible exception of Detroit's passive co-owner William Yawkey), he was courted by all sides looking to get new money into their league. Sinclair reportedly had an opportunity to buy one of the St. Louis or Philadelphia franchises but remained concerned about their long-term value in the face of the Federal League. He also became friendly with Sloufeds owner Phil Ball, a fellow Midwestern self-made millionaire. Ball helped convince Sinclair that the Federal League was a viable option, and for a man who welcomed new challenges, Sinclair found the Federal League an intriguing possibility.

Powers, Sinclair's front man for baseball, had no love lost for Organized Baseball. He still resented the International League owners for voting him out of its presidency several years earlier. For a few years Powers had operated the Motordome in Newark, sponsoring bicycle races without the sanction of the National Cycling Association, cycling's governing body. After competing for some time, Powers merged his operation into the senior organization and left the business.[7] In other words, Powers had a wealthy patron, latent hostility toward Organized Baseball in general and the International League in particular, and experience competing with an existing institution.

Gilmore naturally pounced on Powers and Sinclair, and throughout January 1914 the Federal owners negotiated with the duo on the terms of their entry into the league. Powers wanted to locate a team in Newark, in his home state of New Jersey and in direct competition with the International League franchise located there. Newark also had the advantage of being part of the New

York metropolitan area and permitted Sunday baseball. At the time Sunday baseball games drew the largest crowds, but several states and cities, including New York City, had Blue Laws prohibiting baseball on the Christian Sabbath. Sunday baseball in Newark, it was hoped, would draw huge crowds.

There was just one problem: No current Federal League franchise wanted to be shifted to Newark. The four teams competing with Major League teams were owned by wealthy sportsmen, and none was yet willing to surrender his franchise for little or no compensation. The teams in the four markets competing with Double-A Minor League teams were owned semi-publicly by a large number of local investors. These professionals and businessmen bought into the teams out of civic pride and ego—getting a Major League franchise for their city of which they would be a part-owner—and promises of a healthy return. The solicitations for investment had highlighted how much money men such as Charles Comiskey and John Brush had made through the ownership of their clubs. Many still believed this return awaited them.

On February 4 Charlie Weeghman, William Walker, Phil Ball, Gilmore, and Kansas City manager George Stovall met secretly with Powers. Although the Federals had not yet publicized it, back in the fall the league had notified Kansas City team president Charles Madison that his franchise was forfeited to the league. In early September the league had lent Kansas City $5,000 to meet payroll and demanded they raise $20,000 to cover expenses over the remainder of the season. When the Kawfeds failed to find the additional funds, the league—Ward in particular—covered this amount as well. At a Federal League meeting on October 23, the board of directors declared the Kansas City franchise technically forfeit to the league. According to one Federal League insider, the franchise would be moved to Cleveland.[8]

Gilmore, however, had told Madison that if the stockholders raised $100,000 the franchise could be reinstated in Kansas City. There was also concern over whether the league had strictly followed its defined procedures for stripping a city of its franchise. In any case, the league had continued to act as if Kansas City would be in the league in 1915, including having the team be a party to the anti-trust lawsuit. Now that a wealthy suitor had appeared, it seemed an opportune time to reclaim the Kansas City franchise. Accordingly, the Federal League representatives agreed to sell the franchise to Powers and Sinclair. Kansas City manager George Stovall, a loyal Federal League soldier, agreed to act on behalf of the new owners rather than the existing Kansas City ownership that still believed it had a team. Shortly after this meeting, Gilmore announced that the league had sold the Kansas City franchise to Powers and Sinclair, who were moving it to Newark for the 1915 season. Sinclair paid $25,000 for the franchise rights, and Powers immediately began working with Stovall to fashion his ballclub and determine a site for its ballpark.[9]

Gilmore could not restrain his enthusiasm. He publicly boasted that with Sinclair on board and the shifting of the Kansas City franchise to the New York area, his Federal League was here to stay and his owners were at least as wealthy as those in Organized Baseball:

New York: Harry Sinclair, "reported wealth $10,000,000."

St. Louis: Phil Ball, "estimated wealth $2,000,000."

Brooklyn: Ward Brothers, "reputed wealth $6,000,000."

Chicago: Charles Weeghman, "reputed wealth, $1,000,000."

Pittsburgh: Ed Gwinner, "said to be worth over $1,000,000."

Baltimore: "Federal stock is widely distributed, but the holders include the Mayor and many businessmen. The opposition was driven to take its franchise out of the city."

Buffalo: "Have no millionaires back of them, but they seem to have plenty of money."

Indianapolis: "not weak financially, but has no heavy-hitter in the capitalistic league to support it."[10]

Ban Johnson wasn't buying it. "We feel sure that a year from now there will be no such thing as a Federal League. There has been no demand for a third Major League, as the receipts of the Federal League have proved to us. About all they have increased is a general increase in salaries."[11]

On February 9 Gilmore officially notified Madison that the team had been sold out from under him. But he held out the possibility that Indianapolis, another franchise that had piled up debts to the league, might be substituted. Kansas City's board did not trust Gilmore and had no intention of surrendering its franchise. The club's directors had spent much of the off-season trying to raise additional funds, with plenty of hope but indifferent results. On February 16 one of the team's stockholders phoned Gilmore to grill him on what was happening.

"All I can say to you," Gilmore responded, "is that I feel sure that everything will be all right, and Kansas City will retain its franchise. In fact, it is a hundred to one shot."

"What is the one shot?"

After receiving assurance he was speaking in confidence, Gilmore added the one wrinkle: "I have an option on the Indianapolis Federal League franchise, and am now going to New York and Pinehurst, North Carolina, and will do my best to have the men who want to take the Kansas City franchise take the Indianapolis franchise instead, and I have no doubt that will be accomplished." Gilmore told the director to keep at the money raising and added, "In the meantime if I am interviewed by reporters, I must of necessity deny anything but that the club has been transferred to an Eastern City."[12]

Despite Gilmore's reassurance that they would likely keep their franchise, the Kansas City directors recognized that he was actually stalling them in the hope of making the transfer a fait accompli before they could react. Led by D. J. Haff, a delegation from Kansas City descended upon Gilmore in Chicago on February 25. Their goal was to settle up. When they demanded an accounting of how much they owed, Gilmore produced a paper showing $38,518. Haff disputed this amount, arguing that some expenses were not the responsibility of the team, and pointing out that it was not offset by money owed to the team by the league. Gilmore told them it didn't matter: "he would not accept the money if it was laid on the table."[13]

Haff was prepared for this rejection. The delegation hastened over to the U.S. Circuit Court, where they surprised Gilmore by asking for and receiving a temporary injunction against the transfer of the franchise to Newark. Not surprisingly, this threw the Federal club into chaos. Powers and Sinclair had already purchased a site in Harrison, New Jersey, a suburb across the Passaic River from Newark, and needed to begin construction immediately on a twenty-thousand-seat stadium if it was to be ready by Opening Day. Powers had also made arrangements for the team to report to spring training in Texas in less than two weeks, on March 8. Confusing matters further, Madison's regime had recently sent star southpaw hurler Nick Cullop to Brooklyn for three ballplayers of limited ability, including former manager Bill Bradley. This unequal trade was made as partial payment for the Wards' financial support of Kansas City. Powers and Sinclair, in the process of spending a couple of hundred thousand dollars to put together a team and ballpark in Newark, strenuously objected to this so-called trade.

The judge set the hearing to determine the permanent disposition of the Kansas City franchise for March 8. Meanwhile, Gilmore and Sinclair moved ahead as if the transfer would be sanctioned by the court. Stovall took the team south for spring training, stadium construction proceeded, and, in the interest of league harmony, Ward returned Cullop to KC/Newark at the request of Powers who demanded his star pitcher back. Gilmore also considered that the Federals could lose the case, and kept in his back pocket the idea of substituting Indianapolis as a backup plan.

On March 10 the judge intimated that he would side with Kansas City, and at the request of the parties he granted a continuance to allow them to negotiate a solution. Haff's group proposed that Sinclair and Powers keep the team but leave it in Kansas City. This was a nonstarter; both men wanted to be in the New York metropolitan area. Gilmore suggested paying off the Kansas City investors, but they wanted a Major League team, and in any case Sinclair was not about to pay much more for one of the league's weakest teams. The league and Haff returned to court several days later to affirm that the team could remain in Kansas City. Haff's group also agreed to raise $40,000 to repay the league its cash advances, and with the enthusiasm generated by the court victory, the directors indeed raised $60,000. Accepting the agreement, the judge concurred with the outcome: "I have had difficulty from the beginning in basing the right of forfeiture of the franchise on anything that has been introduced in evidence. It seems to me that the president of the league went beyond his legal rights."[14]

Stalemated on Kansas City, Gilmore, Sinclair, and Powers now turned their attention to Indianapolis, another club in financial difficulty. To secure the franchise, on March 19 the league's executive committee of Gilmore, Ward, and Robertson traveled to Indianapolis to meet with the Hoofeds board of directors. Gilmore claimed that the team was effectively bankrupt and forfeit to the league. Of course, Indianapolis's officers had just seen the results of the Kansas City suit and refused to be bullied into surrendering their franchise.[15]

Despite the brave front, the Indianapolis board knew that they were, in fact, bankrupt and had little hope of financing the 1915 season. To capitalize themselves for the 1914 season the team had raised $50,000 in preferred stock from 394 investors at a 6 percent dividend. The club quickly burned through these funds and could not pay the dividend. The constant clamor from these small and mid-sized investors for their money was a disquieting annoyance to the Indianapolis directors. The team owed roughly $102,000 with little hope of repayment, much less being able to subsidize operations for the coming year.

Some of the debt was owed to the league, which had covered operating costs over the second half of the 1914 season, including $10,000 from the Wards. But this money had come with strings attached: the Wards and others wanted some of Indianapolis's best players. Down the stretch, as the Hoofeds demonstrated a chance to win the pennant, the team quite naturally did not wish to surrender any players. In retaliation, the other owners refused additional financial support, forcing the team's directors to reach into their own pockets to the tune of $26,000. The Indianapolis directors hoped to raise money during the winter but with little expectation of success. Team president Ed Krause spent much of the winter in Florida, leaving the mostly futile fund-raising effort to general manager W. H. Watkins.

After the initial rejection, both sides continued negotiations. Gilmore and Sinclair were pregnant with a stadium in Newark, and the Indianapolis board needed to get out from under its debt. Finally Sinclair agreed to pay $81,000 for the Indianapolis franchise: $76,500 to cover outstanding debts, including the $50,000 in preferred stock and most of the funds lent by the league, and $4,500 for the next year's rent on the ballpark site. None of the funds went to pay back the $26,000 lent by the directors. On March 23 some two hundred stockholders met at the Indianapolis chamber of commerce and unanimously accepted the proposal. Powers and Sinclair finally had a franchise for Newark, fewer than three weeks before Opening Day. Indianapolis attorney and part-owner Edward Gates, who had spent 1914 fighting on behalf of the Federals, did not actively oppose the transfer. He bitterly resented losing Major League baseball in Indianapolis, and as the league's lead attorney he could certainly have thrown up additional roadblocks. But he recognized that the league's survival was at stake and put aside his civic pride to allow Sinclair to get the franchise.[16]

The Wards finally decided enough was enough. They had financially supported two teams, Kansas City and Indianapolis, and possibly a third, Buffalo. They had willingly surrendered Cullop back to Kansas City for the purpose of league harmony. And now the rich newcomers were getting the 1914 championship team. In anticipation of the league meeting on March 26, the Wards staked their claim for Indianapolis/Newark's Benny Kauff and Cy Falkenberg, the best hitter and pitcher respectively on the team. The players, the Wards maintained, were owed to Brooklyn in return for their financial support.

Powers and Sinclair had just paid $81,000 for a Federal League franchise and still had to pay for a ballpark, but at least they had acquired a championship ballclub. Or so they thought. Now they were at risk of losing their two best players to the New York metropolitan area's other team. At the highly contentious league meeting, two of the wealthiest owners in baseball argued for the two players. Sinclair even threatened to withdraw from the league if Brooklyn kept both. The final resolution sent Falkenberg to Newark and Kauff to Brooklyn.

Other issues also demanded attention. Because of his religious beliefs, Robert Ward would not allow his team to play on Sundays. Powers believed that a Sunday game in Newark against Brooklyn would be a huge draw and renewed the pressure on Ward to permit his team to play Sunday games on the road. In the end, Powers had little more success than the owners had had in 1914: Brooklyn would not play on Sundays. The league also needed to determine the disposition of two managers. With the shift of franchises, Kansas City's Stovall was placed in an extremely awkward position. When he took his club to spring training he thought he was working for Powers and Sinclair and that his team would play in Newark. Now he was taking the team back to Kansas City and a group of owners he had seemingly deserted. Stovall, however, had been a loyal Federal Leaguer and a ferocious recruiter for the league. Gilmore did not wish to see him dumped. There was some sentiment for firing another longtime Federal Leaguer, Indianapolis/Newark manager Bill Phillips—despite his winning two consecutive Federal League pennants—and giving the Newark job to Stovall. In the end, Stovall remained with Kansas City, a situation that pleased neither the manager nor the team, and Phillips stayed with Newark. Sinclair had reportedly offered New York Giants manager John McGraw $100,000 to manage his club. This may or may not have been true. Powers would not have wanted to surrender the operational control that McGraw would have demanded. Moreover, it's hard to see McGraw turning down the acclaim that would have come with such a gigantic contract.[17]

While Powers and Sinclair concentrated on Newark, a potential ballpark site in the Bronx was offered up by a realty company near the 177th Street subway station. The company preferred to own the franchise, however, rather than simply sell the site, and the Federals were already committed to Powers and Sinclair.[18] Other observers believed the Bronx would be a much better location than Newark. "Newark is a good Sunday town, but it is very questionable whether it is a good proposition," wrote William Granger in *Sporting Life*. "The Bronx would be an ideal place for the locating of a new club. With a population of something like 600,000 and a growing population it is far and away a better proposition than Newark."[19]

Because of his roots in New Jersey, Powers preferred Newark. Moreover, he felt that by locating the ballpark in nearby Harrison he would be able to draw from a wider area, including Jersey City. The combined population of these North Jersey cities also totaled around 600,000, and Powers felt that they constituted a huge untapped market for Major League baseball. Because Sunday baseball was not generally legal in New York City at the time, Powers also hoped to generate large Sunday crowds of New Yorkers coming over for the game. Harrison Park, by one contemporary estimate, eventually cost $300,000, though more recent scholarship puts the cost of this 21,000-seat steel-and-wood structure at "$100,000 plus."[20]

Robert Ward added another complication for the Federals. After all the money he had spent bolstering the weaker Federal League clubs, Ward believed he had been promised the rights to New York (Manhattan and the Bronx). Exactly how this would play out, given that he already had a team in Brooklyn, was problematic. Ward also preferred Manhattan rather than the Bronx for the Federal League's eventual New York team. Although Ward often supported the Federal League's cause over the narrower interests of his own team, moving into the Bronx with a franchise not owned or controlled by Ward himself would have taken more effort than Powers had time for. Sinclair, however, clearly longed for an eventual New York franchise, and a potential showdown between baseball's two richest magnates loomed.[21]

Organized Baseball was also considering the Bronx. International League president Ed Barrow proposed moving his struggling Jersey City franchise there. Barrow lobbied hard for this move and thought he had lined up the necessary support. Pittsburgh owner Barney Dreyfuss and Brooklyn owner Charles Ebbets both supported the transfer as a way to strengthen the Internationals and put up a roadblock to the Federals. New York Giants president Harry Hempstead, however, controlled the territory for the National League and rejected the request. "Experienced baseball men," the New York Times reported, "are somewhat surprised at the action of the National League in refusing the request of the International League."[22]

With the failure of Barrow to gain a foothold in the Bronx, Ward became more open to the borough. "What the Bronx wants and will get within a year is a big league club," Ward boasted. "And the Federals will be the organization that locates there." He and his fellow owners had clearly given the matter some thought and investigation. "It wouldn't do to locate a ballclub above 161st Street in the Bronx because of the lack of proper traffic facilities. A club would have to locate on the edge of the Harlem River, but I won't discuss sites now. Only say that the Feds will be here next year and as a Major League."[23]

One of the big headaches for the Federals was what to do with all the players they had signed. Because many of the contracts were guaranteed for more than one year, the Federal League clubs couldn't simply release the players. What's more, an outright release of players who had jumped to their league despite the threat of being blackballed would send a discouraging message to potential future jumpers. During 1914, therefore, Federal League in-season rosters often swelled beyond twenty-five players, the 1913 Major League baseball limit. Large rosters were not only unwieldy but also expensive.

Robert Ward pushed the obvious solution: create a relationship with a Minor League. Ward and the other owners pursued this throughout the off-season with little success. It would obviously be a hard sell; the potential rewards for a Minor League switching to the Federals would need to offset the risks of being ostracized by Organized Baseball. During spring training, Brookfeds business manager Dick Carroll met with representatives from the Single-A Southern League. He convinced four of the eight owners to throw in with the Federals but could not line up the fifth and deciding vote. When it became clear that the Federals could not partner with an existing league, Ward led the effort to organize their own Minor League.

The best opportunity presented itself in New England, served by three Minor Leagues, the class B New England League, the class B Eastern Association, and the class C Colonial League. Lower Minor Leagues at the time were notoriously unstable, and these three were particularly vulnerable. Ward successfully wooed the Colonial League and added a couple of larger cities from the class B leagues. Once the reconstituted league was in place, Robert Ward put his nephew Walter in charge, and headquartered it in Providence. The Federals now had a Minor League of their own, but unlike the organized Minors, which were independently owned and were required to cover their own costs, the Colonial League represented one more business that had to be subsidized by the wealthier owners.[24]

The central battleground, however, remained the Major League ballparks and the courts. A favorable decision from Judge Landis would reenergize the Federals, throw confusion into some of Organized Baseball's more confrontational tactics and contract clauses, and give the Federals new leverage in pursuing players. Without such a ruling, the Federals would have to continue to toil under a status quo in which the Majors were clearly winning the struggle for favorable press and star players. If Landis continued to delay his verdict, could the Federals maintain fan interest over a second season?

13

A Long Summer

The failure of the Federals to land any high-profile players over the winter—and the reneging of many they thought they had—diminished public interest as the league moved into its second season. The season openers on April 10 drew well—announced crowds of 15,000 in Brooklyn; 20,000 in Baltimore, 15,000 in Chicago, and 11,000 in Kansas City—but there seemed a less celebratory feel to the games when compared to those of 1914.[1] In a letter to Garry Herrmann, Ban Johnson summarized his reading of early-season interest in the Federals. As the most vehement of the new league's opponents, Johnson naturally took satisfaction in its struggles. But he was also a realist and in a private letter would not have sugarcoated a situation that called for more aggressive countermeasures:

> I have made no effort this spring to get a record of the exact attendance at the Federal League games. Mr. Hedges has written me from time to time relative to the situation in St. Louis, and I have quite an accurate knowledge of what the Club is doing in Chicago. The patronage at St. Louis is about on par with what it was a year ago. The North Side club has fallen far short of the showing made last spring. The conditions are so bad in Buffalo that Robinson [sic] had threatened to move the club to another city. The Baltimore papers, editorially, have called upon the fans to support the Federal League, as they hope to maintain a Major League club in that city. Ward's business in Brooklyn has amounted to nothing up to date. The patronage at Harrison, N.J. was quite satisfactory at the opening and the first two Sundays. Since then the attendance has dropped to Minor League levels.[2]

Johnson recognized that for the Federal League to call it quits, the wealthiest owners backing the league had to be convinced of its ultimate futility. He took it upon himself to befriend Phil Ball and Robert Ward, two of the key Federal League owners. And though one can be cynical about Johnson's initial motives, the friendship he formed with Ball was genuine and lasted many years.

In mid-March 1915 a mutual acquaintance arranged a secret meeting between Johnson and Ward in Chicago. Johnson wanted to convince Ward of the futility of his venture. He analyzed baseball's geography in detail, identifying all the cities, both Major and Minor, that could not support two and three clubs. Ward said little and listened politely. He respected Johnson's knowledge and likely agreed with many of Johnson's points. Neither made any specific propositions to the other, and "nothing important transpired," but it was clear that Ward was willing to listen to other options.[3]

Shortly thereafter, Johnson ran into Ball in McTeague's Restaurant in St. Louis. The press gave this meeting the gloss of an important conference, supposedly including a discussion of Ball's interest in buying the Cardinals. In fact, it was simply a "pleasant chat," with no mention of such a purchase.[4] A couple of weeks later, when Comiskey and Johnson were in St. Louis for the season opener there with the White Sox, they met with Ball for an hour to discuss the overall baseball situation. Johnson reciprocated a week later, inviting Ball to be his guest at the White Sox home opener on April 22. Johnson wanted the anti-trust lawsuit dropped, and Ball wanted Armando Marsans released from his injunction and a return of the other players the Federals had signed during the off-season. Although Johnson later denied that anything concrete had been agreed upon, actions by Federal and Organized Baseball executives over the next few days suggest otherwise.[5]

Ball and his attorney, Montague Lyon, met with Johnson again the next day. Buffalo president William Robertson and Ward also came to Chicago for a conference with Ball, Weeghman, and Gilmore to discuss possible settlement terms. According to one report, Johnson had tentatively worked out a deal whereby Ball would purchase the Cardinals, Weeghman would acquire the Cubs, and Ward would purchase the Dodgers. The remaining Federal League clubs would be merged into Organized Baseball, presumably in the high Minors. If Charles Taft refused to sell the Cubs, Johnson would reportedly amalgamate the St. Louis Browns and the Sloufeds, break the National Agreement, and force the National League into a fight. Of course, all concerned denied the specifics of any plan that reached the press. Moreover, Johnson was surely trying to maneuver Ball away from the Federals, and Ball may have been acting on his own to acquire the Cardinals. His fellow Federal League owners may have hastened to Chicago simply to figure out what was going on.[6]

Of the higher Minor Leagues, the International remained the most troubled. It had been chased out of its largest market, Baltimore, after the 1914 season, when Dunn finally moved his franchise to Richmond. The league remained under pressure from the Federals in Buffalo and Newark. During the off-season Rochester president C. T. Chapin thought the league should fold two teams, though he did not identify which two. The *Washington Post* reported, "Do not be surprised to hear that the International League has decided to suspend operations indefinitely. Unless a miracle is performed by President Edward G. Barrow, the announcement will soon be made that the league will not attempt to play a championship schedule this year. . . . It was learned from a reliable source yesterday that the International League has reached a crisis. The National Commission has been forced to refuse financial assistance to the Buffalo club."[7]

The desperate International League owners wanted out of the fight. Faced with imminent bankruptcy, their loyalty to Organized Baseball took a back seat. Four owners secretly contacted Brooklyn Federals owner Robert Ward regarding a separate peace accord. Their proposal would amalgamate the International League franchises in Brooklyn, Newark, and Baltimore (then in the process of moving to Richmond) into the Federal League teams in those cities and another into Pittsburgh. The remaining four franchises would be on their own, most likely comprising the nucleus of a re-formed International League.[8] This proposal had little interest for Ward and Gilmore. They assumed that the International League was failing and saw no reason to agree to any settlement that did not include the Major Leagues. In retrospect, it is difficult to gauge whether the International League owners would have gone through with this scheme once the full financial leverage and moral authority of Organized Baseball was brought to bear on them. It was a mistake, however, for the Federals not to take this overture more seriously. The pressure on Organized Baseball to settle on more favorable terms would have increased dramatically if they had been able to cleave the International League from Organized Baseball and bring some of its owners into their ranks.

The opening of the season confirmed the fears of the International League's owners. Many teams struggled at the gate, particularly the two in the New York metropolitan area. With five Major League teams in the area—the New York Giants and Yankees, Brooklyn Dodgers, Ward's Brooklyn Tip-Tops, and Sinclair's Newark Peppers—very few fans were interested in the Minor League Newark or Jersey City teams. Faced with a burst of Major League fever in Newark, the International League franchise left town early in the season for Harrisburg, Pennsylvania. Jersey City drew only two hundred to five hundred fans per game, and

The National Commission, the governing body of baseball, had three voting members (seated): National League president John Tener, Chairman Garry Herrmann (also president of the Cincinnati Reds), and American League president Ban Johnson. The trio was assisted by Treasurer John Bruce and Secretary A. J. (Joe) Flanner (standing). (Courtesy of the Dennis Goldstein Collection)

its owners, including ex–Yankee owner Frank Farrell, simply quit and forfeited the franchise to the league.

The initial excitement in Newark wore off quickly, and as the season moved along Newark's attendance proved extremely disappointing. Powers and Sinclair blamed the lack of transportation facilities. They wanted the trolley lines extended and a spur installed to the entrance of Harrison Park. The streetcar company, though, had little interest in paying for a spur unless it would generate ridership, a reticence that reflected a lack of confidence in the long-term viability of the team at the Harrison location. An angry Sinclair declared at a meeting with the trolley company on July 7 that unless the line were extended to the park, he would have no choice but to move the team out of Newark. The threat seemed to work. Several days later the county granted the Public Service Corporation the right to lay tracks over the Jackson Street bridge, bringing the streetcar line to within a block of the ballpark.[9]

Elsewhere, attendance lagged as well, and by midsummer it was clear to the Federals that they were in trouble. Attendance was below 1914 levels, Landis still refused to rule on the anti-trust case, and several teams were having difficulty meeting their financial obligations. Kansas City's reprieve from the courts had done nothing to clear away the concern that even a recapitalized Kawfeds club could survive the season, particularly in its Minor League ballpark. League attorney Edward Gates took it upon himself to explore the possibility of shifting the franchise to Cincinnati. In early May, when the Reds were on a road trip in St. Louis, representatives from the Federals approached several players to sound them out on the possibility of jumping to a Federal League team located in Cincinnati. The response must have given Gates some reassurance because several days later he traveled to Cincinnati to meet with Harry Spinks, owner of a ballpark across the river in Bellevue, Kentucky. Gates and a couple of representatives from Kawfeds executive Charles Madison discussed the price of securing the suburban Cincinnati site to build a new Federal League park. Surveyors evaluated the site for the construction of new stands, and a tentative plan was devised that would have the Kawfeds play their existing schedule in Kansas City until the ballpark was completed, then move to Cincinnati. When news of the meeting became public, Gilmore was forced to deny any potential move. In any event, the shift never moved past these initial conversations.[10]

Fans had also deserted the Tip-Tops. Even Charles Ebbets, the normally fretful owner of the Dodgers, was feeling sanguine. Ebbets boasted to his fellow National League owners that the Dodgers were outdrawing their cross-town competitors by roughly five to one. He listed one example of a June Saturday game, typically a high attendance day, for which the Tip-Tops took in a gate of only $651: 45 at $1.00, 319 at 75 cents, 428 at 50 cents, and 611 at 25 cents. Ebbets, always looking for an angle, concluded the letter by reminding his fellow owners that "it is our duty to do everything and anything to retain the advantage the National League now enjoys in Brooklyn . . . accordingly, if you have any players to dispose of that might strengthen us, I would be pleased to hear from you."[11]

St. Louis was also playing to mostly nonexistent crowds. On July 5 manager Fielder Jones resigned, purportedly over his frustration with shoddy umpiring and his confrontation with Gilmore over the issue. Another inside report, however, gave an additional reason. When Jones joined the club, he had demanded and received a small ownership interest. With the financial struggles of the new league, not only did his stock not pay a dividend but Jones was also subject to capital calls to meet expenses. Only after Ball assured him that he would not have to contribute more capital did Jones rescind his resignation.[12]

The Federals publicly blamed most of their attendance woes on the weather, which was terrible in the summer of 1915. Poor weather hurt attendance at all baseball games, of course, but it seemed particularly to affect the schedule of the less established Federal League. In Chicago, for example, it rained twenty-three of twenty-eight days in late April and early May, requiring the postponement of eleven of twenty-four games. Every Eastern team had at least one game postponed during its trip through Chicago.[13]

Bad weather also curbed the funds raised by the Chifeds for the Eastland Disaster benefit game. On July 24 the SS *Eastland*, a Great Lakes excursion boat, overturned in the Chicago River, killing more than 800 of the 2,500 passengers in one of the Great Lakes area's worst maritime disasters. Weeghman declared July 29 "Eastland Sufferers' Day" to raise money for the victims and their families. He hoped to bring in close to $10,000 through various activities, including a donation of five cents from every admission. But despite heavy advertising, the game generated only $995, mainly due to another day of poor weather.[14]

The Federals' Minor League experiment, the Colonial League, was also struggling. On July 9 two of its eight clubs folded, leaving a six-team circuit to finish the season under a revised schedule. What's more, an agent of Organized Baseball was attempting to pilfer some of its players and restart an affiliated league. To maintain fan interest, players were often transferred from team to team to keep the pennant race close. In the end, the Colonial League probably fared no worse than many other low Minor Leagues in 1915. But the Major Leagues could let many of the others fail without material consequence to their own survival or prestige. The Federals were effectively stuck with their creation through the end of the season, which mercifully came on September 6.

Despite, or possibly because of, their many problems, the Federal League's leadership continued to sell their vision. On Sunday, June 20, several of the league's top money men—Gilmore, Sinclair, Robert Ward, and Pittsburgh's Edward Gwinner and Corry Comstock—traveled to Boston to meet with a group looking for a Boston franchise in their league. The prospective Boston syndicate reportedly included onetime star Boston outfielder Hugh Duffy and eyed a ballpark site in the Forest Hills section of town.[15] Nothing ever came of this overture, though the fact that such a large contingent of Federals went to the meeting suggests that negotiations may have been fairly advanced.

As attendance dwindled, discipline also began to erode as players sensed the precariousness of their league. Once one of the Federals' most aggressive recruiters, Howie Camnitz continued to deteriorate emotionally. Pittsburgh released him early in the season after a fight with another guest in a hotel. Even then, Camnitz did not go quietly. He showed up at the park every day and filed suit for lost wages. Gwinner had little sympathy. "I see in his notice to us that he says 'tender the club my services.' Why, Camnitz has not been in condition to pitch a good game of ball this season, so I don't think he could give us his services."[16] A bitter Gwinner later blamed the Federal League's attendance problems on players who "milked us to the last ounce; and then having us bound to contracts calling for large sums of money, and knowing they could collect, they indulged in a large-sized joy ride. . . . The public, which knows baseball . . . refused to be bilked by a bunch of confidence artists who could, but wouldn't, play baseball."[17]

The Major Leagues, on the other hand, experienced a slight rebound in attendance in 1915. They continued to lose money but at a slower rate than in 1914, causing the owners to revisit some of their more drastic cost-cutting moves. Before the season, the Major Leagues had reinstituted in-season roster limits. The American League had returned to the standard twenty-five-man roster, but the more stressed Nationals decided to cut the roster to only twenty-one. Dropping from an unlimited roster in 1914 to twenty-one represented a significant inconvenience to the clubs. It limited roster flexibility, a situation that became even more acute when injuries struck, and it exposed more players to the lure of the Federals. To counteract these two inconveniences, in mid-July the National League introduced the concept of the "disabled list," still in effect today: an injured player could be placed on the list and another player brought in to restock the roster to twenty-one. Once the player was healthy, he could be reinstated, and another player would have to be released or optioned to the Minors. (The procedure did not last. The next year the league eliminated the disabled list, and it was not reestablished until 1941.)[18]

The bounce-back in attendance did not affect enforcement of the blacklist, which remained in full effect. Ban Johnson, in particular, continued his vindictiveness toward any player, especially the lesser players, who left Organized Baseball for a shot with the Federals. In April he sent a tiny five-line clipping from the *Chicago Tribune* to Garry Herrmann about an obscure pitcher named Henry Keupper who had jumped a low Minor League team in 1913 to join the Sloufeds. Keupper had recently been released by St. Louis and reported back to his Minor League squad. Johnson concluded his short cover letter, "Under no circumstances should this man be permitted to return to Organized Baseball."[19]

As Major League losses continued, several owners examined their options. In Cincinnati, the Fleischmanns in particular were tiring of the baseball war. When one Warren Carter from Pasadena, California, showed up in July and asked if he could buy a controlling interest in the Cincinnati franchise, they agreed to hear him out. After negotiation, Herrmann gave Carter a thirty-day option on a 51

percent controlling interest for $255,000. It got interesting when a Charles Bult-
man, claiming to represent Carter, approached Weeghman regarding his interest
in purchasing the Reds. "When I did not warm up to the proposition," Weeghman related, "it was suggested that we get president Gilmore." After listening
to his proposition, Gilmore turned Bultman down, "as we do not wish to break
up any league." The whole scheme would have been highly problematic in any
case. Herrmann would have fought in court, almost surely successfully, any sale
that threatened to move the Reds to another league. Moreover, once news of the
offer to Weeghman became public, Carter denied that Bultman was in any way
representing him. Had there really been some sort of play, Gilmore would almost
certainly have called on Sinclair for financial help in executing it.[20]

On July 23 the key Federal League owners met in Chicago to discuss the huge
losses all were absorbing and consider ways to turn the situation around. They
considered three expedients: signing new players, placing a team in New York
proper, and reducing ticket prices. At the conclusion of the meeting Gilmore
announced that they would not be expanding to Boston in 1916, but he did say
that they would be moving into New York proper. To emphasize their commitment, Gilmore affirmed that the league would move its headquarters to New
York effective August 1. No other new initiatives were presented, but Gilmore
did say they would be making a splash in the next few days. Numerous rumors
were about, surely planted by the Federals, that several top players, including Ty
Cobb, Babe Ruth, Eddie Collins, Grover Alexander, Frank Baker, Vic Saier, Larry
Gardner, Stuffy McInnis, and Chick Gandil, were considering the Federals.[21]

It soon became clear that the extent of the Federals' player acquisition scheme
was to raid the American Association. The truce with the American Association
had ended some time earlier, and the Federal owners hoped an infusion of top
Double-A players would generate renewed interest. "Sure we're going to be aggressive [going after players]. We've always been aggressive," said Edward Gates,
trying to minimize the comedown. "But if you think the Pittsburgh Club's going out to grab more Organized Ball stars now you're wrong. We've got enough
stars now. What we're going to do now is pull a Connie Mack and develop
some youngsters."[22] Several teams in the American Association were behind on
paying players, and Gates and Gilmore believed this made them free agents. "I
am informed," said Gilmore, "that the players, holding that this failure has rendered void their contracts, believe they are at liberty to sign with us or anybody
else."[23] Manager Fielder Jones grabbed standout outfielder Pete Compton from
the cross state Kansas_City American Association club. Once again, however,

Organized Baseball counterattacked quickly and effectively. Kansas City owner George Tebeau immediately filed for an injunction against Compton's defection. "The case will be thrown out of court at the first hearing," Compton claimed. "The club owes me $460 and cannot pay it. . . . I went into the office four days ago and demanded the $500 due me. George Tebeau handed me $100 saying it was every cent they had, and it was taken at the gate that day."[24]

Nevertheless, after Compton appeared in a doubleheader for the Terriers, the court ruled that he belonged to Tebeau's club. It turned out that his existing contract had a provision requiring written notice "whenever either party considered a breach to exist," which the court upheld as a valid provision not adhered to by Compton.[25] Interestingly, the blacklist, banning any player who jumped to the new league from returning to Organized Baseball, was conveniently ignored after the court victory. "If the temporary injunction was made permanent," Tener rationalized, "Compton must be allowed to play on the Kansas City team in spite of the fact that he has taken part in one [sic] Federal League game in St. Louis."[26] Tebeau was more forceful, saying that Compton would continue to play with his club regardless of the blacklist. When another outfielder, Sammy Meyer, jumped Tebeau's club for the Brookfeds, Tebeau sought and won an injunction against any agents from the Federals who tried to lure his players away.

The Federals fared little better with pitcher Sanford Burk. After two games for the Pittfeds, the Indianapolis American Association club secured an injunction preventing him from pitching for the Federals in violation of his contract. The Federals did manage two minor successes in raids on the International League: the Sloufeds landed Rochester third baseman Art Kores, and Pittsburgh came up with Providence's Ralph Comstock.[27] These fringe Major League–caliber players, however, had little chance of reinvigorating interest in the Federal League. More than anything, they highlighted the level of irrelevance to which the league was in danger of falling.

Ticket price cutting also floundered after some initial enthusiasm. At the July 23 meeting Ball and Sinclair had pushed the idea; the other owners had little interest in devaluing their product, and the plan was voted down six to two. By early August, however, as attendance continued to decline, the six dissenters rethought their opposition. On Saturday, August 7, Sinclair unilaterally reduced ticket prices in his bleachers from 25 cents to 10 cents and drew 15,000, a huge Federal League crowd for the time. The next day Newark drew 18,000 for Sunday's game. The other teams soon followed; most dropped ticket prices from 25 cents to 10 cents in the bleachers, 50 cents to 25 cents in the pavilion, and 75 cents to 50 cents in the grandstand. Box seats typically remained at $1.00.[28]

The Wards had still another plan to enhance attendance: night baseball. In early September, Gilmore and the Wards announced they would try night games in Washington Park for the final series of the season against Buffalo. Installation of the poles and supports began on September 11, and on September 28 they were completed and ready for the lights themselves. Ward hoped to have the lights in and ready for a night game the next day. But it was not to be; beset by technical difficulties, the lights were not ready in time for the series.

The Wards and Gilmore still hoped to capture some value from the costly installation of the lights. To highlight the potential of night baseball, they arranged an exhibition game between two semi-professional teams on October 26. The Federals turned the game into a spectacle, bringing in many of the league's principals. In addition to Gilmore and the New York–area contingent of George Ward, Walter Ward, and Harry Sinclair, Weeghman and Gwinner came to New York for the game. While not perfect, the lights worked adequately. It took some adjustment to reduce the glare and outfield shadows, but the game went smoothly and all the dignitaries in attendance pronounced the exhibition a success. They even went so far as to declare that many games in 1916 would be played under the lights. As it turned out, the first Major League night game would not occur until 1935.[29]

Despite the Federals' difficulties that summer, at least one young magnate seemed to be enjoying himself. Walter Ward, son of George and nephew of Robert, had graduated from Yale just four years earlier and was now, in name only, secretary of the Brookfeds. Young Ward was both good-looking and rich, and assumed that these two qualities could always get him out of trouble. On the team's first trip to Pittsburgh in 1915 he hooked up with an attractive brunette, the daughter of an unidentified former Major Leaguer. The two "became the talk of Pittsburgh's night life," and the girl "was at all times supplied with plenty of money and her wardrobe consisted of the best outfits that money could buy."

When Brooklyn next traveled to Pittsburgh on July 31, Ward and the girl picked up where they had left off. Eventually, George Ward had had enough; he dismissed Walter as team secretary and sent him home. Walter, however, was having too much fun and returned to Pittsburgh to resume his relationship with his new girlfriend. Much to Ward's chagrin, however, she now threatened him with blackmail: if he wanted "to keep her quiet," he needed to pony up $10,000. When Ward refused, the girl and her accomplices went to the local authorities, who ordered Ward held on what were described only as "serious charges." Exactly what these charges were remains unknown—possibly the girl was underage, and this was a setup from the beginning. Under threat of jail, Ward sought out R. H. Jackson, the attorney for the Pittfeds and a friend of the Wards. He was at one time the district attorney for Allegheny County and later disbarred. He reportedly "fixed up" Ward's case by paying $1,000 in ten $100 bills, and Ward escaped home unscathed.

Still, young Ward couldn't seem to stay out of trouble. In 1922 he shot and killed a nineteen-year-old sailor; he pleaded self-defense and asserted that his victim had shot at him. Ward further claimed that the sailor and two other men were blackmailing him—exactly why was never revealed—but the two accomplices never turned up. The case quickly became one of the most sensational murder mysteries of the decade. There were many holes in Ward's story, but after several years of legal posturing he was eventually tried for murder and acquitted. Interestingly, when authorities went back to look at the records of the Pittsburgh case, they could not be found. Ward himself later secretly disappeared to Cuba to live on a family estate. A recent review of the case suggested there may have been a homosexual angle to the blackmail and killing.[30]

While the Federal League continued to sweat out Judge Landis's delay, two other court cases were finally resolved. In July 1915 the New York Supreme Court ruled on Organized Baseball's appeal of the Hal Chase case. A year earlier, Judge Herbert Bissell had ruled that Chase was free to sign with Buffalo because of the ten-day clause in his contract. The Superior Court upheld the initial decision that the existence of the ten-day clause voided the contract, and thus Chase rightfully belonged to Buffalo. The ruling went on, more ominously for the Federals, to conclude that Organized Baseball was not in violation of anti-trust laws because baseball was not commerce.[31]

Armando Marsans also had his case resolved. Throughout the first half of the 1915 season, Marsans remained the only player under injunction who was not playing in Organized Baseball. Around the time the Federals filed their anti-trust suit in January, Phil Ball's lawyer, Montague Lyon, reportedly received an assurance from federal judge David Dyer that he would review the Marsans injunction in St. Louis between January 18 and 30. The Federals, however, chose to roll the Marsans injunction into the Landis anti-trust case and did not appear before Dyer. Ultimately, this proved an unfortunate decision for Marsans personally and the Federals in general. As the parties waited on Landis, Marsans refused to return to Cincinnati.[32] Finally, in late June, Marsans's lawyers petitioned Landis to rule just on the Cuban star's case. Landis offered some initial encouragement that he might reach a decision shortly, but instead he continued to stall.[33]

In early August, Marsans and his attorney, former Kawfeds president Charles Madison, did what they should have done back in January. They moved the case back into federal court in St. Louis and asked Judge Dyer to dissolve the injunction. "All the officials of the Federal League are his friends and political friends also and are very well connected," wrote one old St. Louis baseball wag to Herrmann. He suggested the Reds pick up lawyer Chester Krum, who had once represented Dyer's son on an embezzlement charge, to join their legal team. For his advice, he asked for a season pass to the Cardinals games.[34]

Herrmann quite possibly should have listened to this advice. Dyer removed the injunction, though he gave the Federals a less than complete victory. Gilmore, Gates, and Madison had hoped that Dyer would declare the contract invalid because of the ten-day clause. Instead, as often happened in these cases, the judge ruled in such a way as not to set a precedent. Dyer based his ruling on one of the more obscure arguments raised by Charles Madison—namely, that at one spot in Marsans's contract with the Reds the year was filled in as "1914" and not "1914–1916," as in other places. Dyer therefore concluded that Marsans's contract had expired after the 1914 season and that he was now free to play with the Sloufeds.[35] The Federals had clearly made a tactical mistake by subsuming the Marsans situation into the larger anti-trust case before Landis. Had they pushed earlier to get Dyer to rule, they might have freed Marsans to play and removed the stigma of having the Major League baseball contract validated by a temporary injunction from a federal judge.

Throughout the summer Joe Tinker targeted another disgruntled American League star, slugging Indians outfielder Joe Jackson, who was under contract through 1916. Tinker reportedly offered $10,000 per year and requested a copy of Jackson's contract so he could look for potential loopholes. In mid-August, Jackson was finally ready to jump. He wired Tinker to come to Cleveland and take him along to the Chifeds series in Baltimore. Tinker realized that he was likely to be recognized in Cleveland, leading to a counteraction from Cleveland's management, but he decided to risk the trip as the only way to get the fence-sitting Jackson to skip. Unfortunately for Tinker, events played out as he feared. A couple of players recognized Tinker and alerted Cleveland owner Charles Somers. Once Somers realized the danger, he went to Jackson's house and attempted to tie him up with a long-term contract. In this pursuit he had an unlikely ally in Jackson's wife, who didn't want Jackson to jump to the Federals. She encouraged him to sign for an additional three years at $6,000 per season, a respectable salary for the prewar days but well below market value with the competition from the Federals. Although Jackson had promised Tinker he would be on the train to Baltimore, the pressure from Somers and his wife was too much. Jackson re-signed with Cleveland.[36]

Even at this bargain price, the cash-strapped Somers could not afford to pay his slugging outfielder. "I couldn't hold Jackson and was likely to lose him to the Federal League," Somers complained a little disingenuously. "The only thing left for me to do was to dispose of him for as much as I could get."[37] Somers contacted White Sox owner Charles Comiskey, a man always willing to spend money for top ballplayers. Somers and Comiskey were old friends from the founding of the American League, when Somers helped bankroll several teams including Comiskey's. Now the tables were turned. Comiskey was happy to help out his old benefactor, and in late August he sent Somers $31,500 and three useful players for Jackson. While the Federals were not getting the players they wanted, they were clearly having an effect on the balance of power in the American League. Two of the league's best players, Collins and now Jackson, had switched teams primarily to prevent their defection to the Federal League.

On Labor Day, Buffeds director Walter Mullen introduced a new capital-raising scheme to build local support and finance the struggling club. In an offering memorandum that would never qualify under today's securities laws, the team offered preferred stock for only $10 per share and the right to pay for it on an installment plan over four months. For every two shares of preferred stock, the investor would also receive one share of common stock. The sales pitch claimed that the team had attracted 123,620 people to the ballpark to date, surely an exaggeration.

"Think of the value of the Buffalo franchise five years from now," the offering advised.

> The Buffalo Federal League Club has an issue of Preferred Stock amounting to $125,000.
>
> The club now owns its own beautiful plant, all paid for, and costing in the neighborhood of $85,000.
>
> The club also owns contracts with ballplayers whose purchase prices, according to Organized Baseball standards, would aggregate a total of about $100,000 more.
>
> The club also owns a franchise in the Federal League, and that's worth a hundred thousand dollars.
>
> The man who buys stock in the Club today is getting $250 worth of assets for every $100 he invests.
>
> These assets make the business a cash business—over the wicket every day in quarters and halves and dollars—it comes in silver and bills.[38]

As Buffalo looked to recapitalize, Gilmore continued to advertise the coming invasion of New York in 1916. On September 13 he declared that he had options on two sites in New York and would be announcing the site for 1916 any day. Later that month, a Kansas City scout disclosed that the Kansas City franchise was slated for the move to New York. Baltimore director Ned Hanlon confirmed that because of its persistently weak financial backing, the league saw Kansas City as the most expendable franchise.[39]

After a sleepy summer at the gate, the Federal League's fans woke up to a great final weekend, particularly in Chicago. Pittsburgh entered the weekend with a half-game lead on St. Louis and one and a half on Chicago. To add to the excitement, Pittsburgh and Chicago were to play a doubleheader in Pittsburgh on Saturday and then, after an overnight train ride, the final game of the season on Sunday in Chicago.

Table 13.1. Standings After Games of Friday, October 1, 1915

Pittsburgh Rebels	85	64	.570
St. Louis Terriers	86	66	.566
Chicago Whales	83	65	.561

Tie games, common because of darkness and rainouts, did not count in the standings, and teams did not generally make them up. The team with the best winning percentage would be awarded the pennant. Chicago swept the two Saturday games, edging into the lead (see table 13.2).

Table 13.2. Standings After Games of Saturday, October 2, 1915

Chicago Whales	85	65	.567
Pittsburgh Rebels	85	66	.563
St. Louis Terriers	86	67	.562

Whoever won the Sunday game between Chicago and Pittsburgh would capture the pennant. Weeghman, however, had another idea. The scheduled Friday game between the two teams in Pittsburgh had been rained out; Weeghman suggested that the game be made up on Sunday in Chicago as part of a doubleheader. This was ingenious; he now had only to split a doubleheader to win the pennant. Pittsburgh naturally opposed this proposition, but Gilmore sided with his Chicago pal. He ruled that if Pittsburgh did not play a doubleheader, he would rule both games forfeit.

On Sunday in Chicago, in front of an announced crowd of 34,212—the news reports described the fans as crammed into every nook and cranny of the ballpark—the Whales lost the first game but came back to win the second, and the pennant, 3–0. The final standings represented one of the closest "Major League" races ever (see table 13.3).

Table 13.3. Final Standings

Chicago Whales	86	66	.566
St. Louis Terriers	87	67	.565
Pittsburgh Rebels	86	67	.562

Before the end of the regular season, Gilmore again challenged the Major Leagues to be allowed to play in the World Series, and was once again met with resounding silence. Ban Johnson did little more than admit to the papers that they had received Gilmore's letter and that Herrmann would "acknowledge" it. Now that he had finally captured his pennant, Weeghman also challenged the Major Leagues to include his Whales in the postseason. He even enlisted Chicago politicians in his lobbying effort. But Weeghman's appeal also fell on deaf ears. At the same time Rube Foster of the black Chicago American Giants once again challenged Weeghman to a postseason series; once again he received no reply.[40]

The 1915 season had been a huge disappointment for the Federal League, though the final weekend salvaged some enthusiasm. But no last-minute attendance boost could offset the massive financial losses that the league had suffered. In 1915 Major League attendance rebounded slightly to just above 300,000 per team; the Federals, though no official figures were ever released, likely fell off. One reasonable estimate placed Kansas City at the top of the Federal League's attendance with 180,000 and Brooklyn at the bottom with 50,000. And with their reduced ticket prices, the revenue from these patrons would have been further depressed. One respected sportswriter suggested that several Federal League teams made money, but this is belied by available data. Kansas City lost $35,332 despite leading the league in attendance. Ball admitted to losses of $94,000 in St. Louis. Pittsburgh's owners claimed they were losing roughly $10,000 per month, a loss of $60,000 over the six-month season. At the end of the season, Buffalo was more than $50,000 in debt, and the directors needed to raise $100,000 from the stock sale to keep the team afloat. Baltimore (see table 13.4) lost more than $64,000.[41]

Table 13.4.   Baltimore Financial Results, 1915

Receipts		
Home	34,742.77	
Road	23,769.36	
Season tickets	449.00	
Concessions	6,480.18	
Miscellaneous	1,831.30	
		67,272.61
Expenses		
Player salaries	71,369.72	
Player bonuses	6,083.33	
Traveling expenses	13,707.44	
Rent	4,333.33	
Interest	3,973.20	
Federal League assessment	6,143.00	
Other expenses	25,898.16	
		131,508.18
Net Profit		(64,235.57)

Most of the Federal owners hoped to broker some sort of settlement with Organized Baseball in the off-season. In total, Edward Gwinner and Corry Comstock had lost about $225,000 in Pittsburgh. Most important, the league's two wealthiest backers, Sinclair and the Wards, were tiring of their baseball venture. Ward had lost more than $650,000 bankrolling the league: he had invested $373,000 in his Brooklyn team, lent $220,800 to the league and his club, advanced another $59,000 to the league, and provided untold thousands of additional funds that were never properly documented. Gilmore later admitted that, including 1913, the Federal League as a whole lost roughly $2,500,000. Nonetheless, both Sinclair and Ward still held considerable fortunes that could be used to backstop another year of operation or at least bluff the possibility.[42]

On October 18, however, tragedy struck the Federals. Robert Ward, the league's banker, died suddenly at age sixty-three from heart ailments caused by neuritis (general nerve inflammation) and rheumatism. It is impossible to overstate his loss to the Federals; only Sinclair remained wealthy enough to bankroll the league. "He was the backbone of the Federal League and the blow is likely to prove fatal to the organization," Ban Johnson gloated. "I had a talk with him last spring at which time I was given to understand that he would be glad to get out of the league. I think it was the Federal League that put him under the sod as he could not stand the strain of worries and losses."[43] Blaming his death on the (literal) trials and tribulations of the Federals seems extreme, but there can be no exaggerating the impact of Ward's death. Weeghman had lost much of his smaller fortune, and the other Wards were not nearly as committed to the baseball venture as Robert. The Federals would continue publicly to show their commitment to opening in 1916 and putting a team in New York, but only the most hidebound observers could fail to recognize their dire straits.

14

The Final Countdown

Several years later, in a seminal court case explored in the next chapter, Federal League president Jim Gilmore testified that by June 1915 the moneyed Federal League investors had concluded that under current operating conditions the Federals would not be financially viable for many years. A small subgroup of owners had decided that the best way to change the existing dynamic and force some sort of accommodation with Organized Baseball was to reemphasize the transfer of a franchise to New York proper, preferably Manhattan, with the Bronx also a possibility. In Gilmore's version of this tale, there was never really any intent to spend the money necessary to secure a site and build a stadium, but the bluff had to be convincing. Organized Baseball, particularly the New York teams, needed to sweat. The select faction of Federal League owners in on the ruse included the Wards, Harry Sinclair, Edward Gwinner, Corry Comstock, and Gilmore. Comstock, part-owner in Pittsburgh, was a close friend and business associate of Robert Ward. By not telling the other league executives the true nature of the plan, they obviously reduced the chance of exposure but also risked angry repercussions later in the event of a botched settlement.

As Gilmore told the story, throughout the fall of 1915 the Federals talked up their proposed New York invasion and, to add credibility, searched for a site. Once again, Kansas City was leaked to the press as the franchise to be transferred. Although the Kawfeds had drawn well in 1915, Kansas City's small population, far western geographic location that made travel more expensive and complicated, and, most important, lack of strong financial backing made it the logical franchise to move. After suffering additional financial losses in 1915, the league anticipated little resistance from local investors who were no longer willing to fund the club. In any case, Gilmore's cabal did not really expect to have to transfer the team.[1]

Gilmore's testimony is not convincing. Most obviously, it is hard to imagine how a group this large could have kept a secret from the rest of the league, given the many conferences it held. The two younger Wards, Walter in particular, were not known for their reserve. Moreover, these owners did not act as if they had given up on the league: the ticket price experiment and the assault on the Double-A Minor Leaguers indicated continued interest. Also, any cabal would almost surely have required participation from Charlie Weeghman and Phil Ball, two of the league's key owners. Finally, Robert Ward, known to be one of the most upstanding men in baseball, who had previously stood with the league when Organized Baseball tried to peel him away, would have been unlikely to run a New York bluff without the knowledge of his fellow owners. When he died on October 18, the remaining moneyed owners unquestionably began rethinking the future of their league, and at that point the New York invasion may have turned into a bluff. But before November, the New York initiative was almost surely real.

As further evidence, on October 30, 1915, Gilmore sent a letter to Baltimore president Carrol Rasin encouraging him for the coming season: "Also hope that your club is signing up some good talent for the coming year. I have wonderful faith in Baltimore as a Major League city, and know if you can get a fighting team there and keep it in the race, you will draw wonderful crowds and easily pay expenses."[2] It's one thing to exclude someone from the bluff plan; it's quite another to encourage them to act as if it didn't exist.

Irrespective of whether a small group decided to bluff the Major Leagues to a peace settlement, most of the Federal League owners were looking to settle if they could get anything close to acceptable terms. The Major League owners as well, particularly those in the National League, wanted resolution. They had lost thousands of dollars, and the explosion of player salaries had dramatically increased expenses, raising the bar for break-even attendance. (See table 14.1 for a sample of salary increases.)

To feel out the Federal League owners, in August Boston Braves owner James Gaffney invited Jim Gilmore, Harry Sinclair, Corry Comstock, and George Ward ostensibly to tour the Braves' new ballpark. Over the next couple of months the Federal and National League owners continued with exploratory conversations over what it would take to make peace. During the World Series, Gaffney engi-

Table 14.1. Increases in Major League Salaries (1913–1915)

Player	League	Team	1913	1915
Joe Benz	AL	Chi	2,400	6,500
Buck Weaver	AL	Chi	2,500	6,000
Ray Chapman	AL	Cle	2,400	3,500
Donie Bush	AL	Det	4,200	6,000
Ty Cobb	AL	Det	12,000	20,000
Ray Caldwell	AL	NY	2,400	8,000
Fritz Maisel	AL	NY	2,100	4,800
Roger Peckinpaugh	AL	NY	2,400	6,000
Ed Sweeney	AL	NY	5,500	8,000
Ray Fisher	AL	NY	3,000	6,667
Walter Johnson	AL	Was	7,000	12,500
Clyde Milan	AL	Was	5,550	8,500
Bill James	NL	Bos	2,400	6,000
Rabbit Maranville	NL	Bos	1,800	6,000
Dick Rudolph	NL	Bos	2,900	7,500
Lefty Tyler	NL	Bos	2,700	5,400
Jake Daubert	NL	Brk	5,000	9,000
Nap Rucker	NL	Brk	4,000	4,500
Zack Wheat	NL	Brk	3,300	5,350
Bill Killefer	NL	Phi	3,200	6,500
Fred Clarke	NL	Pit	15,000	15,000
Honus Wagner	NL	Pit	10,000	10,000
Ivey Wingo	NL	STL	2,600	6,500

Source: House Report, page 52; outline of testimony of Chairman Herrmann of National Commission in suit of Baltimore Federal League Club v. American League, et al.

neered a secret meeting in Philadelphia, the first real attempt at an agreement since the spring. For the conference, Gilmore, Sinclair, Ball, and Gwinner traveled to Philadelphia to meet with Tener and Herrmann. While meeting in the Bellevue-Stratford Hotel, the group invited Ban Johnson, having dinner in the hotel with Yankees co-owner Jacob Ruppert, to join them. Johnson agreed only on the condition that Gilmore be sent out; he didn't trust or like the glib Federal League president. As evidence of the desperation of the Federals to get an audience with the full National Commission, the owners agreed to this humiliating condition.[3]

With the attendees now in place, Sinclair proposed that as the basis for a settlement, both established leagues expand to ten teams. The American League would accept the Pittsburgh and Brooklyn Federal League franchises while Baltimore and Newark would join the National; Kansas City and Buffalo would be folded; Weeghman would buy the Cubs, and Ball would purchase one of the two St. Louis franchises. Surprisingly, Ban Johnson, typically an obstructionist on settlement, showed tentative interest in this proposal, but the National League

Tammany Hall–connected Boston Braves owner James Gaffney showing his new stadium to Federal League executives Corry Comstock, Robert Ward, Harry Sinclair, and James Gilmore. (Courtesy of the Dennis Goldstein Collection)

had little interest in substituting American League for Federal League competition in Pittsburgh and Brooklyn.[4]

Over the next few weeks various Federal League and Major League executives continued with exploratory, clandestine discussions. To coordinate the meetings, the Federal League owners deputized a committee of Weeghman, Ball, Gilmore, and Sinclair to confer with Organized Baseball representatives. At the Federal League meeting on November 9 in Indianapolis, the Baltimore delegates quizzed Gilmore, Sinclair, and Weeghman on the status of these discussions. The three told Baltimore's Rasin that they had been talking with Major League owners but had nothing of substance to report. Baltimore director and attorney Stuart Janney asked Gilmore, Weeghman, and Sinclair point-blank whether there was any truth to the rumors of peace. All three replied that there was no truth in them, but the manner of their response "did arouse some suspicion" among the Baltimore contingent.[5]

The Federals also officially announced that the Kansas City franchise had been forfeited to the league and was being moved to New York for the 1916 season. For the next several weeks, rumors swirled about the ballpark's potential location. Gilmore promised a forthcoming announcement, but it was repeatedly delayed for mysterious reasons. Finally, on November 29, the Federals announced

that they had secured from the Pinkney estate a site in Manhattan located between 142nd Street and 145th Street near Fifth Avenue and the Harlem River.
The reported $1.25 million price for the land was enormous for the time. When
one considers that the cost of building the stadium was in the neighborhood of
$480,000, the scale of the commitment the Federals were putting forward was
staggering. The economics were so large that the new Yankees owners, who reportedly had had an opportunity to acquire the site for $800,000 to $1 million,
turned it down. The team would need to draw around 600,000 fans for the deal
to make financial sense.[6]

The question of who would own the team and front these exorbitant costs
needed to be addressed. Gilmore refused to name a buyer for the Kansas City
franchise, preferring to enigmatically allude to investors from various cities.
Fortunately for the Federals, however, they had Sinclair, a man rich enough to
pull it off. Sinclair had also occasionally expressed an interest in owning a team
in New York. In early December the Federals released one of the more plausible
scenarios in which Sinclair would get the New York team, and Powers, with a
syndicate of New Jersey investors, would buy him out of Newark.

Comstock, the named architect and engineer overseeing the ballpark, also
needed to manage the political process of closing the streets that ran through the
site. Without the city's abandonment of the streets, no stadium could be built.
Not surprisingly, opponents of the Federal League planned to object to the street
closings as a way to delay or possibly halt construction. Nevertheless, Comstock
prevailed in securing tentative permission from the Board of Aldermen to close
the necessary streets. He also prepared extensive plans and worked the newspapers to publicize his progress.[7]

On December 13, with Sinclair in his New York office, Gilmore received a call
from National League president John Tener. The National Leaguers were in a
meeting and wanted Gilmore to "come over and fix this thing up."

"I told you the other day," Gilmore responded, "I would not have anything to
do with it, and I will not talk about it."

"Is Sinclair around?" Tener asked.

"Yes, he is right here."

"Will he come?"

"I don't know. I will have to ask him."

"Here, Harry," Gilmore spoke loudly so the other end of the phone connection could hear, "these people want you to come over and talk to them. Do you
want to go?"

Sinclair put his mouth close to the phone and said, "We might as well go and hear what they have to say."[8]

So Gilmore and Sinclair headed over to Tener's office about 3 o'clock in the afternoon. There they found the National League fully represented by Garry Herrmann (Cincinnati), Barney Dreyfuss (Pittsburgh), Schuyler Britton (St. Louis), Charles Ebbets (Brooklyn), James Gaffney (Boston), William Baker (Philadelphia), Harry Hempstead (New York), and Charles Thomas on behalf of Charles Taft (Chicago). After a fruitful discussion, the group went out to dinner at the Republican Club to continue the negotiations.

Gilmore and Sinclair wanted each existing Federal League franchise to receive a payoff or have the right to acquire an existing Major League team. After reaching a tentative agreement for Brooklyn, Chicago, and Pittsburgh, Gilmore asked for a $200,000 payoff for Baltimore. The others laughed at him. Gilmore later defended his request with Sinclair by arguing that he thought it best to start high. He also felt that the Baltimore owners might be satisfied with getting their club into the International League. By the end of the evening the gathering had come up with a nonbinding settlement outline:

1. Sinclair or a representative (assumed to be Weeghman) could buy the Cubs, with the National League assuming $50,000 of the purchase price.
2. The National League would pay $10,000 per year for twenty years to the Wards, technically as rent on Washington Park, subject to the American League doing likewise for a total of $400,000 (equivalent to $229,000 on a present-value basis at a discount rate of 6 percent).*
3. The National League would pay $25,000 to the Pittsburgh Federal League club, subject to the American League doing likewise.
4. All players with the Federal League would be eligible to return to Organized Baseball. The Federal League would continue to assume the obligations of all their contracts and dispose of their services as they might determine.
5. The Federal League would withdraw the anti-trust suit still before Judge Landis.[9]

No agreement was reached regarding Newark, but Sinclair knew that he would be protected. As to St. Louis, Sinclair was close to Ball and knew that

---

*Money paid over time is not worth as much as a lump sum paid up front. To equate a stream of payments to a single payment, termed the "present value," one "discounts" the payments at an applicable discount rate, typically equal to the interest rate for a financial instrument of a similar term and credit quality. Discounting twenty years of payments of $20,000 per year at 6 percent, a reasonable interest rate for the era, equates to a present value of $229,000.

Ball was in conversations with Ban Johnson and the owners of the two St. Louis clubs. He was convinced that Ball would be satisfied with a chance to buy one of these teams. Somewhat unfairly from a competitive standpoint, the Federal League owners who bought into the Major Leagues would be permitted to keep the rights to their Federal League players as well. Thus the 1916 Cubs and whichever St. Louis team Ball purchased would each represent an amalgamation of two Major League teams.

With this tentative agreement in place, Gilmore, Sinclair, and the National Leaguers had the task of convincing the remaining parties to accept it. With Buffalo and Kansas City forfeited to the league, Gilmore and Sinclair had to persuade Weeghman, Gwinner, the Wards, Ball, and Rasin, Hanlon and the rest of the Baltimore contingent. The first three would be simple: Weeghman would receive the chance to purchase the Cubs, and the Wards and Gwinner would receive total payments of $400,000 and $50,000 respectively. Gwinner thought he should receive more but was done funding a money-losing ballclub. The Baltimore delegation would be the most difficult. They did not want a Minor League franchise or a monetary payoff; they wanted Major League baseball for their city. If possible, the Federals also hoped to recover something for the Buffalo franchise, which still had an intact ownership group.

National League owners had long wanted to get the woman out of their fraternity and thought they had an arrangement with Helene Britton to sell the Cardinals to Ball. But at the most recent league meeting she had changed her mind. The other owners appeared too gleeful at her looming exit and pushed too hard. Britton would not be intimidated and refused to sell. Nevertheless, the National League's other seven owners were not concerned about this issue as it related to the settlement: Britton could change her mind again, and there was always the other St. Louis franchise, perennially struggling, for Ball to buy.[10]

To bring the American League on board, the National Leaguers immediately sent Dreyfuss to Chicago to address the American League meeting then in session. He circulated copies of the tentative agreement, telling the American League owners that the National League owners had reached a settlement with the Federals and imploring them to go along with it. After considerable debate the American Leaguers agreed that it made an acceptable framework for a settlement. They deputized a delegation of Charles Comiskey, Jacob Ruppert, Charles Somers, Joseph Lannin, and Ban Johnson to travel to New York to meet with the National League and Federal League owners and hammer out a definitive agreement. The delegation left immediately for a final showdown, now scheduled for December 17 at the Waldorf-Astoria. When they arrived in the late morning, the American League delegation immediately went into conference with their National League counterparts.

Meanwhile, Gilmore had been busy with his owners. On December 16 he notified Weeghman to come to New York, and wired Rasin, "You and Hanlon be at Biltmore in morning. Important."[11] The two also brought Stuart Janney, a team director and attorney, to act as an additional adviser. The Baltimore representatives later said they had no idea what was about to occur, which seems believable. On November 1 Gilmore sent Baltimore secretary Harry Goldman a letter asking him to "make out a statement of the approximate cost to operate your club during the next season. In other words, I would like an idea of how much cheaper you can operate in 1916 than you could in 1915."[12] As late as November 30 Gilmore forwarded a letter to Goldman recommending a player with his note at the bottom: "Better investigate."[13]

Upon arrival in New York on the morning of the 17th, Rasin and Janney went directly to the Biltmore Hotel, where they met with Gilmore. The Federal League president told them that the 1916 season was "all off" and that he and "certain others" of the Federal League had met with the Major League baseball owners and worked out settlement terms. When they pressed Gilmore for details, he remained vague. Rather than discuss the settlement terms with the two Baltimore representatives alone, Gilmore deferred the discussion until he could include the other Federal League executives, who were already preparing for the meeting with Organized Baseball later that day.

The Federal Leaguers all met in a suite at the Biltmore. "It was not a meeting," Rasin described the conference, "but a fist fight. That's about all it was." The Federal League representatives included Weeghman, William Ward, Comstock, and Sinclair in addition to Gilmore. Not surprisingly, after they confirmed that the league was in fact shutting down and received the details of the settlement, the Baltimore contingent was furious. They asked what had been done for Baltimore, and the answer was simple: not a thing. Sinclair, Weeghman, and Gilmore further disclosed to Rasin, Hanlon, and Janney that they would meet with Organized Baseball representatives later that afternoon to authorize a final settlement. Rasin demanded that he be allowed to go along and see what proposition he could get "to take back home." Two discrepancies would come back to haunt the Federal Leaguers later: First, could this be construed as an official meeting of the Federal League? Second, was the foursome of Sinclair, Weeghman, Gilmore, and Rasin granted decision-making authority for the meeting with Organized Baseball? Gilmore, Ward, and Comstock later testified "yes," but Rasin and Janney had no such recollection; they did not feel they had surrendered any of their authority. Regardless, it's hard to blame either side: the Federals, exclusive of Baltimore, saw this as their last opportunity to get the best deal they could; Baltimore's representatives wanted the league to continue or wanted a Major League franchise, neither of which was now really possible.[14]

After the confrontation with their fellow Federal League executives, Hanlon, Rasin, and Janney hustled to the nearby Waldorf-Astoria to lobby Herrmann. Hanlon and Herrmann talked about old times. After this small talk, Janney complained to Herrmann that Baltimore seemed to be excluded from the peace settlement. He and his colleagues felt that Baltimore should get a Major League team as part of the settlement. Herrmann assured Janney that Baltimore would be dealt with fairly by the National Commission. Janney mentioned that he had heard Washington might be on the market and that both St. Louis teams were having financial difficulties. Herrmann acknowledged that the St. Louis Cardinals might be for sale and might be transferable to Baltimore, but this would be subject to the league owners, possibly at a future meeting. Furthermore, this would make three teams in the West and five in the East, creating an unbalanced schedule. Herrmann offered that it might be possible to secure the Baltimore club a franchise in the International League. This was discussed in a general way but clearly was not what the Baltimore representatives wanted.[15]

The full meeting of the leagues' representatives began at 9:10 p.m. on December 17, 1915. Herrmann assumed the chair. He read a statement, drafted by Washington president Ben Minor, and agreed to by the Organized Baseball magnates earlier that day: "That it is the sense of the National and American Leagues of Professional Baseball Clubs, in convention assembled, that the National Commission be authorized on behalf of the two leagues, to carry the agreement as outlined and read to you by the Secretary [the tentative December 13 agreement], into effect, and that the two committees appointed respectively by the National and American Leagues be discharged." The resolution, Herrmann added, had been unanimously adopted.

"I can say for the Federal League," Gilmore responded, "that the committee represented here tonight was appointed with full authority to discuss this proposition with you, and conclude any agreement that we might come to, and we are ready to open up and talk and see what can be done."

Herrmann jumped right in: "The agreement I suppose speaks for itself. Shall we take it up paragraph by paragraph?"

After further procedural issues, Herrmann asked National League secretary John Heydler to read the first paragraph: "First: That the National League representatives on their part agree that if Mr. Sinclair or his representatives or assigns [which was to be Weeghman] purchase the Chicago National League Club, the National League of Professional Baseball Clubs will assume fifty thousand dollars of the purchase price."

Herrmann acknowledged that this was purely a National League matter and that they agreed.

Heydler then read the next three provisions: $20,000 a year for twenty years to the Wards, structured as lease payments for Washington Park; $50,000 to the Pittsburgh Federals; and the Federal League's retention of the player contracts with the right to "dispose" of the players to Organized Baseball. The first provision elicited some conversation on the details, and the second was readily agreed to. Herrmann, however, wanted clarification on the third: "We would want to get some information as to what the contracts are, and with whom, having in mind that we would want to exercise that option or not."

"As I understood it the other night," Sinclair responded, "this was more or less a tentative agreement. We did not have to go into the details of the situation. . . . It seems to me just on that particular point, that there are a great many conditions that would be necessary to be embodied in that paragraph."

"Is your idea," Gilmore added, "we should submit to you a complete list of their salaries and so forth?"

The meeting had reached its first impasse. The Federal Leaguers did not wish to allow Organized Baseball to water down the agreement, particularly as it had never been fully ratified by the Federal League owners—essentially what they hoped to accomplish at this meeting.

After caucusing by the National Commission, National League attorney J. Conway Toole tried to move the meeting forward: "The point of it is that a committee without authority from any Organized Baseball body entered into an agreement or memorandum, as you call it, on the part of the National League, and with a suggestion that the American League was to approve it. Now, Mr. Gilmore and Mr. Sinclair entered into it on the part of the Federal League."

"No," responded Sinclair, clarifying, "Mr. Gilmore and myself stated that we had not any authority to represent the Federal League."

"But now you have that authority, Mr. Sinclair," Toole replied.

"Now we have that authority," Sinclair assured him. Much was later made of the fact that Rasin did not dispute this statement.

"Does the Federal League ratify what you did that night as far as it goes?" Toole asked.

"Not in the present shape it is in," Sinclair responded—at which point it became clear that this meeting would not simply be a reading of the memorandum with agreement to each point.

Not surprisingly, several Organized Baseball owners asked Sinclair to clarify his statement. Was he backing off from the tentative agreement?

"Do I understand," asked Yankees owner Jacob Ruppert, "that the Federal League objects to these agreements that were made here a week ago with the National League?"

"We do not," Sinclair reassured him.

"I believe if the National Commission would meet us in a body," Gilmore expanded, "there would be no trouble in going along with threshing out this matter."

A long discussion then ensued as to whether the owners ought to delegate to the Commission or some other committee the authority to work out the details. Eventually, since they were all together, the magnates settled on calling in their lawyers to help draft an agreement.

"While we are waiting, shall we go ahead with the other paragraphs?" Herrmann suggested. Sinclair wanted to revisit the issue of ownership of the Federal League player contracts. Herrmann restated the issue to his fellow owners: "they [the Federal League owners] want to be given an opportunity to dispose of [i.e., sell to Organized Baseball clubs] their surplus players." All agreed with the concept and went on to discuss the time limit for which the Federals could control the players. Eventually they settled on Opening Day 1917.

With this discussion concluded, Heydler read paragraph five: that the terms of the memorandum were only a general understanding and subject to the agreement of the American League and others of interest. A short clarifying discussion ensued as to who exactly were "others of interest." As this dialogue wound down, Heydler read the final paragraph of the tentative agreement, which declared that nothing would be final until the anti-trust suit, still tentatively pending before Judge Landis, was withdrawn.

"We will have to wait until our attorney comes, Mr. Chairman, before we decide upon that question," Gilmore told Herrmann, and the room took a brief recess as they waited for Janney. Gilmore was probably more interested in having a roomful of baseball owners pressure Janney to agree to withdraw the suit than in his actual legal opinion.

A sportswriter from the *Baltimore Sun* tracked down Janney at the Biltmore and told him the others were looking for him and that "it looked as though

Baltimore could get a National League franchise if he went over there and asked for it."

When Stuart Janney joined the conference at 10:20 p.m., he immediately launched into a long plea for Baltimore as part of the peace settlement: "Baltimore has a population of 750,000 or 800,000 people, including the suburbs. . . . We are willing to purchase and pay for a franchise in the Major Leagues, if we can get it, and we want that to be the main keynote of our situation this evening. . . . In a city of that size [meaning Baltimore], if there is going to be peace, it ought to be a permanent peace, and if it is to be a permanent peace you do not want to leave open a community of that size. . . .

"We are not venturing to suggest to you gentlemen just what franchise we think that would be. You could work that out probably better than ourselves, but that is our starting point." Janney continued along these lines for several minutes. His monologue was not surprising, given that Baltimore had not been a party to the draft agreement, but it certainly moved the meeting off topic from a quick dispatch of its final paragraph.

"Of course, you realize that in so far as the National League is concerned," Herrmann replied, hoping to move past the issue, "its circuit is fixed by constitution and cannot be changed without unanimous consent."

"I appreciate that," Janney replied.

"And assuming now, for the moment that the league would consent to a change of circuit [i.e., a franchise shift]," Herrmann continued, "then you would have to make an arrangement with some club in that league to get their franchise so to speak."

"Yes," Janney understood.

"If that consent should not be obtained," Herrmann tried to discourage Janney, "if the league did not give unanimous consent, or you could not make arrangement with the National League club, that would end the proposition at once."

"I think if you start off with a proposition as to whether or not the National League would consent to a transfer of one of its franchises." Janney unveiled his plan: "I hesitate to suggest to name one, because I do not know the feeling very well of those who may be interested in the particular franchise I might mention, but if you would consent to the transfer of one franchise to Baltimore, and, of course, probably you would have to know exactly what franchise you were dealing with before you could intelligently give your consent, therefore I would suggest we conclude what arrangement we had in mind. Shall I mention the particular franchise?"

"No," popped up Gilmore, who had little interest in having the settlement potentially derailed by a futile debate over Janney's idea of purchasing an existing National League franchise and transferring it to Baltimore.

"We understand that one can be bought," Janney pushed, "and if that could be done, and consent given to the transfer to Baltimore, then our problem is solved, and the city in question would not be without baseball either."

"I do not know what franchise of the National League you refer to," replied Herrmann disingenuously, trying to end Janney's appeal, "but speaking as a member of this committee or of the National Commission or as Chairman of this meeting, I will say right now, in so far as the National League is concerned, the Cincinnati club would not vote for a change of its circuit at this time and unless they did, it could not be put into effect, that proposition. There are other National League Presidents here, and they may be heard on that."

"Do you think, Mr. Herrmann, that they had the Cincinnati franchise in mind?" Ban Johnson asked wryly.

"I do not believe he has. If he has, he has not discussed it with me."

"What National League franchise has he in mind?" asked Ebbets. It was late, the owners were well oiled, and the huge losses from the Federal League war were about to be a thing of the past. Janney was in a tough spot; he wanted something from the owners, so he had to be deferential, and no one else in the room (except Rasin) cared to reopen the agreement at this point.

"I do not know," Herrmann again professed.

"Really, the question of what franchise," Janney continued, "I should suppose that would be a question of negotiations with the individuals who owned that franchise, but if we could get your permission to negotiate, I would be glad to say privately to the Commission, and talk over with them, but I hesitate in a company such as this to make a statement as to what franchise I have in mind."

"I move that the Chairman call the roll of the National League and find out which franchises are for sale," joked Boston owner James Gaffney, to general laughter.

Herrmann turned to Gaffney. "Would you vote to change the circuit regardless of what franchise?"

"Not to Baltimore, absolutely no."

Ashley Lloyd and Ebbets each added "no" for the Giants and Dodgers respectively.

"I should hardly suppose it is necessary, after so many have said no," Janney conceded, "and it takes unanimous consent, and it is all 'noes.' It seems to be a unanimous refusal."

"The American may be willing, I do not know," Herrmann said.

"What will you give for a franchise?" asked White Sox owner Charles Comiskey, joining the fun.

"It depends on which one," responded Janney reasonably.

"I will sell you a good one," Comiskey told him.

Everyone laughed, and Janney doggedly persisted. "I will deal with you."

"All right, what would you give me for it?"

"Comiskey is a businessman alright," snorted Ebbets, and the room again chuckled.

Janney continued to push: "I think that is a matter we ought to discuss at some length and in some detail."

"What do you think the White Sox are worth?" asked Comiskey, completely enjoying himself.

Gilmore piped up, "I think they are worth about $600,000."

Janney said he would take it.

"You will not," Comiskey told him. "We're going to leave the concrete there. Baltimore does not want a Major League franchise."

"What do they want, Mr. Comiskey?" Janney asked him.

"They want a lot of 'guts' to protect the Minor League clubs; that is all. They have to prove they are a Minor League city yet."

"No, and that is just the reason, that they are not, and I would like to ask you whether if you put a Minor League in Chicago, you would get 200 people out to see the games."

"Yes, we tried it out, and we tried it in your town at the same time."

"What is that?" Janney asked.

"We tried it in your town at the same time, and I am awfully glad I met you before you bought the franchise," Comiskey mocked wryly. "Don't buy any Major League franchise for Baltimore, and don't pay a hell of a price for a Minor League franchise."

The other owners laughed heartily at this jibe, but Janney persisted. "That is true, there is a big difference."

"There is not a big difference, there is not a big difference at all."

"If you put a Minor League in a Major League town, it don't pay," Janney tried to explain.

"Well, what would you give for a franchise in Baltimore?" Comiskey pursued. "Suppose we could blow life into [John] McGraw, [Joe] Kelley, [Hugh] Jennings and all those players that you had there and could not support," he further taunted, referring to Baltimore's great National League teams of the 1890s. "Put them back there. What would you give for those players if we would guarantee that they would play good ball in Baltimore for ten years, what would you pay for them and how loyally would you support them?"

"We would support them well," Janney defended.

"What crowd would you draw?"

"We would draw sufficient to enable us to pay $250,000 for a franchise."

"That is just the proper price for a Minor League franchise," Comiskey ridiculed.

Everyone laughed except Janney, who forced himself to remain polite because he had not yet given up hope of convincing the owners to sell him a franchise to move to Baltimore. "Mr. Comiskey, in Chicago, with the standing that your club has there, I will say that your franchise is worth more than that."

Comiskey was having too much fun to let the matter lie. "Now, just a moment. I am telling you what you would give, if you had a guarantee they would play. That is a supposition, I am saying that, but we did that, we did that, and how many people do you imagine you would play to in Baltimore?"

"We would play to sufficient—"

But Comiskey demanded specifics: "Yes, but just give a rough guess. This is an argument. Would you play to 100,000?"

"We would play to over 200,000."

"Well, you had that condition and you played to 96,000." This was a little bit unfair. In 1898, Baltimore's last year in the National League, according to modern estimates, the team played to 123,000 fans, and the team had drawn well during the mid-1890s.

"I know that," Janney conceded, "but you know the circumstances that were there at that time, and baseball is very different today than it was then." This was true: the existence of only one league and syndicate ownership, allowing individual owners to have an interest in more than one franchise, severely depressed attendance at the close of the 1890s.

Comiskey refused to concede the point: "No, no, the conditions are just the same."

"I think you will find during the Federal League season, even though playing at the tail-end, we played to more of a crowd than in a number of cities," Janney pointed out.

Comiskey persisted with the nineteenth-century results: "You had Jennings, you had McGraw, you had Kelly, and you had all those men, and you had a franchise in the American League [sic] and you had a big town to draw from, and you played to 96,000 people! Now, don't buy any Major League franchise."

"We played to a great deal more than that," Janney responded.

"You played to 96,000 people, and you can get the facts, because the same people are in control now, in the Federal League."

Janney tried another tack: "Now, money talks in a situation of that sort, and as I say we are prepared to back up with proper guarantees as to the number of people it will draw, and revenue it will pay. Of course, we cannot guarantee the people." In other words, Janney was offering to guarantee certain minimums to the other clubs for their share of gate receipts on road trips to Baltimore.

"Of course, you can't guarantee the people; the people will not come out," Comiskey kept on.

Janney was clearly growing annoyed: "We would not be putting ourselves behind it if we did not know we could do it. What is your theory about Baltimore? What do you want to do?"

"Baltimore, a Minor League city and not a hell of a good one at that," Comiskey told him.

"That's right," echoed Ebbets, who had been partially responsible for the destruction of the Baltimore team of the 1890s when its best players were transferred to Brooklyn and the franchise folded.

"As sure as you are sitting there now, and your friends will tell you," Comiskey egged Ebbets on. "Charlie, show them what you have got in Baltimore. You are the best evidence in the world. Tell them what you drew in Baltimore. What is the good of getting up here and talking about buying a Major League club for Baltimore? A Major League club to start off with, without anything, is worth $600,000 or $700,000. You have not the slightest idea of paying $600,000 or $700,000, have you?"

"There are some in the two leagues that can be bought for less than that," piped up Rasin.

"There are plenty of them that can be bought for less than that," echoed Janney.

Ebbets rejoined that even Ned Hanlon didn't think Baltimore was a Major League city: "When he [Ned Hanlon] quit Baltimore and came to Brooklyn he said, 'Baltimore is not a Major League city.' We lost money in Baltimore operating the club with the same players that Mr. Comiskey speaks of." Hanlon may have said this at some point in the past, but since then he had tried several times to get Major League baseball back to Baltimore and had been willing to make a significant financial investment.

"There are very specific circumstances that brought that about," Janney again told him.

"Nothing peculiar about it; it is a Minor League city, positively and absolutely, and will never be anything else," Ebbets replied.

"That is your opinion."

"Sure that is my opinion, because I had a piece of experience and lost money down there."

"But money has been lost in other towns also in baseball."

"Not in Major League cities," Ebbets replied falsely.

"Yes, they have been [sic] lost in other towns that are Major League cities," Janney told him.

"It is one of the worst Minor League towns in the country." Ebbets would not let up on Baltimore.

Janney still tried to make his case: "It will never be a Minor League town because the people feel naturally—"

"You have too many colored population to start with," Ebbets interrupted. "They are a cheap population when it gets down to paying money at the gate."

"They come across, I think, in good shape," Janney responded, finally giving in to the hopelessness of the debate. "This is perfectly futile, of course. It requires your consent and I am not going to try and convince you when you are so set in your views."

"Well, the Baltimore representative is certainly entitled to this hearing," chimed in Herrmann, turning to Janney, "but it must be very evident that a condition of this kind that you seek cannot be brought about, unless you," turning to Johnson, "the American League would do it."

"Mr. Herrmann," Johnson teased to general laughter, "will you please recall that at the conference at Philadelphia, Baltimore was awarded to the National League," referring to the settlement negotiation back in October in which Sinclair had proposed adding Baltimore and Newark to the National League and Pittsburgh and Brooklyn to the American.

"Can I recall it, do you say?" asked a confused Herrmann.

"I say you must recall it," replied Johnson.

"No, I do not think I was present at that time. I got in afterward." Herrmann still misunderstood.

"We were to have two ten-club circuits, and Baltimore was awarded to the National League, wasn't it?" Johnson reminded him.

"I think you and Mr. Ball fixed that up," Tener clarified.

"Along with Newark," Johnson further clarified.

"Oh, you mean recently. I thought you meant originally," Herrmann finally understood.

"And you approved of it for a little while," Tener added. "I did not know whether you were in earnest or not, that you would give us Baltimore and Newark, and Mr. Sinclair remembers that."

"Newark is a pretty good town," Sinclair chimed in.

"We were to have Pittsburgh and Brooklyn, and we accepted," Johnson added.

"With the ten-club league," clarified Ebbets.

"You were awarded Baltimore and Newark," Johnson reiterated.

"Don't you think, Mr. Johnson," Sinclair asked, "that that would have had some considerable value to the National League?"

"I think so," Johnson agreed.

"Newark and Baltimore," Sinclair looked for confirmation.

"Oh, yes," Johnson added sarcastically as a gibe at the National League, to general laughter.

"Which one would have been an advantage to us?" Tener asked. New to the long history between the National and American leagues, he didn't understand that Johnson was teasing the Nationals, and he wanted clarification. "Both of them?"

Johnson had tired of the Baltimore discussion and mocked Herrmann again: "Mr. Herrmann evidently forgets the recent conference when cities were awarded, and he overlooked that entirely."

Gaffney finally tried to get the meeting back on track: "How far have we got down in the agreement, Mr. Chairman?"

"We've gotten all through with it. We have read it all," Herrmann told him.

Janney finally changed his tack. "Might I suggest this? You will note that there is absolutely nothing in the proposals that have been before the league with reference to Baltimore. Would it be within the purview of the National Commission to take up the question of some other method of settlement to meet the Baltimore situation if the one we have suggested is not agreeable?"

The Organized Baseball owners agreed, but Herrmann made it clear that "the Major League proposition is impossible at this time." Gilmore quickly named Weeghman and Sinclair along with himself to represent the Federals in hashing out the final agreement.

With the Baltimore situation tabled and a committee in place to complete the settlement, Toole revived the question of the withdrawal of the anti-trust suit. He pushed for quick action. The Federal Leaguers, not surprisingly, preferred to delay the withdrawal until the final settlement had been signed. After a lengthy discussion, both sides decided to punt the issue until the next morning.[16]

In spite of Ban Johnson's constant bombast regarding the evils of the Federals, he and Phil Ball had developed a surprising friendship. By late 1915, as it became clear that a settlement was inevitable, Johnson wired Ball to discuss the end game. Shortly before the National League reached its provisional agreement with the Federals, Ball met with Johnson and Chicago White Sox owner Charles Comiskey at the Union League Club in Chicago. Ball held firm that in any settlement he agreed to, all the Federal League players would have to be reaccepted into Organized Baseball. Johnson had already resigned himself to this request and further pursued Ball's interest in purchasing the Browns. The American League president, who still held considerable sway over the ownership of his league's teams, particularly those that were struggling and undercapitalized, assured Ball that he would get him an option on the club. Although not an official part of the settlement, providing Ball with the opportunity to purchase a Major League ballclub was an important and necessary component of any final peace agreement.

Johnson prevailed on Robert Hedges, who in early December agreed to give Ball an option to purchase the Browns on the condition that he put up $30,000 before Christmas. Ball agreed, and Hedges sent one of his stockholders to fetch the deposit. Meanwhile, Organized Baseball and Federal League owners had negotiated the Federal League out of existence. With the official demise of the Federal League and the reestablishment of the Major Leagues' monopoly, Hedges's group hesitated to sell the franchise. The stockholder collecting the option money didn't show at the office of Ball's lawyer until 4 p.m. and then said he had to go home for Christmas.

"How about the $30,000?" Ball asked.

"The banks are all closed, and you can't get it now," he grinned.

Ball opened a drawer where he had the money. "Here it is," he said, and held out the money. The Browns' representative refused to take it, then knocked it to the floor.

"It's okay," Ball replied. "If you don't take it, the woman who cleans up this place will," and he walked out. Before leaving, the Browns' stockholder picked up the money, and Ball had his option.[17]

Several days after the big meeting at the Biltmore, Gilmore, Weeghman, and Sinclair traveled to Cincinnati to meet with the National Commission and wrap up the agreement. Because nearly all points had been thoroughly hashed out or agreed to on December 17, the meeting went relatively smoothly. At the end, two outstanding issues remained: what to do about the outstanding contract obligations to the Federal League players—this was a significant obligation, potentially around $300,000 for seventy or so players—and how to resolve the Baltimore, and possibly Buffalo, situations. As to the players, Sinclair stepped up and agreed to assume responsibility for the contracts of players not on Pittsburgh, Chicago, or St. Louis. He correctly assumed that some of these contracts had value and that he could sell players back to Organized Baseball to recoup some of his exposure. As to Baltimore and Buffalo, the Federal League representatives had little interest in delaying or risking a settlement for the benefit of Baltimore or the near-bankrupt Buffalo franchise, but they also recognized that Baltimore, in particular, might imperil the peace agreement unless mollified.

One proposal involved amalgamating the Federal League Buffalo ownership into the International League's club and granting an International League franchise to the Baltimore Federal Leaguers; Baltimore's International League team had abandoned that city for Richmond after the 1914 season. International League president Ed Barrow, however, remained determined to obstruct any possibility of the Federal League owners gaining a foothold in his league. He had just spent two years struggling to keep the International League intact. His memories were too recent and too bitter to turn franchises over to his recent adversaries. The Buffalo International franchise had weathered the storm against the Federals, and he saw no reason to force it to surrender a share to them now. Jack Dunn, who had owned the Baltimore club and had sold a partial interest to Richmond investors when he had moved there, wanted a new club for Baltimore. Barrow supported Dunn over the Federal Leaguers: "I fought everybody for him, even my best friends, and that after I had been warned by some of them that Dunn would someday turn on me. . . . Mr. Dunn was on the verge of committing suicide when it looked as if he might not get back into Baltimore. And to this day [September 1917], Gilmore and Sinclair and certain people in Organized Baseball claim that if it had not been for my stubbornness in holding out for Jack Dunn, the peace agreement settlement would have gone through without a hitch."[18]

On December 22, as the finishing touches to the deal were being made, the negotiators took one more shot at satisfying Baltimore. Rasin and Goldman called Janney to the team's office in the Union Trust Building to tell him that Gilmore was on the phone from Cincinnati. They handed the phone to Janney and asked him to take over.

"Will the Baltimore stockholders take $50,000 in settlement and keep the ball grounds and ball team?" Gilmore asked him.

"Unquestionably, they will not. The ball team and grounds would be a liability, not an asset."

"Then what do you want?"

"If you bring us a proposition of $75,000 and you take the ball team and grounds, then we might consider it."

Gilmore said he would need to confer with the others.

"There is nothing doing on that," Gilmore told Janney when he called back fifteen minutes later. "You better take the other."

"No, we will not take the other."

"Well, what are you going to do about it?"

"Well, we just won't settle, that is all."

"What do you mean?"

"Well, we won't dismiss the suit in Chicago, and we will go on and stand on our rights."

"It does not seem to me you have any rights. All the others [the other teams in the league] have stopped."

"Perhaps it looks that way, but at the same time we are going to stand on our rights, whatever they are, if you don't make a satisfactory settlement," Janney told him, and Gilmore rang off.[19]

The participants signed the final peace settlement later that day. It incorporated the points from the December 13 tentative agreement and included two additional sections:

1. The National and American Leagues would each pay the Newark club (Sinclair) $10,000 per year for the next ten years for a total of $200,000 (equivalent to $115,000 on a present value basis at a discount rate of 6 percent).
2. A seven-person committee would be formed to address the Baltimore and Buffalo situations. The seven included the three members of the National Commission, Gilmore, International League president Ed Barrow (both Buffalo and Baltimore had had franchises in the International League at the start of the Federal League conflict in 1914), and a representative from the Buffalo and Baltimore Federal League teams to be appointed by Gilmore.

This latter committee scheduled its first meeting for January 5, 1916. Barrow, Gilmore, Rasin, Janney, and Buffalo's William Robertson traveled to Cincinnati to meet with the Commission and settle the remaining issues. Janney, however, balked at the authority of the committee. Not unreasonably, he did not wish to submit the final disposition of the Baltimore franchise to a seven-man committee made up of four representatives from Organized Baseball and a clearly hostile Gilmore. Without a Baltimore representative there was clearly no reason for a meeting, and it was temporarily delayed as the Commission members tried to convince Janney to join the negotiations. After first postponing the meeting to Wednesday, the Commission then suggested rescheduling in New York on January 19.

Barrow suffered what appeared to be an attack of appendicitis while in Cincinnati, and was growing increasingly frustrated. After battling for survival against the Federal League franchises for two years, he had little interest now in a compromise with the Federals, which would have involved the Federal League ownership in those two cities acquiring franchises in the International League. Barrow wanted see the existing team in Buffalo prevail and Jack Dunn return to Baltimore. Moreover, Brookfeds manager John Ganzel had signed eight International League ballplayers at the end of the 1915 season, and Barrow believed his league should get these players back without having to pay Sinclair for them. (He was willing to make an exception for players sold to the Major Leagues.)[20]

Upon his return to New York, Barrow announced his resignation from the peace committee: "I have resigned from this committee as there does not seem to be any attempt made by the Federal League to get together. We shall go on with our plans for next season without further considering them."[21] Rasin and Janney still didn't appreciate the weakness of their negotiating position. They now hoped to negotiate a final satisfactory buyout at the meeting on January 19 so that they could make a positive report at their stockholders meeting on January 27. Rasin supposed he still had some negotiating leverage because the Federals had not yet formally requested Landis to dismiss the lawsuit, and the signed settlement anticipated a resolution of all the Federal League franchises (except the forfeited Kansas City club). But the settlement with Organized Baseball satisfied the other Federal League owners, and they had no interest in revisiting it. Furthermore, the Major League owners believed they had paid more than enough and had little patience for additional demands. "I am of the opinion we will not have a meeting in New York on the 19th," Herrmann wrote Janney, "as nothing new has developed which would warrant us getting together at the time."[22] Clearly, the Commission was through with Baltimore.

For their stockholders meeting on January 27, the Baltimore directors prepared a report on the status of the franchise. After rehashing their sense of abandonment, the directors recommended "pushing" the suit still pending with Judge Landis—though they surely realized by this time that Landis had little interest in ruling against Organized Baseball. Alternatively, they recommended "a new proceeding be instituted at once to recover triple damages under the Clayton [Antitrust] act," and be authorized to raise an additional $50,000 to cover legal costs.[23]

Days later, a Maryland congressman passed along a letter from a disgruntled Baltimore shareholder to the Justice Department, asking the government to intervene in the baseball settlement because it was in violation of the anti-trust laws. The attorney general's office had little interest in getting involved and responded several days later "that the transaction does not appear to constitute any ground for action by the department."[24]

An embittered Gwinner also expressed unhappiness with the settlement. In Pittsburgh he had lost well over the $50,000 he had been allotted as part of the settlement. "I was willing to go along until the Federal League became a paying proposition," Gwinner complained, "but when my partners saw fit to 'feather their own nest' and drop me overboard, I decided that baseball politics were too much for me, and so I am out." To placate Gwinner, the negotiators assured him he would have an opportunity to purchase a Major League club. The most obvious candidate was the Cleveland Indians, now controlled by the lenders who had taken it from the financially strapped Somers and wanted their debts repaid. In the end, Gwinner refused to meet the $560,000 price—$350,000 in cash and an assumption of $210,000 in debt—mandated by the bankers controlling the team. Johnson could have arranged this sale, but he had little interest in another former Federal League owner in his league, and after Gwinner's pursuit fell short, he swiftly maneuvered the Indians to another friendly owner.[25]

On February 7, 1916, the attorneys for Organized Baseball, the Federal League, and the Baltfeds appeared before Judge Landis for the official dismissal of the anti-trust lawsuit filed the previous January. Janney, on behalf of Baltimore, did not object to the dismissal as long as it did not limit their future rights to bring suit. In his closing statement, delivered orally, Landis offered his thoughts on the case. The self-satisfied judge clearly had never had any intention of ruling against Organized Baseball:

> From the court's own knowledge of the subject matter of your litigation, resulting from thirty years' acquaintance with the subject matter of your litigation, beginning before most of you gentlemen who were in that litigation knew anything about any such thing as baseball, convinces the Court that an appropriate order on this application for a temporary injunction reaching to the extent that that or-

der would have to reach in view of the state of the record, would have been if not destructive, vitally injurious to the subject matter of litigation. [The last clause of this rambling sentence strongly suggests that Landis believed the facts supported the Federals.] . . . And so the question which I had to decide, in addition to the legal questions submitted by that application, was whether or not I would forthwith enter an order that would be vitally injurious if not destructive of this subject. . . . I decided after taking counsel with my own judgment . . . that this court had a right . . . to postpone the announcement of any such order, and that is the reason that the entry of that order was postponed.[26]

The Federal League was no more. After two costly years of struggling for players and acceptance, the Federal League owners succumbed to the institutional advantages of Organized Baseball: a blacklist, a standard player contract that the courts would not invalidate despite its apparent violation of the anti-trust statues and other contract law precedents, a close relationship with the press, and an established Minor League arrangement that provided for mutual support and a regular supply of player talent. To extract roughly $700,000 from Major League baseball's owners as the price for disbanding represented a notable achievement for Gilmore, Sinclair, and Weeghman. The settlement, however, left several loose ends. How one of these, Baltimore's continuing dissatisfaction, was resolved would shape baseball for many years to come.

15

Aftermath

Charlie Weeghman had nearly exhausted his financial resources during his two years of fighting Organized Baseball. Now he had an option to purchase the Cubs, but he and his partner William Walker needed to come up with the $500,000 purchase price in a very short period of time. For a chunk of the capital, Weeghman leaned on a couple of his restaurant suppliers for $50,000 each: J. Ogden Armour, whom he had already tagged for a loan in 1915, and chewing gum magnate William Wrigley. But after raising $350,000, Weeghman ran out of sources.

In desperation he turned to Albert Lasker, a Chicago advertising executive whom he did not know but of whose interest in baseball and ability to raise money Weeghman was well aware. He explained to Lasker that his option on the Cubs expired the next day and that he needed $150,000 by 10 a.m. Lasker told Weeghman he'd think about it overnight. The next morning he agreed to put in the necessary $150,000 on two conditions: he would be allowed to approve the board of directors, and his personal attorney would be the team's attorney. Weeghman had little choice but to accept. At the initial organizational meeting Lasker vetoed one of Weeghman's choices for director and demanded that Wrigley and Armour, whom he knew personally, be on the board. Neither Armour nor Wrigley really wanted to be involved; they had invested money primarily to help out one of their biggest customers. Wrigley eventually accepted, but Armour substituted the head of one of his company's divisions. Weeghman still controlled the team, but now he had powerful men sitting beside him.[1]

As the new owner of the Cubs, Weeghman joined the owners' fraternity and met Brooklyn owner Charles Ebbets socially for the first time.

"Glad to shake hands with you," Ebbets told Weeghman, "even if you did take Tinker away from me. You know they blamed me for causing the Federal League."

"It was an injustice," Weeghman responded, "for it was Charles Webb Murphy who really caused the Feds. He gave Mordecai Brown such a raw deal that I agreed to subscribe $5,000 to put a new Chicago club in the field, and by the way, I've been paying ever since."[2]

As normalcy returned to Major League boardrooms, several owners and executives found themselves confronting leftover problems from the Federal League war. Ban Johnson and several American League magnates believed they had overpaid in the settlement. They convinced themselves they had gone along with it out of a sense of duty to the National League and the Minor Leagues, but now they blamed Garry Herrmann for pushing the settlement from his position as Commission chairman. Johnson several times postponed the annual National Commission meeting (typically held in Cincinnati on the first Monday of the New Year) while he considered his options, including trying to replace Herrmann as chairman. Johnson was eventually persuaded by several owners not to "kick up a fuss so soon after the conclusion of the peace."[3] But owing to the resentment caused by the Federal League settlement and subsequent events, the Commission would never again operate as authoritatively as it had pre–Federal League.

Harry Sinclair was rumored to be shopping for a Major League team, and several owners saw visions of a large payday, hoping they could sell their franchise for a large amount and recover their losses. James Gaffney wanted to sell the Braves, and Sinclair could have purchased them if he wished. The Reds and the bankrupt Indians were also available. Sinclair, however, had seen the bright lights of New York and wanted the Giants franchise; otherwise, he was done with baseball. He offered Harry Hempstead $1 million for the Giants, a huge amount for the time, but Hempstead demanded $1.3 million (another report put Hempstead's price even higher: $1.5 million for 62 percent of the team, effectively valuing the franchise well above $2 million). Sinclair wasn't interested in baseball at any price; he declined Hempstead's demands and went back to his oil business.[4]

Of all the owners, Schuyler Britton seemed to have the most difficulty returning to normalcy. After the mania of the Federal League war subsided, his resentment at playing second fiddle to his wife seemed to consume him. Britton began drinking heavily and staying out late. The couple separated several times in 1916, and Helene later testified that he "frequently struck her." The final break came on November 7 when Schuyler came home at 2 a.m. only to find himself locked out. After almost breaking down the door, once Helene let him in, he "nearly set fire to the house" as he waved his cigar around in a drunken frenzy. That night the couple had their final argument; either Helene kicked him out or Schuyler finally left on his own, but in any event he never returned.[5]

The Federal League settlement left the former league's owners responsible for their player contracts. This was a bit of a two-edged sword: on the one hand, it made them liable for the contracts that were guaranteed for 1916; on the other, it gave them the opportunity to sell the contracts, and hence the rights to the player, to the highest bidder. Weeghman and Ball simply kept their players and amalgamated them into the Cubs and Browns respectively. Sinclair controlled his own players from Newark, plus he had assumed the contracts of the bankrupt Kansas City and Buffalo franchises and Brooklyn's from the Wards.

Sinclair and Pittsburgh's Edward Gwinner immediately began marketing their players to Organized Baseball. Gwinner put together a letter which he sent to all the owners, promoting his players and listing their salaries. Ed Konetchy had a guaranteed salary (i.e., no ten-day clause) of $7,000 for 1916 and 1917; Frank Allen was under contract for $5,500 for 1916; Elmer Knetzer, referred to as the "iron man of the league," was due $4,500; Ralph Comstock, "a spit ball pitcher, has a contract for 1916 and 1917 with a salary of $3,750 with the ten day clause out"; Sanford Burk was at $3,000 for 1916; and Marty Berghammer had a contract for 1916 and 1917 at $3,600 per season. Garry Herrmann offered a typical response, not necessarily with respect to the specific players, but in tone: he didn't want Comstock, Konetchy, or Burk; he might be interested in Allen or Knetzer, but their salaries were too high, and he would want Gwinner to cover part of their pay. Gwinner eventually found a taker: the Boston Braves purchased Allen, Knetzer, and Konetchy for $13,000.

The two New York teams were the most active. The new Yankee owners spent $37,000 to purchase Lee Magee and two others. The Giants, baseball's wealthiest franchise, finally landed Benny Kauff and several others, including future Hall of Famer Edd Roush. In total the Giants spent $48,500 on Sinclair's players. In sum, the Major Leagues spent $129,150 purchasing player contracts from the Federal League owners. The Minors too purchased some of the players, though there is no record of how much was spent; in any case, it would have been significantly less than what the Majors spent. The prices paid by the wealthy New York clubs were well above prewar prices and in line with the star player sales between Major League teams during the Federal League war. This new pricing level seemed to establish a baseline for the remainder of the decade, culminating in the sale of Babe Ruth to the Yankees for $100,000.[6]

The Cincinnati Reds hoped to land Vin Campbell, a solid twenty-eight-year-old outfielder coming off two promising seasons with the Federals. Campbell, however, came from a well-to-do family and chose to quit baseball and run his businesses. He also sued the Newark club for $8,269, which he claimed was owed him on his 1916 guaranteed contract. Sinclair elected to defend the case in court. He and his attorneys argued that because Campbell had turned down opportunities to join Major League teams, he had invalidated the guarantee. Over a year later the case finally came to trial, and the jury found for Campbell, awarding the onetime outfielder $5,597. That Campbell's contract was renewed in September 1915 further belies Gilmore's later claim that Sinclair and others were running a big bluff regarding the league's status for 1916.[7]

Several of the most ardent Federal League supporters and recruiters never made it back to the Majors. Although the peace accord technically removed the player blacklist, several of the more aggressive player-managers appear to have been singled out. Rebel Oakes, a capable center fielder and only twenty-nine, never again played in the Majors. Neither did Harry Lord, the Buffeds manager and third baseman in 1915, or George Stovall, the Kawfeds first baseman and manager. All three eventually found employment in the Minor Leagues as player-managers but left Organized Baseball after only a couple of years. The *Hartford Courant* wrote, "No official blacklist has been placed against them . . . but there is a presumption that [they] have been blacklisted—banished from the scenes where they once flourished."[8] Steve Evans too—flaunter of the $1,000 bills after the world tour—never made it back to the Majors, despite being only thirty years old and a star with the Federals.

Kauff's legal case for his $5,000 bonus was still dragging through the court system at the time of his sale. When he learned he had been sold to the Giants, he demanded $5,000 of his sale price to cover the bonus. Not surprisingly, Sinclair had lost enough money already and had no interest in giving any more to Kauff. Kauff soon recognized the futility of his arguments, the lawsuit petered out, and he enthusiastically joined the Giants.[9]

Kauff's attorney (ironically, John Montgomery Ward) took up the cases of two other players after the settlement. Outfielder Claude Cooper and third baseman Bill Bradley had both signed three-year contracts with Brooklyn in 1914. In 1916 neither Bradley, managing at the class D level in the Minors, nor Cooper, struggling with the Phillies, were being paid anything close to Brooklyn's guaranteed salary. John Montgomery Ward sued William Ward, the son of his old employer, for the players' 1916 salary. The two cases apparently never came to trial, indicating that William Ward and the players probably settled. In 1915 Bradley actually played for Kansas City, implying that the Wards continued their financial support, possibly covering Bradley's salary, throughout the 1915 season.[10]

In one of the odder outcomes of the player redistribution, Rupert Mills refused a buyout of his contract. Mills had signed with Powers and Sinclair in 1915 off the Notre Dame campus for two years at $3,000 per season. With the demise of the Federals, Newark offered him $600 as a buyout for the second year of his contract. Mills refused the buyout offer, and the two sides failed to reach agreement. Mills demanded that he be paid for 1916, and in response Sinclair demanded that Mills honor his contract. Thus Mills would show up at Newark's now quiet Harrison Park at 8:55 a.m. to start his "work day," take a break for lunch, and return from 2 to 6 p.m. Eventually, both sides tired of the charade, and in July they agreed to a buyout of the remainder of Mills's contract. Mills reportedly signed with Detroit but never appeared for them and in 1917 wound up in the Minors.[11]

With the Federals gone from the scene, the baseball owners began rolling back salaries to pre–Federal League levels. As the players recognized the full extent of the retrenchment, they grew increasingly restless. Union leader Dave Fultz hoped to use this frustration to build solidarity in his union. The environment during World War I also provided a favorable window for unions. The demand for goods from the belligerent European powers increased the call for workers at the same time the war shut off the huge supply of cheap immigrant labor from Eastern and Southern Europe. As workers felt more secure and emboldened in their jobs, union membership surged and strikes increased.

On October 30, 1916, Fultz presented a list of five demands to Organized Baseball:

1. Teams must pay players under contract who were injured while playing. [This was purely a Minor League issue; the Major Leagues did not suspend players who were injured while playing.]
2. When a Minor League player is given his five-day notice and released, he shall be immediately free to sign with any other team.
3. Minor league players shall have traveling expenses paid to spring training camps. [This was done for all the Major League players and about three-quarters of the Minor Leaguers.]
4. When a player brings a complaint against a team before the National Commission for adjudication, the Commission must provide the Players Fraternity with a copy of the club's defense.

5. Because Minor League teams often ignored adverse rulings, Fultz insisted that the National Board [the Minor League equivalent of the National Commission] enforce its awards if and when it went against a club.[12]

Fultz viewed these concessions as eminently reasonable and was shocked when the Minor Leagues refused him an audience. In fairness to the Minors, they generally operated on a shoestring budget, particularly the lower leagues, and had not yet rebounded from the shellacking they had taken during the Federal League war. In 1916 Major League baseball attracted more fans than it had in 1913, before the war. The Double-A American Association, on the other hand, the only Minor League for which we have attendance data, remained 25 percent below its 1913 levels. And while forty Minor Leagues started the 1914 season, at the end of the 1916 season there were only twenty-two.[13] The Minor League owners would have had little interest in dickering with a union under any circumstances; under the existing economic hardship they were even less inclined.

Fultz reacted by asking for support from the Major League owners—specifically, the National Commission. He had spent the last four years working with the Commission and believed—incorrectly—that he had built up a measure of goodwill with Ban Johnson, John Tener, and Garry Herrmann. But the Major League owners tolerated the union only as long as the Federal League was around, and would be happy to see it fold, something Fultz never fully internalized. As reported in *Sporting Life*, "When asked whether the removal of the Federal League from the field would lessen the influence of the Fraternity, Fultz said: 'I don't think so. I think the club owners are feeling more kindly toward us now than they did a few years ago.'"[14] The Commission simply sidestepped Fultz's request, saying this was purely a Minor League matter in which they had no intention of getting involved. Over the next couple of weeks Fultz dug in his heels and became increasingly belligerent over Organized Baseball's refusal to address these issues. Finally, he threatened a player strike.

It's hard to believe that Fultz could have been so tone deaf to his union and to the Major League owners. His Fraternity consisted solely of players in the Majors, Double-A, and Single-A; his five demands affected mainly players at Single-A and below. He led a union of players unhappy with the large salary cuts being imposed upon them. How could he ask them to risk their livelihood for a purely Minor League matter and hope to hold them together in the face of the ferocious response they would face from Organized Baseball? "These Minor League matters are not trivial," Fultz declared, defending his decision, "and are of as much importance to the Major League players as to the Minors. There are

about 5,000 Minor League players, and only something like 360 big league players. And sooner or later each of those 360 will go back home to the Minors or
retire from the game."[15] These were hardly inspiring words.

Nevertheless, in the calm of winter following the 1916 season, Fultz, who
had built up a fund of goodwill and trust with the players over the past four
years, persuaded six hundred to seven hundred of them to sign pledges that
they would not sign contracts for the 1917 season until cleared by Fultz. He
set February 20, 1917, as the effective strike date; if the demands were not met
by then, the players would not report to spring training. Fultz also worked to
maintain union solidarity. When pitcher Slim Sallee signed a contract in violation of the Fraternity's edict, Fultz expelled him. For additional support, Fultz
looked outside baseball and approached labor leader Samuel Gompers about
joining his umbrella union, the American Federation of Labor. Gompers initially voiced encouragement for Fultz's appeal and said he favored a strike by
ballplayers if they felt it was necessary.

Organized Baseball's leaders couldn't believe that Fultz was willing to put his
union at risk and that the players would actually strike over such minor matters.
As Fultz grew increasingly inflexible, the owners saw an easy opening to break
the union. Knowing the Major League players would not hold out over Fultz's
demands, they turned up the heat. Ban Johnson spoke for the owners when he
blistered the Players Fraternity:

> We never again shall listen to any proposal he [Fultz] may offer. We invite him to
> carry out his bluff. I, personally, do not believe the players are back of Fultz. I think
> he has been using the power to send out statements without authority from the
> players themselves. The American League will see that Fultz is crushed—driven out
> of baseball. The American League has been fair with its players and will continue
> to treat them fairly without the aid of Mr. Fultz.[16]

In January and February, as players received their contracts in the mail and
with growing pressure to sign, many began deserting Fultz. As early as mid-
January, many of the players on the two New York teams had signed. In early
February only three National League clubs still had at least nine unsigned players. Gompers seemed to have lost interest in incorporating the Players Fraternity
into his organization, costing Fultz a potentially valuable ally. Without outside
support and with his player solidarity eroding, Fultz now hoped only for a
face-saving exit. He asked the National League owners if he might address their
meeting on February 13; they turned him down flat. The magnates understood

that this was an opportunity to crush the union once and for all, and had no interest in a compromise or a strategic retreat by the Players Fraternity. Shortly thereafter, they made it official: the owners severed all relations with the union. Claiming the Players Fraternity had violated it first, they abrogated the Cincinnati Agreement of January 1914.

Organized Baseball would no longer recognize, tolerate, or negotiate with any organization of players. Fultz recognized the players' predicament and surrendered, releasing them to sign contracts so that the staunchest Fraternity supporters would not be left without jobs. This abortive strike effectively ended the Players Fraternity. Without a credible threat of organized action, it had no leverage with which to bargain on any possible future issue. The shockingly quick disintegration of the Players Fraternity cost the players their best chance until the 1960s for a union that might offer real protection from the vagaries of baseball's owners.[17]

It is hard to understand Fultz's decision to risk a strike over relatively trivial Minor League work rules. Because many of the Major League players had absorbed large pay cuts, they may have been willing to take collective action, but only for issues directly affecting their pocketbook. To expect the players, unaccustomed to organized protest, to strike against angry, prepared, and counterattacking employers for five uninspiring demands was naive. Fultz also completely misread the owners' intransigence. After some early triumphs, he came to believe that the owners accepted the Fraternity as a legitimate partner and would yield if he pushed hard enough. He never seemed to appreciate that almost all his previous success was due to the threat of the Federal League. Without the Federals, the owners could bring the full weight of their societal and financial positions to bear without fear of consequences.

Could the Players Fraternity have survived as a viable entity if run differently? It seems unlikely. The baseball magnates, like owners in other industries, despised and feared collective action by employees, and without significant competition for player services the owners had little to fear from hard-line tactics. Even if the union had survived a few years, the end of World War I aborted many of the federal government's labor-friendly policies, leaving unions unprotected from employer abuses. Finally, sports are a particularly difficult arena in which to build the solidarity necessary for collective bargaining. Because of an ingrained loyalty to team and a heightened sense of individual accomplishment, players need a sustained organizing campaign to prepare them for the rigors of collective action. All that being said, the Major League owners and the National Commission continued to pay lip service to the union during the 1916 season.

Had the Fraternity concentrated solely on the most egregious individual cases of player exploitation at the Major League level and stayed away from unimportant confrontations, some sort of independent union might have survived.

Once the final attempt at a successful resolution of the Baltimore situation broke down in January 1916, the club's shareholders soberly realized that the door to Major League baseball in their city, or even what they considered a reasonable settlement, was shut. The shareholders, the fans—the entire city—felt betrayed. For the third time in fewer than twenty years, Baltimore had lost its Major League team. With no other avenues open, on March 29, 1916, the club filed suit in U.S. District Court in Philadelphia against Organized Baseball and their onetime Federal League brethren to recover their losses. They asked for $300,000 in damages, which, under the anti-trust statutes, would be trebled to $900,000. The principal charge in the lawsuit was conspiracy, perhaps best articulated by sportswriter James Isaminger: "that they [Organized Baseball] bought off other Federal League clubs, but left Baltimore out in the cold." With the filing of this suit, Organized Baseball halted its promised payments to the other Federal League owners. As the Major Leagues saw it, they had negotiated a settlement with the Federal League owners; any remaining liability to the Baltimore franchise was the responsibility of the Federals.[18]

Organized Baseball again called on George Wharton Pepper to defend them. When the case finally came to trial in June 1917, Pepper's main defense was familiar: baseball was not interstate commerce and thus did not come under the federal anti-trust statutes. Baltimore's attorneys, led by Stuart Janney, concentrated on the peace negotiations themselves, arguing that they effectively represented a conspiracy because they shut out the Baltimore representatives. Pepper had one more card to play. In the midst of the trial, Organized Baseball's attorneys introduced the stenographic minutes of the settlement conference at the Biltmore. He highlighted the section where Sinclair had said "Yes" when asked if he was representing the entire circuit, and Rasin had raised no objection. Pepper claimed that Rasin, representing Baltimore, was therefore in tacit agreement with everything that ensued. This testimony undercut Janney's main argument. After seeing this evidence, Janney gave up the suit. "Your honor, may I make a statement?" he requested. "After full consideration of this case last night by counsel for the plaintiff, circumstances have arisen which makes us desire to discontinue it. I desire to ask leave of the court, therefore, formally to file a motion of discontinuance. I would say that there has been no settlement in the case."[19]

Despite Janney's protestations, the Baltimore contingent had been negotiating behind the scenes with Organized Baseball's representatives, led by Pepper and National League attorney John O'Toole. With the weakening of their case, the Federals became more willing to settle. In early August, O'Toole presided over a full-blown settlement conference at the Waldorf-Astoria in New York between the National Commission and several National League owners on one side and Janney and key Baltimore representatives on the other. Despite some optimism that an agreement could be reached, Johnson and Tener were not willing to grant Baltimore a Major League team or ante up an amount of money sufficient for the Baltimore owners.

With the failure of these negotiations, the Baltimore shareholders reconsidered the issue and in September 1917 reinstituted their case along much broader lines. The new suit focused more broadly on all the anti-trust violations in addition to concentrating on the conspiracy charge. Much like the January 1915 case in front of Judge Landis, Baltimore's attorneys highlighted the myriad ways that Organized Baseball had interfered with the Federal League. They pointed out how the reserve clause and blacklist had combined to thwart players from moving to the new league.

Ban Johnson remained convinced that Baltimore's lawsuit was simply a tactic to get a settlement out of Organized Baseball, which had little to fear from the courts. Johnson had many contacts throughout baseball and cultivated them for whatever inside dope he could find. He passed on to Herrmann information that a man named Wicks, a onetime secretary of the Newark club, had visited with a private banker and Baltimore stockholder named Hirschberg. According to Wicks, Hirschberg told him that the Baltimore Federals had no expectation of getting a favorable decision but hoped to compel Organized Baseball to come across with a settlement.[20]

Sinclair, Gwinner, and the Wards apparently also believed that little would come of the Baltimore suit or that they could buy off the Baltimore stockholders. In February 1918, with the Baltimore action still pending, attorneys for the three Federal League owners reached an agreement with O'Toole on behalf of the Major League owners that they would release the first installment of the settlement proceeds, held up since early 1916 when Baltimore filed its initial suit. The implied quid pro quo was that the three owners agreed to take on some of the risk of a verdict in favor of the Baltfeds.[21]

To defend the suit the American League, reflecting Ban Johnson's sanguine outlook on the trial, engaged Washington owner and attorney Ben Minor to look after their interests. The National League took the suit much more seriously and reengaged George Wharton Pepper and Samuel Clement Jr. to manage the case. As the trial date neared, Johnson began complaining about legal fees, another indication that he was not particularly worried about the outcome. He told his National League counterpart John Heydler (who had taken over for John Tener) that Minor would represent the American League for roughly $2,500. He was shocked that Herrmann estimated the National League legal bill at $15,000.

With the trial scheduled to begin in March 1919, Johnson and his American League counterparts suddenly became concerned over the possibility of an adverse ruling. Johnson relented and the three commissioners agreed that Pepper should be the lead attorney, regardless of the additional cost. Pepper agreed to take the case under several conditions: he would act for both leagues and be paid by both; if the trial ended and he could return to Philadelphia by March 15, he would charge $20,000 if they won and $5,000 if they lost; if the trial went to March 16 or beyond, the fee would be substantially increased; $5,000 would be paid in advance; and traveling and living expenses in Washington would be covered.[22]

Pepper, recognizing the potential strength of Baltimore's case, suggested that the Major League club presidents attend the trial to demonstrate to the court that they took the allegations seriously. To encourage them, National League president John Heydler highlighted some of the more damning evidence. Testimony from Runt Walsh, Monte Prieste, and George Maisel "showed how for a period of years they were shunted around from club to club, or from coast to coast, as in Maisel's case." Also, a typical letter from Montreal owner Sam Lichtenhein to a player who had just jumped to the Federal League was "a bad spot in evidence." Heydler pointed out that the Baltimore attorneys were leaning heavily on the monopoly and conspiracy portion of their case and introducing as evidence the player purchase and repurchase agreements between the Majors and Minors. Heydler believed that Organized Baseball now oversaw this much better than before 1913. But he was concerned that the Federal League attorneys would be presenting the full career history of various players, which would include years before 1913.[23]

As the trial began, Pepper fretted over the venue. He felt he was in a "courtroom unfriendly to the interests of my clients."[24] He was right. After reading the depositions and hearing two weeks of testimony, Associate Justice Wendell Stafford of the D.C. District Court instructed the jury "(a) that the appellants were engaged in interstate commerce; (b) that they attempted to monopolize, and did monopolize, a part of that commerce principally through what is called the 'reserve clause' and ineligible list features of certain agreements [the blacklist], but (c) left it to the jury to say whether the appellants had conspired together to destroy, and did destroy the Federal League."[25]

Under these instructions the jury had little choice but to find for the plaintiff. Clearly many of Organized Baseball's actions violated the anti-trust laws; if the law applied to baseball, they were surely guilty. The jury awarded the Baltimore Federals $80,000 in damages; under the provisions of the Sherman Antitrust Act the award was trebled to $240,000. Baltimore was also awarded its legal costs of $24,000. Thus, in total, the Baltimore shareholders received a verdict for $264,000.

After the trial Heydler sent a memo to his league's presidents summarizing the result. Although disappointed, he reported that Pepper felt that the judge's instruction that professional baseball was commerce could not be sustained in a higher court. Publicly Johnson and Heydler professed confidence they would prevail on appeal and outlined the consequences if they didn't. "The verdict, of course, is a blow to baseball," Johnson said, "but we are not particularly distressed, as it was nothing more than we expected under the circumstances. We were bound to appeal no matter what the amount of damages was."[26] Heydler also remained confident: "There is nothing that cannot be remedied by higher court, if error has been made. . . . The game is not affected by this decision except in its business aspects, and I believe the public has little interest in those."[27] If Organized Baseball did lose on appeal, Johnson and Heydler foresaw the reseparation of the American and National leagues and the termination of the National Agreement establishing the relationship between the Majors and Minors.

The National Commission also released a formal statement minimizing the impact: "The decision made by Justice Stafford that Organized Baseball violated the prohibitions of the Sherman act was not rendered in a suit by the United States to dissolve the combination. The decision, therefore, necessitates no modification of the system under which Organized Baseball is operating. . . . All clubs and players are accordingly advised that business will proceed as usual and that all legal contracts must be lived up to."[28]

In the months after the jury award, a settlement seemed likely. Both sides had strong reasons to consider one. Baltimore's attorneys recognized that further appeals would be costly and, more important, that they could lose. At the same time a settlement offered Organized Baseball the opportunity to get out relatively cheaply, admit no wrongdoing, and continue business as usual. In the fall, Edwin Goldman, an attorney from the Baltimore legal team, approached Pepper asking for settlement terms. Pepper talked the issue over with O. M. Clement, one of the

American League's attorneys, who thought they should settle. Pepper believed Organized Baseball would ultimately prevail, but "several of the questions are novel" and he could be mistaken. Pepper suggested to Heydler that one possibility would be to settle for the actual amount of the verdict, without the treble damages, on the further condition that Organized Baseball would admit to no violation of the Sherman Act.[29]

In late December 1919 Herrmann wrote to Pepper that the National League had decided not to accept the final compromise figure offered by the Baltimore representatives (unfortunately not available in the correspondence) but to continue with the appeal. Once they chose this path, the Major Leagues looked for other ways to cover themselves. Herrmann sent letters to Sinclair, Gilmore, William Ward, and Charles Weeghman stating that in the event the Baltimore Federals eventually won, baseball would look to the Federals for a full indemnity of costs because the trial court had ruled that there was "no basis in fact for the representations made by the Federal League officers that they had authority to bind their constituent organizations."[30]

In October 1920 the much-anticipated case finally reached the appellate court, where Pepper was opposed by a distinguished group of attorneys, including William L. Marbury, a onetime United States Attorney for Maryland. This time, however, Pepper found a much more sympathetic hearing. The court bought into his entire line of reasoning and concluded that "trade and commerce require the transfer of something, whether it be persons, commodities, or intelligence from one place to another. . . . The business in which the appellants were engaged was the giving of exhibitions of baseball. A game of baseball is not susceptible to being transferred. . . . Not until they [the players] come into contact with their opponents on the baseball field and the contest opens does the game come into existence." In other words, baseball was not commerce. The transport of players across state lines was not sufficient to constitute interstate commerce because it was "but an incident to the main purpose of appellants; namely the production of the game. It was for it they were in business, not for the purpose of transferring players, balls and uniforms."

The court could have stopped there but felt it necessary also to defend the actual practices of Organized Baseball: "By means of the reserve clause and provisions in the rules and regulations [meaning the blacklist], said one witness, the clubs in the National and American Leagues are more evenly balanced, the contests between them are made more attractive to the patrons of the game, and the success of the clubs more certain." In the written opinion, Chief Justice Constantine Smyth acknowledged that these provisions "had the effect of deterring players from violating their contracts, and hence the Federal League and its constituent clubs . . . were unable to obtain players who had contracts with the appellants." In other words, Smyth considered the reserve clause a legitimate part of the contract: by implication, players who ignored the reserve clause and joined the Federals were "violating their contracts." Smyth concluded that because the effect of the reserve clause was only indirect, it was valid: "It must be obvious that the restrictions thus imposed relate directly to the conservation of the personnel of the clubs, and did not directly affect the movement of the appellee in interstate commerce. Whatever the effect, if any, they had was incidental, and therefore did not offend against the statute."[31]

The appeal was heard by the court less than a month after the exposure of the Black Sox scandal, in which it was revealed that a number of Chicago White Sox players had accepted money from gamblers purposely to lose the 1919 World Series. The apparent situation of renegade players disgracing the national pastime likely fed into the court's excessive support for the existing order. One can easily envision a judge in the early 1920s fearing that any decision that loosened the reins on player controls would lead to further chaos. Despite Smyth's antitrust background—he had spent four years as a special assistant to the attorney general prosecuting anti-trust cases—he ruled in favor of Organized Baseball.

Smyth's opinion was not as ridiculous at the time as it seems today. Only since the late 1930s has the Supreme Court "repeatedly asserted that any activity which crosses state borders, any activity which uses channels of interstate commerce, or any local activity which even remotely affects other states or interstate commerce comes within the purview of the commerce power."[32] Moreover, "sometimes, as for example in its enforcement of federal antitrust law," wrote one scholar of the Supreme Court under Chief Justice William Howard Taft, "the Taft Court was scrupulous to maintain a proper boundary between federal and state authority."[33]

Nevertheless, even at the time many observers considered Smyth's opinion mistaken. The *Michigan Law Review*, in its own brief summary of the case and relevant legal precedents, argued, "Does it not seem that when a baseball player signs to play not only at the home grounds, but on the fields of the other league members as well . . . the contract has the interstate feature as such an 'essential' element as to come within the Sherman Anti-Trust Act? . . . The interstate travel of the ball players is so 'essential' an element of their contract as to make it interstate commerce."[34]

Baltimore's stockholders and attorneys, led by Edwin Goldman, hoped the U.S. Supreme Court would see the issue more like the author of the *Michigan Law Re-*

view article and Justice Stafford. In their 202-page appeal, the Baltimore attorneys spent much of the document enumerating the injustices of the Organized Baseball structure and "fewer than twenty pages to the substantive antitrust question."[35] Baltimore felt it had been wronged and highlighted every slight.

The lawyers made their final appeal in front of a packed courtroom on April 19, 1922. Pepper described the scene:

> The situation was dramatic. The courtroom was full of interested onlookers who realized that the continuance of the World Series games was at stake. Counsel for the Federal League made the grave mistake of minimizing the real point in the case (the question, namely, whether interstate commerce was involved) and sought to inflame the passions of the Court by a vehement attack on the evils of organization, a few of which were real and many, as I thought, imaginary. I argued with much earnestness the proposition that personal effort not related to production is not a subject of commerce; that the attempt to secure all the skilled service needed for professional baseball is not an attempt to monopolize commerce or any part of it; and that Organized Baseball, not being commerce, and therefore not interstate commerce, does not come within the prohibitions of the Sherman Act.[36]

On May 29 the Supreme Court announced its unanimous decision. Organized Baseball had won: baseball was not commerce and therefore not subject to federal anti-trust laws. In the Court's opinion, Justice Oliver Wendell Holmes wrote, "The decision of the Court of Appeals went to the root of the case and if correct makes it unnecessary to consider other serious difficulties in the way of the plaintiff's recovery." He continued, "The business is giving exhibitions of baseball, which are purely state affairs . . . the transport [of the players, equipment, uniforms, etc.] is a mere incident, not the essential thing." Holmes further followed the appellate court reasoning: "Personal effort, not related to commerce is not a subject of commerce. That which in its consummation is not commerce does not become commerce among the States because the transportation we have mentioned takes place."[37]

Pepper had clearly adopted the correct legal strategy. He had concentrated on the application of the anti-trust statutes as opposed to the unseemliness of his client's actions. In summary, as the Court read the law, for an action to be a violation of the federal anti-trust laws, three features needed to be present: multiple actors, restraint of trade, and interstate commerce. By ruling that the "personal effort" of baseball players was not trade or commerce, baseball couldn't be restraint of trade; by ruling that it wasn't fundamentally interstate in nature, baseball was not interstate commerce. Thus, as Holmes wrote, Organized Baseball could not be in violation of the anti-trust laws because it did not meet two of the three conditions necessary to be subject to them.

Although the principal plaintiff in the suit was the Baltimore stockholders, the Supreme Court decision had a far-reaching effect on the course of baseball labor relations and the sports business in general during the remainder of the twentieth century. Correct or not, baseball was now exempt from federal anti-trust laws. The question remains: Did it matter? Would baseball or other professional sports have evolved differently had the Court determined that baseball was subject to the anti-trust laws? These counterfactual questions are technically unanswerable because they depend on so many secondary effects. Once one assumes a different reality, many other factors are affected as well.[38] With these caveats, it is nonetheless instructive to look at other professional sports, none of which was more than inchoate in 1922.

In the wake of Holmes's opinion, as professional football, basketball, and hockey evolved they conveniently presumed that the anti-trust exemption covered them as well. All the leagues had rules in place that effectively prevented players from becoming free agents at the end of their contract. But in a 1957 decision the Supreme Court ruled that the anti-trust exemption for baseball was an anomaly and not transferable to other professional sports. Yet for the players, making the sports leagues subject to the anti-trust laws did not lead to free agency. The leagues instituted other expedients to limit the impact of the Court's ruling. For example, the National Football League introduced the "Rozelle Rule," named after Commissioner Pete Rozelle, which gave him the power to decide on compensation to a team losing a free agent from the team signing one. The fear of losing one's top players or draft picks as compensation was a strong deterrent against signing players at the conclusion of their contract. Not until the 1970s and 1980s did the other sports begin to face true free agency.

The players benefited indirectly, however, from the emergence of rival leagues in the other professional sports. The anti-trust laws discouraged (or at least tempered) many of the more blatant tactics—such as the blacklist, inducing players to break contracts, and public declarations of the rival leagues' imminent demise—used by Organized Baseball to wreck the Federal League. These laws clearly made a difference. Successful rival leagues emerged in all three other major professional sports. And while none of them lasted longer than ten years, some ended with a merger of some sort in which the established league accepted either all, as in the case of the American Football League, or at least some of the rival league's teams. The existence of these rival leagues obviously benefited the players as the competition for their services helped drive up salaries.

With its anti-trust exemption baseball was effectively immune from this competition. Since the demise of the Federal League, no rival league has emerged to challenge Major League baseball, much less actually force a merger. In the late 1940s, when the Mexican League tried to bolster its status by signing Major Leaguers for big salaries, Organized Baseball could stop any significant player exodus by instituting and enforcing the blacklist. Even in 1960, when a much more populous and prosperous America could support more than the sixteen existing teams, an attempt at a rival league—named the Continental and led by legendary baseball executive Branch Rickey—could not get off the ground. Eventually, the Major Leagues were forced to expand to reflect the growing population in the South and West, but they were never subject to a true test from a rival league. Had the Court ruled against Organized Baseball and placed them under the anti-trust statutes, the Major Leagues would almost surely have faced future challenges. The potential profit and ego satisfaction derived from owning a Major League baseball team would eventually have led another group of wealthy businessmen to try their hands in baseball. A rival league, protected from some of the most egregious actions of Major League baseball, might even have succeeded. In time such a league would probably have folded or been partially merged. The outcome could very well have been Major League teams in the South and West many years earlier and higher players' salaries as the rival leagues competed for their services.

The Minor Leagues also would have turned out differently. It's hard to see the farm system, in which Major League teams gained control of Minor League teams, developing as it did unless baseball was protected from anti-trust laws. Rather than losing their independence in the 1930s and 1940s as the farm-system arrangement evolved, the Minor Leagues might have remained self-sufficient and unallied with particular Major League teams.

Most of the Federal League's personalities disappeared quickly from the baseball limelight. Of the Federal League's owners, only Phil Ball had a lasting affair with Major League baseball, owning the St. Louis Browns until his death in 1933. His partner, Otto Stifel, suffered a much more tragic demise. Although he reportedly owned an interest in several racehorses and a coal mine in addition to his brewery, by the late 1910s Stifel was rumored to be struggling financially. Prohibition decimated his income, and he converted his brewery into a margarine factory, a much less profitable enterprise. In August 1920 he committed suicide by shooting himself in the head. In a series of rambling suicide notes he blamed Prohibition, the banks, and some unscrupulous friends and family members, whom he claimed took financial advantage of him.[39]

When he first gained control of the Cubs, Charlie Weeghman, ever the marketer, in 1916 became the first owner in baseball to allow fans to keep foul balls that went into the stands. But Weeghman ran into hard times during World War I when his lunch-counter business crashed. Many of the young men who had worked downtown and patronized his restaurants joined the military or war-related industries. Weeghman was forced to sell his interest in the Cubs and watch his business slip away. Eventually his wife divorced him, and Weeghman moved to New York, where, with the backing of a couple of baseball owners, Jacob Ruppert of the Yankees and Harry Frazee, formerly of the Red Sox, he opened another restaurant. Weeghman, though, had lost his touch, and the place failed, as did two other later attempts. Once one of baseball's leading characters, Weeghman could never recover his magic after the demise of the Federals.

After two years of almost constant presence in the newspapers, Jim Gilmore returned to life as a small businessman, running a stationery business and taking up golf. Ned Hanlon retired from baseball to work for the Baltimore Parks Board, eventually becoming chairman in 1931.[40] Edward Gwinner, frustrated with the settlement terms, never returned to baseball.

Harry Sinclair went back to the oil business full time, though he couldn't stay away from sports altogether and later became a substantial and successful investor in thoroughbred horse racing. In 1916, without the Federal League to divert his attention, Sinclair consolidated a number of his businesses and several others into the Sinclair Oil and Refining Corporation, becoming one the largest oil companies in the country. His success was briefly interrupted in the 1920s when he went to jail for six months as a part of the Teapot Dome scandal. Sinclair Oil had been awarded the oil rights to government lands in Wyoming, land called "Teapot Dome" because of its geological shape. The company received the rights from Secretary of the Interior Albert Fall without competitive bidding. It later emerged that Fall had been bribed to lease the lands to Sinclair's company, and the resulting scandal, including criminal trials and Senate hearings, was one of the most dramatic and prominent of the twentieth century.

Of the people introduced to Organized Baseball through the Federal League war, Judge Kenesaw Landis may have benefited the most. Major League owners clearly appreciated his response to the Federal League's anti-trust suit. In the wake of the Black Sox scandal and other controversies, when the owners decided that the National Commission was no longer effective as the sport's governing body, they turned to Judge Landis in late 1920 to become baseball's first commissioner. In his position Landis was no pawn of the owners and generally acted independently in support of the best interests of baseball as he saw it. Of course, he typically saw it in a way similar to that of the owners who had hired him. But he did occasionally take the players' side when he felt an owner was improperly holding a player down in the Minor Leagues, and he actively campaigned against the farm system, which he felt was unfair to the players and would hurt the Minors.

A couple of questions still dog the modern baseball historian: Could the Federal League have succeeded, and, more specifically, what would success have looked like? When they embarked on their venture, the Federal League's owners were looking at a history in which new leagues had succeeded or failed relatively quickly. The Union Association and the Players League both had folded after one year; conversely, the American League had clearly established itself as viable after only one season. The American League, however, had two huge advantages: the supply of Major League teams in 1901 had shrunk to a level well below any intelligent measure of demand, and the National League was in complete disarray, the owners feuding with one another and arguing over the structure of the league. The hostility among the National League's magnates left them impotent to offer an intelligent, coherent response to the new American League.

The Federal League had neither of the American League's advantages. While one might argue that the country could support more than the existing sixteen Major League teams in 1914 because of recent urban growth, in fact the Major Leagues were not forced to expand until 1961. Moreover, baseball was not in disarray. Certainly there was unrest—the high Minor Leagues were dissatisfied with their status, and National League owners remained fractious—but these circumstances hardly compared with those at the turn of the century when the American League declared itself a Major League.

It's hard to fault the Federal League's initial organization. The founders lined up a wealthy group of owners that compared favorably with the Majors and certainly exceeded what the American League had started with in 1901. The cities that did not enjoy wealthy owners had a civic form of ownership that raised a significant amount of money and guaranteed strong local interest. What's more, most of the teams lined up first-class ballparks. Although not up the standards of the most recent round of new stadiums, most had either recently been used as a Major League ballpark or were the equivalent of this previous generation of ballparks.

The Federals also made only a few tactical mistakes. Most significant, Gilmore and the owners often advertised player defections too quickly, allowing the

Major Leagues ample opportunity to recapture them. They may also have been better off putting a team in New York or the Bronx, as opposed to Newark and Brooklyn, but this would have been an incredibly expensive proposition. In the end, it's hard to see either of these mistakes as decisive.

While not an unreasonable assumption, the expectation of a short battle may have been the Federal League's greatest miscalculation. In every successful new sports league after 1915—defined as eventual incorporation of some or all of the teams into the preexisting structure—the new league would need to prove itself over a period of years. The working assumption of the existing league at first was always that the upstarts could not compete and would eventually fail. Only after proving its staying power and affecting the existing league by siphoning off revenues and increasing player salaries would the existing league consider some sort of merger. Most of the Federal League's ownership groups believed that if they could persevere for a year or two, they could force their way into Major League baseball. The wealthier owners hoped to buy into the Majors; the civic-owned teams competing in Minor League cities hoped that their city would be recognized as Major League. Had the losses been more manageable, the teams might have been able to hold out longer, but the red ink flowed well beyond expectations and showed no signs of abating.

For the most part, the Federals' financial losses were not due to mistakes. Organized Baseball's aggressive strategy successfully pushed the Federal League's cost of operations beyond what the owners could support. The warlike response to players lured by the Federals, especially those whose contracts had expired and were held to their existing team solely by the reserve clause, surprised and dismayed the Federals. Behind Ban Johnson's leadership, the baseball establishment did not typically resort to legal action when they lost a player; they would go all out to re-sign him, regardless of his new contract status. Once the disputes invariably ended up in court, often as the Federals tried to enforce their contacts, Gilmore and Gates seemed to be legally overmatched. The lack of overriding court victories on the anti-trust front made the Federals' undertaking that much more difficult. A precedent-setting ruling in federal court against Organized Baseball would have given the Federals a chance at more players by nullifying some of their contracts. More important, it would have invalidated the blacklist, removing the key disincentive of jumping to the new league. Had the initial Chief Johnson decision gone the other way and the twenty-player defection occurred, or had Judge Landis ruled for the Federals, they would have earned much-needed breathing room. Just as important, the cost of battling an opponent that could flaunt the anti-trust laws added operating costs that proved almost insurmountable. The salaries the Federals were forced to pay in order to lure players in the face of a possible blacklist and constant meddling by the Major Leagues, the uncertainty resulting from court rulings that often caused the Federals to return players, and the costs of the court battles themselves raised expenses well beyond initial expectations.

Organized Baseball's forceful response, of course, influenced more than just the expense side of the ledger. By contesting every significant player acquisition, the established leagues prevented the Federals from landing any Major League stars still in the prime of their career. Without Major League–caliber rosters, the Federals fell below expectations at the gate. With the exception of Chicago, the Federal League teams in Major League cities could never quite convince the populace that they were truly Major League. Federal League franchises competing against only Minor League competition consistently outdrew their rivals but could not generate enough revenue to support their civic ownership.

After two years of competition, struggling with disappointing revenues and higher-than-projected expenses, most Federal League owners had little interest in continuing. With the death of Robert Ward, only Harry Sinclair still had the wherewithal to bankroll the league, and he had already lost enough money and could envision no positive outcome. The Major Leagues had also suffered, particularly the National, but nowhere near the degree that would force them to accept the Federals as an equal or incorporate some of its teams. As the Major League owners proved after the 1914 season, they might have agreed to some sort of amalgamation of several of the teams into the high Minors, but the Federal League teams in non–Major League cities had no interest in this solution. For the Federals to have succeeded without a sweeping court victory, they needed a long-term strategy. Major League baseball was not about to cave in after only a year or two. And given Organized Baseball's effective response and the consequent extent of the Federals' financial losses, without a completely restructured ownership a longer-term strategy may have been impossible.

The Federals had built a solid organization. They made very few substantive mistakes in their two years of battling Organized Baseball. If such a league could not succeed, how could anyone else? With the end of the Federal League and the subsequent anti-trust exemption, Organized Baseball was free to develop as it did. The continued existence of the reserve clause for another sixty years, the evolution of the farm system beginning in the 1920s and 1930s, the ossification of the franchise landscape—no team would move until 1953, and expansion would have to wait until 1961—all could unfold as they did. By defeating the Federal League on the field and in the courts, Organized Baseball gained immunity from any outside challenge for years to come.

Notes

I used documents and records from three archival sources extensively in researching the Federal League's fight for acceptance. First, the materials associated with the Federal League's January 1915 anti-trust case tried before Judge Kenesaw Mountain Landis, *The Federal League of Professional Baseball Clubs v. The National League, the American League, et al.*, can be found in the National Archives and Records Administration–Great Lakes Region (Chicago). In the notes below, documents from this archive are referred to as "Landis case." Second, the documents and testimony from the suit brought by the Federal League's Baltimore franchise, *Federal Baseball Club of Baltimore, Inc., v. National League of Professional Baseball Clubs, et al.*, 259 U.S. 2000 (1922), which eventually was heard by the Supreme Court, are referred to as Record on Appeal. Third, the August (Garry) Herrmann papers at the National Baseball Hall of Fame and Museum contain numerous letters, legal documents, and other papers from the years when Organized Baseball battled the Federal League. Letters from this collection are referred to by the last names of the sender and recipient, and the date. The Herrmann papers also include the transcript from the Landis case.

Full citations of abbreviated sources may be found in the bibliography that follows.

PROLOGUE: THE OPENING SALVO—DECEMBER 1913

1. *Cincinnati Enquirer*, August 14, 1913.
2. *Cincinnati Enquirer*, August 29, 1913.
3. Daniel Ginsberg, "John Tener," Society for American Baseball Research Biography Project (www.bioproject.sabr.org); Gallagher, 36–38; *Sporting News*, September 10, 1942.
4. *Sporting News*, September 10, 1942.
5. Unidentified newspaper article by Frank Menke, Garry Herrmann Hall of Fame file.
6. *Sporting News*, November 25, 1948, 11; Cook, 176–78.

7. Cook, 178.

8. Bogen, 139.

9. Tinker affidavit, Landis case.

10. Ibid.

11. Ibid.

12. *New York Times*, December 31, 1913.

CHAPTER 1: AMERICA MEETS SPORTS LEAGUES

1. House Report, 21.

2. House Report, 34.

3. House Report, 35.

4. Ibid.

5. Seymour, *Early Years*, 299.

6. *Chicago Tribune*, February 24, 1929.

7. Unidentified newspaper article, January 14, 1932, Charles Somers Hall of Fame file.

8. Armour and Levitt, 41.

9. See Tygiel, 35–63, for a discussion of the evolution of some of these players to owners.

10. Solomon, 231.

11. Greenstein, 1–5.

12. Solomon, 239; Riess, *Touching Base*, 79–81; Lieb, *Baltimore Orioles*, 118; Graham, *New York Yankees*, 5–7; Murdock, 63; Pietrusza, *Major Leagues*, 176.

13. Allen, *Cincinnati Reds*, 75.

14. Cook, 53–54, quoted from *Sporting Life*, March 14, 1908.

CHAPTER 2: RUMBLINGS

1. Maddison, 379 (GDP amounts in 1990 international dollars).

2. Dubofsky, 35.

3. *New York Times*, March 12, 1912, 10.

4. Ibid.

5. Stump, 222.

6. *Chicago Tribune*, April 20, 1913, C1.

7. Wooley, 245; Seymour, *Golden Age*, 71–72.

8. *Sporting Life*, August 6, 1910.

9. *Sporting News*, January 6, 1916, 3.

10. *Miami Herald*, March 9, 1915; Craig, table IX.

11. Quirk and Fort, 391–408.

12. U.S. Bureau of the Census, *Historical Statistics of the United States, Colonial Times to 1970*, Bicentennial Edition, Part 1 (Washington, D.C., 1975), 105–6.

13. Pietrusza, *Major Leagues*, 193.

14. *Sporting News*, May 30, 1912, 1.

15. *Pittsburgh Leader*, January 21, 1914.

16. House Report, 50.

17. *Baseball Magazine*, October 1915, 68.

18. Ibid., 69.

19. Theo. Hewes to William Graves Jr., April 8, 1913.

20. Haller, 213.

21. *Sporting Life*, March 22, 1913, 5.

22. Levitt, *Ed Barrow*, 87.

23. Fullerton to John Powers, March 7, 1913.

24. *Chicago Tribune*, August 25, 1913, 11.

25. Quinn to Johnson, May 29, 1913.

26. Hedges to Johnson, June 4, 1913.

27. Johnson to Herrmann, May 31, 1913.

28. Dreyfuss to Herrmann, September 8, 1913.

29. Barnard to Johnson, June 10, 1913.

30. *New York Times*, June 16, 1913, 7.

31. Gates biographical information: *Indiana and Indianans: A history of aboriginal and territorial Indiana and the century of statehood* (Chicago: American Historical Society, 1919); Dunn, *Jacob Piatt*, p. 1702 at http://genwiz.genealogenie.net/lake_maxinkuckee/lots_cot tage_history_east/alfred_b_gates.htm; Courts and Lawyers of Indiana, 1916, 1257–58.

32. Johnson to Herrmann, August 2, 1913.

33. Gary Jones to Robert Hedges, August 25, 1913.

34. Johnson to Herrmann, August 5, 1913.

35. Johnson to Herrmann, August 2, 1913.

36. Johnson to Herrmann, August 5, 1913.

37. Quoted in Luse, 147.

38. *Sporting Life*, August 9, 1914, 1.

39. *Chicago Tribune*, January 18, 1914, B3.

40. *Sporting News*, August 19, 1915, 1.

41. *Sporting News*, November 23, 1944.

42. Barnard to Johnson, August 4, 1913.

43. Johnson to Herrmann, September 5, 1913.

CHAPTER 3: GOING MAJOR

1. *Chicago Tribune*, October 15, 1913.

2. *Sporting Life*, February 14, 1914.

3. *Sporting News*, November 26, 1914.

4. *Chicago Tribune*, January 3, 1914.

5. *Sporting Life*, November 22, 1913.

6. *Sporting Life*, November 15, 1913, 12.

7. Johnson to Herrmann, December 17, 1913.

8. Watkins, 875–881; Riess, *Sport in Industrial America*, 167.

9. Lieb, *Boston Red Sox*, 116; Quirk and Fort, 4000–401.

10. Tinker affidavit, Exhibit H, Landis case.

11. *Sporting Life*, December 6, 1913; *Chicago Tribune*, January 4, 1914.

12. Dreyfuss to Herrmann, December 1, 1913.

13. *Sporting Life*, January 31, 1914, 8.

14. Johnson to A. J. Flanner, January 13, 1914.

15. Dreyfuss to Herrmann, January 8, 1914.

16. Ball biographical information: *Baseball Magazine*, "Messrs. Stifel and Ball"; *New York Times*, October 23, 1933, 15; *Sporting News*, October 20, 1932, 5; *Sporting News*, October 26, 1933.

17. *Sporting News*, November 10, 1938, 11; *Chicago Tribune*, April 26, 1914; *New York Times*, November 3, 1938; Shea, 18.

18. *Baseball Magazine*, September 1915, 56.

19. *Sporting Life*, December 6, 1913.

20. Unidentified newspaper clipping, January 12, 1914, Herrmann papers.

21. White, 22–23; Selter, 8.

22. Okkonen, 54.

23. Plaintiff brief, Record on Appeal, 22; *Sporting News*, February 5, 1915; Okkonen, 57; *Sporting Life*, April 25, 1914.

24. Willis E. Johnson in the *St. Louis Globe-Democrat* quoted in Thomas, "Federal League Park (St. Louis)."

25. *Chicago Tribune*, January 28, 1914; Joan M. Thomas, "Federal League Park (St. Louis)," Society for American Baseball Research Biography Project (www.bioproject .sabr.org); Okkonen, 63; correspondence with Ron Selter.

26. Selter, 141–43.

27. Dreyfuss to Herrmann, May 23, 1914.

28. H. D. Seekamp (treasurer and business manager, St. Louis Cardinals) to Herrmann, May 20, 1914.

29. Dreyfuss biographical information: Lieb, *Pittsburgh Pirates*, 41–47; Sam Bernstein, "Barney Dreyfuss," Society for American Baseball Research Biography Project (www .bioproject.sabr.org); Bonk and Martin, 62–64; Woolley, 248.

30. Woolley, 248.

31. Lieb, *Pittsburgh Pirates*, 46–47.

32. *Sporting Life*, December 6, 1913.

33. *Hartford Courant*, January 7, 1914, 19.

34. *Chicago Tribune*, January 12, 1914, 10; *Sporting Life*, January 17, 1914, 8; *New York Times*, January 14, 1914.

35. Brown affidavit, Landis case; Herrmann affidavit, Landis case.

36. Brown affidavit, Landis case.

37. House Report, 53.

38. Edwards, 341.

39. Robert A. Margo in Susan B. Carter, et al., *Historical Statistics of the United States: Earliest Times to the Present* (Cambridge: Cambridge University Press, 2006), vol. 2, 271–72.

40. Alexander, *Ty Cobb*, 116.

41. *Chicago Tribune*, December 3, 1913, 18.

42. Somers affidavit, Landis case.

43. *Washington Post*, January 14, 1914, 8; *Boston Globe*, January 25, 1914, A17; Dreyfuss affidavit, Landis case; *Washington Post*, January 10, 1914, 8.

44. *Sporting Life*, April 11, 1914, 13; Oakes affidavit, Landis case; Britton affidavit, Landis case.

45. *Chicago Tribune*, January 25, 1914, B1.

46. Baker biographical information: *New York Times*, December 5, 1930; Lieb and Baumgartner, 102–3; unidentified newspaper clippings, Baker Hall of Fame file.

47. Baker affidavit, Landis case.

48. *Chicago Tribune*, January 13, 1914, 14.

49. *Los Angeles Times*, January 29, 1914, III 1.

50. *Washington Post*, May 6, 1914, 8.

51. *Chicago Tribune*, January 13, 1914, 14.

CHAPTER 4: A REAL PLAYERS UNION

1. Fultz biographical information: Principally from unidentified newspaper clippings, Fultz Hall of Fame File.

2. Unidentified newspaper clipping, Fultz Hall of Fame File.

3. Levitt, *Ed Barrow*, 113.

4. Dan Daniel, unidentified newspaper clipping, Fultz Hall of Fame File, January 26, 1944.

5. *Sporting Life*, January 10, 1914, 1, 3; Potts, 33–38; Record on Appeal, 103–6.

6. *Sporting Life*, January 10, 1914, 3.

CHAPTER 5: THE BATTLE FOR CHICAGO

1. *Sporting Life*, January 10, 1914, 15; *Chicago Tribune*, January 23, 1914, 14.

2. *Chicago Tribune*, January 19, 1914, 12.

3. *Chicago Tribune*, January 20, 1914, 10.

4. Unidentified correspondence from Charles Murphy, Herrmann papers.

5. *Chicago Tribune*, January 18, 1914.

6. *Sporting Life*, January 10, 1914.

7. *Chicago Tribune*, January 19, 1914.

8. Chivington to Herrmann, February 3, 1914.

9. Herrmann to Dreyfuss, January 23, 1914; transcript of telephone conversation between Dreyfuss and Hempstead, January 23, 1914, 5 p.m.

10. *Sporting News*, February 5, 1914.

11. *Washington Post*, May 3, 1914, S2.

12. Lenny Jacobsen, "Charles Murphy," Society for American Baseball Research Biography Project (www.bioproject.sabr.org); Bill Bailey, unidentified newspaper clipping, Charles Murphy Hall of Fame File.

13. Bogen, 123–25; Jacobson, "Charles Murphy"; Gregory Ryhal, "Frank Chance," Society for American Baseball Research Biography Project (www.bioproject.sabr.org).

14. *New York Times*, August 13, 1912, 10; *New York Times*, September 29, 1912, S1.

15. *Boston Globe*, November 29, 1912.

16. *New York Times*, February 15, 1914, S1.

17. *New York Times*, February 12, 1914, 10; *Baseball Magazine*, August 1914, 108.

18. *Baseball Magazine*, August 1914, 32.

19. *Chicago Tribune*, February 14, 1914, 14.

20. *Chicago Tribune*, February 13, 1914.

21. Jacobsen, "Charles Murphy"; *New York Times*, February 22, 1914, S1; *Chicago Tribune*, February 22, 1914, 1.

22. *Sporting Life*, February 28, 1914, 1; *Boston Globe*, March 19, 1914.

23. *Chicago Tribune*, February 15, 1914, B1.

24. *Washington Post*, March 4, 1914, 8.

25. Shea, 40.

26. Kush, 10; Operative Report, May 13, 1914, in Johnson to Herrmann, May 22, 1914.

27. *Chicago Tribune*, April 23, 1914, 17.

28. Lane, "R. B. Ward," 108.

29. Lane, July 1915; *Sporting Life*, October 30, 1915, 12; *Sporting Life*, October 23, 1915, 9; *New York Times*, October 20, 1915, 13; unidentified newspaper clippings, Ward Hall of Fame file.

30. *Baseball Magazine*, July 1915, 31.

31. Ibid., 30.

32. Unidentified Joe Vila article, in Johnson to Herrmann, August 24, 1914.

33. Ebbets biographical information: Solomon, 155; John Saccoman, "Charlie Ebbets," Society for American Baseball Research Biography Project (www.bioproject .sabr.org); McCue, 36; *Sporting News*, August 19, 1915, 1; Graham, *Brooklyn Dodgers*.

34. Solomon, 251; Armour and Levitt, 20.

35. Solomon, 245–46, 251–52, 265; Graham, *Brooklyn Dodgers*, 12–13; McCue, 36–37; Saccoman, "Charlie Ebbets"; Armour and Levitt, 15–20.

36. Okkonen, 52; Heydler to Herrmann, May 12, 1914; *Sporting Life*, February 21, 1914, 8; *Sporting Life*, February 28, 1914, 8.

37. *Sporting Life*, February 28, 1914, 8.

38. *Sporting Life*, August 5, 1916.

CHAPTER 6: ORGANIZED BASEBALL RESPONDS

1. Charlie Weatherby, "Bill Killefer," Society for American Baseball Research Biography Project (www.bioproject.sabr.org).

2. *Chicago Tribune*, January 19, 1914.

3. *Chicago Tribune*, January 22, 1914, 8.

4. *Los Angeles Times*, January 22, 1914.

5. Farrell affidavit, Landis case; Cole affidavit, Landis case.

6. Cole affidavit, Landis case.

7. Ibid.

8. *New York Times*, January 26, 1914; *New York Times*, February 5, 1914; Farrell affidavit, Landis case; Cole affidavit, Landis case.

9. *Sporting News*, March 5, 1914.

10. Tinker affidavit, Landis case.

11. Hedges biographical information: Golenbock, *Spirit of St. Louis*, 56–57; Steve Steinberg, "Robert Hedges," Society for American Baseball Research Biography Project (www.bioproject.sabr.org); Lieb, *Baltimore Orioles*, 184–85; Quirk and Fort, 4000.

12. *New York Times*, December 9, 1914; *Leslie's Illustrated Weekly*, December 31, 1914.

13. Ebbets to Herrmann, January 7, 1915; *New York Times*, February 13, 1914.

14. Johnson to Herrmann, February 20, 1914.

15. Bulletin No. 1, Relative to Protection of Player and Territorial Rights of Clubs and Leagues Under the National Agreement, undated.

16. *Sporting Life*, February 6, 1915, 7.

17. Gilmore affidavit, Landis case.

18. Johnson to Herrmann, February 17, 1914.

19. Johnson to Herrmann, February 28, 1914.

20. *Washington Post*, March 4, 1914, 8.

21. Record on Appeal, 197–99.

22. *New York Times*, October 13, 1913, 1.

23. *New York Times*, October 25, 1913, 2.

24. Kaese, 122–30.

25. Unidentified newspaper clipping, August 25, 1932, Gaffney Hall of Fame file.

26. Competiton for players from around-the-world tour: Gay, 143–44; *Sporting Life*, March 14, 1914, 3, 9, 11; *Sporting Life*, November 20, 1915, 7; *Sporting News*, March 12, 1914; *Los Angeles Times*, March 6, 1914; Elfers, 237–44.

27. *Sporting Life*, March 14, 1914, 3.

28. Ibid.

29. Elfers, 240; *Sporting Life*, March 14, 1914, 11.

30. Doolan affidavit, Landis case; Baker affidavit, Landis case.

31. Elfers, 241.

32. *Sporting Life*, March 14, 9.

33. *Chicago Tribune*, March 9, 1914, 13.

34. *Sporting Life*, April 11, 1914, 13; *Boston Globe*, March 19, 1914, 7.

35. Johnson to Herrmann, April 8, 1914.

36. Johnson to Herrmann, March 28, 1914; Irv Goldfarb, "Howie Camnitz," Society for American Baseball Research Biography Project (www.bioproject.sabr.org); *Los Angeles Times*, April 5, 1914, VII 1; Dreyfuss to Herrmann, March 27, 1914; *Sporting News*, April 9, 1914; *Boston Globe*, March 19, 1914.

37. Johnson to Herrmann, March 28, 1914.

38. Dreyfuss to Herrmann, March 27, 1914.

39. Stovall's pursuit of Hamilton: *Sporting Life*, April 18, 1914, 10; *Sporting News*, November 14, 1951, 15; *Sporting Life*, April 25, 1914, 12–13; *Sporting News*, April 23, 1914, 2; Hedges affidavit, Landis case; *Hartford Courant*, April 16, 1914, 18.

40. *Sporting Life*, April 18, 1914, 10.

41. *Sporting Life*, April 25, 1914, 12–13.

42. *Washington Post*, March 3, 1914, 8; Thomas affidavit, Landis case.

43. *Chicago Tribune*, April 2, 1914.

44. *Chicago Tribune*, April 11, 1914.

45. Levitt, *Ed Barrow*, 92–93.

46. Johnson to Herrmann, June 27, 1914.

47. Johnson to Herrmann, June 15, 1914; Johnson to Herrmann, January 26, 1915.

48. Unidentified newspaper clipping, Herrmann Hall of Fame File.

49. Johnson to Herrmann, April 3, 1914.

50. Tener to Johnson, April 10, 1914.

51. Spink to Johnson, April 14, 1914; Spink to Johnson, May 6, 1914.

52. Price to Johnson, February 14, 1914.

CHAPTER 7: THE SEASON OPENS

1. *New York Times*, March 8, 1914.

2. Pepper biographical information: www.archives.upenn.edu/people/18000s/pepper _geo_wharton.html; Pepper, 20–24.

3. *Federal Reporter*, vol. 215 (West Publishing Co., 1914), 168–73.

4. *Grand Rapids Herald*, April 11, 1914, 10, quoted in *Stereoscope*, Winter 2003, 6.

5. *Chicago Tribune*, April 11, 1914.

6. Ibid.

7. Toot, 86–89.

8. Toot, 86–89; *Washington Post*, May 6, 1914, 8.

9. *Sporting Life*, April 25, 1914, 12.

10. Barrow to Herrmann, May 2, 1914; *Sporting Life*, April 25, 1914, 12.

11. *Los Angeles Times*, April 15, 1914.

12. *St. Louis Times*, unidentified date, Herrmann papers; *Chicago Tribune*, April 17, 1914.

13. *Chicago Tribune*, April 24, 1914; Dreyfuss to Herrmann, April 28, 1914; Dreyfuss to Herrmann, April 30, 1914.

14. Dreyfuss to Herrmann, April 28, 1914.

15. Stein to Herrmann, May 29, 1914.

16. *Chicago Daily News*, April 24, 1914.

17. McGill to Johnson, July 5, 1914; *Boston Herald*, May 3, 1914; Thomas Chivington to Herrmann, January 28, 1915.

18. *Sporting News*, January 27, 1916, 3; *Chicago Tribune*, April 28, 1914.

19. Griffith affidavit, Landis case.

20. Oakes affidavit, Landis case.

21. *Sporting Life*, May 30, 1914, 1.

22. *Chicago Tribune*, June 5, 1914; *Sporting Life*, May 30, 1914, 1; *Sporting Life*, June 13, 1914, 1.

23. *Chicago Tribune*, June 15, 1914; *Baseball Magazine*, March 1915; *Sporting Life*, January 9, 1915; Huhn, 104–5.

24. Operative reports, included in Johnson to Herrmann, May 22, 1914.

25. Ibid.

26. Toot, 89.

27. *Sporting Life*, June 13, 1914, 3.

28. *New York Sun*, June 5, 1914.

29. Sanborn decision: *Federal Reporter*, vol. 216, 1915, 269.

30. *Sporting Life*, July 4, 1914, 2.

31. *Chicago Tribune*, July 18, 1914.

32. Chase's jump to the Federal League: Kohout, 134–36; *Sporting Life*, July 4, 1914, 3; Wiggins, 130–31.

33. State of New York, Supreme Court, Erie County, Opinion of Hon. Herbert P. Bissell, July 21, 1914.

CHAPTER 8: THE STRUGGLE CONTINUES

1. Harry Conover, *Evening Mail* article, undated, sent by John Heydler to Major League owners, July 31, 1914.

2. Charles Thomas to Herrmann, July 1, 1914.

3. Travis Hoke to Robert Hedges, no date.

4. Lieb, *Baltimore Orioles*, 128.

5. Mack to Johnson, May 21, 1914; Johnson to Herrmann, May 22, 1914.

6. *New York Times*, June 20, 1914.

7. Levitt, *Ed Barrow*, 95–96.

8. Barrow to Herrmann, June 6, 1914.

9. *Chicago Tribune*, June 21, 1914.

10. Barrow to Herrmann, June 26, 1914.

11. *Sporting News*, June 25, 1914.

12. Heydler to Herrmann, June 25, 1914.

13. Johnson to American League owners, confidential memorandum, August 8, 1914.

14. Heydler to Herrmann, July 4, 1914.

15. *Sporting News*, July 16, 1914.

16. Dunn to Herrmann, July 13, 1914.

17. Joe Vila, unidentified newspaper article, in Johnson to Herrmann, August 24, 1914.

18. Fleischmann to Herrmann, July 21, 1914.

19. Somers to Herrmann, May 21, 1914.

20. *New York Sun*, August 18, 1914; *Seattle Post-Intelligencer*, August 17, 1914; *Sporting News*, August 20, 1914.

21. Robert McRoy to Herrmann, August 17, 1914.

22. Dreyfuss to Herrmann, July 2, 1914; *Pittsburgh Post*, July 2, 1914.

23. D. P. Peterson to Robert Hedges, June 24, 1914.

24. W. N. Ferguson to James McCaffrey, October 13, 1914.

25. Johnson to American League owners, confidential memorandum, August 8, 1914.

26. *New York Evening Sun*, September 20, 1914.

27. James McGill to Herrmann, September 17, 1914; Johnson to Herrmann, September 19, 1914.

28. *Sporting Life*, October 24, 1914, 12.

29. *Chicago Tribune*, February 18, 1916, 16.

30. Johnson to Herrmann, February 10, 1915.

CHAPTER 9: A POSSIBLE SETTLEMENT

1. Herrmann to Cantillon, August 17, 1914.

2. Cantillon to Herrmann, August 19, 1914.

3. McRoy to Herrmann, September 1, 1914.

4. Gilmore affidavit, Landis case; Cantillon to Herrmann, September 3, 1914.

5. Lannin to Johnson, September 12, 1914.

6. Herrmann to Cantillon, September 9, 1914.

7. Herrmann to Johnson and Tener, September 14, 1914.

8. Dreyfuss to Herrmann, September 16, 1914.

9. Herrmann to Johnson, October 14, 1914; Herrmann to Weeghman, November 14, 1914.

10. Robert Ward affidavit, Landis case.

11. Robert Ward affidavit, Landis case; Johnson to Herrmann, September 10, 1914.

12. Lannin to Johnson, September 27, 1914.

13. *New York Sun*, October 3, 1914.

14. *New York Times*, October 2, 1914, 9.

15. *New York Times*, October 2, 1914; *New York Times*, October 3, 1914; *New York Sun*, October 3, 1914; *Boston American*, undated; *Boston Post*, October 4, 1914.

16. Robert Ward affidavit, Landis case.

17. Robert Ward affidavit, Landis case; Lannin affidavit, Landis case.

18. Lannin affidavit, Landis case.

19. Cantillon affidavit, Landis case.

20. Herrmann to Johnson, October 17, 1914.

21. Unidentified newspaper clipping, Herrmann Hall of Fame file; *Chicago Tribune,* October 19, 1914; *Chicago Tribune,* October 20, 1914, 8.

22. Herrmann to L. H. Carstans, November 4, 1914.

23. Hempstead to Herrmann, November 4, 1914.

24. Unidentified newspaper clipping, November 10, 1914, Herrmann Hall of Fame file.

25. Herrmann to Weeghman, November 14, 1914.

26. Gilmore affidavit, Landis case; Weeghman to Herrmann, November 13, 1914.

27. Herrmann to Tener, November 14, 1914.

28. Telegram, *Daily News* to Herrmann, November 23, 1914.

29. *New York Times,* November 12, 1914.

30. Dreyfuss to Herrmann, November 19, 1914.

31. Herrmann to Weeghman, December 5, 1914.

CHAPTER 10: PLAYER REINFORCEMENTS

1. Helene Britton biographical information: Borst, 25–30; Thomas, "Helene Britton"; Woolley, 249; Lieb, *St. Louis Cardinals,* 46–48.

2. Borst, 27.

3. Bresnahan affidavit, Landis case.

4. Robert Ward affidavit, Landis case.

5. Dreyfuss affidavit, Landis case; Jones affidavit, Landis case; *Sporting Life,* October 24, 1914, 14.

6. Steve Steinberg, "Ray Caldwell," Society for American Baseball Research Biography Project (www.bioproject.sabr.org); *New York Times,* September 13, 1914; *Sporting Life,* October 24, 1914, 15.

7. Ebbets to Herrmann, January 3, 1915.

8. Ebbets affidavit, Landis case.

9. Herrmann to Berghammer, November 4, 1914.

10. Britton affidavit, Landis case.

11. Perritt affidavit, Landis case.

12. Huggins affidavit, Landis case.

13. *St. Louis Times,* October 13, 1914.

14. Britton to Herrmann, October 15, 1914; Hedges to Johnson, October 15, 1914; Britton affidavit, Landis case.

15. Hedges to Johnson, October 15, 1914.

16. Johnson to Herrmann, October 29, 1914.

17. *New York Times*, December 9, 1914; *Leslie's Illustrated Weekly*, December 31, 1914.

18. *Chicago Tribune*, February 11, 1915.

19. Barrow to International League owners, December 7, 1914; *New York Times*, December 9, 1914.

20. *Sporting Life*, February 6, 1915, 10.

21. *Boston Herald*, September 19, 1914.

22. *Sporting Life*, October 24, 1914, 15.

23. Swift, 236; Lieb, *Connie Mack*, 181–82; Wiggins, 169–70.

24. Mansch, 151; Wiggins, 169–70.

25. *Baseball Magazine*, April 1915, 58; *Washington Post*, December 4, 1914, 1.

26. *Baseball Magazine*, June 1915, 58.

27. *Baseball Magazine*, April 1915, 59.

28. Ibid., 61.

29. *Washington Post*, December 6, 1914.

30. *Sporting Life*, December 12, 1914, 9.

31. *Hartford Courant*, December 3, 1914, 16.

32. Johnson's jump to the Federal League: *Baseball Magazine*, April 1915, 53–62; Thomas, 129–39; Huhn, 114–17; Murdock, 79–80; Deveaux, 42–44.

33. *Baseball Magazine*, March 1916, 31–32.

34. Huhn, 114.

35. *Baseball Magazine*, April 1915, 62.

36. *Washington Post*, March 15, 1915.

37. *Sporting Life*, January 30, 1915, 9.

38. Thomas, 136.

39. *Washington Post*, February 5, 1938.

40. Exhibit B: *Cincinnati v. Marsans*, May 3, 1915, in Petition of St. Louis Federal League, June 28, 1915.

41. Unidentified newspaper clipping, January 16, 1915.

42. Marquard contract.

43. Herrmann to Johnson and Tener, December 19, 1914.

44. Unidentified newspaper clipping, Hempstead Hall of Fame file.

45. *Sporting Life*, February 13, 1915, 9.

46. *Sporting Life*, April 10, 1915.

47. *New York Times*, January 8, 1915.

CHAPTER 11: ANTI-TRUST ATTACK

1. J. G. Taylor Spink, 40–41; Pietrusza, *Judge and Jury*, 153–56.

2. Herrmann to Griffith, January 5, 1915; Minor to Herrmann, January 8, 1915; Griffith to Herrmann, January 8, 1915; Minor to Herrmann, January 12, 1915.

3. "Outline of Bill," Herrmann Hall of Fame file.

4. Ibid.

5. *Chicago Tribune*, January 21, 1915; Pietrusza, *Judge and Jury*, 155–56.

6. Trial transcript, Landis case, Herrmann Hall of Fame file.

7. *Sporting Life*, February 6, 1915, 8.

8. Johnson to Herrmann, January 27, 1915.

9. *Boston Journal*, January 22, 1915.

10. Powers to Herrmann, January 23, 1915.

11. Powers to Herrmann, January 30, 1915.

12. *New York Times*, February 22, 1915; Cappy Gagnon, "Ed Reulbach," Society for American Baseball Research Biography Project (www.bioproject.sabr.org).

13. *Sporting Life*, March 13, 1915, 8.

14. McGraw recruitment of Kauff: *Sporting Life*, May 8, 1915, 1; Alexander, *John McGraw*, 185–86; Pietrusza, *Major Leagues*, 241; Kauff, 19–22; *New York Times*, April 30, 1915; *New York Times*, May 1, 1915; David Jones, "Bennie Kauff," Society for American Baseball Research Biography Project (www.bioproject.sabr.org); Watkins, 202–3.

15. Unidentified newspaper clipping, Herrmann papers.

16. *Sporting Life*, May 8, 1915, 1.

17. *Sporting Life*, May 22, 1915, 13.

18. Kauff, 20.

CHAPTER 12: OWNER REINFORCEMENTS

1. *Sporting Life*, February 13, 1915; Levitt, *Ed Barrow*, 178–82.

2. Unidentified newspaper clipping, Herrmann Hall of Fame file, January 16, 1915.

3. Sinclair biographical information: Lane, "Harry Sinclair"; Sinclair Oil Corporation, 13–20; www.kshs.org/portraits/sinclair_harry.htm; *Sporting News*, November 21, 1956; newspaper clippings, Sinclair Hall of Fame file.

4. Lane, "Harry Sinclair," 28–29.

5. *Sporting News*, August 19, 1915, 1.

6. Sinclair to Powers, January 5, 1914.

7. *New York Times*, February 7, 1915, 35.

8. *Washington Post*, December 28, 1915.

9. *Sporting Life*, March 13, 1915, 1; *Sporting Life*, February 13, 1915, 8; *Sporting Life*, March 20, 1915, 9.

10. *Boston Post*, February 21, 1915.

11. *Sporting Life*, February 27, 1915.

12. *Sporting Life*, March 20, 1915, 8.

13. Ibid., 8.

14. *New York Times*, March 16, 1915, 12; *Sporting News*, March 18, 1915, 2; *Sporting Life*, April 10, 1915, 9.

15. *Sporting News*, March 25, 1915, 1.

16. *Sporting News*, April 1, 1915, 5; *Sporting Life*, January 30, 1915, 10.

17. *Sporting Life*, March 6, 1915; Alexander, *John McGraw*, 182.

18. Price to Johnson, February 14, 1914; *Sporting Life*, February 20, 1915, 9.

19. *Sporting Life*, February 20, 1915, 9.

20. *Sporting Life*, January 8, 1916, 10; Okkonen, 59.

21. *Sporting Life*, February 20, 1915, 9; *Sporting Life*, April 10, 1915, 8.

22. *New York Times*, February 10, 1915.

23. *Sporting Life*, April 17, 1915, 9.

24. *New York Times*, March 18, 1915.

CHAPTER 13: A LONG SUMMER

1. *Sporting Life*, April 17, 1915, 8.

2. Johnson to Herrmann, May 19, 1915.

3. *Sporting Life*, April 10, 1915; Johnson to Herrmann, April 5, 1915.

4. Johnson to Herrmann, April 5, 1915; *Commercial Tribune*, April 4, 1915.

5. *Sporting Life*, April 24, 1915, 1; *Sporting Life*, May 1, 1915, 1; Murdock, 115; *Sporting News*, May 13, 1915, 4.

6. *Boston Herald*, April 24, 1915; *Sporting Life*, May 1, 1915.

7. *Washington Post*, January 28, 1915.

8. *New York Times*, April 5, 1915.

9. *New York Times*, July 9, 1915; unidentified newspaper clipping, Herrmann papers, July 13, 1915; *Sporting Life*, July 17, 1915, 6.

10. *Cincinnati Commercial Tribune*, May 14, 1914.

11. Ebbets to Tener, Baker, Britton, Dreyfuss, Gaffney, Hempstead, Herrmann, and Thomas, June 21, 1915.

12. *Sporting Life*, July 24, 1915, 1, 3.

13. *Sporting Life*, June 5, 1915, 11.

14. Unidentified magazine article, Weeghman Hall of Fame file.

15. *Sporting Life*, June 26, 1915, 10.

16. Quoted in Irv Goldfarb, "Howie Camnitz," Society for American Baseball Research Biography Project (www.bioproject.sabr.org).

17. *Sporting Life*, February 17, 1917, 9.

18. *New York Times*, July 13, 1915, 9; *Boston Globe*, July 13, 1915, 7; Clifford Blau, members.dslextreme.com/users/brak2.0/dl.htm.

19. Johnson to Herrmann, April 13, 1915.

20. *Sporting Life*, August 21, 1915.

21. *Sporting Life*, July 24, 1915, 1; *Sporting Life*, July 31, 1915, 1.

22. *Sporting Life*, July 24, 1915, 1.

23. *Sporting Life*, July 31, 1915, 6.

24. Ibid.

25. *Sporting Life*, August 14, 1915, 6.

26. Ibid.

27. Wiggins, 246–48; *New York Times*, July 29, 1915.

28. *Sporting Life*, August 21, 1915, 6; Pietrusza, *Major Leagues*, 243; Joan Thomas, "Federal League Park (St. Louis)," Society for American Baseball Research Biography Project (www.bioproject.sabr.org).

29. *Sporting Life*, November 6, 1915, 3; *Christian Science Monitor*, October 16, 1915, 30; Kermisch, 50–51.

30. *New York Times*, May 30, 1922; www.brookspeters.com/20008/07/the-millionaire-and-the-sailor.

31. *Sporting Life*, July 17, 1915, 6.

32. *Sporting Life*, January 23, 1915, 2.

33. Toot, 121.

34. Joseph Hornbacher to Herrmann, August 20, 1914.

35. Toot, 123; *Sporting Life*, August 28, 1915, 8.

36. *Baseball Magazine*, "The Famous Joe Jackson Deal"; Fleitz, 102–3; Allen, *American League Story*, 82; *Sporting Life*, August 28, 1915, 9.

37. *Baseball Magazine*, "The Famous Joe Jackson Deal," 32.

38. Offering memorandum in letter from Robert McRoy to Herrmann, September 12, 1915.

39. *Sporting Life*, September 18, 1915; *New York Times*, September 24, 1915, 9.

40. *New York Times*, September 20, 1915, 7; *Chicago Tribune*, September 21, 1915, 11.

41. *Sporting News*, January 1, 1916; *New York Times*, October 27, 1915; Overfield, 55.

42. Record on Appeal, 394; *Chicago Tribune*, February 18, 1916, 16; *New York Times*, May 6, 1917.

43. *Sporting Life*, October 30, 1915.

CHAPTER 14: THE FINAL COUNTDOWN

1. Record on Appeal, 340–41.

2. Record on Appeal, 376.

3. *Sporting News*, August 19, 1915, 1; *Sporting News*, October 28, 1915, 1; *Sporting News*, August 25, 1932.

4. Record on Appeal, 416, 413; minutes, 158, 159; *New York Times*, October 11, 1915.

5. Record on Appeal, 303, 321.

6. *New York Times*, November 30, 1915, 11, 20.

7. Record on Appeal, 390.

8. Record on Appeal, 340–41.

9. Record on Appeal, 169–70.

10. *Sporting News*, January 6, 1916, 5.

11. Record on Appeal, 303.

12. Record on Appeal, 325.

13. Record on Appeal, 326.

14. Record on Appeal, 201–2, 301–2, 341–42, 389–90, 387.

15. Record on Appeal, 304, 416.

16. Minutes of the Waldorf-Astoria settlement meeting, December 17, 1915, appended to respondent's brief in Record on Appeal, 105–79. (Note that the dialogue has been edited to omit redundant or not germane portions.)

17. *Sporting News*, October 20, 1932, 5.

18. *Rochester Democrat*, September 19, 1917.

19. Record on Appeal, 306–7, 349.

20. *Sporting Life*, February 12, 1916.

21. Levitt, *Ed Barrow*, 106.

22. Record on Appeal, 313.

23. Record on Appeal, 323–24.

24. *New York Times*, January 11, 1916.

25. *Sporting News*, December 30, 1915, 3; Levitt, *Ed Barrow*, 105; *New York Times*, December 24, 1915; *Sporting Life*, January 8, 1916, 13; *Sporting Life*, January 22, 1916, 12.

26. William Harridge to Herrmann, February 9, 1916.

CHAPTER 15: AFTERMATH

1. *The Reminiscences of Albert Davis Lasker*, 1950 (Oral History Collection of Columbia University), 68–75; Cruikshank and Schultz, 156–60; Gunther, 117–18.

2. *Sporting Life*, January 22, 1916.

3. *Sporting Life*, November 11, 1916, 9.

4. Unidentified newspaper clipping, James Gilmore Hall of Fame File; *Sporting Life*, January 22, 1916, 5; *Sporting News*, January 6, 1916, 3.

5. Borst, 25–30; Thomas, "Helene Britton."

6. Gwinner to Herrmann, January 21, 1916; Herrmann to Gwinner, January 22, 1916; Record on Appeal, 568–69.

7. *Sporting Life*, January 22, 1916, 7; *Sporting Life*, August 5, 1916, 4; *Washington Post*, October 17, 1917, 8.

8. *Hartford Courant*, March 12, 1916, 17.

9. *Baseball Magazine*, May 1916.

10. *Sporting Life*, August 5, 1916, 4; *Hartford Courant*, August 1, 1916, 19.

11. Kermisch, 33.

12. *Sporting Life*, November 11, 1916, 4; *Sporting Life*, December 2, 1916, 4.

13. Hearings, 1394.

14. *Sporting Life*, February 12, 1916, 11.

15. *Sporting Life*, December 16, 1916, 11.

16. *Sporting Life*, January 20, 1917, 6.

17. Demise of players union: *Sporting Life*, February 17, 1917, 3; Lowenfish, *Imperfect Diamond*, 94–95; *New York Times*, January 14, 1918, 13; Levitt, *Ed Barrow*, 112–17.

18. *New York Times*, January 28, 1916, 7; Hailey, 71; James Isaminger, *Philadelphia North American*, June 16, 1917.

19. Ibid.

20. Johnson to Herrmann, November 3, 1917.

21. *Christian Science Monitor*, February 16, 1918, 18; *Washington Post*, February 16, 1918, 8; *New York Times*, February 24, 1918, 31; *Chicago Tribune*, February 24, 1918, A2.

22. Pepper to Tener, July 28, 1917; Johnson to Heydler, February 21, 1919; Heydler to National League clubs, February 19, 1919; Pepper to Heydler, March 5, 1919.

23. Heydler to National League clubs, February 19, 1919; Heydler to National League club presidents, March 29, 1919.

24. Pepper, 357.

25. Court of Appeals of the District of Columbia decision, *Federal League of Professional Baseball Clubs v. The National League, the American League, etc.*, December 6, 1920.

26. *New York Times*, April 14, 1919, 10.

27. Heydler to National League club presidents, April 14, 1919.

28. *New York Times*, April 15, 1919, 12.

29. Pepper to Heydler, November 8, 1919.

30. Herrmann to Pepper, December 12, 1919; Herrmann to Sinclair, March 2, 1920.

31. Court of Appeals of the District of Columbia decision.

32. "Monopsony in Manpower," *Yale Law Journal*, 609.

33. Post, 1636.

34. *Michigan Law Review*, 867–69.

35. Alito, 91.

36. Pepper, 359.

37. U.S. Supreme Court decision, *Federal Baseball Club of Baltimore Inc., v. National League of Professional Baseball Clubs, et al.* (259 U.S. 200 [1922]).

38. Legal scholar Ed Edmonds points out that baseball's anti-trust exemption was not really ratified until the Supreme Court's *Toolson* decision in 1953. When New York Yankees farmhand George Toolson challenged the reserve clause, baseball's anti-trust posture again came under scrutiny. In the years following the *Federal Baseball* decision, as the Court redefined interstate commerce and its definition of labor, it could have reversed *Federal Baseball*. Instead, in *Toolson* the Court invoked the principle of *stare decisis* (respecting the precedent of earlier court rulings) and ruled they would not overturn the exemption granted in the *Federal Baseball* case.

39. *Kansas City Star*, August 18, August 20, August 25, 1920; *Moberly* (Mo.) *Monitor—Index*, August 18, 1920; *Moberly* (Mo.) *Democrat*, August 22, 1920.

40. Zack Triscuit, "Ned Hanlon," Society for American Baseball Research Biography Project (www.bioproject.sabr.org).

Bibliography

NEWSPAPERS

(Articles from many newspapers were examined; those below were searched comprehensively.)

Atlanta Constitution
Boston Globe
Chicago Defender
Chicago Tribune
Los Angeles Times
New York Times
Sporting Life
Sporting News
Washington Post

ANNUALS

Reach's Official Baseball Guide. Philadelphia: A. J. Reach, 1912–1922.
Spalding's Official Baseball Guide. New York: American Sports Publishing, 1912–1922.

GENERAL

Abrams, Roger L. *Legal Bases: Baseball and the Law.* Philadelphia: Temple University Press, 1998.
Alexander, Charles C. *John McGraw.* New York: Penguin Books, 1989.
———. *Our Game: An American Baseball History.* New York: Henry Holt, 1995.
———. *Ty Cobb.* New York: Oxford University Press, 1984.

Alito, Samuel A., Jr. "Federal Baseball Club of Baltimore, Inc. v. National League of Professional Baseball Clubs." *Baseball Research Journal.* Society for American Baseball Research (Fall 2009).

Allen, Lee. *100 Years of Baseball.* New York: Bartholomew House, 1950.

——. *The American League Story.* New York: Hill and Wang, 1962.

——. *The Cincinnati Reds.* New York: G. P. Putnam's Sons, 1948.

——. *The National League Story.* New York: Hill and Wang, 1961.

Armour, Mark A., and Daniel R. Levitt. *Paths to Glory: How Great Baseball Teams Got That Way.* Washington, D.C.: Brassey's, 2003.

Barber, Frederick Courtenay. "The Star Ball-Players and Their Earnings." *Munsey's Magazine,* 1913.

Barrow, Edward Grant, as told to John Drebinger. "Why the Yankees Won't Break Up." *Liberty,* March 16, 1940.

Barrow, Edward Grant, as told to Arthur Mann. "Baseball Cavalcade." *Saturday Evening Post,* April 24, 1937.

Barrow, Edward Grant, with James M. Kahn. *My Fifty Years in Baseball.* New York: Coward-McCann, 1951.

Baseball Magazine. "Famous Magnates of the Federal League, A Series Devoted to the Leaders of the New Circuit: Messrs. Stifel and Ball, the Joint Owners of the St. Louis Feds" (November 1915).

——. "Famous Magnates of the Federal League, A Series Devoted to the Leaders of the New Circuit: Messrs. Weeghman and Walker and How They Gained Success" (September 1915).

——. "Ten Cent Baseball" (November 1915).

——. "The Famous Joe Jackson Deal" (March 1916).

Betts, John Rickards. "The Technological Revolution and the Rise of Sport, 1850–1900." *Mississippi Valley Historical Review* (September 1953).

Bjarkman, Peter C., ed. *Encyclopedia of Major League Baseball—American League.* New York: Carroll and Graf, 1993.

——, ed. *Encyclopedia of Major League Baseball—National League.* New York: Carroll and Graf, 1993.

Bogen, Gil. *Tinker, Evers, and Chance: A Triple Biography.* Jefferson, N.C.: McFarland, 2003.

Bonk, Dan, and Len Martin. "Bourbon, Baseball and Barney." *A Celebration of Louisville Baseball in the Major and Minor Leagues.* Society for American Baseball Research (1997).

Borst, William. "The Matron Magnate." *Baseball Research Journal.* Society for American Baseball Research (1977).

Boxerman, Burton A., and Benita W. Boxerman. *Ebbets to Veeck to Busch: Eight Owners Who Shaped Baseball.* Jefferson, N.C.: McFarland, 2003.

Broeg, Bob, and William J. Miller Jr. *Baseball from a Different Angle.* South Bend, Ind.: Diamond Communications, 1988.

Browning, Reed. *Cy Young: A Baseball Life.* Amherst: University of Massachusetts Press, 2000.

Brown, Warren. *The Chicago Cubs.* New York: G. P. Putnam's Sons, 1946.

———. *The Chicago White Sox.* New York: G. P. Putnam's Sons, 1952.

Bucek, Jeanine, et al. *The Baseball Encyclopedia.* 10th edition. New York: Macmillan, 1996.

Bulger, Bozeman. "The Baseball Business from the Inside." *Collier's* (March 25, 1922).

Bulger, Bozeman, an interview with Colonel Huston. "A Big League Club Owner Tells the Truth." *Liberty* (September 27, 1924).

Burk, Robert F. *Much More Than a Game: Players, Owners, and American Baseball Since 1921.* Chapel Hill: University of North Carolina Press, 2001.

———. *Never Just a Game: Players, Owners, & American Baseball to 1920.* Chapel Hill: University of North Carolina Press, 1994.

Chandler, Alfred D., Jr. *Strategy and Structure: Chapters in the History of Industrial America.* Cambridge, Mass.: MIT Press, 1962, 1990.

Chusid, Irwin. "The Short, Happy Life of the Newark Peppers." *Baseball Research Journal.* Society for American Baseball Research (1991).

Cook, William A. *August "Garry" Herrmann: A Baseball Biography.* Jefferson, N.C.: McFarland, 2008.

Cooper, John Milton, Jr. *Pivotal Decades: The United States 1900–1920.* New York: W.W. Norton, 1990.

Corey, Lewis. "Problems of the Peace: IV. The Middle Class." *Antioch Review* (Spring 1945).

Craig, Peter S. "Organized Baseball: An Industry Study of a $100 Million Spectator Sport." Unpublished thesis, Oberlin College, 1950.

Creamer, Robert W. *Babe: The Legend Comes to Life.* New York: Fireside Books, 1992.

———. *Stengel: His Life and Times.* New York: Fireside Books, 1990.

Cruikshank, Jeffery L., and Arthur W. Schultz. *The Man Who Sold America.* Boston: Harvard Business Review Press, 2010.

Danzig, Alison, and Joe Reichler. *The History of Baseball: Its Great Players, Teams and Managers.* New York: Prentice Hall, 1959.

Deadball Committee of the Society of American Baseball Research. *Deadball Stars of the American League,* edited by David Jones. Dulles, Va.: Potomac Books, 2006.

———. *Deadball Stars of the National League,* edited by Tom Simon. Dulles, Va.: Brassey's, 2004.

Dellinger, Susan. *Red Legs and Black Sox.* Cincinnati: Emmis, 2006.

De Santis, Vincent P. *The Shaping of Modern America, 1877–1920.* 3rd edition. Wheeling, Ill.: Harlan Davidson, 1989.

Deveaux, Tom. *The Washington Senators, 1901–1971.* Jefferson, N.C.: McFarland, 2001.

Deveney, Sean. *The Original Curse: Did the Cubs Throw the 1918 World Series to Babe Ruth's Red Sox and Incite the Black Sox Scandal?* New York: McGraw-Hill, 2010.

Dewey, Donald, and Nicholas Acocella. *The Ball Clubs.* New York: Harper Perennial, 1996.

———. *The Biographical Encyclopedia of Baseball.* Chicago: Triumph Books, 2002.

Di Salvatore, Bryan. *A Clever Base-Ballist: The Life and Times of John Montgomery Ward.* New York: Pantheon, 1999.

Drucker, Peter F. *The Essential Drucker: The Best of Sixty Years of Peter Drucker's Essential Writings on Management.* New York: HarperCollins, 2001.

Dubofsky, Melvin. *Industrialism and the American Worker, 1865–1920.* 3rd edition. Wheeling, Ill.: Harlan Davidson, 1975, 1985, 1996.

Duquette, Jerold J. *Regulating the National Pastime: Baseball and Antitrust.* Westport, Conn.: Praeger, 1999.

Eckler, John. "Baseball—Sport or Commerce?" *University of Chicago Law Review* (Autumn 1949).

Edwards, Elisha Jay. "The New Salaried Class." *American Monthly Review of Reviews* (July–December 1905).

Elfers, James E. *The Tour to End All Tours: The Story of Major League Baseball's 1913–1914 World Tour.* Lincoln: University of Nebraska Press, 2003.

Federal Baseball Club v. National League of Professional Baseball, 259 U.S. 200 (1922), Record on Appeal.

The Federal League (website). www.toyou.com/fl/index.cfm.

Fetter, Henry D. *Taking on the Yankees: Winning and Losing in the Business of Baseball, 1903–2003.* New York: W. W. Norton, 2003.

Finch, Robert L., L. H. Addington, and Ben M. Morgan, eds. *The Story of Minor League Baseball.* Columbus, Ohio: National Association of Professional Baseball Leagues, 1953.

Fleitz, David L. *Shoeless: The Life and Times of Joe Jackson.* Jefferson, N.C.: McFarland, 2001.

Forman, Sean. Baseball Reference Website. www.baseball-reference.com.

Foster, John B., ed. *A History of the National Association of Professional Baseball Leagues, 1902–1926.* Columbus, Ohio: National Association of Professional Baseball Leagues, n.d.

Fullerton, Hugh S. "Baseball—The Business and the Sport." *American Review of Reviews* (April 1920).

———. "Earnings in Baseball." *North American Review* (June 1930).

Fultz, David. "The Baseball Players Fraternity and What It Stands For." *Baseball Magazine* (November 1912).

Gallagher, Robert C. "John Tener's Brilliant Career." *Baseball Research Journal.* Society for American Baseball Research (1990).

Ginsberg, Daniel E. *The Fix Is In: A History of Baseball Gambling and Game Fixing Scandals.* Jefferson, N.C.: McFarland, 1995.

Goldman, Robert M. *One Man Out: Curt Flood versus Baseball.* Lawrence: University Press of Kansas, 2008.

Golenbock, Peter. *The Spirit of St. Louis: A History of the St. Louis Cardinals and Browns.* New York: St. Martin's, 1996.

———. *Wrigleyville: A Magical History Tour of the Chicago Cubs.* New York: Spike, 2000.

Gordon, John Steele. *An Empire of Wealth: The Epic History of American Economic Power.* New York: HarperCollins, 2004.

Grace, Kevin. "Cincinnati's King of Diamonds—Garry Herrmann." *Baseball in the Buckeye State.* Society for American Baseball Research (2004).

Graham, Frank. *The Brooklyn Dodgers.* New York: G. P. Putnam's Sons, 1945.

———. *McGraw of the Giants: An Informal Biography.* New York: G. P. Putnam's Sons, 1944.

———. *The New York Giants.* Carbondale: Southern Illinois University Press, 2002

———. *The New York Yankees.* Carbondale: Southern Illinois University Press, 2002.

Greenstein, Fred I. "The Changing Pattern of Urban Party Politics." *Annals of the American Academy of Political and Social Sciences, vol. 353, City Bosses and Political Machines* (May 1964).

Gunther, John. *Taken at the Flood: The Story of Albert D. Lasker.* New York: Harper & Brothers, 1960.

Hailey, Gary. "Anatomy of a Murder: The Federal League and the Courts." *National Pastime.* Society for American Baseball Research (Spring 1985).

Haller, Mark H. "Organized Crime in Urban Society: Chicago in the Twentieth Century." *Journal of Social History* (Winter 1971–1972).

Ham, Eldon L. "Aside the Aside: The True Precedent of Baseball in Law; Law, The Residue of Luck—or, Who's Not on First." *Marquette Sports Law Review* (Spring 2003).

Hardy, Stephen. *How Boston Played: Sport, Recreation, and Community, 1865–1915.* Knoxville: University of Tennessee Press, 2003.

Hofstadter, Richard. *The Age of Reform: From Bryan to FDR.* New York: Vintage, 1955.

Huhn, Rick. *Eddie Collins: A Baseball Biography.* Jefferson, N.C.: McFarland, 2008.

James, Bill. *The Bill James Historical Baseball Abstract.* New York: Villard, 1986.

———. *The New Bill James Historical Baseball Abstract.* New York: Free Press, 2001.

———. *The Politics of Glory.* New York: Macmillan, 1994.

James, Bill, and others, eds. *Bill James Presents . . . STATS All-Time Major League Handbook.* Morton Grove, Ill.: STATS Publishing, 1998.

———. *Bill James Presents . . . STATS All-Time Baseball Sourcebook.* Morton Grove, Ill.: STATS Publishing, 1998.

Johnson, Lloyd, and Miles Wolff, eds. *The Encyclopedia of Minor League Baseball.* 2nd edition. Durham, N.C.: Baseball America, 1997.

Johnston, Alva. "Beer and Baseball." *New Yorker,* September 24, 1932.

Kaese, Harold. *The Boston Braves.* New York: G. P. Putnam's Sons, 1948.

Karst, Gene, and Martin J. Jones Jr. *Who's Who in Professional Baseball.* New Rochelle, N.Y.: Arlington House, 1973.

Kauff, Bennie. "The Inside Story of Bennie Kauff's Holdout." *Baseball Magazine* (May 1916).

Kavanagh, Jack. *Walter Johnson: A Life*. South Bend, Ind.: Diamond Communications, 1995.

Kavanagh, Jack, and Norman Macht. *Uncle Robbie*. Cleveland: Society for American Baseball Research, 1999.

Keener, Sid C. "Baseball's Rags-to-Riches Story." Parts 1–6, *St. Louis Star Times* (January 1946).

Kennedy, David M. *Over Here: The First World War and American Society*. New York: Oxford University Press, 2004.

Kermisch, Al. "From a Researchers Notebook." *Baseball Research Journal*. Society for American Baseball Research (1986).

Kieran, John. "Big-League Business." *Saturday Evening Post*, May 31, 1930.

Kohout, Martin Donell. *Hal Chase: The Defiant Life and Turbulent Times of Baseball's Biggest Crook*. Jefferson, N.C.: McFarland, 2001.

Koppett, Leonard. *Koppett's Concise History of Major League Baseball*. Philadelphia: Temple University Press, 1998.

Kush, Raymond D. "The Building of Wrigley Field." *Baseball Research Journal*. Society for American Baseball Research (1981).

Kutler, Stanley I., ed. *Encyclopedia of the United States in the Twentieth Century*, 4 volumes. New York: Charles Scribner's Sons, 1996.

Lahman, Sean. *Baseball Player Database*. www.baseball1.com.

Lane, F. C. "The Big Man of the Minor Leagues." *Baseball Magazine* (February 1918).

———. "The Enormous Financial Hazards of Running a Major League Baseball Club." *Baseball Magazine* (January 1923).

———. "Famous Magnates of the Federal League, A Series Devoted to the Leaders of the New Circuit: R. B. Ward, the Master Baker, Vice-President of the Feds." *Baseball Magazine* (July 1915).

———. "Famous Magnates of the Federal League, A Series Devoted to the Leaders of the New Circuit: Harry Sinclair, Oil Wizard, the Live Wire of the Feds." *Baseball Magazine* (August 1915).

———. "The Sensational Evers Deal." *Baseball Magazine* (August 1914).

Lane, F. C., an interview with Colonel Ruppert. "Baseball's Master Builder." *Baseball Magazine* (October 1936).

Leuchtenburg, William E. *The Perils of Prosperity, 1914–1932*. Chicago: University of Chicago Press, 1958.

Levitt, Daniel R. *Ed Barrow: The Bulldog Who Built the Yankees' First Dynasty*. Lincoln: University of Nebraska Press, 2008.

———. "Ed Barrow, the Federal League, and the Union League." *National Pastime* (2008).

Lewis, Franklin. *The Cleveland Indians*. New York: G. P. Putnam's Sons, 1949.

Lieb, Fred. *The Baltimore Orioles*. Carbondale: Southern Illinois University Press, 2005.

———. *Baseball as I Have Known It.* New York: Coward, McCann & Geoghegan, 1976.

———. *The Baseball Story.* New York: G. P. Putnam's Sons, 1950.

———. *The Boston Red Sox.* New York: G. P. Putnam's Sons, 1947.

———. *Connie Mack.* New York: G. P. Putnam's Sons, 1945.

———. *The Detroit Tigers.* New York: G. P. Putnam's Sons, 1946.

———. *The Pittsburgh Pirates.* Carbondale: Southern Illinois University Press, 2003.

———. *The St. Louis Cardinals.* Carbondale: Southern Illinois University Press, 2001.

Lieb, Fred, and Stan Baumgartner. *The Philadelphia Phillies.* New York: G. P. Putnam's Sons, 1953.

Link, Arthur S., and Richard L. McCormick. *Progressivism.* Wheeling, Ill.: Harlan Davidson, 1983.

Longert, Scott. "The Players' Fraternity." *Society for American Baseball Research* (2001).

Lord, Walter. *The Good Years: From 1900 to the First World War.* New York: Bantam, 1969.

Lowenfish, Lee. *The Imperfect Diamond: A History of Baseball's Labor Wars.* New York: Da Capo Press, 1991.

———. "The Latter Years of John M. Ward." *The National Pastime.* Society for American Baseball Research (1983).

Luse, E. Vernon. "The Federal League of Baseball Clubs." *Road Trips.* Society for American Baseball Research (2004).

Maddison, Angus. *Contours of the World Economy, 1–2030 AD: Essays in Macro-Economic History.* Oxford: Oxford University Press, 2007.

Mansch, Larry D. *Rube Marquard: The Life and Times of a Baseball Hall of Famer.* Jefferson, N.C.: McFarland, 1998.

May, Henry F. *The End of American Innocence: A Study of the First Years of Our Own Time 1912–1917.* Chicago: Quadrangle Paperbacks, 1959.

McCraw, Thomas K. *American Business, 1920–2000: How It Worked.* Wheeling, Ill.: Harlan Davidson, 2000.

McCue, Andy. "A History of Dodger Ownership." *The National Pastime.* Society for American Baseball Research (1993).

McDonald, Kevin. "Antitrust and Baseball: Stealing Holmes." *Journal of Supreme Court History,* vol. 2 (1998).

Mercer, Sid. "The Colonel." Parts 1 and 3–6, *New York Journal and American* (January 14–20, 1939).

Michigan Law Review. "Constitutional Law—Monopolies—Baseball Club Not Engaged in 'Trade' or 'Commerce'" (June 1921).

M.L.C. "Baseball and the Law—Yesterday and Today." *Virginia Law Journal* (November 1946).

Mohl, Raymond A. *The New City: Urban America in the Industrial Age, 1860–1920.* Arlington Heights, Ill.: Harlan Davidson, 1985.

Murdock, Eugene. *Ban Johnson: Czar of Baseball.* Westport, Conn.: Greenwood Press, 1982.

Nathanson, Mitchell J. "The Sovereign Nation of Baseball: Why Federal Law Does Not Apply to 'America's Game' and How It Got That Way." *Villanova Sports & Entertainment Law Journal* (2008).

Neft, David S., Richard M. Cohen, and Michael L. Neft. *The Sports Encyclopedia: Baseball 2001*. New York: St. Martin's Griffin, 2001.

Obojski, Robert. *Bush League: A History of Minor League Baseball*. New York: Macmillan, 1975.

Okkonen, Marc. *The Federal League of 1914–1915: Baseball's Third Major League*. Garret Park, Md.: Society for American Baseball Research, 1989.

Okrent, Daniel, and Harris Lewine, eds. *The Ultimate Baseball Book*. Boston: Houghton Mifflin, 1988.

Overfield, Joseph M. *The 100 Seasons of Buffalo Baseball*. Kenmore, N.Y.: Partners' Press, 1985.

Palmer, Pete, and Gary Gillette, eds. *The 2006 ESPN Baseball Encyclopedia*. New York: Sterling Publishing, 2006.

Paxon, Frederic L. *American Democracy and the World War: Pre-War Years, 1913–1917*. New York: Cooper Square, 1966.

Pepper, George Wharton. *Philadelphia Lawyer: An Autobiography*. Philadelphia: Lippincott, 1944.

Pietrusza, David. *Judge and Jury: The Life and Times of Judge Kenesaw Mountain Landis*. South Bend, Ind.: Diamond Communications, 1998.

———. *Major Leagues: The Formation, Sometimes Absorption and Mostly Inevitable Demise of 18 Professional Baseball Organizations, 1871 to Present*. Jefferson, N.C.: McFarland, 1991.

Pietrusza, David, Matthew Silverman, and Michael Gershman, eds. *Baseball: The Biographical Encyclopedia*. Toronto: Sports Media Publishing, 2000, 2003.

Porter, David L., ed. *Biographical Dictionary of American Sports: Baseball*. Westport, Conn.: Greenwood Press, 1987.

Porter, Glenn. *The Rise of Big Business: 1860–1920*. 2nd edition. Wheeling, Ill.: Harlan Davidson, 1977, 1992.

Post, Robert. "Federalism in the Taft Court Era: Can It Be 'Revived'?" *Duke Law Journal* (March 2002).

Potts, R. F. "The Great Cincinnati Meeting." *Baseball Magazine* (March 1914).

Quirk, James, and Rodney D. Fort. *Pay Dirt: The Business of Professional Sports Teams*. Princeton, N.J.: Princeton University Press, 1997.

Record on Appeal. *Federal Baseball Club of Baltimore, Inc. v. National League of Professional Baseball Clubs, et al.* (259 U.S. 200 [1922]).

Reidenbaugh, Lowell. *100 Years of National League Baseball*. St. Louis: Sporting News Publishing, 1976.

Ribet, Barrie. "The Chicago Baseball Wars." *Baseball Research Journal*. Society for American Baseball Research (1999).

Riess, Steven A. "The Baseball Magnates and Urban Politics in the Progressive Era: 1895–1920." *Journal of Sports History* (Spring 1974).

———. *Sport in Industrial America*. Arlington Heights, Ill.: Harlan Davidson, 1995.

———. *Touching Base: Professional Baseball and American Culture in the Progressive Era*. Urbana: University of Illinois Press, 1999.

Robinson, Ray. *Matty: An American Hero*. New York: Oxford University Press, 1993.

Rock, Patrick. "Kansas City Packers." *Unions to Royals: The Story of Professional Baseball in Kansas City*. Society for American Baseball Research (1996).

Rothe, Emil H. "Was the Federal League a Major League?" *Baseball Research Journal*. Society for American Baseball Research (1981).

Seebrook, Martin. "Shades of the Federal League!" *Baseball Digest* (March 1955).

Selter, Ronald M. *Ballparks of the Deadball Era*. Jefferson, N.C.: McFarland, 2008.

Seymour, Harold. *Baseball: The Early Years*. New York: Oxford University Press, 1960.

———. *Baseball: The Golden Age*. New York: Oxford University Press, 1971.

———. "Limited Representation Used Only by Big-League Players." *Industrial Bulletin* (April 1960).

Shapiro, Michael. *Bottom of the Ninth*. New York: Times Books, 2009.

Shatzkin, Mike, and Jim Charlton, creators and developers. *The Ballplayers: Baseball's Ultimate Biographical Reference*. New York: Arbor House, 1990.

Shea, Stuart, with George Castle. *Wrigley Field: The Unauthorized Biography*. Dulles, Va.: Potomac Books, 2004.

Sigman, Shayna M. "The Jurisprudence of Judge Kenesaw Mountain Landis." *Marquette Sports Law Review* (Spring 2005).

Sinclair Oil Corporation. *A Great Name in Oil: Sinclair through Fifty Years*. New York: F. W. Dodge/McGraw Hill, 1966.

Smelser, Marshall. *The Life That Ruth Built: A Biography*. New York: Quadrangle, 1975.

Smith, David, et al. Retrosheet (website). www.retrosheet.org.

Solomon, Burt. *The Baseball Timeline: The Day-by-Day History of Baseball, From Valley Forge to the Present Day*. New York: Avon Books, 1997.

———. *Where They Ain't*. New York: Free Press, 1999.

Spink, Alfred H. *The National Game*. Carbondale: Southern Illinois University Press, 2000.

Spink, J. G. Taylor. *Judge Landis and 25 Years of Baseball*. St. Louis: Sporting News Publishing, 1974.

Stout, Glenn, and Richard Johnson. *Red Sox Century: One Hundred Years of Red Sox Baseball*. Boston: Houghton Mifflin, 2000.

———. *Yankees Century: 100 Years of Yankees Baseball*. Boston: Houghton Mifflin, 2002.

Stump, Al. *Cobb: A Biography*. Chapel Hill, N.C.: Algonquin Books, 1994.

Sullivan, Morgan A. "'A Derelict in the Stream of the Law': Overruling Baseball's Antitrust Exemption." *Duke Law Journal* (April 1999).

Sullivan, Neil J. *The Minors: The Struggles and the Triumph of Baseball's Poor Relation from 1876 to the Present*. New York: St. Martin's, 1990.

Swift, Tom. *Chief Bender's Burden.* Lincoln: University of Nebraska Press: 2008.

Szymanski, Stefan, and Andrew Zimbalist. *National Pastime: How Americans Play Baseball and the Rest of the World Plays Soccer.* Washington, D.C.: Brookings Institution Press, 2005.

Thernstrom, Stephan, and Peter R. Knights. "Men in Motion: Some Data and Speculations about Urban Population Mobility in Nineteenth-Century America." *Journal of Interdisciplinary History* (Autumn 1970).

Thomas, Henry W. *Walter Johnson: Baseball's Big Train.* Washington D.C.: Phenom Press, 1995.

Thorn, John, Phil Birnbaum, Bill Deane, et al. *Total Baseball: The Ultimate Baseball Encyclopedia.* Toronto: Sports Media Publishing, 2004.

Toot, Peter T. *Armando Marsans: A Cuban Pioneer in the Major Leagues.* Jefferson, N.C.: McFarland, 2004.

Topkis, Jay H. "Monopoly in Professional Sports." *Yale Law Journal* (April 1949).

Tygiel, Jules. *Past Time: Baseball as History.* New York: Oxford University Press, 2000.

U.S. Bureau of the Census. *Historical Statistics of the United States: Colonial Times to 1970,* Bicentennial Edition, 1975.

U.S. House of Representatives. *Hearings Before the Subcommittee on the Study of Monopoly Power of the Committee of the Judiciary: Organized Baseball* (82nd Cong., 1st sess., 1952).

———. *Report of the Subcommittee on the Study of Monopoly Power of the Committee of the Judiciary: Organized Baseball* (82nd Cong., 2nd sess., 1952).

Voigt, David Q. *American Baseball, Volume 1: From Gentleman's Sport to the Commissioner System.* State College: Pennsylvania State University Press, 1983.

Watkins, George P. "The Growth of Large Fortunes." *Publications of the American Economic Association* (November 1907).

Wayman, Joseph M. "Federal League Legacies." *Baseball Research Journal.* Society for American Baseball Research (1997).

White, G. Edward. *Creating the National Pastime: Baseball Transforms Itself, 1903–1953.* Princeton, N.J.: Princeton University Press, 1996.

Wiebe, Robert H. *The Search for Order, 1877–1920.* New York: Hill and Wang, 1967.

Wiggins, Robert Peyton. *The Federal League of Baseball Clubs: The History of an Outlaw Major League, 1914–1915.* Jefferson, N.C.: McFarland, 2009.

Willes, Ed. *The Rebel League: The Short and Unruly Life of the World Hockey Association.* Toronto: McClellan and Stewart, 2004.

Woolley, Edward Mott. "The Business of Baseball." *McClure's Magazine* (July 1912).

Wright, Marshall D. *The American Association.* Jefferson, N.C.: McFarland, 1997.

———. *The International League: Year-by-Year Statistics, 1884–1953.* Jefferson, N.C.: McFarland, 1998.

Wrigley, William, Jr. "Owning a Big-League Ball Team." *Saturday Evening Post* (September 13, 1930).

Yale Law Journal. "Monopsony in Manpower" (March 1953).

———. "Organized Baseball and the Law" (June 1937).

Zimbalist, Andrew. *Baseball and Billions: A Probing Look Inside the Big Business of Our National Pastime.* New York: Basic Books, 1994.

———. *May the Best Team Win: Baseball Economics and Public Policy.* Washington, D.C.: Brookings Institution Press, 2003.

Zingg, Paul J. *Harry Hooper: An American Baseball Life.* Urbana: University of Illinois Press, 1993.

Index